Asian Security
in the 1980s

Asian Security in the 1980s

Problems and Policies for a Time of Transition

Richard H. Solomon, ed.

OG
&H
Oelgeschlager, Gunn & Hain, Publishers, Inc.
Cambridge, Massachusetts

International Standard Book Number: 0-89946-037-2

Library of Congress Catalog Card Number: 80-16914

Second printing 1982, West Germany

Library of Congress Cataloging in Publication Data

Conference on East Asian Security in the 1980s, Santa Monica, Calif., 1979.
    Asian security in the 1980s.

    Includes index.
    1.   Asia—Politics and government—Congresses.   2.   Asia—Defenses—Congresses.   3.   Asia—Economic conditions—1945-   —Congresses.   4.   Asia—Relations (general) with the United States—Congresses.   5.   United States—Relations (general) with Asia—Congresses.   I.   Solomon, Richard H., 1937-
II.   Title.
[DS35.C66   1979]   355'.03305   80-16914
ISBN 0-89946-037-2

The research described in this report was sponsored by the Department of Defense under Contract MDA903-77-C-0115, monitored by the Assistant Secretary of Defense (International Security Affairs).

Art on the jacket adapted by Clifford Stoltz from "The Waves at Kanagawa" by Katsushika Hokusai. Permission granted by the Blackburn Museum and Art Gallery. Jacket design by Clifford Stoltz.

CONTENTS

FOREWORD

East Asia, the locus of America's last three military conflicts, has experienced dynamic economic growth and startling political change in the past decade. The transformation of U.S. relations with the People's Republic of China from confrontation to normalization, and Japan's emergence as an economic superstate now giving consideration to possible changes in its security posture, are but two of the most dramatic developments of the 1970s in this vital region. And yet, during this period, America's attention turned elsewhere. Unburdened of Vietnam, U.S. national security policymakers focused on other international concerns: political instability and arms balances in the Middle East; the modernization of NATO's defenses; changes in the U.S.-Soviet strategic relationship; and problems in developing areas such as Africa.

This shift of emphasis and attention, reinforced by the U.S. decision to withdraw its ground forces from the Republic of Korea, generated concern and confusion among America's Asian allies and friends. Was the United States relinquishing its security role in East Asia? Had a new period of American isolationism begun? Or was the United States just readjusting its priorities back to a traditional "Europe first" orientation?

Such questions had hardly been expressed before a series of developments served to refocus U.S., and world, attention on Asia. An increasingly large U.S. trade deficit with Japan generated political tensions so acute as to threaten the future of the relationship which has been central to America's involvement in the region since World War II. And in late 1978 fighting broke out again in Indochina, first between two recently allied communist states, Vietnam and Kampuchea (Cambodia), and not long thereafter between China and Vietnam. The Soviet Union involved itself in these conflicts, initially by establishing formal economic and treaty ties with Hanoi, and then by providing materiel, logistic, and intelligence support to Vietnamese forces operating on two fronts against the Khmer and the Chinese. In early 1979 the prospect of new Sino-Soviet military tensions, if not open conflict, appeared to be heightened as each of the communist powers sought ways of supporting its regional ally.

These events were followed by a summit meeting of European, American, and Japanese leaders in Tokyo in the summer of 1979 to address economic issues, the problem of Indochinese refugees, and the implications of a reconsideration of the decision to withdraw U.S. ground forces from Korea. American officials sought to reaffirm their intention to sustain the U.S. role in Asian affairs, although they did not fully define the future direction of American policy toward the region.

It was amidst these troublesome developments and ambiguities about U.S. intentions toward East Asia that Rand convened a conference of more than fifty senior government officials and analysts. They came from most of the important non-communist countries of East Asia as well as from points within the United States to assess the political, economic, and military trends that are likely to affect the region's security in the 1980s. The conference was designed to stimulate a dialogue that would clarify U.S. policy alternatives. With the support of the Office of the Assistant Secretary of Defense and The Rand Corporation itself, a dozen papers were commissioned to serve as the basis for three days of discussion which took place in Santa Monica in mid-January 1979.

This volume contains the conference papers updated as of the early fall of 1979, and a summary of the discussions. Together, they present an unusually diverse and rich exchange of views, bringing into focus both Asian and American perspectives on the forces affecting security along the rim of the Western Pacific. An initial, overview chapter, prepared with the benefit of the conference papers and discussions, describes U.S. policy choices toward the region.

These materials were first published as a Rand Report in December 1979, just a few days before the Soviet invasion of Afghanistan, and a few weeks after the taking of the American embassy and hostages in Teheran. While these events focused attention on the Persian Gulf and Indian Ocean, they also stimulated a period of profound rethinking of security needs by the countries of East, Southeast, and West Asia, as well as by the United States. Despite the rapid movement of events, the analyses in this volume remain highly relevant to an assessment of security trends throughout the Asian region.

We expect these materials to prove useful in at least three ways: by contributing to a better understanding of the issues that will shape near-term Asian security; by aiding in the assessment of specific policies that the United States and its allies might pursue; and by serving as a basis for rethinking U.S. military force postures for the Pacific theater.

Donald B. Rice
President
The Rand Corporation

ACKNOWLEDGMENTS

The creation of this volume attests to the interest and insights of the various authors who contributed their time and energies, amidst busy professional schedules in some cases dominated by official responsibilities, in support of this effort to assess Asian security trends and policy issues for the 1980s. The Rand Corporation is indebted to each of them for their contributions to the enterprise.

At the same time, particular recognition is due a number of people who supported the convening of the conference from which this book has grown, and others who assisted in producing and editing the publication. Donald B. Rice, Rand's President, both encouraged the conference and sustained the writing effort with the Corporation's own limited research funds. Ambassador Morton Abramowitz, while Deputy Assistant Secretary of Defense, originally urged the convening of the conference. I am indebted to him, to his successor Michael Armacost, and to Assistant Secretary of Defense David McGiffert, for their partial sponsorship of the conference and publication effort.

I wish to acknowledge the assistance of a number of my colleagues for their important contributions to the production of this report: Jonathan Pollack and Anna Ford for invaluable research assistance; Janet DeLand for her editorial contributions; and Mary Yanokawa for unflagging support in all the demands of convening the conference, working with the various authors, and typing the manuscript. I am also grateful for typing assistance provided by Nancy Challman, Sandra Dougharty, Kay McKenzie, Diane Reingold, Linda Daly, Jan Iverson, Mary Maloney, and Janet True.

I am also indebted to D. Michael Landi, Paul F. Langer, Nicholas Platt, Jonathan Pollack, and Strobe Talbott for substantive and editorial guidance, particularly in the preparation of Chapter 1.

While I must bear responsibility for limitations in the organization and substantive focus of the conference and volume, and for any errors of fact or interpretation in the initial chapter, this report is above all a collective effort. I am grateful for the active support and intellectual stimulation of the many people who contributed to it.

Richard H. Solomon
June 1980

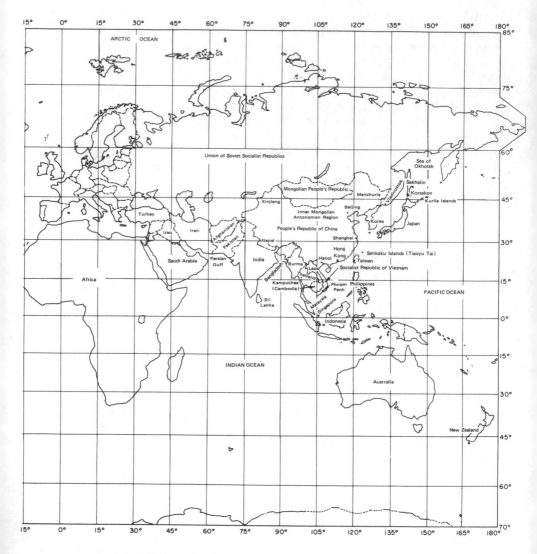

Map 1—The Asia-Pacific region and neighboring areas of Sino-Soviet influence

Chapter 1

AMERICAN DEFENSE PLANNING AND ASIAN SECURITY: POLICY CHOICES FOR A TIME OF TRANSITION

Richard H. Solomon[1]

ASIAN COLLECTIVE SECURITY, ANTI-HEGEMONY, OR DETENTE?

For more than a decade, the premises underlying America's post-World War II involvement in Asian security affairs have been going through a fundamental transformation. The central element in these changes has been the breakdown of the Sino-Soviet alliance and its evolution since the late 1960s into a military confrontation and worldwide geopolitical rivalry.

The Nixon Administration's establishment of a dialogue with Chinese leaders in 1971 symbolically shattered the communist-capitalist lines of conflict in Asia that dated from the Korean War period and established a new political context for an effort to disengage the United States from the Vietnam conflict. The Carter Administration's completion of the process of normalizing relations with the People's Republic of China (PRC), in combination with Tokyo's signing of a Sino-Japanese friendship treaty and China's turn to Japan and the West for development capital and technology, capped a decade of dramatic changes with the potential for a fundamentally new pattern of international alignments in the political, economic, and security affairs of Asia.

These transformations in relations among the major powers were paralleled by no less startling changes in the Asian region itself. History's irony has been most evident in the rapid deterioration of China's relations with Vietnam. What in the early 1970s had been an alliance "as close as lips to teeth" is now a bitter military confrontation, a situation punctuated by the thirty-day Sino-Vietnamese border war in the early winter of 1979. The security implications of the new Chinese-American relationship were highlighted by PRC Vice-Premier Deng Xiaoping's (Teng Hsiao-p'ing's) triumphal normalization visit to Washington in January 1979, just prior to the Sino-Vietnamese military clash—a timing which stimulated questions about U.S. support for Beijing's (Peking's) action and concerns about the possibility of a Sino-Soviet war and its impact on U.S.-Soviet relations.

Less spectacular changes now confront the United States and its Asian allies and friends with major new choices of security strategy and political alignment. These include rapid economic growth in Japan, South Korea, Taiwan, Hong Kong, and Singapore of more than 7 percent per year for most of the 1970s, and the quiet training of generations of scientific and managerial talent that have made East Asia the most rapidly developing region of the world. States formerly dependent on

[1] Richard H. Solomon is director of The Rand Corporation's research program on International Security Policy, and head of the Social Science Department. From 1971 to 1976 he served on the staff of the National Security Council, having previously been a professor of Political Science at the University of Michigan.

1

American protection for their security are gradually acquiring the resources to play a substantial role in managing their own defenses.

American awareness of many of these changes was dimmed during the decade of the Vietnam War. With the end of the conflict in the mid-1970s, U.S. interests in the region seemed well-served by a period of inactivity. Policymakers and the public turned their attention to other concerns—domestic inflation, energy and international monetary problems, adverse trends in the strategic military balance and NATO-Warsaw Pact deployments, SALT II, and the Middle East negotiations. These issues had been overshadowed by the divisive and draining Indochina conflict and required attention after a period of neglect. Yet in only three or four years we have come to see new sources of insecurity and conflict in Asia: a growing Soviet naval presence in the Pacific and Indian Oceans; extension of the Moscow-Beijing feud to ravaged Indochina; heightened prospects for nuclear proliferation in potentially volatile areas such as Korea; and the possibility of conflicts over offshore natural resources that run from the fishing grounds off Sakhalin Island to the oil-rich sea floor of the South China Sea.

The most disturbing aspect of these developments is the prospect they hold for once again involving Asia in the disputes of the great powers. The trend most likely to shape the pattern of Asian security issues in the 1980s is the further extension of the Sino-Soviet conflict into the affairs of the region. Moscow doggedly attempts to build an "Asian collective security" coalition which will give the USSR access to the area and constrain Chinese, and American, power. Its efforts are reinforced by growing Soviet naval and air deployments to the Asian theater and the opportunistic establishment of bilateral political ties and security treaties—most recently with South Yemen, Afghanistan, and Vietnam—in order to create a regional base structure. The Chinese, in response, are making parallel efforts to construct a countercoalition of states allied on the theme of "anti-hegemony," opposed to the further extension of Soviet influence into Asia.

The basic choice in America's security planning for Asia in the 1980s is how to relate to these opposing strategies of the major communist states: Should we join with the Chinese in a global effort to constrain the Soviet Union's imperialistic impulses, and in the process risk polarizing the affairs of Asia around the Sino-Soviet dispute; or should we remain aloof from the Moscow-Beijing feud and seek to account for American interests and the security of our allies—the Republic of Korea (ROK), Japan, the Philippines, and the ANZUS countries[2]—through the strengthening of a "loose Oceanic alliance" of friendly and like-minded states?[3] The alternative chosen will influence many of the specific policy choices that will give shape to America's role in Asia in the coming decade.

At the same time, a clear choice in a regional security strategy will not be ours alone to make. The concerns of our allies will influence many decisions. Difficult choices involving the risk of conflict may be forced upon us by the initiatives of others; and alternatives may be foreclosed by events beyond our control. But in an era of rapid political and economic change, and as yet relatively unstructured responses by the United States and other powers involved, it is important to clarify the major trends affecting Asian security, the policy alternatives that are likely to

---

[2] Australia and New Zealand.

[3] See the analysis by Noel Gayler, pp. 54, 60, and 67 below.

come before us, and the impact on American and allied interests of different courses of action.

The closest thing to an organizing theme in U.S. Asian policy in recent years has been a derivative of Washington's Soviet-oriented policy of détente: the attempt to normalize relations with former adversaries such as China and Vietnam. At the same time, there has been an uncertainty and lack of coherence to specific American actions which stands in marked contrast to Moscow's persistent, if not highly successful, efforts to contain the expansion of Chinese influence, and Beijing's attempt to engage the United States, Japan, and the NATO countries in a new security alignment designed to counter Soviet "social-imperialism." This reflects a shattering of the policy consensus which had existed in the United States from the Korean War into the 1960s on the need to contain and isolate expansionist Asian communist states allied to the Soviet Union—a major result of our Vietnam agony and the disintegration of the Moscow-Beijing alliance.

Efforts to reestablish a sense of policy direction were part of the process of disengagement from Vietnam. The Nixon Administration's "Guam Doctrine" of 1969 asserted the premise that "the way we could become involved [in another Asian war] would be to attempt withdrawal [from the region] because, whether we like it or not, geography makes us an Asian power."[4] President Ford's "Pacific Doctrine" of 1975 sought to reformulate an Asian policy based on "a balance among the major powers, strong ties to our allies in the region, an easing of tensions between adversaries, the self-reliance and regional solidarity of smaller nations, and expanding economic ties and cultural exchanges."[5]

Conceptualizing and gaining public support for an appropriate set of political, economic, and military policies that would give form to these general assertions, however, has proven to be a difficult task. Despite official pronouncements that "our nation has recovered its self-confidence at home, and we have not abandoned our interest in Asia,"[6] the region has taken third or fourth place in a set of American foreign policy priorities now focused on European security issues, the strategic balance, and the Middle East. There is a profound division of opinion among American leaders about how to deal with the global Soviet challenge and about the place of China in a national security strategy. There is also a feeling among many U.S. officials that American interests, for the moment at least, are relatively well served by conditions in Asia. And although there is ample evidence that the United States remains actively engaged in the political, economic, and security affairs of the region,[7] recent U.S. policy initiatives suggest uncertainty of purpose and a desire to limit American involvement in Asian affairs.

[4] Richard M. Nixon, "Informal Remarks in Guam with Newsmen" (July 25, 1969), in *Public Papers of the Presidents of the United States: Richard Nixon*, U.S. Government Printing Office, Washington, D.C., 1971, p. 546.

[5] "President Ford's Pacific Doctrine," Department of State News Release, Washington, D.C., December 7, 1975, p. 3.

[6] Secretary of State Cyrus Vance, "United States and Asia," Department of State News Release, Washington, D.C., June 29, 1977, p. 1.

[7] Senior U.S. officials have repeatedly asserted in recent years the view that the current situation in Asia is favorable to the interests of the United States and its allies, that America intends to remain an Asian power, and that the United States is strengthening its military presence in the area at a level appropriate to the requirements of regional stability. See, for example, the speech by Secretary of Defense Harold Brown on American defense policy delivered to the Los Angeles World Affairs Council, February 20, 1978, *Los Angeles Times*, February 21, 1978; Keyes Beech, "Mondale Says U.S. Determined to Stay a Pacific Power, Cites 7th Fleet Buildup," *Los Angeles Times*, September 3, 1979; Richard Holbrooke, "East Asia Today and in the Decades Ahead," speech delivered to the Women's National Democratic Club, November 27, 1978.

As a number of the contributors to this volume point out, there is a widespread concern in Asia that the United States cannot be depended upon to meet its regional security commitments.[8] This reflects an assumption that the lingering influence of the Vietnam War experience, reinforced by a shifting Soviet-American power balance, continues to immobilize political support in the United States for an activist foreign policy. This perception is also the result of a series of recent American actions that have created confusion or uncertainty about our Asian security policy. Most important of these has been the unilateral announcement in 1977 that all U.S. ground troops would be withdrawn from the ROK, and the subsequent reversal of this decision in the spring of 1979 as a result of Congressional pressures and new intelligence information about North Korean troop strength.

There also has been uncertainty about American intentions toward China. The delay of some years in completing the process of normalizing U.S.-PRC relations suggested to some Asians an inability on the part of the United States to accomplish what most states of the region had already achieved. More recently, a concern has arisen that the development of U.S.-PRC security cooperation on the theme of anti-hegemony will either provoke the Soviet Union or take precedence over America's traditional alliance relationships in Asia. There are also worries that the economic tensions in Japanese-American relations will become so acute as to alienate the Japanese and impel them in the direction of a more independent and nationalistic foreign policy.

An effective American Asian security policy for the 1980s—one which will gain domestic political support and the confidence of our allies—will require greater clarity regarding four issue areas: First, a clear U.S. strategy for dealing with the global Soviet challenge, and greater consensus on the issue of how to relate to China in the "triangular" context of Sino-Soviet relations and the Sino-Soviet dispute. Second, an assessment of regional trends that will affect Asian security in the coming decade. Third, evaluation of American and allied military requirements, as well as economic and political policies, for responding to both global and regional security threats. And fourth, an awareness of the concerns and interests of friendly and allied states in Asia as they will affect American policy choices.

This volume is designed to contribute to a clarification of American policy alternatives regarding Asian security for the coming decade, primarily by assessing the major political, economic, and military trends in the region. As a basis for the series of analytical chapters that follow this introduction, the subsequent discussion seeks to identify the qualities of what will be a time of transition for Asia. By evaluating the major factors that will influence regional security, we can then define the policy choices that the United States and its allies will face as they try to shape a coherent set of political, economic, and defense programs designed to enhance their security and realize other interests in the region.

A Shifting U.S.-Soviet Military Balance. For most of the three decades following World War II, American policy planners saw Asian issues in the context of U.S. strategic military superiority over our primary Cold War adversary, the Soviet Union. They could take some comfort from the knowledge that the United States enjoyed a position of predominance in nuclear and naval forces in Asia. Moreover, the Soviet-American competition was seen by those planners to be cen-

---

[8] See pp. 105, 166-167, and 176-178 below.

tered predominantly in Europe. At the time of the Korean and Vietnam Wars, for example, a major concern was that deep American involvement in conventional military conflicts in Asia would draw U.S. defense capabilities and attention from Europe, where the Soviets had the capabilities and incentives to challenge the United States directly. For this reason, consideration was given to ways of rapidly disengaging U.S. forces from combat in order to be able to respond to possible Soviet challenges in the NATO theater. (Such a disengagement, however, was never effectively implemented.)

The coming decade will require an entirely different set of assumptions about the Soviet-American military balance in both strategic and regional forces, and of the place of Asia in the global U.S.-Soviet rivalry. Many experts believe that for at least several years in the early 1980s America's Minuteman strategic missiles will be vulnerable to a Soviet first strike. This factor, in combination with Moscow's conventional military preponderance in Europe and an active Soviet civil defense program, compromises the assumption that Soviet leaders seek only "strategic parity" or "equal security." Such military trends, if unchallenged, may make the United States more cautious in situations where American and Soviet interests clash.

At the same time, this shift in the pattern of "superpower" military capabilities is likely to make the Soviets more assertive. Recent direct and proxy Soviet interventions in the Third World—from Africa and the Middle East to Indochina—have occurred in circumstances less favorable to the USSR than those Soviet leaders may enjoy in the 1980s.

The Soviet Union's ability to project military force into Asia at all levels of conflict is also growing. The recent deployment to the Soviet Far East of Backfire bombers and SS-20 intermediate-range mobile nuclear missiles is transforming the theater nuclear balance. Soviet ground forces numbering more than 45 divisions, deployed primarily along the Sino-Soviet frontier, are now being supplemented by paratroop and amphibious units in the Maritime Provinces and on offshore islands. These units give Moscow new capabilities for intervention in Japan and Korea, as well as in China.[9] Strengthened Soviet long-range aviation[10] and naval assets in Asia are gradually expanding Moscow's ability to *project* power, to go beyond the missions of threatening the security of U.S. bases in Asia, the Seventh Fleet, and America's ballistic missile submarines. As several contributors to this volume observe, there is growing concern among Asian leaders that the Soviet Union is now creating a capability to threaten the security of the sea lanes and to intervene in support of friendly states and proxy forces—as Moscow has done recently with Vietnam in its conflict with Kampuchea (Cambodia) and China.

The degree of caution, or assertiveness, that these new military circumstances will induce cannot be predicted—in part because the United States has the ability to remedy some of the presently unfavorable military trends. Moscow's past behavior, however, suggests greater efforts in the future to project the influence of the USSR unless Soviet power is checked by some countervailing capability. There may also be an inclination on the part of regional states to accommodate their policies

[9] See Russell Spurr, "The Soviet Threat: Ominous Implications of Red Power Plays," *Far Eastern Economic Review,* June 23, 1978, pp. 73-76; and William Chapman, "Japan Reports Soviet Buildup on Disputed Island," *Washington Post,* September 27, 1979.

[10] With capabilities for intelligence collection, anti-shipping operations, and transport.

to the growing Soviet military presence if it is not countered by the United States or some coalition of countries.

Interdependence in Security Affairs. "Interdependence" entered the American vocabulary of international affairs in the 1970s, largely as a result of the oil crisis and economic problems in relations with allies such as Japan. This perspective is likely to gain enhanced significance in the coming decade. As noted above, the shifting power balance between the United States and the Soviet Union is likely to impel greater efforts at coalition-building to compensate for the limited security capabilities of any given country. Indeed, it was such a consideration that led self-reliant China to pursue its opening to the United States, Japan, and Western Europe after the Soviet invasion of Czechoslovakia in 1968 and border clashes along the Sino-Soviet frontier the following year. As Mao Zedong (Mao Tse-tung) rhetorically inquired of Henry Kissinger, "If neither side [the U.S. or China] had anything to ask from the other, why would you be coming to Peking? If neither side had anything to ask, then why ... would we want to receive you and the President?"[11]

Soviet efforts to isolate China largely backfired, as Beijing succeeded during the 1970s in broadening its international contacts and establishing normal relations with Tokyo, Washington, and the capitals of Western Europe. To date, the anti-hegemony theme in this proto-coalition of China, Japan, the United States, and Europe is muted and ambivalent, particularly as far as military affairs are concerned. But if Soviet threats to the security of these states continue to increase, it is likely that this emergent entente will acquire a more explicit character as a defense alliance.

The smaller states of Asia, understandably, are reluctant to be drawn into this evolving pattern of great-power contention. Yet events are carrying them in a direction contrary to their desires. The Vietnamese, presumed by all to be fiercely independent, have allied themselves by formal treaty to the Soviet Union in order to gain some protection from Chinese pressures as they pursue the goal of a Hanoi-dominated federation of the Indochina states.[12] In reaction, the countries of ASEAN (the Association of Southeast Asian Nations)—Thailand, Malaysia, Singapore, the Philippines, and Indonesia—contemplate more active forms of security cooperation in order to resist the pressures of an expansionist Vietnam. As with the new pattern of great-power relationships, the evolution of ASEAN as a security coalition will be shaped by the threat the Association faces.

Interdependence will be more than a matter of greater collaboration in security affairs. Evolving economic relationships are reinforcing new patterns of security cooperation—as well as straining old alliances. China's turn to the West and Japan has been motivated, in part, by the desire to gain access to advanced technologies, investment capital, and new markets that will facilitate economic modernization. Continuation of the remarkable growth of the economies of South Korea, Taiwan, Hong Kong, and Singapore, along with the future growth of the ASEAN economies, is highly dependent upon continuing investment from Japan, the United States, and Western Europe, as well as on unimpeded access to their markets for local manufactures. And the stability of the U.S.-Japanese alliance in the 1980s will be

---

[11] Henry A. Kissinger, *White House Years*, Little, Brown, Boston, 1979, p. 1060.
[12] Ibid., pp. 468-469, and passim; also, p. 155 below.

tested by the effectiveness with which the two countries cope with the structural economic transformations required to end the massive trade imbalances that have created political pressures for protectionist measures.

The vitality of East Asia will be affected, as well, by developments beyond the region: by the stability of access to Middle Eastern energy supplies; and by the impact of the tide of Islamic fundamentalism on those states with sizable Muslim populations—Indonesia, the Philippines, and Malaysia.

National Interest, Not Ideology, as an Aligning Force. The 1970s has seen the substantial erosion of ideology as an aligning force in international politics, and this has certainly occurred in the affairs of Asia. The normalization of Sino-American and Sino-Japanese relations and the economic rationalization of China's post-Mao Zedong economic and social policies have diminished, at least for the present, the communist-capitalist lines of cleavage in Asian political and economic relations. In contrast, as a number of contributors to this volume observe, conflict in Asia is now "East-East" rather than "East-West" in character, as former socialist allies China and Vietnam, and China and the Soviet Union, contest the extension of each other's influence with the threat or use of arms.

National interest has replaced ideology as the orienting force of international relationships in Asia. As Takuya Kubo notes, this can be a healthy thing as long as a spirit of independence is tempered by a sense of responsibility for cooperative measures designed to enhance regional security and economic progress.[13] The question for the coming decade is whether the force of nationalism will remain benign, or whether it will fuel territorial disputes, resource rivalry, and destabilizing approaches to security—e.g., through arms races and nuclear proliferation. In this regard, there remains latent concern in Asia about the future evolution of Japanese defense policy in the direction of a more assertive nationalism—a prospect which, as Soedjatmoko comments, could be accelerated by the present strains in U.S.-Japanese economic relations and the diminished credibility of the American security presence in Asia.

The Non-Military Determinants of Security. While military factors will, of course, continue to be a major element in regional security affairs, one aspect of the "transitional" quality of current developments in Asia is that emerging social, political, and economic factors will produce new tensions and international alignments which ultimately may lead to regional conflicts.

The economic dynamism of the non-communist Sinitic societies—South Korea, Japan, Taiwan, Hong Kong, and Singapore—has created a stabilizing prosperity. Nonetheless, these states remain vulnerable to recession or dislocations induced by unreliable access to energy supplies or markets in the United States and Europe. If, as Herman Kahn suggests, the developed countries of the West are entering a period of economic malaise, current protectionist pressures will only increase. And as economic development proceeds in the multi-ethnic societies of ASEAN, resentment against the more visible wealth of the entrepreneurial "Overseas Chinese" could stimulate communal violence—particularly if Islamic fundamentalism takes hold in Malaysia or Indonesia. Vietnam already has paid a significant economic price for the expulsion of its skilled and commercially active Chinese minority.

Barring a major economic catastrophe, East Asia is likely to remain the world's most dynamic region of growth in the coming decade. And while this will inhibit

---

[13] See p. 93 below.

internal political unrest and contribute to the expansion of constructive trading relationships, the growing scientific and industrial capacities of the states of the region also hold the potential for intraregional arms manufacturing and transfers, and for nuclear proliferation. Leslie Gelb concludes that regional arms sales are not a matter of concern at present, although failure of the United States to manage economic and security relations with its traditional Asian allies could stimulate disruptive trends toward such transfers and/or proliferation.

The United States retains the capability to shape in a constructive manner emergent economic and defense programs in Asia. Unlike the Soviet Union, which projects its influence in the region almost exclusively through military means, the United States has the political and social access, and the scientific and economic resources, to interact with the countries of Asia on a broad range of issues. [14] To do so effectively, however, will require greater constancy of purpose in security affairs, such as military assistance programs, and a willingness to incur the domestic political costs associated with various structural economic readjustments. For example, a liberal textile import quota for China would enable the PRC to earn the foreign exchange with which to purchase more American industrial goods, although such a policy would affect domestic producers and the interests of our traditional foreign suppliers.

And finally, as Guy Pauker's analysis emphasizes, the 1980s will be a critical period for the states of the region in dealing with population growth and a concomitant sluggishness in agricultural production. Despite decades of effort to solve these problems, the Chinese were unable to sustain per capita grain consumption in 1978 at anything more than a 1957 level;[15] and Indonesia has become the world's major importer of rice as a result of production shortfalls and a population growth rate approaching 3 percent. While the social and political effects of such problems may not be felt in a highly disruptive form for some years, the 1980s may be the last time certain countries can attempt to deal with population and food problems in a manner that does not generate extensive human misery and political turmoil.

NEW SOURCES OF REGIONAL INSTABILITY AND CONFLICT

Apart from the major trends discussed above, East Asian security in the 1980s will be shaped by a range of specific factors, some of which are regional "spillovers" of global trends, and some of which are problems unique to Asia. The eight sources of potential instability or conflict described in the following pages are the factors most likely—in some unfolding combination—to threaten the peace and security of East Asia in the coming decade.

[14] For example, in 1977 the United States provided a market for 25.7 percent of Asia's exports and furnished 14.6 percent of its imports. The Soviet Union provided only 1.2 percent of Asia's imports and accounted for 1.9 percent of its exports. (International Monetary Fund, *Direction of Trade, Annual 1971-1977.*)

[15] "Decisions of the Central Committee of the Communist Party of China on Some Questions Concerning the Acceleration of Agricultural Development" (December 22, 1978), *People's Daily,* October 6, 1979, p.1.

The Sino-Soviet Conflict

The Moscow-Beijing rivalry will be the major "structural" factor shaping the evolving pattern of regional political alignments and prospects for military conflict.

During the 1960s the Sino-Soviet feud was confined largely to political maneuvering within the international communist movement and to the gradual military buildup along the Sino-Soviet frontier which culminated in the border clashes of 1969. The 1970s have seen the feud extended to involve appeals by the Soviets and Chinese to non-communist states from Europe to Asia as the two countries maneuver against each other in a bitter contest of containment and counter-containment.

The first major realignments in the non-communist world associated with this political competition were the opening of Sino-American normalization negotiations in July 1971 and the signing of the Soviet-Indian Peace and Friendship Treaty in the early fall of that same year—just prior to the Indo-Pakistani war of November.[16] Subsequent years saw little progress by Moscow in its persistent efforts to enlist support for an anti-Chinese coalition, although Beijing, once admitted to the United Nations, made significant progress in broadening its political access to the international community. The last two years of the 1970s, however, have seen major developments in the pattern of political realignment around the two communist powers. In August 1978 Tokyo and Beijing signed a Peace and Friendship Treaty that included an expression of common opposition to "hegemony." An agreement on the full normalization of Sino-American relations reached at the end of 1978 contained explicit reference to the same theme. On Moscow's side of the strategic equation, 1978 saw Soviet-oriented coups in South Yemen and Afghanistan and the signing of a Soviet-Vietnamese Peace and Friendship Treaty in the face of serious political and military tensions between Beijing and Hanoi.

These political realignments have not, to date, been accompanied by major military actions, although reports persist of clashes along the Sino-Soviet frontier. Moreover, both sides continue to strengthen their military positions. The Russians are upgrading the weaponry deployed with more than 45 divisions that threaten the Chinese; and Beijing sustains its counterdeployment of more than 70 divisions. The Soviets have positioned SS-20 IRBMs in eastern Siberia in a way that threatens not only China but also Japan and other Asian states as far south as Indonesia. Moscow's construction of the Baikal-Amur Mainline (BAM) Railroad is designed to strengthen Soviet logistical capabilities in the sensitive Chinese border area, as well as to accelerate the economic development of Siberia. And there are persistent reports of Moscow's intention to build a major naval facility at Korsakov on Sakhalin Island as well as Soviet pressures on Vietnam to establish permanent air and naval facilities at Danang and Cam Ranh Bay.

China's military response to the Soviet buildup is only now taking form. A defense modernization program begun in 1975 was sidetracked during the turmoil surrounding political attacks on Deng Xiaoping and the subsequent purging of the "Gang of Four." The Chinese now seem firmly embarked, however, on a broad-scale approach to economic development and the gradual modernization of their military

---

[16] Henry Kissinger has now revealed that in the context of the Indian attack on Pakistan (an ally of both China and the United States), President Nixon communicated to PRC leaders his intention to assist China if Beijing came to Pakistan's aid, and as a result the Soviet Union—India's ally—initiated military action against China. The security aspect of "triangular politics" thus dates from November 1971. See Kissinger, *White House Years*, pp. 910-911.

establishment. This effort includes substantial purchases of advanced industrial technology from Japan, the United States, and Europe, and interest in European military hardware such as combat aircraft, anti-tank and air-to-air missiles, and component systems, e.g., aircraft and marine engines. To date, however, no major weapon system has been sold to Beijing.[17]

The question for the 1980s is how far the Russians and the Chinese will proceed in the political and military dimensions of their geopolitical maneuvering. Despite talks initiated between Beijing and Moscow in September 1979 to reduce tensions, the Soviets can be expected to persist in efforts to gain allies on China's periphery. Iran, Afghanistan, Pakistan, and North Korea are likely to be high-priority, if unstable, targets of opportunity. Taiwan and the ASEAN states will be less promising candidates. And it remains to be seen whether Moscow's presently most promising point of access in Asia—Vietnam—will be converted into a permanent Soviet military presence on China's southern frontier.

Similarly, it is not clear how successful Beijing will be in constructing what Deng Xiaoping has termed an "Eastern NATO" in its relations with Japan and the United States, or how far the Europeans (and the Americans) will go in selling military equipment and defense-related technologies to the Chinese. Such developments are most likely to occur in reaction to threatening moves on the part of the Soviet Union. And the possibility of some limited Soviet military action against the PRC during the coming decade—perhaps in the form of large-scale border clashes conducted in a period of heightened Sino-Vietnamese tensions—cannot be ruled out.

As we conclude in the final section of this analysis, the basic policy problem for the United States and its Asian allies in the 1980s is how to conduct relations with Moscow and Beijing in the context of their enduring enmity. A significant reduction in Sino-Soviet tensions resulting from the current discussions would presumably dampen down the Moscow-Beijing rivalry in Asia; and this would contribute to regional stability. Such a development seems unlikely, however, in view of Moscow's penchant for projecting Soviet influence through military power. The Sino-Soviet conflict is most likely to remain bounded by the two extremes of rapprochement and war, with the most likely prospect being an ongoing political rivalry with persistent military tensions.

The U.S.-Soviet Long-Term Competition

As a result of the full normalization of China's relations with Washington and Tokyo, it will become increasingly difficult during the coming decade to separate the elements of global Soviet-American competition from those of regional competition in Asia. The great failure of Soviet policy during the 1960s and 1970s was to have provoked into life a long-feared two-front strategic challenge. The coming decade may see the realization of a Sino-Japanese-American coalition for political, economic, and perhaps even defense cooperation. Although the United States is now unburdened of its "two-front" security problem—at least in the form of a Sino-Soviet alliance—American defense planners must worry about the Soviets

---

[17] It has been reported that British leaders told PRC Premier Hua Guofeng, during his visit to London in November 1979, that they would sell the PRC about 70 of their Harrier jump-jet fighters. No purchase agreement has yet been signed, however. See Leonard Downie, Jr., "Britain Tells Hua It Is Willing to Sell Harrier Jets," *Los Angeles Times*, November 2, 1979, p. 27.

redeploying some of their "Chinese" divisions to Europe as reinforcements during a NATO-Warsaw Pact conflict. In sum, the 1980s will see the increasing "globalization" of what thus far have been regional Asian security issues.

As one example of this trend, during the 1970s the gradual strengthening of Soviet naval forces in the Pacific seemed designed to threaten the carrier task forces and ballistic missile submarines of the U.S. Seventh Fleet. While these two missions will remain central to the operations of the Soviet Pacific Fleet, the deployment of the new Kiev-class aircraft-carrying ASW cruiser *Minsk* to the Pacific region in 1979 signifies that Moscow is gradually assembling new and substantial power-projection capabilities. These new capabilities will not only threaten the security of key strait passages that traditionally have been the focus of U.S. and allied naval defense strategy, they already give Moscow some ability to intervene in regional disputes on behalf of client states (as it has done in Vietnam).

These capabilities also mean that the Soviets are building the capacity to threaten the security of the sea lines of communication which are so essential to the commerce of the island nations of the region and their access to energy resources. The growing Soviet military presence will further challenge the ability of the United States to reinforce its Asian deployments in times of crisis. In the coming decade, the United States and its allies will have to consider new approaches to countering the growing Soviet military presence in Asia—a problem which will be substantially compounded should Moscow establish permanent naval and air basing facilities in Vietnam.

Once Again, Indochina

The Indochina Peninsula seems fated to be an area of enduring tension if not overt conflict, and a place in the Asian political landscape where the interests of the great powers converge. It is uncertain how the present military conflict between Vietnam (backed by the Soviet Union) and Kampuchea and China will be resolved, but the outcome will have a significant impact on the security not only of the combatants themselves but also of the ASEAN states. Continuing conflict in Indochina is the factor most likely to poison the Asian security environment and provoke heightened Sino-Soviet tensions in the 1980s.

Hanoi failed in its attempt of late 1978 to wage a quick military campaign which would unseat the Chinese-backed Pol Pot regime in Kampuchea and replace it with a government friendly to Vietnam. And while Beijing's thirty-day punitive border war did not inflict a military defeat on the Vietnamese, it did impose on Hanoi all the military and economic burdens of a two-front security threat and the anticipated political costs of enduring Chinese enmity. It also put the Vietnamese in a position of near total dependence on Soviet security assistance and economic aid for their war-ravaged economy—an international isolation that has been compounded by the collapse of U.S.-Vietnamese normalization talks and international reaction to Hanoi's expulsion of its ethnic Chinese minority and military operations in Kampuchea.

The future evolution of this new phase of the seemingly endless conflict on the Indochina Peninsula is not easily predicted. Vietnam will pursue a new dry-season campaign against the remaining Pol Pot forces, and the Chinese will seek ways of sustaining the guerrilla insurgency against Vietnamese troops in Kampuchea and Hanoi's client Heng Samrin regime. How far the insurgency will spill over into

Thailand, already burdened with a major influx of Khmer refugees, will probably be related to Thailand's role as a sanctuary or source of resupply for the Pol Pot forces. If Hanoi succeeds in destroying the insurgency and consolidating control of Kampuchea for Heng Samrin, the Vietnamese could then wage a guerrilla campaign against the Thai in retribution—although Hanoi will have to consider the prospect of a strong reaction from the ASEAN countries and from the United States. Moreover, the Chinese will continue to oppose the extension of Hanoi's influence beyond Vietnam through some combination of support for guerrilla forces in Kampuchea, perhaps the opening of a second insurgent front in Laos, and maintenance of a conventional military threat on Vietnam's northern frontier.

An unlikely prospect at present is for a change in policy and/or government in Hanoi to a regime that is both more inclined to repair relations with China and limit dependence on the Soviet Union. Were such a development to occur, however, Beijing would almost certainly seek to improve its presently poisonous relations with the Vietnamese.

What can be said with some assurance is that a situation of continuing insurgent warfare and military tension in Indochina will be the context most favorable for the Soviet Union to extend its military presence in Southeast Asia. The great danger in the coming years for virtually all states with interests in Asia is that the Sino-Vietnamese conflict will escalate to a point that precipitates a direct Sino-Soviet military clash. The challenge to the PRC and the United States is to attempt to influence events in a direction that will decouple Indochina from further great-power intervention. At present such a development would require the unlikely circumstances of a neutralization of Kampuchea (perhaps under Prince Sihanouk's leadership) or a new regime in Hanoi that is inclined toward establishing a balanced relationship between Beijing, Moscow, and Washington.

Korea: The Shifting Power Balance Between North and South

The enduring military confrontation between North and South Korea—a major source of tension in East Asia for the past three decades—will likewise not disappear in the 1980s. However, the coming decade will see a significant transformation in the power balance between the two adversaries. The productivity and technical sophistication of the South Korean economy continues to grow rapidly, in marked contrast to the stagnating, defense-oriented system in the North. Per capita income in South Korea surpassed that of the North in the mid-1970s, and the ROK has developed extensive trading ties abroad. Although the military balance presently favors the North, South Korea should be able to strengthen an effective deterrent military force through its own weapons production capabilities and the continuing presence of American ground forces, aircraft, and naval units. In short, a significant shift will occur in the relative power positions of North and South Korea which, if managed properly, could stabilize the confrontation on the Peninsula. Given the shared interests of the ROK, the United States, China, Japan, and probably the Soviet Union as well, in preventing another Korean War, efforts to achieve such a stabilization are likely to elicit broad support.

There are, however, several factors which will make the coming decade a period of some danger in Northeast Asia. The aging Kim Il-sung could come to believe that he faces a "last chance" opportunity to use military force to reunify the Peninsula, or at least to disrupt the trends toward ever-increasing North Korean inferiority relative to the ROK in political, economic, and even military terms. Should such a view materialize during a time of apparently irresolute or distracted American support for the security of the ROK, political turmoil in Seoul growing from the recent assassination of President Park Chung Hee, and perhaps encouragement of Pyongyang by a Soviet Union so concerned about the evolving pattern of Sino-Japanese-American relations that it wants to stir up trouble, the presently favorable situation could be upset by a North Korean military initiative. Pyongyang's belief that the South was approaching the acquisition of atomic weapons and a delivery system capable of threatening North Korea's existence could also reinforce a "now or never" view of present trends.

As the Korean situation evolves in the coming decade, the "deterrence equation," to use Richard Sneider's term, will require careful management by all parties concerned if the confrontation between North and South is not to become a renewed source of conflict with serious effects on the security of the region. And while military issues will remain central to South Korea's security, the 1980s may well see new opportunities for a negotiated stabilization of relations between North and South. The combination of North Korean economic weakness, political isolation, and unfavorable military prospects could lead Kim Il-sung—or more likely his successors—to accept the temporary reality of two Korean societies in return for broadened political recognition and inclusion of North Korea in the expanding Asian economic community.

China Irredenta

Throughout the 1970s Beijing's concerns about Soviet encirclement led Chinese leaders to set aside certain territorial disputes in order to create conditions for a broad united front against "hegemony." The one exception to this pattern was China's military takeover of the Paracel Islands from South Vietnamese forces in January 1974—an initiative that did much to poison Beijing's relations with Hanoi. Most observers of the Sino-Soviet and Sino-Vietnamese disputes would hold that China's territorial claims in these conflicts reflect political maneuvering more than a determined effort to reclaim lost lands. However, Beijing's presently muted territorial claims on the eastern periphery of the PRC are likely, over the longer term, to be sources of tension if not conflict between China and its neighbors.

Since the early 1970s the Chinese have asserted their claim to the Tiaoyu Tai or Senkaku Islands north of Taiwan in the East China Sea, while at the same time urging Japan to set aside this territorial dispute in favor of unity on other issues. This position was reaffirmed during the negotiations for the Peace and Friendship Treaty in 1978. And although Beijing has warned Japan and South Korea against joint exploitation of undersea oil resources on the continental shelf in the Yellow Sea, the Chinese have indicated that they are prepared to reserve their claim as long as Tokyo and Seoul do likewise.

Although PRC leaders were unwilling to foreswear the use of force in resolving the Taiwan issue as part of a normalization agreement with the United States, in the interest of building a positive relationship with Washington they took an accommodating position on the future of the island (as they continue to do regarding the status of Hong Kong and Macao as well). Deng Xiaoping has asserted that it will take decades, if not longer, to reunify (rather than "liberate") the island with the mainland, and that Taiwan can maintain its social, economic, and political systems so that its people will suffer no loss in their present status. Beijing adopts a similar position of unyielding assertion of a territorial claim with reservation of efforts to enforce it with respect to the Spratly Islands in the South China Sea—territory contested by Vietnam and the Philippines, and lightly garrisoned by troops from Taiwan.

China's currently accommodating position on these residual territorial issues reflects not only a desire to minimize conflicts with the United States, Japan, and certain other neighboring states in the context of the Soviet challenge, but also its limited military capabilities for enforcing claims. However, Beijing's swift air and naval takeover of the disputed Paracel Islands indicates that the Chinese will forcefully pursue their claims when circumstances are favorable and military means are available.

The issue for the 1980s is not whether China will rapidly acquire the military assets to conduct complex offshore air and naval campaigns in support of these unresolved territorial disputes, but whether actions of other parties will force Beijing's hand on issues the Chinese would prefer to reserve for more opportune circumstances. A Taiwanese move to assert their independence of China, or the less likely development of Taiwan turning to the Soviet Union for protection against PRC pressures, could impel Beijing to take ill-prepared and costly actions to the detriment of currently moderate and accommodating policies. Similarly, efforts by neighboring states to exploit offshore resources in areas contested by the PRC would very likely sour the current political atmosphere and provoke Chinese countermeasures.

Territorial Disputes and Resource Rivalry

Paralleling China's unresolved territorial claims are a range of similar disputes which could cause serious tensions in Northeast and Southeast Asia in the coming decade. Among these are the Soviet-Japanese conflict over the four islands of Habomai, Shikotan, Kunashiri, and Etorofu in the Southern Kurile chain off Hokkaido—a dispute that continues to block the conclusion of a peace treaty between the two countries[18]—and associated conflicts over fishing rights in the Seas of Japan and Okhotsk and the Bering Sea. The delimitation of Exclusive Economic Zones of control over continental shelf resources remains contested by China, Japan, and South Korea; and several islands in the Gulf of Siam persist as points of potential conflict among Vietnam, Kampuchea, and Thailand.[19] These territorial claims will acquire heightened salience as efforts to promote undersea oil exploration are expanded during the 1980s. And Indonesia's border differences with Papua-New Guinea could cause problems in Jakarta's relations with Australia and the United States.

While none of these territorial issues is likely in itself to be the cause of major conflict, any of them could catalyze other sources of dispute (e.g., Soviet concerns about the direction of Japanese and PRC foreign policies, or the Vietnam-Kampu-

---

[18] The dispute over what the Japanese call the "northern territories" deepened in 1978 when the Soviets began to garrison the islands. See Henry Scott Stokes, "Soviet Force on Isle Protested by Japan," *New York Times*, October 3, 1979.

[19] These territorial disputes are discussed in detail by Guy Pauker on pp. 231-247 below.

chea conflict). In the absence of a successful conclusion of the Law of the Sea negotiations, resolution of associated territorial claims, and delimitation of the boundaries of Exclusive Economic Zones, these issues will remain sources of regional tension and insecurity.

The Strains of Economic Growth

The remarkable economic dynamism of the non-communist states of Asia is not only a source of growing strength and self-confidence, but—as Herman Kahn asserts in Chapter 9—is also cause for considerable optimism in assessing the future. At the same time, this very dynamism presents certain problems of growth, balance, and the evolution of new relationships which, if not handled properly, could have a negative effect on regional security. Five aspects of the present economic situation are cause for particular attention, if not concern:[20] problems of market competition and related protectionist pressures; competition for available investment capital, technology, and skilled manpower; the securing of energy supplies, especially petroleum, and related sea transportation routes; protection of the economies of the region against the effects of global recession; and prospects for weapons development and arms transfers—including the problem of nuclear proliferation—which come with the growing technological sophistication and industrial productivity of the more advanced states of the region.

As economic growth proceeds, the most natural economic complementarity will be betwen the advanced industrial states and the less-developed countries (LDCs), between those who can supply natural resources and inexpensive labor and those with the industrial capacity to provide advanced technologies and markets for raw materials and consumer goods. Thus, prospects are favorable for the growth of trade between Japan and China, the United States and China, perhaps between Taiwan and China, and between the industrial superpowers and the ASEAN states. Such economic complementarity will be constrained, however, by the various protectionist measures invoked by the developed countries as they seek to ease the impact on their domestic industries of less-expensive imports from the LDCs—textiles, clothing, electronics, and the products of newly developed light industries. Such protectionism will inhibit structural readjustments in Japan, the United States, and Western Europe that would help these advanced economies "mesh" with those of the developing states of Asia.

We also note Soedjatmoko's concern about the potential for disruptive radicalization of the "North-South" dimension of Asian economic relations as the poorer countries press their quest for a new international economic order that would provide improved terms of trade for their raw material exports, greater control over "common" offshore resources, and more favorable terms of access to development capital and technology.[21] At the present time it is not clear that events in Asia are moving in this direction; but developments beyond the region—such as a radicalization of the oil-exporting states of the Middle East growing from the present turmoil in Iran—could combine with political changes in one or a number of the key countries of Southeast Asia to produce an atmosphere of economic confrontation between the developing and the developed states.

[20] See the detailed analysis of East Asian economic trend by Harald Malmgren, pp. 200-215 below.
[21] See pp. 173-175 below. See also Guy J. Pauker, *Military Implications of a Possible World Order Crisis in the 1980s*, The Rand Corporation, R-2003-AF, 1977, especially pp. 10-35.

Economic tension will also be evident *between* the developing countries as they contend for export markets, capital, and energy supplies. The prospect of successful offshore oil exploitation in Asia provides some hope for regional protection against the possible disruption of Middle East oil imports. At the same time, the previously noted territorial conflicts raise questions about whether Asian oil can be developed without compounding tensions between China and rival claimants to offshore resources.

As the Korean and Taiwanese economies continue to expand, these two countries will increasingly compete with each other, and with Japan, for American markets currently dominated by the Japanese. And as Beijing pursues its dramatic new economic development program—which various sources estimate could absorb several tens of billions of dollars in foreign investment by the mid-1980s—the ASEAN states will become increasingly concerned about the ability of their new industries to compete with cheap Chinese manufactures and their access to capital and technology from the United States and Japan. A major challenge of the 1980s is to develop a combination of bilateral and multilateral economic institutions, in support of market forces, that can cope with the divisive side effects of economic modernization that is likely to proceed apace.

Among the developed countries, the balance-of-payments problem which continues to burden Japanese-American relations reflects the difficulty of developing complementary market structures where cultures and social systems are so different. While trade problems have not yet generated a protectionist reaction in the United States strong enough to degrade relations between the two countries, it is not clear that leaders in either Washington or Tokyo will be able to resist the domestic political forces that seek to obstruct the adjustments in economic policy which would resolve trade and related monetary problems. Several authors in this volume note concern in Asia that American political and economic pressures on Japan will eventually generate a political backlash among the Japanese which could seriously disrupt U.S.-Japanese relations and drive Japan in the direction of closer ties with either China or the Soviet Union, or impel the country toward a more assertive and nationalistic foreign policy. Such developments can be minimized only by a continuing process of consultation on economic and other issues between Washington and Tokyo.

Security issues deriving from the present phase of economic growth in the region are those related to trends in weapons research and development, production, and transfer. While Japan continues to foreswear an export-oriented arms industry, Korea and Taiwan are establishing a capacity to produce such conventional weapons as light arms, artillery and ammunition, mines, tanks, and light naval craft in quantities that far exceed their own needs. The 1980s could see an increase in weapons sales within the region which would stimulate local arms races. Similarly, Taiwan, South Korea, and Japan each have the scientific talent and industrial capacity to eventually develop advanced military systems such as missiles and atomic weapons.

One of the major challenges to formulating a U.S. security policy appropriate to Asian conditions in the coming decade is the need to sustain a sufficiently credible American defense presence so as to prevent the growth of potentially destabilizing trends in arms research, development, production, and transfer.

Domestic Political Instabilities

As the revolution in Iran of the winter and spring of 1979 illustrates all too clearly, rapid economic growth and defense modernization may generate social and political turmoil that in turn can rapidly undermine regional security arrangements. Apart from the long-term effects of population-growth and food-production problems, which continue to burden several Southeast Asian states, there is the enduring issue of rural-urban social polarization resulting from the uneven distribution of wealth in the early stages of industrialization. Moreover, recently urbanized populations are particularly vulnerable to the disruption of trade-related economic activity and the concomitant prospect of demagogic political appeals by revolutionary political leaders. There is a high probability that the coming decade will witness domestic political instability in a number of key Asian states which could disrupt regional security arrangements. Two factors are particularly relevant in making this assessment: the prospect for leadership-succession crises in states with weakly institutionalized political systems; and the possibility of ethnic or communal tensions exacerbated by political and/or economic developments.

Only three non-communist countries in Asia—Japan, Australia, and New Zealand—have political systems that are clearly capable of smoothly managing leadership successions. Singapore and Malaysia may also be countries in this category. Five states seem particularly vulnerable to disruptive leadership crises in the coming decade: South Korea, Taiwan, the Philippines, Indonesia, and—to a lesser degree—Thailand. In each of these countries the second generation of post-World War II leadership faces the task of managing the transition from highly personal, centralized, and authoritarian rule to more participatory and institutionalized political forms. The assassination of South Korean President Park Chung Hee in November 1979 has already precipitated this problem in the ROK. It seems unlikely that the Chiang, Marcos, Suharto, or Kriangsak leaderships will escape the difficulties of this process, with its attendant potential for domestic turmoil, outside intervention, and disruption of the larger pattern of regional security arrangements.

Ethnic or communal tensions seem particularly likely to develop in four countries: Taiwan, the Philippines, Indonesia, and Malaysia. In Taiwan, the political mobilization of the Taiwanese majority is growing as a result of their substantial economic power. The recent American withdrawal of diplomatic recognition from the Nationalist government is likely to further weaken the legitimacy of the aging "mainlander" ruling elite. While both "mainlander" and Taiwanese communities continue to share an interest in preventing domination of the island by the communist government in Beijing, political and economic developments could impel the Taiwanese to press for self-rule, if not independence. This process may be catalyzed when the strong and visible leadership of Chiang Ching-kuo passes from the scene. Political turmoil on the island, or a Taiwanese move toward independence, could prompt some form of intervention by Beijing and lead to strained relations between the PRC and the United States and Japan.

In Malaysia and Indonesia, enduring ethnic, economic, and political differences between Muslim and Chinese elements of the population could be exacerbated by some combination of growing Islamic fundamentalism, a resurgence in external encouragement of the now-dormant communist insurgencies, and tensions resulting from the process of economic modernization. There is some indication that the

Soviet Union may be stimulating such tensions through Arab collaborators in order to disrupt what it sees as an unfavorable trend toward ASEAN solidarity and resulting efforts to limit the Soviet presence in the region.

The communist countries of Asia will also face the prospect of domestic political instability and leadership crises. We have already commented on the possible impact of the anticipated demise of Kim Il-sung on Korean security. China is also likely to go through a period of political instability in the 1980s as the Communist Party continues to adjust to the passing of Mao Zedong. Reports persist of tensions between Party Chairman Hua Guofeng (Hua Kuo-feng) and thrice-rehabilitated Vice-Premier Deng Xiaoping. And while there now appears to be a leadership consensus in support of the national security and economic development policies that have led China to seek close relations with Japan and the West, Beijing's thirty-year history of leadership feuds and abrupt policy changes gives limited confidence that current policies, which are so favorable to the United States and its allies, will long endure. The Soviet Union, as well, will soon experience a period of leadership change holding the potential for political instability and possible modifications in Moscow's policies affecting Asian security.

While it is unlikely that Soviet and Chinese leaders will suddenly repair their enduringly bad relations, a reduction in Sino-Soviet hostility, if accompanied by diminished geopolitical maneuvering by Moscow and Beijing against each other, would be a positive contribution to the security of Asia. Conversely, a deterioration in Sino-Soviet relations to the point of war, or another period of political instability in Beijing which again turned the Chinese "inward" upon themselves, would profoundly alter the present political climate in Asia.

Of all the trends that are likely to shape regional security in the 1980s, the least amenable to American influence—and the most likely to undermine what at present is a relatively promising situation—is the pattern of domestic political instabilities that could emerge in the coming decade.

AMERICAN SECURITY POLICIES FOR EAST ASIA IN THE 1980s

Beyond consideration of the many factors that will influence Asian security in the 1980s, there remains the problem of the United States—in collaboration with its allies and friendly states—formulating an appropriate set of policies to support their respective and collective interests in the region. Political diversity and the varied nature of Asian problems make it unlikely that one overarching "grand design" for Asia can be formulated. The most fundamental security issue for the United States—how to respond to the regional spillover of the Sino-Soviet dispute in the context of the global Soviet-American rivalry—is a problem that may have limited relevance to the interests of regional allies. And "local" problems may rank low on the U.S. security agenda. In order to identify the major components of an American security policy for the region, the following discussion explores several enduring problems which will shape America's involvement in Asian affairs, suggests certain broad conceptual approaches to a security strategy for the region, and then specifies a set of concrete policy choices.

Problems in Formulating a Coherent American Policy for Asia

Historians of America's relations with Asia have observed several elements of continuity in our approach to the region: a strong interest in commercial development and a fascination with the *potential* of the China market which contrasts with the *reality* of our predominant commerce with Japan; a desire to see Asian nations strong enough to resist the designs of imperialist powers, particularly those who would seek to deny American access to the region; special concern for China's security, its "territorial and administrative integrity" as it was phrased in the "Open Door" Notes of 1899; and efforts to maintain a balance of power in the area, at times through arms control arrangements such as the Washington Conference on Naval Limitations of 1921-22. Of particular significance in contemporary circumstances, America's involvement in Asian security affairs has been characterized by a repetitive or cyclical pattern of periods of reluctance to commit U.S. power in support of self-proclaimed security and commercial interests, followed by deep military involvement—most recently in World War II, Korea, and Vietnam—succeeded by another period of reticence or withdrawal.[22]

Such themes have current relevance as the United States seeks to develop a new defense posture that will reconcile the contradictory pulls of our continuing interests in Asia with a changeable public mood at times inclined to minimize an American security presence and at other times prepared to support forceful intervention in regional affairs. It is not clear that a policy concept can be formulated which will reconcile these conflicting impulses and changing moods, much less one that has the simple coherence of Moscow's vague notion of "Asian collective security" or Beijing's unambiguous appeal for an "anti-hegemony" coalition. America's global and regional security interests are highly varied; and Asia presents a changing and diverse set of defense problems and political relationships which contrast with the U.S. experience in Europe. Moreover, certain characteristics of the Asian environment inhibit the development of a coherent concept for American defense planning which would go much beyond the very general notion of preserving a regional balance of power and preventing domination of the area by one state or a coalition of powers hostile to American interests.

Uncertain Adversaries, Unclear Lines of Confrontation. Since the disintegration of the Sino-Soviet alliance, and with the more recent normalization of U.S.-PRC relations, the sources of threat to American interests in Asia have diffused. Whereas the sharp political-military demarcation between the NATO and Warsaw Pact states in Europe has been blurred only slightly by détente and American diplomacy in Eastern Europe, the one clear line of military confrontation in Asia toward which defense planning can be oriented is the heavily armed boundary between North and South Korea. The main lines of conflict in the region are now between the communist states—disputes such as the Sino-Vietnamese rivalry, in which Americans have little incentive to become involved.

This situation is likely to change during the 1980s, however. The growing Soviet military presence in Asia—in particular, Moscow's strengthened naval deployment—is becoming a major source of concern in Washington as well as in friendly Asian capitals. New Soviet theater nuclear forces, air assets, and an en-

[22] See, for example, A. Whitney Griswold, *The Far East Policy of the United States*, Yale University Press, New Haven, 1964, especially Chap. XI.

hanced capacity to threaten the security of the sea lanes will become major issues in American and allied defense planning. And as several contributors to this volume note, there has already been a basic reassessment of the notion that U.S. Seventh Fleet assets can be safely shifted from the Pacific to the Persian Gulf, the Mediterranean, or the Atlantic in times of crisis. Aside from the fact that such a naval redeployment would be vulnerable to attack in transit, its greater weakness is that it would substantially degrade the ability of the United States to secure the sea lanes so vital to Japan and our other Asian allies.[23]

Several contributors note Moscow's difficulty in translating military resources into political and economic influence; and this has led some analysts to question the seriousness of the Soviet military threat to Asia. But such a perspective is unlikely to persist in the 1980s, largely as a result of Soviet actions. The primary source of insecurity in the region, and the driving force behind the political realignments now tending to repolarize Asia, is the heightened political-military rivalry between Moscow and Beijing; and the Soviets are the more powerful and assertive element in the contest. As a result, the Soviet Union is likely to be seen by most Asians as the most threatening and disruptive presence in the region, despite persisting distrust of Chinese intentions in some quarters.

Regional Political and Economic Diversity. In contrast to Europe's postwar political and economic unity, around which the NATO alliance was formed, Asia is a region of considerable geographic and cultural diversity, and limited economic and political integration. States of Northeast Asia with well-developed economic ties and shared security interests, such as Japan and South Korea, are constrained in the development of cooperative defense relations by the burden of past history. Japan and China only recently have begun to explore the security implications of a shared concern about the expansion of Soviet power; and both countries are limited in the development of regional security roles by the legacy of World War II (in the case of Japan) or by support for communist insurgencies and limited military resources (in Beijing's case).

Disparate security requirements further limit the development of integrated defense planning for the region—particularly between the states of Northeast and Southeast Asia. And while ASEAN gives promise of a regional approach to economic development, there is great reluctance to transform this young organization into an instrument of defense cooperation.

For the United States this situation has meant, and will continue to require, a largely bilateral approach to Asian security issues (with the one exception of the ANZUS alliance). The American defense presence in the region will continue to "bridge" states reluctant to deal with each other directly in security matters and will mediate the gradual projection of Japanese and Chinese power beyond their immediate defense needs. In the absence of one clear and present threat to the security of the region, American defense relations will be characterized by diversity of form and varied degrees of involvement.

America's "European" Orientation

Despite the fact that the last three wars fought by the United States took place in Asia, Americans continue to have a Europe-oriented conception of national

---

[23] See p. 60 (especially footnote 5), 66, 83, and 88 below.

security. The influence of the public's predominantly European cultural background, sense of history, and geographic perspective is only gradually being modified by the impact of U.S. economic ties to Asia, the increasing ease of travel to the Pacific region, and the fact that American security planning in a world of ICBMs and the global reach of Soviet power can no longer be limited to European alliances. All the same, even though U.S. commerce with Asia now exceeds that with any other part of the world, Asia has yet to acquire its proper weight in the American national consciousness. Although U.S. trade with the region surpassed commerce with Europe in the mid-1970s—as a result of a dramatic increase in imports, as is illustrated in Figs. 1 and 2—the ratio of capital investment in Europe to capital investment in Asia is more than 5 to 1 (as shown in Fig. 3), presumably because of the relative ease of doing business in an area that is culturally familiar and more readily accessible, and where political and economic stability contribute to a favorable investment climate.

To these factors must be added the weight of the Vietnam experience. The American public continues to lack confidence that it can understand, much less cope effectively with, a culturally distant region of the world. Current frustrations in dealing with the turmoil in Iran reinforce the public's inclination to avoid being pulled once again into seemingly endless conflicts in unstable Asian countries that do not appear to have direct relevance for America's security. All the same, the effects of the Vietnam trauma seem finally to be dissipating. The public calls ever more clearly for demonstrations of American strength and leadership abroad. Congressional leaders express renewed willingness to pursue important national objectives in Asia, as is most evident in recent Senate opposition to the withdrawal of U.S. ground forces from Korea—despite the impact of "Koreagate" and some public support for the withdrawal.

In addition to the influence of public opinion, there is some uncertainty in the minds of American government officials and defense planners about the exact role our Asian relations should play in a global security strategy: Given the Sino-Soviet dispute, is there a new linkage between European defense and the now positive relations between Beijing, Tokyo, and Washington? Will the extension of Soviet, Japanese, and Chinese military power into the region contribute to stability in Asia, or to a new phase of arms competition and political rivalry? And will the growing industrial power and weapons-production capability of such states as South Korea and Taiwan help to stabilize the confrontations that have been major points of regional instability over the past three decades, or will they be new sources of instability?

In sum, it is unlikely that under present circumstances a "grand concept" can be formulated that would readily shape American security planning for the region or that would be accepted by enough Asian states to constitute an effectively integrated effort. Nonetheless, several general orientations toward U.S. involvement in Asian security affairs can be identified which will influence specific policy choices and give some measure of coherence to otherwise disparate actions and apparently uncoordinated relationships.

Three Approaches to an Asian Security Strategy

One remarkable quality of this period of transition is that the United States has real choices in structuring its future role in regional security affairs. Certain alter-

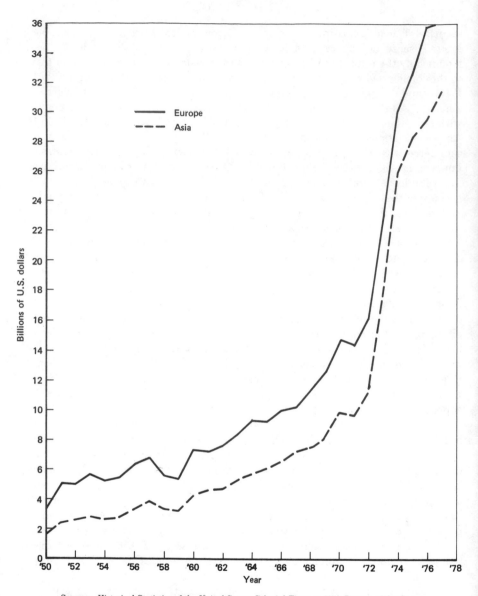

SOURCE: *Historical Statistics of the United States; Colonial Times to 1970*, Bureau of the Census, U.S. Government Printing Office, Washington, D.C., 1975; and *Statistical Abstract of the United States; 1973, 1978*, U.S. Department of Commerce.

Fig. 1—U.S. exports of merchandise to Europe and Asia, 1950-1977

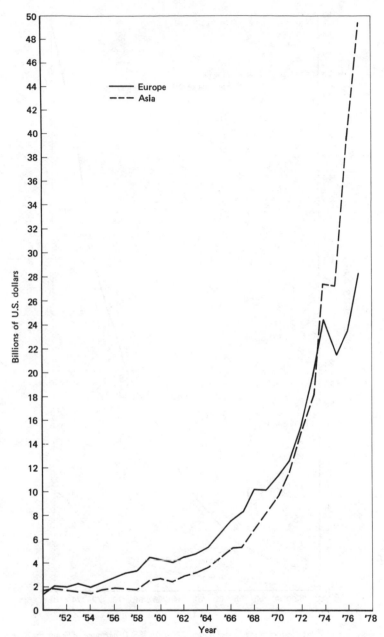

Source: *Historical Statistics of the United States; Colonial Times to 1970*, Bureau of the Census, U.S. Government Printing Office, Washington, D.C., 1975; and *Statistical Abstract of the United States; 1973, 1978*, U.S. Department of Commerce.

Fig. 2—U.S. imports of merchandise from Europe and Asia, 1950-1977

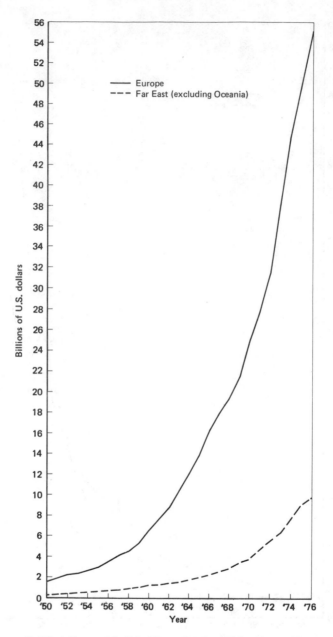

SOURCE: *Statistical Abstract of the United States, 1957-1978*, U.S. Department of Commerce.

Fig. 3—U.S. direct investments in Europe and the Far East, 1950-1976

natives are constrained by public resistance to involvement in distant sources of conflict, but others are reinforced by a concern among government officials that American interests will not permit another period of withdrawal from regional defense responsibilities. The primary sources of choice are changes occurring in the region itself: the heightened capability of various states (especially Japan and Korea) to assume greater security responsibilities; and the interest of others, primarily China, in encouraging a more active American role in global security affairs.

One thoughtful analysis suggests that the United States has three basic choices of strategy in its approach to Asia.[24] The first is a "minimalist" or "limited involve-ment" pattern in which the United States would restrict its direct security presence to the key alliance with Japan and limit its naval deployments to mid-Pacific island bases from which it can secure the strategic submarine fleet. In effect, this approach would "uncover" America's commercial, cultural, and political involvement in Asia on the assumptions that the security of allies such as Korea and the Philippines is not in serious jeopardy, that there is no real threat to the security of the sea lanes, and that American influence in the region can be limited to economic, political, and cultural activities.

The second choice is to join forces with the Chinese in an active "united front" designed to limit the extension of Soviet influence into Asia and counterweight Moscow's growing military capabilities for strategic and regional action through concerted efforts by the PRC, the United States, Japan, and the NATO states.

The third alternative is to limit America's formal security commitments to its traditional Asian allies but maintain an active "forward" military presence in the region, applying U.S. defense resources in a flexible and responsive way that pre-serves an equilibrium of power without being provocative to Moscow or seeking to deny Soviet access to the region for non-disruptive purposes of commerce and cultural relations.

While the "limited involvement" strategy reflects a now-changing public mood and the policy positions of a few in official positions, it is largely a straw man against which to test alternatives. It is an unsupportable view, given American interests in Asia; and it is unworkable, given the likely evolution of regional trends in the absence of a mediating American security presence. A viable security strategy is likely to combine elements of coalition activity among the major powers of the region with the flexible application of U.S. defense assets in response to challenges to regional stability. The full significance of these choices, however, can be grasped only by considering in detail the practical policy alternatives we will face in the 1980s.

Ten Policy Choices for an American Security Strategy in Asia

1. Develop Security Ties with China? The great strategic dilemma for the United States is how to proceed in developing relations with the PRC now that political normalization has been achieved. From the perspective of America's secu-rity interests, the fact that we do not have a political and military confrontation

---

[24] See Robert A. Scalapino, "Approaches to Peace and Security in Asia: The Uncertainty Surrounding American Strategic Principles," *Current Scene*, U.S. Consulate-General, Hong Kong, Vol. XVI, Nos. 8 and 9, August-September 1978.

with the Chinese—as we had for three decades—gives the United States considerable strategic flexibility. We no longer face a two-front security challenge from the combination of Soviet and Chinese power. Consolidating and strengthening cooperative U.S.-PRC relations in political and economic areas, along with social and cultural exchanges, will have a positive effect on America's global position and on the Asian environment irrespective of whether the United States and China develop an active program of security cooperation.

Proceeding beyond the present U.S.-PRC relationship into areas of defense collaboration, however, presents issues of considerable complexity. Will a China that is strengthening its military forces with help from the United States and its allies also maintain an active role in constraining the expansion of Soviet power, or will PRC leaders seek to reduce Soviet pressures on them through some negotiated accommodation with Moscow? Will Soviet leaders, fearing the formation of a U.S.-PRC-Japanese-Western European coalition against them, lash out in some way to fragment this proto-alliance—perhaps, as William Hyland suggests, through military action against the weakest member of the coalition, China? What strains will U.S.-PRC security cooperation place on America's relations with her traditional Asian allies? And will a Sino-American security relationship, a "united front against social-imperialism," repolarize Asian affairs around the Sino-Soviet feud?

Given such considerations, the United States should proceed with caution in developing the security aspects of the U.S.-PRC relationship. While completion of the normalization process has tilted the United States toward the anti-hegemony side of the strategic rivalry between Beijing and Moscow, steps toward the development of defense cooperation with the Chinese—ranging from policy coordination and intelligence-sharing to sales of defense-related technologies and weapons systems, to the ultimate measure of joint defense planning—should be taken in response to Soviet actions that threaten U.S. and PRC interests.

The United States should avoid actions that convey to Moscow an intent to develop a security relationship with the Chinese irrespective of Soviet actions. If there is some constraining effect on Soviet aggressiveness in the present Sino-American relationship, it is more in the *anticipation* of a U.S.-PRC alliance than in practical measures that could strengthen China's defenses. The United States must convey a sense to Soviet leaders that they are able to influence the pace and direction in which U.S.-PRC relations evolve; that restraint on their part will be met with concomitant restraint in Sino-American security cooperation, while Soviet actions that threaten Chinese and American interests will provoke heightened U.S.-PRC cooperation.

From this perspective, current American policy on the issue of possible arms sales to China seems inappropriate. The policy, as articulated by Secretary of State Vance, is that while the United States will not itself sell military equipment to the PRC, it will not object to its allies doing so. [25] This position is problematic in a number of respects: It does not conform with the Administration's expressions of concern for the development of a "strong and secure" China,[26] and it minimizes

[25] See Secretary Vance's news conference of November 2, 1977, in *Department of State Bulletin*, November 1977, p. 715.

[26] See, for example, President Carter's toast to Deng Xiaoping during the Vice-Premier's visit to Washington, as reported in the *New York Times*, January 30, 1979; and Vice-President Mondale's speech at Beijing University on August 27, 1979, in the *New York Times*, August 28, 1979.

incentives for Chinese leaders to sustain close ties to the United States and Europe. It is a policy that Moscow probably interprets as duplicitous: The United States *says* it will not sell arms to China, but Washington probably is encouraging such sales by its European allies. This policy encourages the Soviets to put political pressure on the Germans, British, and French to not sell arms to the PRC; and at the same time, it minimizes Moscow's incentives for restraint in dealings with the United States by decreasing concerns about possible responses we might undertake with the Chinese.

In contrast, an American policy that held open the *possibility* of U.S. arms sales to China, while developing a record of such sales only in response to Soviet actions that threaten U.S. and PRC interests, would be a more realistic expression of America's intent to counter such actions. It would also provide greater incentives for Soviet restraint. And while there are problems in implementing such a concept, it is a better declared policy than alternatives which either are not credible or assert the intent to arm China irrespective of Soviet actions.

The recent record of Soviet actions in Africa, the Middle East, and Asia gives little confidence that Moscow will show restraint in the absence of some countervailing pressure. The strategic challenge to the United States and its traditional Asian allies, and to China, in the 1980s will be to strengthen the potential for creating such a countervailing force without gratuitously provoking Soviet actions that would repolarize the region and increase the possibility of military conflict.

2. Enhancing Defense Cooperation with Japan. The past several years have seen a remarkable change in the willingness of the Japanese official community and public to openly discuss the country's security requirements: to consider the previously taboo issue of active defense cooperation with the United States; and to think about an expansion of Japan's defensive military capabilities. Japanese defense planners now talk about developing a national security budget in excess of 1 percent of GNP[27] and assert their responsibility to speak out on international issues. The Fukuda government's willingness to conclude a Peace and Friendship Treaty with Beijing in 1978, in the face of strong Soviet objections, represents an important turning point in Japan's post-World War II role in international affairs.

How should the United States respond to this new assertiveness in Japanese thinking about security issues? Because the U.S.-Japanese defense relationship remains healthy—and indeed today is receiving less criticism than ever from domestic and foreign sources—the response will depend on how the two countries can transform what thus far has been a protectorate relationship into a working alliance between equals. There are ample opportunities for genuine defense cooperation as the two sides confront the sources of regional insecurity considered earlier.

High priority must be given to managing the economic tensions associated with the bilateral balance-of-payments problem so that political pressures do not degrade the security alliance. The two countries must also ensure that the pattern of regional economic growth supports their political and security objectives in Asia. Washington and Tokyo will find it in their common interest to coordinate policies for dealing with such issues as Korean security, relations with China and the Soviet Union, and regional resource rivalry, but the United States must make special efforts to overcome its past poor record for genuine consultation with the Japanese.

[27] See pp. 106-108 below.

Public and official attitudes in Japan will no longer tolerate a "second class" or subordinate status in relations with the United States, and there will be increasing sensitivity to American actions that imply either a lack of awareness of Japanese interests or unreliability in the U.S. commitment to Japan's defense.

In the area of military planning, Japanese concerns about the growing Soviet naval and aircraft deployments in the Pacific, and the security of the sea lanes, are clearly shared by the United States. The question for the 1980s, as Japan expands its Self-Defense Forces, is how far the two sides can proceed in coordinating the use of military assets for air defense, anti-submarine warfare, and sea lane security within the framework of the Mutual Security Treaty.

Despite the "Nixon shock" on China policy of 1971, the process of normalizing U.S.-PRC relations unburdened Japan of one of the major sources of tension in its postwar foreign policy: Chinese criticism of the Japanese-American security alliance. Since 1973 the Chinese have actively encouraged Japan to sustain defense ties with the United States; and it seems likely that Beijing will continue to support this position throughout the coming decade. The common problem for Washington and Tokyo in their dealings with the PRC will be to coordinate the potential for security cooperation with the Chinese so as to remain in control of the effects of the China relationship on the Soviet Union.

3. The U.S. Military Force Structure in Asia. Since the end of America's involvement in the Vietnam War, U.S. military forces in Asia have been designed for deterrence rather than war-fighting. Indeed, as one informed policymaker on American defense matters has observed, "No clear and carefully delineated U.S. defense posture in Asia has emerged in the wake of Vietnam," apart from an effort to limit American involvement in future conflicts on the Asian mainland to the employment of air and naval power in support of indigenous ground forces.[28]

The analyses in this volume underscore the complex purposes that American military forces in Asia must serve, in combination with the political and economic instruments of U.S. foreign policy. The strategic submarine fleet in the Pacific must be secured against a growing Soviet naval presence so as to maintain the integrity of our nuclear deterrent. We must confront, along with our allies, growing Soviet theater nuclear forces and counter their threat to American bases in the region. Conventional U.S. air, naval, and ground forces must help deter renewed conflict in Korea and Indochina (against Thailand). They must be maintained at a level that will overcome the diminished credibility of the American military presence in the region (and allay suspicions that they might be redeployed in a time of crisis to Europe or the Middle East), discourage incentives for nuclear proliferation that might derive from a lack of confidence in U.S. security guarantees, ensure the security of the sea lanes, and minimize prospects for conflict over offshore resources.

Our military assistance and arms sales programs must strengthen the defense capabilities of our allies and friends at a level appropriate to regional threats, without being so constrained as to stimulate a search for other sources of supply or so forthcoming as to provoke local arms races. In short, the American military presence in Asia in the 1980s must be responsive to a full range of challenges—from

---

[28] [Senator] Sam Nunn, "What Forces for Asia? What Forces for Europe?", *The Washington Review of Strategic and International Studies*, Vol. I, No. 1, January 1978, p. 15.

helping to maintain the strategic balance and deterring conventional conflict among great and regional powers to discouraging proxy interventions and enabling allies to deal with insurgent threats.

Several specific military challenges are likely to necessitate adjustments in the U.S. force posture in Asia in the 1980s. As Soviet theater nuclear forces grow, it will be necessary to consider ways of countering threats to allied military forces and American bases. As Soviet naval forces deployed in the Pacific increase—and if the USSR acquires naval and air bases in Vietnam—we will have to consider measures that will sustain sea lane security in order to reassure allies about our ability to help protect their routes of commercial transport and the military logistical lines that sustain their defenses. We will also have to counter Moscow's enhanced threat to our strategic submarine fleet in the Pacific. To be specific, consideration should be given to the addition of a third or fourth carrier task force to the Seventh Fleet, particularly in view of the heightened demands for naval assets in the Indian Ocean and the Mediterranean resulting from instabilities in the Middle East. And strengthened Soviet air deployments in Asia will require increased air-defense support for allied and friendly states.

In view of the Carter Administration's decision to postpone further withdrawals of American ground forces from Korea, it does not appear necessary at the present time to consider increases in infantry or marine deployments to Asia. It will be important to sustain current ground-force levels, however, if the credibility of American defense commitments in the region is to be enhanced. U.S. military assistance and arms sales programs will assume heightened importance for strengthening the ability of key allies to deal directly with conventional military threats (such as South Korea now faces) and insurgencies (as Thailand is again contending with).

4. Regional Arms Control. East Asia has not been the focus of efforts in recent years to promote arms control agreements, although the great powers and some regional states have sought to minimize destabilizing conventional arms races and the proliferation problem through unilateral action. This situation may well change in the 1980s, however. Assuming there is a SALT III negotiation, or that progress is made in conventional arms talks in Europe (the Mutual and Balanced Force Reduction—MBFR—talks), it is likely that theater nuclear and conventional force issues will arise that will concern not only U.S. and Soviet Asian deployments but also the forces of our allies and friendly states.

In pursuing such negotiations, the United States will have to be particularly sensitive to the potential for strains in relations with allies and friends as third-party issues are raised in the context of Soviet-American negotiations. Japan, for example, will worry about degradation of the American nuclear umbrella resulting from discussions on theater nuclear issues; and there will be sensitivity to the manner in which U.S. forward-based systems affect Japan's commitment to the three nuclear principles of non-development, non-transfer, and non-deployment. The Chinese will be concerned about Soviet-American agreements on nuclear testing and deployment issues which will enable Moscow to constrain the PRC's defense modernization program—or at least to put Beijing on the political defensive. The Chinese will also worry that any Washington-Moscow agreement to reduce Soviet tank deployments in Europe might just enable the Soviet Union to increase its armored forces on the Sino-Soviet frontier.

As noted earlier, the Korean situation may be evolving to a point where Pyongyang will see its interests served by an agreement stabilizing the present military balance between North and South. In such a circumstance, it might be possible to negotiate an arms-control arrangement for the Korean Peninsula. In the absence of such an opportunity, however, the United States will have an important role to play in unilaterally sustaining the military balance between North and South by way of the American military presence in the ROK, as well as through military assistance and arms sales programs to Seoul.

In recent years, the United States has conducted its military assistance and arms sales programs, and has deployed (or decided to withdraw) its forces abroad, as if there were no relationship between such policies and either conventional arms transfer patterns or incentives for nuclear proliferation. In several instances, however, the United States has put itself in the position of simultaneously generating questions about the reliability of its defense commitment and pressuring foreign governments not to acquire certain conventional weapons systems or nuclear reactor fuel-reprocessing facilities.

To the degree that dampening conventional arms races and preventing nuclear proliferation remain priority foreign policy goals, the United States may have to adopt more active and visible defense measures in its security relations abroad. The capability for indigenous development and production of sophisticated conventional arms and nuclear weapons in several Asian states may pass beyond American influence in the coming decade. This will sharpen the tradeoff between the credibility and strength of U.S. defense relationships and pressures for conventional arms acquisition and nuclear proliferation.

5. Minimizing Vietnam's Role as a Soviet Proxy. Soviet success in using Cuban troops as forces of proxy intervention in Africa may tempt Moscow to encourage Vietnam to play a similar role in Asia—initially by denying Kampuchea to Chinese influence, and then perhaps by seeking to destabilize Thailand and (with the help of an Arab client state) other ASEAN countries where Muslim-Chinese communal tensions persist (e.g., Malaysia and Indonesia). The fluidity of the current conflict in Indochina makes it difficult to assess future trends, but if—as seems most likely—Vietnam succeeds in consolidating control over Kampuchea, Hanoi could decide to press on against Thailand. In such circumstances, the United States, the ASEAN states, and China will have to consider actions that would support the Thais and bring pressure to bear on the Vietnamese. A major risk, of course, is that such actions will heighten Soviet pressures against the Chinese, and thus once again require American officials to consider ways of enhancing PRC security.[29]

The preferred outcome in Indochina, from the point of view of American interests, is the reestablishment of a neutral government in Kampuchea—perhaps under Prince Sihanouk's leadership. It now seems unlikely that a constellation of forces will emerge from the present chaos and violence in that savaged country to make possible such a development, but Indochina has produced equally unanticipated surprises before. In appropriate circumstances, the United States retains the option—which was politically foreclosed by Hanoi's invasion of Kampuchea—of recognizing Hanoi and assisting in the reconstruction of Vietnam's economy.

6. ASEAN: A Security Coalition for Southeast Asia? While the ASEAN countries resist burdening their institution of political and economic cooperation with defense responsibilities, the possible evolution of the current Vietnam-Kampuchea conflict could lead the member states to re-evaluate their security require-

---

[29] See footnote 16 on p. 9 above.

ments. One former senior government official from the region has asked why, if Moscow develops proxy forces (e.g., Cuba) for its expansionist aims, should not the United States encourage the development of "proxy defense" forces by friendly states?

The interests of the ASEAN countries and the United States would be best served by a resolution of the present violence in Indochina, by Hanoi's return to the tasks of reconstructing Vietnam, and by great-power acceptance of the region as an area of "peace, freedom, and neutrality." Reality, however, may not be so kind as to support such a development; and the 1980s may see Vietnamese aggressiveness, externally supported insurgencies, and domestic political instabilty in one or more countries of the region combining to present ASEAN with difficult security problems. The choice will then be whether to address those problems in some collective framework or as individual states reinforced with external assistance.

7. Korea: Managing the "Crossover" in Power Relationships Between North and South. As noted in the previous analysis of the Korean situation, a major shift in economic and military power relationships between North and South is now taking place. Yet the prospect for instability in Korea remains high, given the political uncertainty now evident in the South and the possibility of a "last chance" military initiative by the aging Kim Il-sung.

The United States has a strong interest in encouraging the evolution of the Korean situation in a direction that will help stabilize the Peninsula. The now-reversed decision to withdraw the U.S. Second Division from the South probably raised doubts in Kim Il-sung's mind about the credibility of the American defense commitment to the ROK. It also increased incentives in the South for proliferation. And given the temptation to the North that a situation of political turmoil in Seoul could provide, the United States must exercise special care in the application of its human rights policy, particularly as it cannot apply the policy with equal vigor in Pyongyang as well as in Seoul.

In the 1980s the United States will have to simultaneously maintain the military balance on the Peninsula and develop a joint policy with Seoul that will draw Pyongyang into a constructive economic relationship in return for acceptance of the present division of the country (pending some future joint and peaceful solution to the reunification problem). In this regard, the now fully normalized U.S.-PRC relationship and Beijing's currently accommodating position on the Taiwan issue hold out new hope for at least latent Chinese support of such a policy. But the United States must maintain its role as sustainer of the military equilibrium on the Peninsula to provide a framework within which a political accommodation can take place.

8. Responding to Internal Political Instabilities. Some of the most troubling aspects of the Asian security environment that are least amenable to U.S. influence are the sources of domestic political instability—leadership succession crises, ethnic tensions, and insurgent movements—which can rapidly disrupt the security of an entire region. We have noted the vulnerabilities of a number of Asian states to leadership transitions and insurgencies or communal violence. The question is what, if anything, American policy can do to minimize the impact of such developments on regional security. The short answer is "not much"; and those sources of influence the United States does possess are most effectively applied in a preventive manner, not in times of crisis.

If there is any lesson to be learned from Vietnam, it is that direct American intervention in an insurgent conflict is more likely to undermine the development of an indigenous capability to cope with the problem than it is to make the problem go away.

Three forms of influence that the United States does have are political support for the indigenous leadership (including pressures to improve human rights conditions), military assistance designed to strengthen internal security forces, and the ability to apply political and military pressures when an insurgent movement is clearly receiving assistance across an international boundary. This third form of action requires little comment, although if one of the ASEAN states becomes the target of insurgent pressures supported by Hanoi, the question will be whether the Association, rather than the United States, should take the lead in collectively responding to the threat.

By assisting in the development of internal security forces, the United States will continue to face the dilemma of wanting to see friendly governments acquire the capability to cope with threats to their domestic political stability, even while the development of these forces can work to create or enhance the very tensions—through suppression of domestic sources of political opposition—that they are designed to limit. There is no generally applicable solution to this dilemma; it must be managed on a case-by-case basis. Similarly, no standard or simple answer can be given to the question of how to use the application or withdrawal of expressions of American support for a particular leader. Such expressions of support are one of the basic tools of influence in the conduct of foreign relations, and decisions regarding their use must remain the responsibility of the White House and senior State Department officials.

One observation might be made, however, about the human rights policy as an element in our dealings with foreign governments. The impression has been created in recent years that use of the human rights issue is shaped largely by domestic American political considerations—a Congressman's need to develop constituent support for himself, or an Administration's effort to mobilize backing for a given foreign policy. While public support is without question an important factor in the conduct of foreign relations, a primary consideration must be the impact of a human rights position on the internal stability of the country concerned. A legitimate rationale for the application of such a policy, and a criterion for its use, must be whether pressures for improving the human rights of a given people will inflame political tensions and heighten prospects for political instability, or whether they will move a government to broaden its popular base and enhance stability.

Other reactions to America's recent use of the human rights issue in foreign relations are that we apply it to our allies and friends more vigorously than to our adversaries (e.g., South Korea as opposed to the totalitarian North) or to defenseless allies but not to states from whom we want something (e.g., the Philippines as opposed to Saudi Arabia). There is also a feeling that the policy inappropriately seeks to apply American political standards to countries with very different cultural and institutional backgrounds.[30] Such attitudes tend to generate resentment and cynicism rather than ameliorating the problems the policy is presumably designed to address.

[30] See p. 94 below.

9. Defusing Resource Rivalries and Territorial Disputes. The various sources of dispute over territory and access to offshore natural resources in Asia will probably remain points of confrontation in the 1980s, even as the countries involved may seek to defer resolution of their differences in the interest of more immediate goals (as the Chinese and Japanese have done in the case of the Senkaku or Tiaoyu Tai Islands). American policy, as well, is likely to be one of minimizing involvement in disputes that are not of direct relevance to U.S. interests and for which there are no ready solutions. Washington, for example, properly discourages American oil-prospecting firms from conducting explorations in disputed offshore areas of the Yellow, East, and South China Seas.

American security interests may be served in the coming decade, however, by more active efforts to encourage the negotiated resolution of such sources of dispute as delimitation of the boundaries of Exclusive Economic Zones. The interest of China and Japan in heightening their economic cooperation, combined with unique American capabilities for undersea oil and mineral exploitation, may provide the basis for collaborative resolution of these sources of dispute.

10. Moderating the Strains of Economic Development. The coming decade is likely to be a time of continuing strong economic growth for many of the states of East Asia, and of new regional investment and trade patterns as Japan and the United States deepen their involvement in China's economic development. This constructive process, however, will generate problems that existing bilateral and multilateral institutions may not be able to resolve. These include the security of access to energy supplies, a growing potential for destructive market competition and protectionism, uneven access to development capital, and unbalanced trade patterns. The following problems seem to require particular attention if economic strains are not to have a disruptive impact on political relationships and regional security:

- China's recent turn outward to the international community, particularly to Japan and the United States, for development capital may create some imbalances in regional investment. Washington and Tokyo have a special interest in seeing that this does not happen and, in particular, that the ASEAN states maintain the momentum of their development programs.
- Recent events in the Middle East and Gulf states illustrate once again the vulnerability of the developing and industrial countries to disruption of energy supplies. China's interest in exploiting its oil and coal reserves for export, as well as other opportunities for offshore oil exploration in Asia, may provide new opportunities for buffering the region against the disruption of energy imports.
- The growing interdependence of the economies of East Asia, both within the region and in relations with various developed countries in other parts of the world, may require some new multilateral mechanism to deal with the "growing pains" of these evolving relationships. The developing countries will enter a period of enhanced competition for markets in the developed world; and the developed countries will have to go through a period of difficult structural economic adjustments to alleviate the political pressures of economic protectionism and to respond to new opportunities for

the export of manufactured goods to the more advanced developing economies of Asia.

Existing international economic mechanisms, such as UNCTAD (the United Nations Conference on Trade and Development), the GATT (General Agreement on Tariffs and Trade), the Asian Development Bank, and ESCAP (the United Nations Economic and Social Commission for Asia and the Pacific), may be inadequate forums for dealing with these issues. There is a growing sense that an institution such as the OECD[31] should be constructed for Asia. Several specialists have proposed an OPTAD—an Organization for Pacific Basin Trade and Development.[32] Such an instrumentality could facilitate discussion and the formulation of policies to cope with the economic strains that are a sign of the continuing vitality of the non-communist economies of Asia, and also with potential sources of tensions which could degrade cooperative political relations and eventually cause security problems.

CONCLUSION: A POWER EQUILIBRIUM OR RENEWED POLARIZATION IN EAST ASIA?

The above areas of policy choice do not constitute a coherent program for East Asian security in the 1980s, but they do exhibit one predominant theme: the catalyzing influence that actions of the Soviet Union will have in shaping the direction of policy in many of these areas. The Chinese, who have long stressed self-reliance in their efforts to modernize, have turned to the United States and other countries of the West largely because of their fears of Soviet encirclement. Recent policy pronouncements from Beijing and the initiation of talks with Moscow suggest renewed interest in post-Mao Zedong China in moderating tensions with the Soviet Union. Continuing Soviet pressures against the PRC, however, will drive the Chinese in the direction of closer security cooperation with the West.

While American policymakers are currently chary of such issues as arms sales to China, continuing Soviet military modernization and interventions—either direct or by proxy—in areas of the world of concern to U.S. interests will gradually shift attitudes toward support for more active and overt forms of security cooperation with Beijing. And the Japanese, as the analyses in this volume document, have reached a major turning point in their post-World War II foreign and security policies. The direction they take will be influenced, above all, by the threat they feel from the Soviet Union—now identified in the defense "White Papers" as the country's major security concern.

Lesser disputes of the Asian region—the Korean military standoff, the continuing conflict in Indochina, internal political and ethnic instabilities, and areas of territorial and resource conflict—have their own dynamic. Yet they provide contexts into which the Soviet Union has demonstrated a willingness to intervene in other parts of the world. This is not to lay at Moscow's doorstep responsibility for

---

[31] See p. 216 (especially footnote 4) below.

[32] See the discussion of this issue by Harald Malmgren on p. 214 below; see also *An Asian-Pacific Regional Economic Organization: An Exploratory Concept Paper*, Committee on Foreign Relations, U.S. Senate, July 1979.

all the world's ills, but only to point out the unavoidable fact that the Soviets have the concerns, the capabilities, and the record of initiatives which make the USSR the country most likely to challenge the security interests of the major and regional states of Asia.

In the absence of such a challenge, the countries of the region would likely pursue their own separate interests in loose forms of collaboration—in the process stimulating their own local conflicts as well. An equilibrium of relationships would probably emerge with only limited relevance to the interests of the great powers. The more likely prospect, however, is for a worldwide series of Soviet initiatives that will tend to repolarize the region around the Sino-Soviet feud and the U.S.-Soviet global competition.

This is the great change we anticipate for the 1980s in the security affairs of Asia. Unlike the 1950s, when the Sino-Soviet alliance polarized the region around Soviet and American security coalitions, or the 1960s, when the Chinese tried to go their own way and build a third pole in international relationships around the "newly emerging forces" of the Third World, the 1970s has seen the Chinese turn toward the West to counter the heightened military and political challenge from Moscow and to accelerate their economic modernization. The 1980s will very likely see the evolution of this still-latent security coalition of the United States, China, Japan, and the countries of Western Europe in response to the growing and assertive power of the Soviet Union.

PART I

THE INFLUENCE OF THE GREAT POWERS

Chapter 2

THE SINO-SOVIET CONFLICT:
A SEARCH FOR NEW SECURITY STRATEGIES

William G. Hyland[1]

Shortly after Soviet Premier Khrushchev's political demise in October 1964, Chinese Premier Zhou Enlai (Chou En-lai) paid a brief visit to Moscow. Zhou ostensibly was attending the celebration of the October Revolution. In fact, he was on a reconnaissance mission to determine whether basic Soviet policies were to be changed in the wake of the Khrushchev purge. According to one account, probably apocryphal, in the course of Zhou's conversations with Soviet leaders, Minister of Defense Rodion Malinovsky turned to the visiting Premier and said, "Now it's your turn to get rid of Mao." There is no indication of the degree of Zhou's indignation; but in any event, the Chinese obviously did not follow Malinovsky's advice.

The point of this story is that fifteen years ago it was still possible to regard the split between the Soviet Union and the People's Republic of China (PRC) as a temporary phenomenon resulting in some measure from the forceful personalities leading each of them. The Chinese thought it at least worthwhile to explore the possibility of a shift in Soviet policy by dispatching Zhou to Moscow—a conciliatory gesture in its own right. At the same time, the Soviets apparently thought that some change might be brought about simply by removing Mao Zedong (Mao Tsetung). The failure of Zhou's brief mission was a turning point. The Brezhnev regime was not prepared for an accommodation; but neither was it simply "Khrushchevism without Khrushchev," as it has often been depicted in Chinese propaganda. In fact, Brezhnev and his colleagues began to introduce some important changes in their policy toward Beijing (Peking) which indicated that they considered the Chinese a serious challenge to the political and security interests of the Soviet Union.

THE SOVIET UNION'S POST-KHRUSHCHEV CHINA POLICY

Where Khrushchev had relished polemicizing with the Chinese and set some store by his ability to persuade other communists of the righteousness of his own cause, the Brezhnev regime downgraded the purely polemical aspects of the contest with Beijing. Whereas Khrushchev brought primarily political and psychological pressures on China, without any real threat of military action, the Brezhnev regime began building up its military forces, with the implicit threat of intervention. Where Khrushchev wanted to win over the majority of the communist movement and reestablish Soviet preeminence, the Brezhnev regime came to see the contest

[1] William G. Hyland is a Senior Fellow at the Georgetown Center for Strategic and International Studies. He formerly served as a staff member of the National Security Council, Director of the Bureau of Intelligence and Research of the Department of State (1973-74), and Deputy Assistant to the President for National Security Affairs (1975-76).

in more conventional power terms. In short, in the years that followed Khrushchev's removal, the Soviet leadership began to pursue policies designed to contain and counter Chinese influence. The conflict was transformed from a ideological contest into a power struggle between two potential enemy states.

Diplomatically, the Soviets moved to improve their dealings with Japan in the 1960s, especially in economic relations. They intervened in the Indian subcontinent in 1965 to mediate the India-Pakistan dispute—not to resolve the Kashmir issue, but to isolate China. In Vietnam, the new Soviet regime became more actively involved, extending greater military assistance and pressuring China, via Hanoi, to make some accommodation to permit the transit of Soviet military supplies across Chinese territory. And the Soviets may even have made some appeals to anti-Mao factional leaders in China—e.g., Liu Shaoqi (Liu Shao-ch'i)—for a joint policy on Vietnam.

Most important, the new Moscow leadership began a systematic buildup of military strength along the Sino-Soviet frontier. Some increase in the number of Soviet divisions began almost immediately in 1965. The Soviets had about 12 understrength divisions for immediate operations against the Chinese in 1964. In the four years that followed, this force was almost doubled, including, for the first time, the deployment of 1 to 2 divisions in Mongolia. And between 1967 and 1972 the number of divisions again doubled. By 1972 the Soviets had deployed about 600,000 troops along China's northern periphery. Subsequently, the buildup continued, although more in materiel than in manpower. By the early 1970s nearly 45 divisions were stationed along the Soviet-Chinese border or in immediate reserve. These forces were supplied with about 6,000 tanks and 4,000 tactical aircraft. It is estimated by U.S. government agencies that about one-quarter of all Soviet military forces were now aligned against China.[2]

Against this backdrop of growing strength, the Soviet intervention in Czechoslovakia in August 1968 and the promulgation of the Brezhnev doctrine of limited sovereignty for socialist states had ominous implications for Beijing. In this period, the appreciation of the Soviet military threat began to play a role among the contending factions of the Cultural Revolution. Some Chinese leaders believed it would be prudent to conciliate the Soviets, while others advocated unrelenting opposition.[3] Whatever the internal differences among the Chinese, by 1968 or 1969 the Soviet problem could no longer be ignored or talked out of existence. The Soviets had set forth a claim to protecting the socialist gains of other countries, as they interpreted them; and they had used the Red Army to enforce the doctrine. Obviously, if China was straying from the path of Marxism-Leninism, then the Soviets might find a pretext for military intervention.

In this light, the Daimansky or Zhenbao (Chen-pao) Island crisis of March 1969 is still difficult to explain. Why should the Chinese take the initiative in starting a military confrontation in the wake of the Soviet invasion of Czechoslovakia? A number of explanations have been offered, but the significant point is that the Soviets quickly exploited the incident, first by publicizing it and then by staging a

---

[2] See Central Intelligence Agency, National Foreign Assessment Center, *Estimated Soviet Defense Spending*, SR-78-10121, June 1978.

[3] For two analyses of possible factional alignments in the Chinese leadership, see Thomas M. Gottlieb, *Chinese Foreign Policy Factionalism and the Origins of the Strategic Triangle*, The Rand Corporation, R-1902-NA, July 1977, and Kenneth G. Lieberthal, *Sino-Soviet Conflict in the 1970s: Its Evolution and Implications for the Strategic Triangle*, The Rand Corporation, R-2342-NA, July 1978.

bloody reprisal. In the months that followed, there was growing speculation about a Soviet attack on China, and the credibility of these rumors was sufficient to cause the U.S. government to initiate some contingency studies and to issue to Moscow veiled warnings about the consequences of a Soviet attack on the Chinese.[4]

A showdown meeting was held between Soviet Premier Kosygin and Zhou Enlai in Beijing in September 1969, following the funeral of Vietnamese leader Ho Chi Minh. This encounter temporarily eased the crisis, but at the cost to the Chinese of agreeing to open negotiations without preconditions. For Moscow, it seemed that pressure politics had paid off. True to their diplomatic style, the Soviets attempted to cash in on their immediate gains by offering the most minimal concession in return for a virtual Chinese capitulation. The Chinese proved more adroit in the maneuvering that followed. Sporadic negotiations continued into the 1970s, marked by increasingly broad and more generous Soviet offers and growing Chinese recalcitrance.

This also was the period of ascendancy of the Chinese Defense Minister Lin Biao (Lin Piao), and it is possible that the Soviets saw in Lin a potential negotiating partner. Apparently Lin resisted the conclusion that the dispute with the Soviets was irreparable and held out against the obvious countermove—later initiated by Mao and Zhou Enlai—of an opening toward the United States. Until Lin's fall in September 1971 and the establishment of a Beijing-Washington dialogue in that same year, the Soviets played what essentially was a waiting game in their dealings with the Chinese and the United States. In retrospect, it seems that Moscow underrated Beijing's "American alternative," or at least did not take it seriously enough to forestall it by a major improvement in its own dealings with the United States. In both 1970 and 1971 the Soviets kept their relations with Washington in reserve. Tensions in 1970 grew over the Suez, over Jordan, and over a Soviet submarine base in Cuba. SALT remained stalled until May 1971. Indeed, in this period Moscow's preferred policy was to deal with the Europeans—especially West Germany —to the exclusion of the United States. Soviet success in dealing with Germany in 1970 and the slight improvement in relations with the United States when the SALT deadlock was broken in early 1971 may have led Moscow to believe that China was being effectively isolated. At one point in 1970, Soviet leaders blatantly proposed to Washington a sort of Soviet-American alliance against "provocative attacks" by third countries, clearly implying China.[5]

In any event, at the 24th Soviet Party Congress in March 1971—which saw the unveiling of Brezhnev's "peace program"—the Soviet leader still held out to the Chinese the option of an improvement in relations. "The situation demands unity," he said, adding that the USSR was prepared not only to lower Sino-Soviet tensions but to restore friendly relations.

The secret trip of U.S. Presidential Adviser Henry Kissinger to Beijing in July 1971 shattered this strategy. Both Washington and Beijing created new options and gained new leverage. Now it was the Soviets, not the Chinese, who were in danger of being outmaneuvered. Characteristically, Moscow responded to this new reality by increasing the pace and scope of bargaining with both the Americans and the

[4] Roger Morris, *Uncertain Greatness: Henry Kissinger and American Foreign Policy*, Harper and Row, New York, 1977, p. 205.
[5] John Newhouse, *Cold Dawn: The Story of SALT*, Holt, Rinehart and Winston, New York, 1973, p. 189.

Chinese. The Berlin negotiations with the West were quickly completed in August 1971, and a summit meeting with President Nixon was arranged and announced in October. With China, the Soviets tried to revive the abortive border negotiations. The Soviet negotiator ostentatiously returned to Beijing shortly after the Nixon visit, in February 1972. And in March, Brezhnev revealed that the Soviets had made proposals to the Chinese for a non-aggression treaty and a border settlement. Moscow was prepared to settle outstanding differences on the basis of the principles of peaceful coexistence, a concept that the Soviets previously had attempted to restrict as applicable only to non-socialist states. In sum, triangular diplomacy had begun with a vengeance.

The focal point of Soviet efforts, however, increasingly was the United States. A high point of sorts was reached in June 1973 during Brezhnev's visit to the United States. The Soviet leader proclaimed in Washington the irreversibility of détente and signed a new agreement to reduce the danger of nuclear war between the United States and the Soviet Union. Interestingly, Brezhnev subsequently revealed that on the eve of his departure for Washington he had made a similar proposal to the Chinese, which they had not deigned to answer. With U.S.-Soviet relations improving, the Soviets began to revise their view of the Chinese relationship. According to the Nixon memoirs, during Brezhnev's visit to San Clemente the Soviet leader had spoken of China with "only thinly veiled concern."[6] He was worried about a Sino-American military relationship and predicted that in ten years China would be a major nuclear power, with a capability equal to "what we have now." According to Nixon's account, Brezhnev did not think that the Chinese policies would change even after Mao's death: "He was certain that the entire Chinese leadership was instinctively aggressive."[7]

By the summer of 1973, the Soviets had made numerous negotiating offers to the Chinese. They had not compromised on essentials, i.e., they still demanded that China renounce its revisionist claims to Soviet territory, nor would they disengage and withdraw their troops from along the border; but on matters of form and minor border adjustments, the Soviets had sought to demonstrate their flexibility and to put the onus for intransigence on Beijing.

At the Tenth Congress of the Chinese Communist Party in August 1973, however, the Chinese displayed no willingness or interest in moving toward Moscow. Indeed, Zhou Enlai, temporarily in the ascendancy, seemed to be preparing a new policy line stressing the importance of making China into a great power by the end of the century. The Soviets apparently interpreted this meeting as the end of any serious possibility for an accommodation as long as Mao lived. Zhou's anti-Soviet position may have impressed Moscow with the hopelessness of its effort to reduce tensions with the Chinese, as the PRC Premier had long been seen as a possible advocate of a more balanced and moderate foreign policy line. In any case, Moscow had bigger gains to make in the West by pursuing the Helsinki Conference and starting the negotiations on force reductions in Central Europe. Economic credits were beginning to flow to the Soviet Union in some volume, and there were prospects for luring the Americans and Japanese into economic projects in the Soviet Far East (with obvious overtones for Beijing). Moreover, the Chinese leadership

---

[6] Richard M. Nixon, *RN: The Memoirs of Richard Nixon*, Grosset and Dunlap, New York, 1978, p.882.

[7] Ibid.

was still torn by factionalism. The "Gang of Four" initiated its challenge to the pragmatic Zhou Enlai, putting the skillful but ailing Premier on the political defensive. For Moscow, another period of waiting seemed advisable in the East, while efforts proceeded to secure the western flank of the Soviet Union.

As for China, it seems that after the resignation of President Nixon and in the face of a meeting between Brezhnev and President Ford at Vladivostok, there was a short period in which it considered some gestures toward Moscow tactically expedient. In early November 1974 a congratulatory message from the Chinese on the anniversary of the "October Revolution" proposed a non-aggression agreement, renunciation of the use of force, mutual force withdrawals, and a border settlement. Beijing dropped its demand for Soviet recognition of the inequality of the Tsarist treaties. Some Western journalists began speculating about a "reconciliation between Russia and China that is now taking shape."[8] To the surprise of some, Brezhnev brusquely rejected the proposal during a stopover in Mongolia two days before meeting with President Ford at Vladivostok. He construed the Chinese proposal as a demand to recognize "disputed" border areas. For the Soviets, this brushing aside of the Chinese gesture might have been an indicator of their belief that with Nixon gone and with Mao nearing the end of his days, Beijing's adherence to the Chairman's policy of dealing with the United States might be short-lived. One Soviet observer in this period wrote that the "Chinese problem" had ceased to be an issue concerning only the Soviet Union and China (i.e., a bilateral issue) and had become a question of attitude toward the theory and practice of Maoism *and its creator;* and this attitude had become a sort of "watershed between the friends and the enemies of the Soviet Union."[9] The implication was that the obstacle to improvement of Sino-Soviet relations was Mao, and his defeat or demise had become a precondition for any major progress or improvement in those relations.

An interesting line of speculation is that the Soviets may well have come to believe that the group around Jiang Qing (Chiang Ch'ing, Mao's wife)—later to be denounced as one of the "Gang of Four"—was a promising source of weakness in the Chinese leadership. Its opposition to Zhou Enlai, who was espousing a line of building China into a modern power by the end of the century, might have seemed to the Soviets as likely to deepen internal divisions in Beijing. In any case, this radical element in the leadership was likely to jeopardize China's relations with the United States and upset any realistic foreign policy strategy. For Moscow, waiting seemed the best course: Either Jiang Qing would plunge China into another period of chaos; or she would be destroyed and thereby discredit Mao himself. In either case, the Soviets stood to gain ground.

Alternatively, there is some evidence that Zhou and Deng Xiaoping (Teng Hsiao-p'ing) may have wanted to signal to Moscow the possibility of an improvement in relations when they unexpectedly released a captured Soviet helicopter crew on December 27, 1975, after twenty-one months of detention. If so, the Soviet response was not altered. Indeed, at the 25th Party Congress in February 1976, the Soviet leadership explicitly spelled out its waiting game: "The ball is in the Chinese court," was Brezhnev's summary phrase. His address to the Party Congress on

---

[8] Victor Zorza, *Washington Post,* November 14, 1974.

[9] See O. E. Vladimirov, "The Present Stage of the Ideological Struggle Against Maoism," *Problemy Dalnego Vostoka,* No. 3, 1974; translated in *Joint Publications Research Service (JPRS),* No. 63409, November 11, 1974, pp. 136-150.

February 24 contrasted with the more conciliatory line of five years earlier. Whereas in 1971 he had spoken of unity and mutual interest, he now described China as a "reserve" of imperialism engaging in feverish attempts to wreck détente and seeking to provoke a world war. If China was ready to return to a policy based on "genuine" Marxism-Leninism, then Moscow was prepared to meet it with an appropriate response, "corresponding to principles of socialist internationalism" (as opposed to peaceful coexistence). One can only conclude that the Soviets were quite content to wait for the passing of Mao.

POST-MAO EXPECTATIONS AND DISILLUSIONMENT

There seems little doubt that the Soviets anticipated that the death of Mao would open up new opportunities for influencing Chinese policy. Their own experience must have taught them that succession periods are uncertain and, in particular, a time when a new leadership may shed some of the old inhibitions and policy dogmas of the fallen leader. The old myth that the Chinese communists were different, a leadership held together by the searing emotional experience of the Long March, had long since been shattered by the Cultural Revolution. Moreover, during the various post-"liberation" political struggles in China, a succession of figures had appeared—Gao Gang (Kao Kang), Peng Dehuai (P'eng Teh-huai), Liu Shaoqi, Lin Biao—who supposedly were more sympathetic to the Soviets than was Chairman Mao. While great clouds of ideological obfuscation had surrounded these internal political feuds and purges, Moscow had some basis for believing that a more pro-Soviet leader might appear. An observer in Moscow easily could have argued that Mao's policy of hostility toward the Soviet Union had done little for Chinese interests. The PRC's economy, military defenses, and foreign policy were all in need of repair. Soviet military preponderance along the Chinese frontier should have been a factor justifying a revision of Mao's policy of total hostility toward Moscow.

Whatever the reasoning, in the aftermath of the Chairman's death in early September 1976, a pause ensued that was clearly deliberate on Moscow's part. On October 1, 1976, the Soviets published one of their pseudonymous authoritative articles, by I. Alexandrov, which reviewed Sino-Soviet relations in a markedly favorable light. The article asserted that "We are proceeding on the premise that in relations between our states there are no problems which cannot be solved, given a mutual desire in the spirit of good neighborliness, mutual benefit, and consideration of each other's interests."[10] Similarly, in a speech to a Central Committee plenary session on October 25, Brezhnev stated, "I want to emphasize that, in our opinion, there are no issues in relations between the USSR and PRC that could not be resolved in the spirit of good neighborliness. We will act in this direction. The matter will depend on what stand is taken by the other side."[11] The Soviet border negotiator was given a well-publicized return to Beijing, and a Soviet message of congratulations was sent to Hua Guofeng (Hua Kuo-feng) on his assumption of the Party Chairmanship on October 7, 1976.

[10] I. Alexandrov, "Twenty-Seven Years of the PRC," *Pravda*, October 1, 1976; translated in Foreign Broadcast Information Service (FBIS), *Daily Report—Soviet Union*, October 4, 1976, p. C4.
[11] FBIS, *Daily Report—Soviet Union*, October 26, 1976, p. A17.

Until the spring of 1977, the Soviets seemed to hold out some hope for a positive response from the Chinese, or at least acted as if they did. But Moscow's media gradually began to sharpen their polemical comments. On April 22, the anniversary of Lenin's birth, the principal Soviet speaker commented that "regrettably" there had been no change in Chinese policy in "recent time." The ubiquitous I. Alexandrov appeared in print again on May 14 with another article, this time warning of the "unforgivable error" of waiting too late to respond to the Chinese danger until it reaches "disastrous dimensions."[12] The article was keyed to remarks by Hua Guofeng and stressed that the new Chinese leader was emphasizing a policy of "stepping up preparations for war." According to Alexandrov, the Chinese economy was being reorganized on a military footing and defense industries were being given top priority. A few days later, on May 19, the Soviet Foreign Ministry lodged an official protest over a PRC campaign of hostile propaganda directed against the Soviet Union. Chinese foreign policy was said to be dangerously balanced on a "knife edge." A warning about Western blindness to Chinese nuclear ambitions was carried in a long article in the journal of the Ministry of Foreign Affairs, *International Affairs*. This article argued that China's nuclear arms development was being carried out "not without the consent of military industrial circles in the United States, the Federal Republic of Germany, and some arms manufacturers in France, Japan, and Great Britain." The article warned against the illusion that Beijing's expansionism could be diverted in some other direction (i.e., toward the Soviet Union): "But they tend to forget the bitter lesson of the not-too-distant past."[13]

This Soviet reappraisal was not unjustified. The Chinese response was a lengthy article in the July issue of the Party's theoretical journal *Red Flag*,[14] which claimed that the "new tsars" were greater imperialists than the old tsars, and so forth. Clearly, any hopes for a post-Mao "honeymoon" had dissipated. Their ending seemed to coincide with the third rehabilitation of Deng Xiaoping in the same month. This is perplexing. For a time, Deng had been thought of as a "moderate" or pragmatist of the Zhou Enlai school and therefore possibly open to some accommodation with Moscow. On the other hand, Soviet leaders surely must have remembered him as the main spear-bearer for the Chinese in their polemics against Moscow in the early days of the public conflict.

In any event, Hua Guofeng's address to the Eleventh Congress of the Chinese Communist Party on August 12, 1977, was unrelenting in its bitterness toward the Soviets. While repeating standard Maoist charges and slogans against Soviet "social imperialism," Hua claimed that Moscow had not shown one iota of good faith about improving state-to-state relations. Not only had the Soviets made it impossible to achieve anything in the border negotiations, said Hua, but they had whipped up "one anti-China wave after another." The Chinese leader more or less acknowledged that Moscow had harbored some hope for a new policy in Beijing toward the Soviet Union. He stated, "It [Moscow] has been trying by hook or crook

[12] I. Alexandrov, "Peking: A Course Toward Wrecking International Détente Under the Guise of Anti-Sovietism," *Pravda*, May 14, 1977; translated in FBIS, *Daily Report—Soviet Union*, May 16, 1977, p. C6.

[13] Y. Semyonov, "China's Maoist Line," *International Affairs*, No. 7, 1977.

[14] "Soviet Social-Imperialism is the Most Dangerous Source of World War," *Hongqi (Hung-ch'i)*, No. 7, July 1977; translated in FBIS, *Daily Report—People's Republic of China*, July 8, 1977, pp. A1-A10.

to force us to change the Marxist-Leninist line laid down by Chairman Mao. This is pure daydreaming."[15]

Chinese policy assumed an increasingly strident tone in the winter of 1977, and by early 1978 Hua had toughened up his own position. At the National People's Congress in February, he repeated what he had said the previous August, but spelled out the conditions for any improvement in dealings with Moscow:

1. Signing an agreement on maintaining the status quo on the border;
2. Disengaging the armed forces of both sides in the disputed border areas;
3. Entering into negotiations on resolving boundary questions; and
4. Withdrawing Soviet armed forces from Mongolia and the Sino-Soviet frontier areas "so that the situation there will revert to what it was in the early 1960s."[16]

THE NEW PHASE

China's Fifth National People's Congress, convened in March 1978, was clearly a watershed act in that it inaugurated a new phase in PRC domestic development policies, with far-reaching foreign policy consequences. The Chinese leadership set forth a program of economic and military modernization that implied a significant commitment to acquiring technology and financial credits from Japan and from capitalist countries of the West. The underlying geopolitical theme of the decisions of the People's Congress was that China must be prepared to meet the challenge of the Soviet Union by transforming a still backward country into a modern industrial power supported by modern military forces by the end of the century.

This major departure in national development strategy, strongly reminiscent of the Zhou Enlai modernization program of 1973 (with even Stalinist industrialization overtones), was accompanied by a number of initiatives in foreign policy with an openly anti-Soviet thrust: the signing of a Sino-Japanese Treaty of Peace and Friendship on August 12; a tour of Romania, Yugoslavia, and Iran by Party Chairman Hua Guofeng during which Hua spoke out on the necessity of opposing "hegemony"; a visit by Vice-Premier Deng Xiaoping to Japan in September; the increasingly open and dangerous confrontation with Vietnam and the Soviet Union over Indochina; and, finally, the completion of "normalization" of relations with Washington in mid-December. At the same time, the Soviets staged something of a counteroffensive. Pressures on China's position in South Asia were heightened in Pakistan through startling Soviet advances in Afghanistan—culminating in the signing of a treaty with Kabul on December 5, 1978—and greater Soviet assertiveness in Iran. Most significant was Moscow's open political intervention in Indochina through the Russo-Vietnamese Treaty of Friendship and Cooperation, signed on November 3, 1978, which most certainly was the precondition for Hanoi's attack on Kampuchea (Cambodia) in December.

Prior to the outbreak of Sino-Vietnamese hostilities in February 1979, there

[15] Hua Guofeng, *Political Report to the Eleventh Party Congress* (August 12, 1977); translated in FBIS, *Daily Report—People's Republic of China*, September 1, 1977, Supplement 9, p. 31.

[16] Hua Guofeng, "Unite and Strive to Build a Modern Powerful Socialist Country—Report on the Work of the Government Delivered at the First Session of the Fifth National People's Congress" (February 26, 1978); translated in *Peking Review*, No. 10, March 10, 1978, p. 39.

was a strong surge of Chinese economic activity with Japan and the European Economic Community (EEC). At least two countries—France and Great Britain—were bargaining about arms sales. And, of course, the "China card" became a more active strategic factor in American policy. In response, Moscow did not hesitate to warn of the consequences of a European or American military relationship with the PRC.

In sum, at the end of 1978, international political relationships were in a state of considerable flux. A new balance of power seemed to be emerging around a quadruple entente of Western Europe, Japan, China, and the United States, with opposition to the Soviet Union as its major unifying theme.

It is beyond the scope of this analysis to examine all aspects of these complex and fluid relationships. However, in the following paragraphs we examine how they seem to affect the Soviet Union and the Sino-Soviet relationship.

First of all, each of the actors in the "quadruple entente" has consciously and deliberately avoided joining any avowedly anti-Soviet alliance. The Western Europeans have by no means jettisoned their relationships with Moscow; indeed, there has been some political intensification, especially in Soviet-German relations. Nor has the United States, for all the fascination of the "China card," written off the prospect of improving relations with Moscow—as is evident in President Carter's signing of a second SALT agreement during his meeting with Soviet leader Brezhnev in Vienna in June 1979. And the Japanese persist in asserting that their Peace and Friendship Treaty with the Chinese is not directed against the Soviet Union. Nevertheless, each of the three power centers—Japan, the United States, and Western Europe—seems to be pursuing policies that objectively encourage the Chinese in their policy of creating an anti-Soviet coalition.

In some respects, the Sino-Japanese treaty has been the most critical step in this direction (although it was preceded by a sharpening of the conflict in Indochina). As long as Japan was maneuvering between Moscow and Beijing, the Soviets had some hope that economic enticements might keep the Chinese and Japanese at some distance. But as it became clear in early 1978 that the Japanese would not sign a peace treaty with the Soviet Union but would reopen negotiations with Beijing, Moscow began to stress the security consequences for the Soviet Union. Soviet media stressed the following reasons for apprehension: (1) "The signing of a treaty with a clause on hegemony would be tantamount to an official establishment of a military and political alliance between Japan and China—an alliance fraught with serious consequences . . . .. Peking's marshals are long nursing the hope of getting certain types of strategic military equipment from Japan"; (2) "Still more reasons for anxiety are the insistent calls of certain Japanese politicians to set up a Japanese-American-Chinese military political alliance in Asia"; (3) "Japan and China strive traditionally for expansion in Southeast Asia."[17]

Even allowing for the predictable propaganda content of such an analysis, the Soviets nevertheless saw the prospective Sino-Japanese treaty as a geopolitical change of great significance. Increasingly pessimistic Soviet assessments followed the failure of Soviet-Japanese talks and (ironically) the publication of a draft Soviet-Japanese friendship treaty, which was clearly directed against China, including a veiled "hegemony" clause in Article 12:

[17] Moscow Radio Peace and Progress, January 24, 1978; translated in FBIS, *Daily Report—Soviet Union*, January 30, 1978, pp. M2-M3.

The USSR and Japan do not claim and do not recognize anyone's claim to any special rights to advantage in world affairs including claims to domination in Asia and the area of the Far East.[18]

In essence, during 1978 Soviet diplomacy failed in Japan, not because of a lack of skill in drafting treaties, but because Moscow refused to acknowledge the legitimacy of Japan's claim to the "northern territories," four islands of the Kurile chain. Moscow's dilemma was that while returning even some of the islands would conciliate Tokyo, it would also open the door to Chinese claims to revision of the Sino-Soviet border. By refusing any acknowledgment that the Japanese claim could be negotiated, Moscow effectively shut itself out of the diplomatic game.

Soviet diplomacy in 1978 seemed to be peculiarly passive. Even at the time of renewed Sino-Japanese tensions over the Senkaku or Tiaoyu Tai Islands in April, the Soviets were unable to divert the Japanese from their course of negotiating a peace and friendship treaty with the Chinese. Moreover, the treaty was obviously being encouraged by Washington. President Carter wished Prime Minister Fukuda "good luck" in his negotiations with Beijing, a sentiment echoed by National Security Adviser Zbigniew Brzezinski during his visit to China in May. (Interestingly, the Sino-American normalization talks intensified in September after the signing of the Sino-Japanese treaty.) For Moscow at least, a Sino-Japanese-American "bloc" in Asia seemed to be taking shape. The significance of this development was heightened by the appreciation that Japan's official and public mood was shifting toward support of a more autonomous foreign policy and increased self-defense activities. It was no surprise to Moscow that immediately after the signing of the Sino-Japanese treaty, a Chinese military leader visited Japan. A deputy chief of the Chinese General Staff, Zhang Caiqian (Chang Tsai-chien), visited Tokyo in September for six days of talks, including a call at the Joint Staff Council of the Japanese Defense Forces. The visit prompted one Japanese newspaper to editorialize that China seemed determined to step up its efforts to organize an anti-Soviet international front while hoping that Japan, in collaboration with the United States and its European allies, "would maintain military power strong enough to match that of the Soviet Union"[19]—an analysis probably endorsed in Moscow.

During this period, China's interest in obtaining foreign assistance for the modernization of its military establishment was being ever more widely advertised. "The China market is beckoning," stated the London Economist on September 30, 1978, adding that China's voracious appetite "makes for good business and, so long as China and the West agree about Russia, good politics."[20] British interest in trade with Beijing was of course whetted by the much publicized negotiations for the purchase of Harrier jets. This apparent interest on Beijing's part in purchasing Western military hardware and exploring co-production arrangements (including the French "HOT" anti-tank missile) reflected a signal from Washington that European arms sales to China would not encounter American objections.[21]

To date, however, the military implications of China's new relations with Ja-

---

[18] *The Current Digest of the Soviet Press*, Vol. XXX, No. 8, March 22, 1978, p. 11.

[19] *Mainichi Daily News* (Tokyo), as quoted by Bradley K. Martin, *Baltimore Sun*, September 13, 1978.

[20] "What to Sell to China," *Economist*, September 30, 1978, p. 20.

[21] Statement by Secretary of State Vance in London on December 9, 1978, *Department of State Bulletin*, Vol. 79, No. 2022, January 1979, pp. 17-18.

pan, the United States, and Western Europe have been overshadowed by conventional economic ties, highlighted by the signing of two long-term trade agreements with Japan and the EEC. The magnitude of these burgeoning trade relationships is difficult to estimate, as is China's ability to pay for its purchases. A certain amount of idle talk and wishful thinking is probably involved, but recent agreements give some sense of the scope of these activities. China and France signed a seven-year trade agreement in December 1978 that called for almost $14 billion in trade, although this agreement was curtailed somewhat in the summer of 1979. The export credits involved were reported to be worth $6.8 billion. The Nippon Steel Corporation signed a contract with Beijing, also in December 1978, to provide $2.03 billion in equipment for a steel mill near Shanghai, an agreement that was subsequently thrown in doubt as China reassessed her economic priorities and repayment capabilities. The United States and China signed a trade agreement on July 7, 1979, for $8 to $10 billion through 1985. All of this confronts the Soviet Union with the threatening prospect of an alliance, however tentative, between the major power centers on its eastern and western flanks.

CURRENT SOVIET STRATEGY: A "BREAKOUT" IN THE ARC OF CRISIS

How is the Soviet Union likely to cope with this emerging "encirclement"? Moscow initiated a counteroffensive in the fall of 1978. First, a treaty was signed with Hanoi that seemed almost a blank check for the Vietnamese to call for Soviet military assistance. Indeed, well before establishment of the formal treaty, it was obvious that the Moscow-Beijing rivalry had spread to Indochina, thus introducing a new and more dangerous dimension to two decades of Sino-Soviet conflict. With each major power backing a client, the contest inevitably would result in the loss of prestige for one. The formation by Vietnam of a new Kampuchean national front shortly after the signing of the Soviet treaty in November was the forerunner of the outright invasion of December, a shattering defeat for the Beijing-backed Pol Pot goverment in Pnomh Penh and therefore a defeat for China as well.

Another element of the anti-China counteroffensive appeared in Eastern Europe. For the first time in some years, the Soviets began exerting pressure on Romania. The immediate issue was further integration of the military forces of the Warsaw Pact and an increase in defense spending by its members. It was a ploy deliberately designed to start a controversy. The Soviets knew that the Romanians were bound to resist. One can only conclude that Moscow intended this new source of tension, which came immediately after the visit to Bucharest of PRC Premier Hua Guofeng, to be a sharp reminder that flirting with China could involve a heavy price.

These maneuvers must be viewed in the broader context of Soviet global strategy. Surveying the new "quadruple entente," the Soviets could easily perceive that one of the gaps in the "encirclement" was the area that the British used to call "the northern tier," the string of Middle Eastern states running from Turkey to Afghanistan (more recently termed the "arc of crisis"). The Soviets seem to have made a strategic decision to exploit this gap. Their moves have included the remarkable new relationship with Afghanistan, the switch in support from Somalia to Ethiopia and the related intervention with Cuban troops, the signing of a friendship treaty with Turkey in June 1978, the Soviet-inspired coup in South Yemen in that same month, and some probing for an accommodation with Pakistan.

These events do not necessarily reflect a Moscow master plan. A number of unanticipated opportunities have presented themselves; but in some cases local developments have been given a sharp impetus by the Soviets. The key to this strategy is Iran. Moscow's role in the upheavals of the spring of 1979 is not clear, but there should be little doubt that the weakening of Iran and its transformation into a radical Moslem regime has been a major strategic gain for the Soviet Union. It has grave implications for the strategic balance in the Persian Gulf and, by extension, for the security of Saudi Arabia. It cannot be accidental that the Soviets became increasingly active throughout this general area following Hua Guofeng's visit to Iran, issuing contrived warnings to the West against intervention, asserting a Soviet security interest in Iran, and signing a mutual security treaty with Afghanistan. Soviet action in this potentially vulnerable "northern tier" area also indirectly relates to Moscow's problems of dealing with Japan and Western Europe in their support for China. The critical vulnerability of the oil lifeline from the Persian Gulf need not be commented on; it is obvious.

Aside from this gap in the "northern tier," the weakest link in the chain of potential encirclement for the Soviets is Western Europe. Détente in Europe preceded the relaxation of tensions with the United States in the early 1970s. The economic stake for both sides is growing to the point where it is no longer clear which partner has the leverage. But if Moscow's strategy has been to calm its western flank in order to deal with China, it now appears that this strategy is backfiring. Indeed, if the British or other Europeans proceed to sell arms to China, what have the Soviets accomplished? Thus, the Soviets will almost certainly have to devise a European strategy to deal with the European-China links. The choices seem to be either a furthering of détente on the condition that European assistance to China be restrained, or a revival of pressure tactics.

Deepening European détente poses some problems. Almost certainly, the Europeans see the next phase in dealings with the Soviets as involving the military dimension—first, reducing Soviet forces in Central Europe, and second, restraining Soviet theater nuclear forces. What price Moscow might pay and how the negotiations might be arranged is still uncertain. Thus far, the Soviets have shown only a modest interest in addressing such issues, although they have kept the MBFR[22] talks alive. The issue is whether they can strike a bargain with the United States and Western Europe that would reduce their military advantages in Central Europe in return for an understanding on Western relations with China. The risks to the Soviets of even minimal disengagement from Central Europe are severe; no one can foresee the impact on Moscow's control of Eastern Europe.[23] And such a strategic tradeoff would seem to demonstrate the validity of a Western strategy of "playing the China card."

Moscow's alternative is to put on more direct pressure—perhaps already foreshadowed by Brezhnev's warnings to the British about the sale of jets to China.

[22] Mutual Balanced Force Reductions.

[23] Brezhnev's announcement of October 5, 1979, of a unilateral withdrawal of 20,000 Soviet troops and 1,000 tanks seems a calculated gambit to discourage NATO's theater nuclear weapons modernization.

Developing this strategy involves some obvious drawbacks. First, the Soviets have an economic stake in the continuing access to European technology and credits. To jeopardize this access might simply encourage the Europeans to shift to the China market. Moreover, reviving tensions with the Western Europeans without some concurrent alleviation of tensions in the East would seem to be the most risky strategy. But the Soviets may in the end conclude that the threat of new pressures needs to be tried. Germany is particularly vulnerable, as Bonn's policy of using European détente to promote some accommodation with East Germany could be thwarted, with major domestic repercussions in the Federal Republic.

If the Soviets conclude that they cannot make any drastic changes in their European policies, their remaining choices are also unattractive. They could, of course, heighten tensions with the United States, but this seems unwarrantedly risky, as it would have the effect of driving Washington further toward détente with China. Brezhnev's conduct of Soviet foreign policy since President Carter's announcement of normalization of relations with Beijing suggests that Moscow prefers to try a different course of action: namely, to intensify détente with the United States—initially through completion of SALT II and a summit meeting. Since the United States is firmly on record against American arms sales to China,[24] the most productive Soviet strategy would appear to be to use Washington as a restraint on European sales. This is little more than a holding action, but it probably is Moscow's best choice in the near term.

This leaves the problem of China itself. No Soviet leader in his right mind would passively watch the growth of Chinese power sponsored by the United States, Japan, and Western Europe. The critical question for Moscow is whether to try to muddle through, hoping for a new domestic upheaval in China or some strain in Beijing's dealings with the West, or to consider a more drastic alternative: accommodation with the Chinese, or a severe confrontation.

Accommodation, of course, cannot be ruled out. Both leaderships—Moscow and Beijing—are destined for major changes over the next several years, although the Chinese may have somewhat greater continuity than the Soviets. As noted at the outset of this paper, leadership changes have a way of evoking expectations of change, even if those expectations often are unjustified. Each side might conclude that the other will make some changes in the future, and decide simply to proceed without trying to ameliorate the relationship. This is a more satisfactory approach for China than for the Soviet Union; the longer China can continue its military and economic modernization without facing a showdown with Moscow, the better are its chances for playing the global balance of power to its advantage. This is certainly one motive in the diplomatic dialogue of the spring of 1979 which led to the Moscow-Beijing agreement to hold talks in September.[25]

For the Soviets, a delaying game is probably a losing game. The present or future leadership has to consider whether an accommodation with Beijing is really feasible in light of the potential growth of Chinese power. There have been a number of such opportunities in the past that have turned out to be fruitless. There

---

[24] Statement by Secretary of State Vance, op. cit.

[25] Remarks of Vice-Premier Li Xiannian (Li Hsien-nien) to the visiting Japanese Socialist Party delegation on June 17, 1979; translated in FBIS, *Daily Report—People's Republic of China*, August 18, 1979, pp. D2-D3; and Hua Guofeng's Report to the Second Session of the Fifth National People's Congress on June 18, 1979, in *Renmin Ribao (Jen-min Jih-pao)*, June 26, 1979, p. 4; translated in *Beijing Review*, No. 27, July 6, 1979, pp. 30-31; and *New York Times*, July 17, 1979, p. 6.

is considerable evidence that the Soviets consider the conflict with China too fundamental to be papered over. Thus, one cannot rule out the possibility that over the
next several years, the Soviets—much like Stalin in the 1930s—will consider the
option of dealing with the Chinese as the enemy, through some form of military
action.

As for the Chinese, their modernization program seems linked to an active
anti-Soviet policy. But their internal political situation is much too unstable and
uncertain to rule out the possibility of a relaxation of tensions, if not some form of
accommodation with the Soviet Union. Indeed, recent public criticism of Chairman
Mao and the rehabilitation of certain anti-Maoist leaders thought to be "pro-Soviet"—including former Defense Minister Peng Dehuai—suggest the possibility of an
opening for Moscow.

On balance, however, the chances seem slightly better that the 1980s will see
a serious Sino-Soviet confrontation. One reason is that the Soviet military advantage over China is waning. Sooner rather than later the Soviets will have to exploit
their present position or face the serious challenge of a strengthened China allied
to Japan and the West. Moscow has several alternatives should it decide to move
to a military confrontation with the PRC: thrusts into Xinjiang (Sinkiang) Province
or Inner Mongolia; or an invasion across Manchuria, perhaps in coordination with
a Vietnamese attack on China's southern frontier. The risks of a nuclear exchange,
of course, are one major inhibition on such a course of action, although the Soviets
could attack Chinese missile sites first in the hope of eliminating most of China's
retaliatory force (an action that is still within the realm of Soviet capabilities). The
arguments against a military thrust are well known, particularly the danger of
becoming bogged down in China. But a crushing blow, perhaps followed by a rapid
withdrawal—such as the Chinese executed against India in 1962 and then attempted against Vietnam in early 1979—might be a tactical solution to the Soviet
problem. Humiliating China and discrediting its leadership might be seen as a
catalyst to provoking a general realignment of international forces. In February
1979 the Soviets had a pretext for military action against the PRC, but, despite
some bluster, Moscow refrained from any military moves. Indeed the Soviets responded slowly and cautiously during the crisis. The Sino-Vietnamese conflict is not
over, however, and it still could provide the context for a Sino-Soviet clash. But the
immediate result of the crisis seems to have been that both Moscow and Beijing
have decided to test the possibilities of some accommodation through fairly high-
level talks without preconditions.

Whatever the immediate outcome of the new Sino-Soviet discussions, Moscow
simply cannot abide the present alignment of forces in the world. Soviet leaders
probably believe that the international balance of power is incompatible with the
USSR's strategic nuclear position, which has earned the country the right to "equal
security." They have taken some action to forestall this new "correlation of forces,"
or to compensate for it through gains in the Middle East, South and Southeast Asia,
and Africa. They might be able to achieve a new strategic position in the Persian
Gulf and the Indian Ocean which would enable them to threaten the oil lifelines
of the West. This seems to be the preferred Soviet strategy, if only because the
opportunities are there and it is relatively safe.

The alternative of breaking up the Beijing-inspired anti-Soviet coalition by
conciliating its major Western members will probably be tried as well, since it has

the added advantage of minimizing the chances of a Soviet-American confrontation over the Persian Gulf or Indian Ocean areas. But the crucial decision regarding China has yet to be made. It is difficult to see how a significant accommodation between the two powers can be negotiated. It is possible that the future holds the prospect of heightened Sino-Soviet confrontation, including a military clash. The repercussions for Japan and the West—and particularly for the United States—of such a development would be enormous, as would be the implications of a Moscow-Beijing rapprochement. In short, Sino-Soviet relations, after twenty years of deepening hostility, may be in a period of movement. The direction of this movement is yet to be seen, but it is likely to be a major factor shaping the global strategic balance and Asian security relationships in the 1980s.

Chapter 3

SECURITY IMPLICATIONS OF THE SOVIET MILITARY PRESENCE IN ASIA

Admiral Noel Gayler[1]

The foreign policy of the Soviet state advances through both the presence and the use of power. Power is both the shield behind which Soviet interests advance and their armor against encroachment. The Soviet Union's exploitation of power of all kinds is public and quite explicit—the much-advertised "correlation of forces." And military forces are the dominant component of that power.

Soviet concerns are global, and Moscow's claims of interest in problems world-wide are very clear. Foreign Minister Gromyko has said, "There is not a single question of any importance which could at present be solved without the Soviet Union or against its will."[2] In Asia, as in the rest of the world, the Soviet claim to participation in or direction of affairs is backed by power—specifically, by military presence.

For this discussion, we define Asia rather broadly as including not only Northeast Asia and Southeast Asia, but also Pacific Oceania, South Asia, and the Indian Ocean. The security requirements of the various countries of the region are quite diverse, yet they are all interrelated in important ways. Border and internal security in one region is affected by deployable forces in another. All have common concerns about access to and use of natural resources, the flow and pressure of populations, and the security of communications and trade. To consider less than the entire region would be to fractionate what is an integral security context.

We think of security as protection both from external military aggression and from coercion under the threat or implicit threat of such aggression. With respect to Asia, we must consider the security interests of a wide variety of states and peoples: the loose "Oceanic alliance" of the United States, Japan, Australia, New Zealand, the Philippines, and like-minded states in the Western Pacific; the People's Republic of China (PRC); the ASEAN countries; the states of South Asia; and South Korea and Taiwan, which have special security problems. Common to all is a general interest in the uninterrupted flow of commerce and resources, particularly oil, across the seas from the Persian Gulf through the Indian and Pacific Oceans to Asia and the western United States. Taken together, these interests are nothing less than the preservation of the entire political and economic system of these states.

Finally, we must consider the perceived regional security interests of the Soviet Union itself. While the Soviet military presence in Asia is threatening in the eyes

---

[1] Admiral Noel Gayler, U.S.N. (retired), naval officer and naval aviator, was Assistant Chief of Naval Operations for Development, Deputy Director of Strategic Target Planning, Director of the National Security Agency, and Commander-in-Chief, U.S. Pacific Forces. He is currently a member of the Defense Science Board and a consultant to The Rand Corporation and various other research laboratories and groups on technology applications and politico-military affairs.

[2] See Gromyko's speech to the 24th Party Congress on April 4, 1971; translated in Foreign Broadcast Information Service (FBIS), *Daily Report—Soviet Union*, April 6, 1971, p. 77.

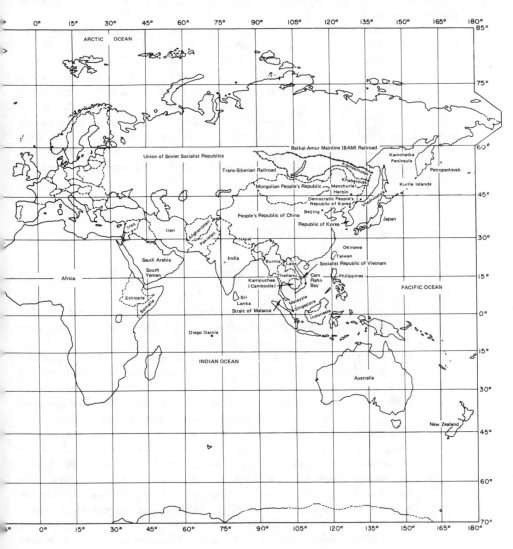

Map 1—The Soviet military presence in Asia

of the states of the region, in Moscow's eyes it is only the expression of legitimate defensive concerns, plus the asserted right to participate in all important political matters worldwide.

Comparison of Soviet military forces with others in Asia cannot be simply an exercise in "bean-counting," totaling and comparing numbers of troops, aircraft, and ships. Functional capabilities, strategy, and political utility are better measures. These are a complex combination of military forces, geography, initiative, resources, and many other factors. Hence, the following discussion will consider the nature and characteristics of Soviet forces, their disposition, their functional capabilities, and their political impact. We will also consider Soviet security strategies and the countervailing strategies open to the states of Asia that are most affected by the Soviet military presence. Finally, we will try to identify the critical issues raised by the Soviet military presence and their implications for American policy and force requirements.

CHARACTERISTICS OF THE SOVIET MILITARY PRESENCE IN ASIA

The Soviet military presence in or directable toward Asia has ten important elements:[3]

- A rapidly assignable allocation of central strategic nuclear forces. Russian intercontinental rockets, submarine-launched guided missiles, and long-range aviation can reach any point in Asia.
- A specifically Asia-directed nuclear force of intermediate-range ballistic missiles, plus the optional carriage of nuclear weapons on bombers and tactical aircraft.
- A China-oriented ground force of more than 45 combat divisions disposed along the common border and most densely deployed opposite Manchuria. Of these divisions, half are at full strength and half are organizations in being at about one-third strength. An integral force of four tactical air armies and one long-range aviation division supports these ground forces.
- Sea and air forces based principally, but not entirely, in the Soviet Far East. The Far East Fleet has 75 submarines (50 of them nuclear), 70 major surface combatants, about 15 intelligence ships, and appropriate fleet support ships (Pacific-based ballistic missile submarines are considered part of the central strategic forces). Naval-subordinated aircraft include missile-carrying patrol aircraft, medium bombers, anti-submarine aircraft, and miscellaneous naval tactical aircraft, totaling one-third to one-fourth of the entire Soviet inventory.
- Readily assignable long-range air forces, paratroop forces, and air-mobile forces. These are deployable in strength, given suitable bases, to the northwest Indian Ocean, the Persian Gulf, and the littoral of the Red Sea.
- A base structure ranging from the well-established major bases at Vladivostok, Petropavlovsk, and Khabarovsk in the Soviet Far East, through

[3] This summary is based primarily on data and analysis provided in *The Military Balance, 1979-1980*, The International Institute for Strategic Studies, London, 1979, pp. 9-11.

politically volatile base opportunities in Ethiopia, South Yemen, and elsewhere, to prepared ocean anchorages in international waters. A recent and highly disturbing possibility is Soviet establishment of operating naval and air basing facilities in Vietnam.

- A Far Eastern military-industrial complex capable of nearly autonomous peacetime support of major military forces. At Komsomolsk is one of the world's great naval construction shipyards. At the same time, logistic support from European Russia, whether by the Trans-Siberian Railway, the Northern sea route, or the Indian Ocean-Pacific sea route is, for various military reasons, fragile. The Baikal-Amur Mainline Railroad (BAM) will alleviate this fragility in some measure, but construction is difficult and far behind schedule. Whether the Soviet logistic structure could withstand the stress of major war is an operational and tactical matter that can be evaluated only by the test of combat.
- The Soviet oceanographic, fishing, and even commercial shipping fleets are essentially paramilitary forces, under direct or indirect control of the Soviet Navy. Military control is also exercised over Soviet civil aviation. Intelligence "trawlers" engage in full-time military intelligence collection.
- Soviet command, communications, and intelligence satellites overlook the entire area. Photographic satellites take detailed pictures of fixed areas on demand, and Soviet electronic intelligence (ELINT) and radar satellites maintain constant surveillance of the Asian region. While these capabilities at present are rather crude, they are a developing threat that may locate and identify naval and air forces with considerable accuracy, unless sophisticated countermeasures are adopted.
- Soviet secret intelligence activities (KGB and GRU) are pervasive in Asia, as they are worldwide. Characteristically, the intelligence effort is immense; the crudity, in some cases, is astonishing; and the effectiveness is difficult to gauge. Because of ethnic, cultural, and linguistic difficulties, these activities may be less effective in Asia than in Europe, but this does not preclude considerable danger from both espionage and covert action in specific circumstances. While the Russians represent themselves as a protection or counterforce against excessive Chinese influence, the evidence is that they are strongly oriented toward political subversion of host countries, in the interest of Soviet state objectives.

The great Soviet military buildup in Asia, which started in the 1960s and continues today, has had two overlapping phases: The first was a rapid quantitative buildup to approximately present force levels; the second is a qualitative improvement program which continues today.

The motivating factors behind this force expansion and improvement effort seem fairly clear:

- The dispute with China.
- Concern for the security of the Soviet Far East.
- Global power competition with the United States, extending to the Pacific-Indian Ocean theater.
- Increasing ambition to influence events in Asia.

The most striking recent changes in the character of Soviet Far Eastern military forces have been qualitative improvements rather than quantitative increases. In its ground forces, Moscow has deployed several new weapons systems, such as the T-62 tank (with 115mm guns), the GM-21 multiple rocket launcher, and the FROG 7 tactical nuclear rocket. Air strength is being upgraded with SU-19 and MiG-23 attack-fighter planes. Naval power is being considerably increased by the continuing replacement of conventional submarines by nuclear submarines and of gun-armed surface ships by missile-armed ships, the deployment of higher capability naval-subordinated patrol and tactical aircraft, and the recent Pacific deployment of at least one of the new Kiev-class aircraft-carrying ASW cruisers.

Less obvious, but perhaps more important, is the improvement in Soviet command, control, and intelligence capabilities in the Far East. Among other developments, space surveillance and communications directly and responsively support operational commanders.

While the great bulk of Moscow's forces in Asia are concentrated in the Soviet Far East, its naval forces have developed effective long-range sea-keeping capabilities, supported by a competent logistic train. The range of Soviet nuclear submarines is nearly unlimited. The unsupported range of some long-range aircraft covers much of the western Pacific and the northern Indian Ocean. The range of other aircraft is limited principally by the political availability of bases—and this is a volatile situation. For example, Soviet bases in Vietnam would transform the sea route security situation in the western Pacific; bases in Pacific Oceania would threaten the ANZUS links; and bases in South Yemen, Ethiopia, or Oman would threaten the security of the Persian Gulf and Suez Canal-Red Sea routes.

As the qualitative capabilities of Soviet forces have increased, those of the United States have remained relatively static. A small number of new fighters, such as the F-14, have been introduced, but in general, American naval forces—both ships and aircraft—are aging. The all-important anti-submarine capability has not kept pace with the growth of the Soviet submarine force. The Air Force is making do with assets of pre-1970 vintage, although a significant but inadequate number of "smart" weapons are on hand. And except for some improvements in missiles and helicopters, the Army is qualitatively very similar to the forces that fought in Vietnam and even in Korea.

Although the United States invented most of the relevant advanced technology for command, control, and surveillance, it lags badly in the actual use of that technology. In addition to a disturbing list of material shortcomings, U.S. forces in Asia are further handicapped by serious constraints on combat readiness. They have funds sufficient for only minor and regional exercises, and the major combined exercises which are a forcing and testing ground for development of strategy, tactics, and doctrine are a thing of the past. This is a particularly dangerous situation in an era of rapid political and technical change.

Soviet Functional Capabilities[4]

The most significant measure of Soviet military forces in Asia is their functional

[4] Nothing in what follows implies U.S. or allied enmity to the Soviet Union or any desire to forge an alliance inimical to the Soviets. It is entirely a discussion of power realities, devoted to establishing a secure situation for all.

capability. While actual capabilities will be decisive in war, perceived capabilities are critical to Soviet political advances in Asia. Military forces are the Soviets' strongest—and almost their only—card. Actual and perceived capabilities are fairly close at the present time, as Asian leaders have become quite sophisticated militarily, especially in the context of their own regions.

The assessment of functional capabilities—the power to carry out military operations—requires consideration of innumerable factors. It certainly includes the absolute and relative sizes of military forces, their physical capabilities, their readiness and training, their logistic support, and their morale. It includes the political framework of conflict and the circumstances in which it is initiated. It also includes those great intangibles, intelligence and leadership, which so often have been the determinants of victory in the past and will be so again in the future. And because conflict is at least a two-handed game, capabilities are relative, not absolute; thus it is essential to estimate the interaction of opposing forces.

Given this mixture of tangibles and intangibles, of quantifiables and unquantifiables, of apples and oranges, we can only assess reasonable bounds to Soviet military capabilities and estimate reasonable best cases (from our standpoint) and worst cases.

We must further divide this assessment into three quite separate situations: a ground-air war between the USSR and China; a sea war against the Oceanic alliance; and a war by Soviet proxy against or within a smaller country.

In ground-air war against China, the Soviets would appear to have a decisive short-term advantage in military capabilities. They are vastly superior in technology, armor, mobility, firepower, and tactical air. Their nuclear superiority is so enormous that it precludes any rational Chinese nuclear initiative. Attacking at times and places of their choosing, there is little doubt that the Soviets could advance hundreds of miles into Chinese territory. This is not to say that they could then subjugate China, were they to attempt so foolhardy a venture. But they could, for example, carve off industrial Manchuria, as far south as Harbin. Whether they could hold this area for the tens of years necessary to make such a venture "profitable," however, is not at all certain. The Japanese, of course, held Manchuria (Manchukuo) until they had lost World War II elsewhere. The Soviet Union has carved out similar imperial holdings in Eastern Europe and the Baltic, but not on such a scale and at as remote a distance from the center of Soviet power.

Defensively, the Soviet Union would appear to be in a fully secure position. It is difficult to conceive of any Chinese offensive that could succeed even briefly against the Soviets' overwhelming defensive military capabilities.

What difference would hypothetical American military assistance to China make in the areas of technology and logistics? After the battle was joined, practically none. But even with a long buildup and with opportunity for Chinese assimilation, it is difficult to visualize U.S. assistance making a major difference in the military capabilities of the PRC relative to those of the Soviets. If Soviet logistics lines are long and vulnerable, American lines are even more so. And if certain American arms have technical superiority, certain Soviet arms have also. It is not clear that Soviet arms are, on balance, inferior to American arms for the requirements of a campaign against China.

The balance of capabilities in a Soviet sea-air war against the loose Oceanic alliance seems far less easy to assess. It is difficult to imagine such a war by itself.

It would almost certainly be a part of a global conflict in which NATO and her allies were locked in combat with the Warsaw Pact.

In the best case, with the alerted allies acting decisively in concert in Europe and in the Pacific, it should be possible to:

- Contain the Soviet submarine threat by mining the key "choke" straits, by air attacks on bases, and by attrition at sea, especially in the waters near Japan.
- Contain or destroy the surface fleet, principally by air action.
- Inflict sufficient attrition on attacking aircraft to make such attacks unprofitable against either Japan or the sea lanes.

In the Indian Ocean, a similar outcome could ensue as the result of an aggressive attack by allied tactical air—mostly carrier-based—on the relatively fragile Soviet base structure.

It appears, therefore, that in a reasonable best-case situation, the sea and air lines of communication can be kept open, Japan can be held secure, the Oceanic alliance can be sustained, and the Russian threat can be contained, albeit with loss. It must be emphasized that this best-case assessment requires a decisive American and allied commitment, as well as combat doctrine, force levels, and logistic support that are not yet evident. It is presently a potential capability rather than an actuality. The military balance in the Pacific is such that relatively small increments in combat forces can have a very great influence on the regional "correlation of forces."

A reasonable worst-case situation could be created by changing only a few military factors:

- A drawdown of allied sea and air forces in the Western Pacific.[5]
- Uncertainty in allied political understanding and doctrine, especially with respect to the use of bases in Japan, resulting in an indecisive reaction to the Soviet threat.
- Failure to have essential materiel (e.g., anti-submarine mines) and logistic support in place.

In this situation, a Soviet naval and air offensive in the western Pacific and the northern Indian Ocean could be expected to be successful, with the following consequences:

- Japan would be isolated by submarine blockade, possibly bombed from the air, and eventually vulnerable to amphibious attack on Hokkaido.

[5] Some might consider using U.S. Pacific forces to supplement American military strength in the European theater. But it is, of course, inconceivable that a war between NATO and the Warsaw Pact would be anything other than global in scope. Nothing in Soviet military doctrine, exercises, or common sense suggests otherwise.

To plan to transfer Pacific forces to Europe or the Middle East in the context of a NATO-Warsaw Pact conflict would only create a soft spot for attack. After the battle was joined, forces could be disengaged and transferred across two great oceans (either way) only at great risk. In any event, transiting forces would be out of action anywhere for the critical opening weeks of crisis or war.

Worse still would be the political consequences of such transfers: the abandonment of Korea and of Japan—our most important single ally in Asia. All hope of stiffening PRC resistance would dissipate, and the ANZUS allies would be placed in grave peril.

- Korea would be denied logistic resupply, and successful defense against an opportunistic attack from the North would be doubtful.
- More than 80 percent of the Middle East oil shipments would be interdicted.
- China would be isolated.
- Taiwan would endure only with Soviet sufferance.
- The Soviet Union would control the sea lines of access to every Asian country.

To repeat, these somewhat apocalyptic consequences are not a prediction of something that will or may happen. They are a potential consequence of Soviet military capabilities in the Far East, relative to those of the United States and its allies, assuming that present trends continue.

Let us now look at Soviet capabilities for the exploitation of civil or factional wars ("wars of national liberation"). These may take the form of support of one element by military supply, or advisers, or combat troops from another country, e.g., Cuba or Vietnam, or a combination of these. Soviet proxy forces might be allies of convenience or ideological comrades, or both. In Asia, the Vietnamese now seem the likeliest such Soviet ally, whether for expansion southward and westward, or for creating a countervailing two-front confrontation with China.

In any type of action, there would be no shortage of appropriate military weapons on the side supplied by the Soviets. There would be no logistics or resupply mission that the USSR could not handle. Soviet problems would be political and would involve forging a reliable and effective alliance with the faction they were supporting. The past record suggests that the Soviets will have considerable difficulty in projecting political influence in Asia. In general, Soviet and proxy military support to a given faction, if not counterbalanced, could make a great or even a decisive difference in a local conflict. Direct Soviet combat involvement would very likely be unproductive.

To predict where and when internal instability might tempt the Soviets to support one national faction in a "war of national liberation" requires a better crystal ball than mine. A look at recent history suggests, however, that the Southwest Pacific region (Thailand, Malaysia, and Indonesia) may not be immune to Soviet pressures. And, of course, Kampuchea (Cambodia) is now subject to direct military action by a Soviet-supported "proxy," Vietnam. In the Indian Ocean area, there is hardly a small state from Ethiopia through Yemen to Afghanistan that could not in some circumstances be vulnerable to internal factional strife, with accompanying Soviet opportunities for subversive action. Nor are the emerging tiny and fragile states of Pacific Oceania invulnerable to such pressures.

Soviet Strategies for the Pacific Region

There seem to be six dominant themes in Soviet strategies in the Far East:

- Containing Chinese power and influence, while at the same time keeping the door open to reconciliation (on Moscow's terms).
- Placing the United States on the defensive and separating it from its Pacific allies, as part of a continuing effort to shift the global balance of power.

- Thwarting the creation of any anti-Soviet coalition in the Far East, especially of Japan, China, and the United States.
- Building up the Soviet Far East as a power center.
- Extending Soviet influence over events throughout Asia.

Moscow has further advocated formation of a relatively formal organization of security in Asia under some form of regional pact or "collective security" arrangement.[6] (The Soviets criticize the idea of a "balance of power" in the region as being unstable and dangerous, and they may well be right.) In advocating a security pact, they provide for inclusion of the four great powers: the Soviet Union, the United States, China, and Japan. China, Japan, and other states have regarded these proposals as a veiled attempt to contain Beijing's (Peking's) influence in Asia and to extend Soviet hegemony or at least legitimize Soviet involvement in the affairs of the region. These states have rejected the concept out of hand; indeed, even Moscow's allies in Asia—North Korea and Vietnam—have failed to support the proposal. At the same time, Moscow also seeks to establish bilateral security relationships, as it has done recently with Afghanistan and Vietnam.[7]

Soviet tactics in support of these strategies have been essentially opportunistic, both reacting to events and attempting to control them. Soviet behavior has been likened to a man running along the hall in an apartment building, trying every door. When he finds one door unlocked, he enters. For example, the Soviets have:

- Maintained a major military capability directed against China.
- Maintained a strong sea/air force directed against the United States and the Oceanic alliance.
- Supported Vietnam in its conflict with China's ally Kampuchea and its related confrontation with the PRC.
- Intervened in South Yemen and Afghanistan in support of Soviet-oriented revolutions.
- Abandoned the lesser Red Sea power, Somalia, in favor of the greater regional power, Ethiopia.
- Persistently advanced the Soviet fishing and trading presence in the South Pacific, South Asia, and the Indian Ocean.
- Exerted increasing military pressure on Japan through reconnaissance activities and demonstrations of Soviet naval presence and amphibious attack capabilities in Northeast Asia.

On the other hand, Moscow has been notably restrained in its recent support for North Korea, probably for complex and long-standing political reasons. This restraint perhaps also reflects a realistic appraisal of the relative strengths of North Korea and South Korea.

A better gauge of the Soviet potential for politico-military maneuvering in Asia may lie in Moscow's recent record of actions in Angola and Ethiopia. There, in the shadow of Soviet military power, Cuban proxies have been a decisive force in local civil wars. The essential preconditions have been an excess of Soviet deployable power over that of the United States, and Soviet willingness to supply arms.

[6] See p.2 above.
[7] See pp. 9, 49, and 50.

FOUR PERSPECTIVES ON REGIONAL SECURITY

Security seems to lie in the eyes of the beholder. One country's "necessary defense measures" represent to another country "aggressive preparations for war." Yet there is a sense in which security has an absolute meaning. It is that situation in which no state or people is coerced by war or the threat of war. In this discussion, we have been talking about the Soviet capability for coercive military action in Asia; but a full understanding of regional security trends requires a look at the other side of the military balance as well, the Soviet Union's view of its own security in Asia.

A comprehensive evaluation of Asian security trends and the implications of the Soviet military presence must therefore consider four points of view:

- That of the PRC.
- That of the global Oceanic alliance of the NATO states, the Pacific allies (the United States, Japan, the Republic of Korea, the Philippines, Australia, and New Zealand), and like-minded states such as Thailand and the other ASEAN countries.
- That of the other Asian countries.
- That of the Soviet Union.

China feels threatened—and objectively is threatened—by the great Soviet offensive military deployment on its borders, combined with Moscow's overwhelming nuclear strength. This threat, and Chinese insecurity, could be neutralized only by a full Sino-Soviet political rapprochement, a major reduction in Soviet forces in the Far East, or a major enhancement in Chinese military capabilities. None of these developments seems likely in the near future. China will continue to attempt to provide for its security by passive measures designed to make itself more "indigestible," by attempting to divert Soviet attention elsewhere, by improving its military forces as it can, and by tentatively embracing anti-Soviet allies or perhaps seeking to minimize Soviet pressures through political talks.

The security position of the Oceanic alliance in Asia is not separable from its global position, but the Pacific, Indian Ocean, and Asian elements of the alliance have enormous and underrated importance. We have here the clearest possible contrast between a potentially disastrous security situation and a very satisfactory one. To sustain policies that would lead to the "reasonable worst case" described above will guarantee that Soviet power will be seen to be dominant in matters of vital concern to the countries affected: their internal security; their economic livelihood; their access to food and raw materials; and the integrity of their territory. While the countries concerned might feel some relief from anticipated Chinese pressures, under worst-case circumstances they would certainly feel the need for some degree of political accommodation to Soviet ambitions. If Washington were to undertake the initiatives and measures necessary to "pull up our socks," however, the situation could be transformed, and the Oceanic alliance could become at once secure and securely allied.

The security perspective of the Soviet Union itself is least explicable in Western eyes. Moscow is building military power of every category at a rate that suggests an attempt to overawe the world, in furtherance of Soviet political objectives. Yet the Soviets seem to feel genuinely threatened in Asia by the potential alliance of the United States, China, and Japan. They seem to have little insight into the fact that the conditions for such an alliance have been created precisely by their own military buildup and political adventures. Their attempts at conciliation through "good neighborly relations" and proposals for "cooperation" have foundered on policy rigidity (as in the case of the four islands in the Kurile chain claimed by Japan)[8] and distrust born of military adventurism in Asia and elsewhere in the world.

IMPLICATIONS FOR REGIONAL SECURITY

We are now in a position to assess the principal implications of the Soviet military presence in Asia:

- Moscow can place major limitations on the freedom of action of any Asian nation, and particularly China, Japan, and Korea.
- The Soviets can, in some circumstances, threaten to coerce any nation dependent on overseas trade or Middle Eastern and overseas oil; they can therefore fracture the Oceanic alliance if it cannot protect itself against the threat to its lines of communication.
- They can, in some circumstances, reduce and constrain American and allied power and influence west of Guam to the vanishing point.
- They can make some difference in the outcomes of factional civil strife in Asia (as they now seek to do in Indochina).
- They can defend the Soviet Far East against incursions by all comers.
- They cannot change the fundamental power relationship between themselves and China. Although the Soviets have military superiority, they are unable to threaten Beijing with the prospect of the conquest of China itself or to neutralize Chinese political influence in the region and world.
- They cannot organize Asia under their hegemony in some form of "collective security" arrangement.

Assessing American and allied military capabilities and their influence on regional security, we find the following:

- The United States and its allies cannot greatly affect Chinese military capabilities, except in the very long term or in symbolic ways.
- The United States cannot greatly affect the internal security affairs of most Asian states facing subversion or civil war.
- The United States can ensure the security of its regional allies against external attack, ranging from the Republic of Korea (ROK) and Japan to the Philippines and the ANZUS states.
- The United States and its allies can keep open vital sea and air lines of communication, but if and only if certain critical political and military needs are met.

[8] See pp. 48 and 74 for further discussion of this issue.

AN ALLIED STRATEGY FOR THE MILITARY SECURITY OF EAST ASIA

There are several moderately useful things the United States can do to enhance Asian security in the coming decade:

- Continue to develop a normal relationship with China, while avoiding any appearance of an anti-Soviet alliance.
- Provide for the continuing military security of Korea.
- Encourage Japan to enhance the capabilities of its forces in the air and sea defense of its home islands. This would provide an important Japanese motivation and a complement to American capabilities, without providing any reasonable cause for unease in the Soviet Union or in the rest of Asia. American and Japanese military capabilities can and should be more fully integrated through enhanced security cooperation.

The most fundamental leverage in regional security lies in control of the sea and air lines of communication. That control is vital to the Oceanic coalition, and it is of great interest to most Asian states. It is not, however, a vital interest of the Soviet Union.[9] Without it, the Soviet Union loses much of its capacity to threaten but is not itself threatened in any vital way.

The key to an allied security strategy is therefore use and control of the sea and air along the littoral of the Pacific Ocean and the Indian Ocean. With it, the allies are in business; without it, they are highly vulnerable to Soviet military pressures. What are the requirements for such control?

- Base availability. Sea and air bases in Japan and the Philippines, and the limited capability at Diego Garcia, are essential. Ground rules for base employment must be as firm and explicit as the political sensibilities of the host countries will permit.
- Base denial. The establishment of Soviet bases in Vietnam, in Pacific Oceania, the Persian Gulf, or the Horn of Africa would pose a great potential threat to sea and air security. Every possible effort should be made to inhibit the establishment of such bases.[10]
- Adequate allied forces to contain and defeat Soviet submarine and air forces and sea-surface forces in Asia.
- Adequate logistic support, including local and allied support arrangements.
- Doctrine, both political and military, providing for the integral defense of sea and air communications.

[9] Soviet views—for example, those of Admiral Gorshkov—are quite different. For Gorshkov, "the sea power of the [Soviet] state ... can counter the oceanic strategy of imperialism." (S. G. Gorshkov, *The Sea Power of the State*, Naval Institute Press, Annapolis, Maryland, 1979, p. 284.) Exactly. But the premises underlying the security strategies of the two sides are fundamentally different. The Soviet state and its contiguous allies are essentially self-sufficient in the sinews of war. The individual countries of the Western alliance are not. Hence, sea control is vital to the West, while it is only a convenience for the Soviet Union. (A special case arises in the logistic resupply of the Soviet Far East. Much tonnage traverses the Indian Ocean, and a limited amount crosses the Northern Sea route. But this is not a vital interest of the Soviet Union, in the same sense as sea communications are to the alliance.)

[10] According to news reports, Soviet Party leader Brezhnev told President Carter at Vienna in June 1979 that the USSR did not intend to establish military bases in Vietnam. See footnote 7, p. 160 below.

An appropriate security doctrine for East Asia in the 1980s should begin with the premise that in local or global war, American Pacific forces will stay in the Pacific and will not be expended in a non-productive attempt to relieve Europe. Moreover, it should be based on an offensive defense: Soviet submarine, air, space, and logistic capabilities can be attacked at their sources. Allied naval and air forces should be coordinated with as close to unified operational control as political considerations will permit; and this operational control should be a feature of peacetime exercises. Some of these exercises should be on a theater scale, and they should be as realistic as possible. Finally, the Asian subtheaters—Northeast Asia, Southeast Asia, Pacific Oceania, the eastern Indian Ocean, and the northwest Indian Ocean—should be treated as the integral military areas that in fact they are. For example, in the event of war, the defenses of Japan and Korea are integral, not separable.

Let us examine allied force requirements in more detail. Since both capability and the appearance of capability are important, it is essential that both deployment and basing be as far forward as possible. Forces "earmarked" for Asia but deployed in the continental United States or the eastern Pacific are of questionable military or political utility. Not only is there political doubt about their availability in time of trouble, they also take significantly longer to bring to bear on regional problems than would forces deployed in the region.

The principal force elements required to contain and defeat submarines in the Pacific and the Indian Ocean are long-range acoustic surveillance, satellite surveillance and data transfer, long-range maritime air, superior nuclear attack submarines, and effective offensive sea mines. Convoy and close escort are no longer practicable in an era of high-performance submarines with long-range weapons. We need to move from close-in defense to long-range subsurface denial and control. In the 1980s, it will be necessary to bring about a massive transfer of effort from surface anti-submarine forces to long-range surveillance and attack, using the most advanced air- and space-based technology available to us.

Similarly, security of long-range heavy air transport needs far more attention than it is now given. Not only are landing strips subject to attack, low-altitude landing approaches can be imperiled by highly mobile surface-to-air missiles such as the SA-7. Furthermore, it is now feasible to make fighter intercepts of large logistic aircraft at great distance from a fighter base—perhaps as far as 2,500 nautical miles.

A long-range airlift capability is the vital prerequisite to sustaining all military capabilities in the Pacific-Asian-Indian Ocean theater. We will be short of such a capacity unless most of the military airlift command can be devoted to that theater. It is vital that heavy transport helicopters be designed for carriage in the largest heavy transports of the C-5 class.

The next major requirement is the ability to quickly establish and maintain tactical air superiority where required, for example, in the approaches to Japan, the Indonesian straits, or the Persian Gulf. This tactical air superiority is necessary to defend our own forces and to project power where needed. It is the dominant element in the all-important political perception of power.

Land-based tactical airpower and sea-based airpower each have important advantages; sole reliance on either would be unwise. Given bases and logistic support, land-based aircraft can be very rapidly deployed and brought into action. Without available bases—the norm in most of the theater—carrier-based air is the only way, and it has important political flexibility.

In view of recent Soviet encroachments in the Red Sea-southern Arabia-Arabian Sea area, a countervailing American sea-air presence has become a necessity. Fleet basing in this area is extraordinarily difficult and costly. Therefore, rather than attempt to maintain permanent major forces in the area, a periodic entry in great strength from both the Pacific and the Atlantic seems a more feasible and more effective strategy. Finally, the theater ground forces in Hawaii, Korea, and Japan (Okinawa), both Army and Marine, should be kept in a high state of mobility and readiness for deployment on short notice.

All of this emphasis on the military capability of allied forces serves the political purpose of redressing the balance with the qualitative improvements in Soviet forces dedicated to or deployable in East Asia. As always, both reality and perception are involved; and some of the needed improvements go more to one than to the other, but they are inseparable. To the extent that vital security is safeguarded, improvements in allied military capabilities will be a political plus.

Major political obstacles to an alliance strategy for East Asian security remain, however. Almost all of our potential maritime allies prefer to keep their options open. They would like to run with the hare and hunt with the hounds, at least until they reach a moment of decision that is much closer to necessity than is now perceived by them. Most would like to avoid too overt a commitment to collective defense. Many have local political fish to fry which, in their eyes, transcend in importance global and theater interests. Many goverments have to contend with indigenous political opposition that limits freedom to plan collectively; and the closer they are to a democratic model of domestic politics, the more important this opposition becomes. For all these reasons, planned, formal, and concerted political-military arrangements of the sort required to maximize security are not now realistic. SEATO is dead, CENTO is moribund, and no one is attempting to revive either alliance.

There is, however, a more useful model: a strong America at the hub of a loose Oceanic alliance. Each spoke is different, from strong and formal treaty alliances like ANZUS, to the somewhat ambiguous provisions of the Japanese security treaty, to relationships that are simply a clear estimate of the self-interest of the potential allies involved. Such a system can be quickly converted, in time of threat, to a political alliance.

Building a military alliance is a more difficult process. It takes time and money, as well as political will. But the way can be paved conceptually and doctrinally by the widest variety of bilateral and multilateral exercises and consultations. The military requirements will then suggest themselves to the potential allies.

We can now summarize the implications of the Soviet military presence in Asia:

- The Soviet presence is a significant threat to the security of the sea lanes, and Soviet forces are capable of limited interventions on behalf of regional allies (such as Vietnam).
- An impression of Soviet military dominance in Asia would be a disastrous political fact if it ultimately were to occur.
- Soviet military capabilities are increasing. They can and must be balanced by qualitative improvements in American forces in the region and by progress toward an effective allied doctrine and security relationships.

At present, military "leverage" in East Asia is very high, and relatively small differences in Soviet or allied strength can produce major shifts in the regional balance of power.

Chapter 4

CHANGING JAPANESE SECURITY PERSPECTIVES

Paul F.Langer[1]

During the past three decades, hardly a year has gone by without one or another Asian nation being violently shaken by internal upheavals or war. While the major powers often have been drawn into these conflicts through direct military involvement, arms supply relationships, or the support of proxy allies, Japan has been able to keep at a safe distance from such turbulence—remaining Asia's lone island of peace and political stability. The conservative Liberal Democratic Party first came to power in Japan more than thirty years ago. Although its hold on power has weakened in recent years, it still rules the country today. During the intervening years, a single-minded national effort to develop and modernize the Japanese economy has proceeded relentlessly and with phenomenal success. This process has transformed what not long ago was a war-devastated, impoverished, resource-poor nation into an astonishingly prosperous one. During 1979 Japan passed an historic milestone when its Gross National Product (GNP) approached the equivalent of $1 trillion—in the process exceeding the Soviet Union in economic power. As Japan enters the 1980s, it stands as the world's second-largest national economic unit.

With all due credit to the vitality, sense of purpose, industriousness, and discipline characteristic of the Japanese people, it is widely recognized in Japan and elsewhere that these astounding achievements would not have been possible without a national security strategy that has proved both effective and cheap. Sheltered against external threats by the American military umbrella, Japan has enjoyed the enviable position of controlling the extent and manner of its political and military involvement with the problems and conflicts of other nations. The post-World War II governments of Japan have tended to remain on the sidelines in international security affairs, placing their faith in the wisdom of U.S. policy and actions. Hence, ever since the end of World War II, the burden of responsibility—as well as the cost—of maintaining a safe international environment around Japan has rested heavily on the United States.

From today's vantage point, such a division of burden-sharing may appear unbalanced in favor of Japan. Yet it must be recognized that the present arrangement is but the logical outcome of Japan's total military defeat in World War II and the consequence of the subsequent far-reaching U.S. policy decision to retain the leading role in shaping the future of postwar Japan. More than three decades have gone by since then. It would be surprising if the American-Japanese alliance relationship did not demand adjustments reflecting changes in the domestic conditions of the alliance partners, in the correlation of their forces, and in the international context in which the United States and Japan must pursue their policy objectives. Recognition of this fact has matured more slowly in Japan than in the United States. However, during the past several years evidence has been accumulating

[1] Paul F. Langer is on the staff of The Rand Corporation, where he specializes in the analysis of Asian policy issues. His writings in this field have been widely published, in the United States and abroad.

that the American-Japanese partnership is entering a new era and that this will also gradually find expression in the field of national security relations.

In Japan, probably more than in the case of other large nations, external forces tend to be the catalyst of major policy changes, since Japan's well-being is so vulnerable to international economic developments largely beyond its control. Today, once more, Japanese policy is in a period of some flux in response to the cumulative effect (experienced with a certain time lag) of international developments. It is legitimate therefore to ask what are the external events prompting changes in the Japanese perspective on the outside world; how these changes might affect Japan's national security policies in the years ahead; and how they might modify, in turn, the U.S.-Japanese military relationship.

An analysis of Japanese debates over national policy suggests a number of major international developments as having triggered Japanese policy reassessments. These include the limited U.S. military disengagement of the past several years in Southeast and Northeast Asia, raising questions about the future thrust of American strategy in the Pacific region and the role assigned by it to Japan; the growing and increasingly conspicuous military presence and involvement of the Soviet Union, globally as well as in the Pacific area; the dramatic Sino-American rapprochement culminating in the resumption of U.S. diplomatic relations with Beijing (Peking); the conclusion in 1978 of the Sino-Japanese Treaty of Peace and Friendship in the face of Soviet warnings; the increasingly ambivalent nature of U.S.-Soviet relations, distinguished by the two superpowers' intensified global competition proceeding in parallel with serious bilateral efforts to reduce the risks of an arms race involving highly sophisticated weaponry; and the recent clash of Chinese and Vietnamese armies, the dramatic reconfiguring of communist force alignments in an area of great importance to Japan, and the meaning of that reconfiguration for the future of the region, for Chinese behavior, and for Japanese attempts to create a fruitful and balanced relationship with both of the big communist powers.

One might also mention in this context the delicate situation on the Korean Peninsula, where the American initiative toward China appears to have created new opportunities as well as new dangers. Also, Japanese perceptions and policies are increasingly influenced by economic-technological issues impinging on the political and military spheres. Two problem clusters deserve special mention here: the issue of natural resources, especially as it pertains to the flow of vital energy supplies in the context of potential instability in the Middle East and of the perceived vulnerability of the sea lanes of communication in the face of the continued buildup of the Soviet naval presence in the Western Pacific; and the growing international tensions generated, in part, by Japan's continuing balance-of-payments surplus with its principal trading partner, the United States, and with the European community. All of these issues have had an increasingly powerful effect on the evolution of Japan's security perspectives, especially as these developments are occurring at a time when Japanese confidence in the ability of the United States to cope with mounting domestic and international problems has already been weakened.

JAPAN'S DEFENSE DEBATE

Much has already been written about the ebb and flow of debates among the Japanese regarding the meaning of national security in the particular circumstances of Japan.[2] While there is no need to go over that same ground again, it does seem useful to identify briefly two major interrelated problem areas central to that debate before examining the impact of external events on Japanese defense perspectives.

Nature and Mission of the Self-Defense Forces. For several years after Japan's surrender, the mood of the Japanese people was reflected in the widely held view that a defeated Japan under an American occupation no longer had need for an indigenous military force to ensure its security from external threats. The adoption of the Peace Constitution (originally suggested by the Occupation authorities), with its outright prohibition of "war potential," was one product of such thinking. For a nation once known for its ready resort to military power as an instrument of national policy, this represented a sharp break with the past. The explanation for the continued broad popular acceptance of the prohibition of "war potential" lies in Japan's World War II experience: The catastrophic defeat in the war created psychological conditions favorable to an outright rejection of military force.

However, confronted in the Korean War and through subsequent international developments with the harsh realities of world affairs, support for extreme pacifist views has steadily eroded in Japan. Today, a limited self-defense effort—vaguely defined as "minimum necessary defense power"—is accepted by the majority of the Japanese people. This does not mean that they or their leaders consider it necessary or advisable for Japan to develop a large military establishment like that of the other great powers, capable of projecting military force into areas beyond its own borders. Economic and political diplomacy remain central to Japan's national security strategy. Under presently prevailing conditions, the Japanese defense debate no longer focuses on the acceptability of a limited self-defense effort, but on the character of and the mission to be assigned to such a force and on the compatibility of that force with the provisions of the Constitution, which in the minds of most Japanese people stands as a guarantor of a democratic, progressive, nonmilitaristic Japan.

Despite certain initial misgivings on the part of the Japanese government, a modestly sized (about a quarter of a million men strong), defensively oriented Japanese military force—created in response to American urging—has been a

---

[2] In addition to numerous articles on the debate and the evolution of Japan's national security policy over the years in *Foreign Policy, Foreign Affairs, Pacific Community,* and other leading international journals, a number of lengthier studies deal with the subject. These include J.A.A. Stockwin, *The Japanese Socialist Party and Neutralism,* Cambridge University Press, London and New York, 1968; Martin E. Weinstein, *Japan's Postwar Defense Policy, 1947-1968,* Columbia University Press, New York and London, 1971; Paul F. Langer, *Japanese National Security—Domestic Determinants,* The Rand Corporation, R-1030-ISA, June 1972; Robert E. Osgood, *The Weary and the Wary: U.S. and Japanese Security Policies in Transition,* The Johns Hopkins University Press, Baltimore and London, 1972; John K. Emmerson and Leonard A. Humphreys, *Will Japan Rearm? A Study in Attitudes,* American Enterprise Institute and Hoover Institution, Stanford, California, 1973; Joachim Glaubitz, *Die Aussen—und Sicherheitspolitik Japans-Grundlagen und Ansätze einer Neuorientierung,* Stiftung Wissenschaft und Politik, Ebenhausen, 1973; and James H. Buck (ed.), *The Modern Japanese Military System,* Sage Publications, Beverly Hills and London, 1975. A basic source of information on Japanese defense policy and planning rationales is the series of White Papers issued by the Japanese Defense Agency under the title *Nihon no Boei.* Most of these volumes have appeared in an official translation, entitled *Defense of Japan.*

reality since the early 1950s. However, the legal status of these Self-Defense Forces (SDF) is clouded, and the government's scope of action remains restricted by the Constitutional prohibition against the development of "war potential." Beyond the legal niceties inherent in attempts to define what is meant by war potential as opposed to self-defense activities, the practical issue is that of the permissible mission of these military forces and the criteria that should determine the limits of their further expansion. Government and opposition agree that "war potential" can be equated with offensive weapon systems and offensive military action. But at a time when the line between "defensive" and "offensive" is often blurred, this definition leaves ample room for divergent interpretations. Much of the Japanese national security debate is generated therefore by the efforts of successive conservative Japanese governments to interpret the Constitution in a flexible way so as to allow for the development of a numerically small, but militarily effective and sophisticated defense force, while the left-wing opposition strenuously resists such elastic reinterpretations.

Closely related to the above issues is the debate over the geographic scope of the SDF's mission. No strong support for a regional military role of the SDF has developed or can be detected, even in the face of major changes in Japan's international environment. The issue is rather the appropriate perimeter within which Japan's forces are to fulfill their defense mission. Should the SDF be allowed to engage in activities beyond Japan's territorial limits in order to ensure the country's security? An all-out prohibition against reconnaissance, intelligence collection, and other activities beyond Japan's territorial boundaries would cripple the military effectiveness of the SDF. An affirmative answer, on the other hand, raises the question of how far the defense perimeter can be safely extended without making the Self-Defense Forces lose their Constitutionally required strictly defensive character.

The Military Relationship with the United States. The seeds of a major domestic controversy were sown when, after regaining national independence in 1952, the Japanese government entered into a formal and exclusive military relationship with the United States. Ever since, the U.S.-Japanese Mutual Security Treaty has been central to Japan's national security strategy. Thus, the internal Japanese debate regarding the previously mentioned contentious aspects of the country's defense policy is profoundly influenced by the nature and condition of the U.S.-Japanese alliance.

It is true that this alliance is mutual only in a very limited sense, since it does not oblige Japan to come to the aid of the United States with military force. Yet, quite apart from the stationing of U.S. forces on Japanese soil, the partnership with the United States exacts a political price from Japan. While it strengthens the very beneficial political and economic ties with the United States, it also creates Japanese obligations perceived at times as onerous, for Japan must lend consistent support to U.S. policies and actions if the American security commitment to Japan is to retain its viability. But American policies and actions are not necessarily or always viewed by the Japanese as directly supportive of Japan's interests, nor are they necessarily judged to be promising or expedient. In many instances, they tend to be politically destabilizing in that they intensify the existing political divisions in Japan.

The alliance of two powers whose military capabilities, missions, and international responsibilities are of quite a different order creates its own difficulties; and these difficulties have been magnified by the fact that the military capabilities of the two partners and their respective national security burdens have remained essentially unchanged over the years, while Japan's economic power has grown immensely both in absolute terms and in comparison with the uneven development of the American economy. Not surprisingly, these circumstances have led Japanese policymakers to reassess the state of health of the American alliance and to reexamine the basic premises on which this alliance and Japan's international strategy rest.

SOME JAPANESE QUESTIONS REGARDING THE BASIC PREMISES UNDERLYING THE AMERICAN ALLIANCE

Ever since the end of World War II, Japan has staked its security on the American military guarantee and on a virtually exclusive political relationship with the United States. While neither of the two nations has ever formally and explicitly articulated the rationale for this arrangement, seen from the Japanese perspective the alliance rests on four major premises: (1) the existence of a *potential*, though primarily indirect, Soviet threat to Japan's security, suggesting in turn the need for deterrence through some form of American military presence in and around Japan; (2) the deterrent effect of the U.S. military presence flowing from the maintenance of a global military balance favoring the United States and from demonstrably superior U.S. military power in the region backed by the political will to employ it in the defense of Japan; (3) U.S. willingness and capacity to shoulder for an indefinite period the resulting financial burden without substantial Japanese contributions to the maintenance of American defense capabilities in the region; and (4) the continuation of a near-identity of U.S. and Japanese national interests allowing the two nations to coordinate their policies and actions in the region effectively. Although none of these fundamental Japanese assumptions has been invalidated by developments that have occurred since the establishment of the security alliance two decades ago, from the Japanese perspective they are being substantially modified by the changing circumstances of the past several years.

A major reason for Japan's well-known reluctance to assume greater responsibility for its self-defense has been the nature of postwar Japan's external threat perceptions. In contrast to America's European allies, the Japanese have had difficulty developing plausible scenarios involving direct military threats to their own security. Rather, concern has tended to focus on indirect threats such as might result from the spillover effect of local conflicts (e.g., in Korea) on the approaches to or along the supply routes leading to the Japanese home islands. Certainly, Japan's geographic position and history have had something to do with this assessment. So does the Sino-Soviet confrontation, which for more than a decade has pitted the military forces of the two communist giants against each other, thus preventing them from uniting against Japan, as was the original intent of the now defunct Sino-Soviet military alliance of 1950. Faith in the overwhelming superiority of American military power over any potential aggressor has been the principal factor that has made postwar Japan feel absolutely secure from external threats—a situation that now may be changing in a fundamental way.

Soviet international behavior in recent years appears to have cast some doubt on the validity of these reassuring conclusions. During the past decade, Japan has observed with concern the development of a more powerful, aggressive, and conceivably expansionist Soviet security strategy, both globally and in the Asian region. This perception has been shaped by a series of events: the fighting along the Sino-Soviet border in 1969; the injection of communist military assistance and armed forces into Third World conflicts in Angola, Ethiopia, Afghanistan, and Vietnam; the continuing buildup around Japan of the Soviet Pacific Fleet and its possible use of the former U.S. naval base at Cam Ranh Bay; and frequent Soviet intrusions into Japanese air space and territorial waters and their implications for Japan's defense (brought home by the startling ease with which a defecting Soviet MiG-25 pilot breached Japan's air defenses in 1976). China's insistence on the great danger of war and on the bellicose nature of the Soviet regime may not be fully shared by Tokyo, but it appears to have had the effect of heightening Japanese concern about the growth of Soviet military power and about Soviet intentions. Moscow's behavior toward Japan, especially the hardening of the Soviet position on the issue of the contested northern territories,[3] has done nothing to reassure the Japanese nor has the Soviet-supported Vietnamese forces' invasion of Kampuchea (Cambodia) and their armed clash with China.

Over the years, periodic Japanese reassessments of the state of the global and regional U.S.-Soviet military balance have further reinforced the impact of the above developments on Japanese security perceptions.[4] References to this matter in the successive issues of the annual government White Papers, entitled *Defense of Japan*, are instructive in that regard and deserve extensive quotation:

> Particularly noteworthy is the increase in nuclear and naval power by the Soviets since the late 1960s.[5]

> In the face of increasing Soviet military strength, the U.S. is attempting to maintain a viable nuclear potential, while increasingly relying on key allies for conventional military capabilities.[6]

> During the past decade, however, there has been a marked expansion of Soviet forces, in striking contrast to a quantitative decline in the previously overwhelming American posture. Although a military balance still remains between the U.S. and the Soviet Union, this has been a significant factor in the recent world military structure, and great attention has been focused on the possible outcome of this trend and its potential effect upon the specific military environments for the security of the West.[7]

> The improvements in the Soviet Union's military capability since the 1960s have not only eased the national security position of the Soviet side, despite this containment policy, but also altered the military balance between the United States and the Soviet Union as well as its structure to some extent.[8]

---

[3] This territorial dispute is a major obstacle to an improvement of Soviet-Japanese relations. It concerns Japanese claims to several small islands (off Japan's northernmost island, Hokkaido), now the possessions of the USSR under its interpretation of the wartime Yalta Agreement. See also pp. 80 and 104 below.

[4] On this point, see Paul F. Langer, "Japanese Elite Assessments of the U.S.-U.S.S.R. Military Balance," in Donald C. Daniel (ed.), *International Perceptions of the Superpower Military Balance*, Praeger Publishers, New York and London, 1978.

[5] Defense Agency, *Defense of Japan, 1976* (White Paper), p. 7.

[6] Ibid., p. 8.

[7] Defense Agency, *Defense of Japan, 1977* (White Paper), p. 7.

[8] Ibid., p. 14.

The Soviet Union has expanded its nuclear deterrent capability against the United States and at the same time has reinforced its military posture in Europe and the Far East. This has been accomplished through improved air defense capability at home, modernization of ground forces and tactical air power, strengthening of naval power and expansion into the outer oceans.

The Soviet force strength, in particular, surpasses that of the United States, and the safety of the sea and air lanes from the U.S. mainland is being jeopardized.[9]

The 'blue water' expansion of Soviet naval power into the outer oceans also is a matter of concern to the national security of Japan which is situated along passage strait routes to the outer oceans...[10]

... the fleet [U.S. Seventh Fleet] has a sufficient anti-submarine capability for its own defense. However, there is reason to conclude that it lacks sufficient capabilities for the protection of large numbers of merchant vessels. It will therefore be difficult to counter completely the Soviet capabilities for severing the sea lanes of communication.[11]

In this context, it should be noted that Japanese assessments of the U.S.-Soviet military balance tend to be derived primarily from American analyses.[12] While authoritative American statements regarding Soviet military capabilities have at times appeared to send out contradictory messages to the Japanese audience, they are read by the Japanese as supporting the view that, in relative terms at least, we have been witnessing a decline in American power over the past two decades. Doubts about America's capacity to exercise global leadership in restraining Soviet advances have become pervasive; so has concern about the gradual erosion of U.S. power.

Direct observation of the growth of the Soviet military presence in East Asia (as evidenced in the buildup of the Soviet Pacific Fleet and Soviet military assistance to Vietnam in its conquest of Kampuchea and defense against China) points in the same direction, viz. that the U.S. and the Soviet Union have reached a point of near-parity and that the trend in the long run may not favor the United States. If the available evidence regarding Japanese uneasiness about the future of the U.S.-Soviet military balance concerns the distant rather than the immediate future, such views seem to be based on an extrapolation of trends and on events not all directly related to matters of an essentially military nature. Japanese judgments about who is militarily ahead often appear to originate in analyses of the broader trends in international affairs, which to the Japanese seem to indicate a relative decline in the overall U.S. power position. One might cite in that context the seeming devolution of U.S. international commitments, as in Korea, and the apparent inability or unwillingness of the United States to stem the injection of Soviet or Soviet-sponsored forces into a growing number of Third World areas. It is not

[9] Ibid.

[10] Ibid., pp. 24-25.

[11] Boeicho (Defense Agency), *Nihon no Boei* (Defense of Japan), July 1978, p. 39. This is the writer's translation from the original Japanese language White Paper; no official English translation is available.

[12] This may account for the rather similar American and Japanese perceptions of Soviet power reflected in a recent Gallup poll conducted in the United States and in Japan. Of the Americans polled, 10 percent viewed the Soviet Union as "the most powerful"; so did 9 percent in Japan. Americans in their majority considered the Soviet Union "one of the most powerful (countries)"; so did the Japanese, with roughly equal percentages—69 percent in the case of the United States and 60 percent for the Japanese. *The Gallup Opinion Index*, January 1979.

so much correlations of military forces that give rise to these concerns, but rather the momentum that has carried the Soviet Union so far forward in so short a time.

Much evidence exists for the contention that such thinking has encouraged the Japanese public to give increasingly serious study to issues of national security, to approach these problems in a realistic fashion, and to reject simplistic solutions.[13] Clearly, the Japanese public's mood is changing.[14] Recent opinion polls convincingly show that the need for the SDF is now overwhelmingly (86 percent)[15] accepted by the Japanese public, not excluding many supporters of the Socialist and Communist Parties. Defense issues that were once taboo are today openly aired in the Diet and in the public media. For the first time, left-wing opposition to Japan's military preparedness program appears to be on the defensive. This is partly due to the Chinese volte-face, with leaders of the PRC now endorsing outright the primacy of the U.S.-Japan Mutual Security Treaty and Japan's need for armed forces, and partly to the Chinese military's open cultivation of contacts with Japanese counterparts.

There are no indications at present, however, that the perceived relative erosion of U.S. power has stimulated a desire among the Japanese to adopt a dramatic reorientation of the long-standing Japanese defense strategy, at the heart of which is the security alliance with the United States. Significantly, in recent months, fewer than 10 percent of the Japanese public wished to see the U.S. security pact abrogated.[16] The available evidence suggests that Japanese policymakers see a growing need for bolstering U.S.-Japanese defense cooperation and thereby preventing a further retrenchment of the American military position in the Far East.

As indicated in the 1978 Defense White Paper, the conclusion is being drawn in Tokyo that under prevailing circumstances Japan must be ready to do more in matters of defense through a strengthening of its own forces, to the extent that political conditions permit, and by making a larger financial contribution to the U.S. defense effort in the region. In an effort to assume a more equitable share of the burden, the Japanese government in 1978 agreed as a first step to increase the financial support for the U.S. military presence in Japan by the equivalent of some $100 million. As a result, the total direct Japanese contribution (base rental fees, replacement facilities, labor costs) reached an annual rate of about $700 million. The Japanese remain convinced that the American security tie is militarily and politically the most advantageous as well as the most cost-effective answer to Japan's national security problem. In view of changing circumstances, they are now willing to admit that in one form or another they must pay a higher price if they wish to continue to base their security on the deterrent effect of a U.S. military presence in and near Japan and on the American guarantee contained in the Mutual Security Treaty.

[13] See Takuya Kubo, "Security in Northeast Asia," pp. 100-101 of this volume.

[14] If anything, the recent trend suggests a modest decline in neutralist sentiment among the Japanese public and continued minimal support for an alignment with the communist side. The most recently available data, gathered in January 1979, show 54.1 percent favoring a Free World alignment (in January 1974 the figure was 27.8 percent); 22.7 percent opting for a neutralist foreign policy and security stance (in January 1974, 31.8 percent); and a mere 1.4 percent favoring alignment with the communist countries (in January 1974, 3.5 percent); the remainder were in the "don't know" column. Seron Chosa (Opinion Survey), March 1974 and March 1979.

[15] Results of an opinion survey made in December 1978 by the Prime Minister's Office. (Asahi Evening News, March 5, 1979). Comparable polls conducted by the same government agency in 1972 and 1975 showed 73 percent and 79 percent of support, respectively.

[16] Ibid.

As to the identity of U.S. and Japanese security interests—the fourth and most essential element of the structure on which the alliance rests—here, too, changes have been occurring in the past few years, and the consequences are clearly evident. For reasons related to the negative impact of Japanese export surpluses on the U.S. balance of payments, it has become more difficult to harmonize U.S. and Japanese economic interests. The friction resulting from American efforts to restrict Japanese exports and to open up the Japanese market more widely to American goods has made Japan view U.S. actions and strategies more critically. This phenomenon is no longer entirely limited to the economic sphere. While the two nations continue to agree on the fundamental purpose and general thrust of their national policies, Japan now inclines to follow its own counsel with regard to lesser matters. The question for the 1980s is whether U.S. and Japanese cooperative efforts can prevent economic issues from spilling over into the more fundamental political and security dimensions of the U.S.-Japan tie.

JAPAN'S SECURITY STRATEGY AND THE COMMUNIST POWERS

Ever since the Japanese regained the freedom to determine their own policies in 1952, and apart from the central importance of the U.S. security tie, relations with China and the Soviet Union have been Japan's principal foreign policy concerns. During the first years after Japan's reappearance on the international scene, Tokyo's options for dealing with the two communist powers were limited by their common hostility toward Japan and its American ally, as codified in the anti-Japanese and anti-U.S. Sino-Soviet alliance of 1950. The subsequent development of the Sino-Soviet conflict, however, produced a new situation. It also created a policy dilemma for Japan.

While the Sino-Soviet conflict had the effect of improving Japan's bargaining position, it also had the effect of raising the level of tension throughout the Far East. Since the early 1960s, Japan has faced conflicting pulls from Moscow and Beijing, forcing it to engage in a precarious balancing act, often described as "equidistant diplomacy."

The problem of developing a consistent strategy has been further aggravated by the tendency of Chinese and Soviet policymakers (especially the latter) to shift back and forth between the application of hard and soft policy lines in their attempts to influence Japanese policies.

In this Sino-Soviet contest over Japan, the Chinese clearly have enjoyed political, psychological, and economic advantages that Soviet diplomacy has never been able to develop. Nevertheless, until the American opening to China in 1971 made a new relationship between Tokyo and Beijing a distinct possibility, Japan's relations with both communist powers remained unsatisfactory for all parties concerned. Although Moscow had succeeded in the 1950s in establishing diplomatic relations with Tokyo, it subsequently boxed itself in through the Soviet leadership's adamant refusal to negotiate a return of Japan's Soviet-occupied northern territories—in Japanese eyes, a sine qua non for a peace treaty. The convulsions caused by the Chinese Cultural Revolution and the Taiwan problem, on the other hand, set natural limits to any improvement of Sino-Japanese relations.

The Nixon Administration's establishment of a political dialogue with China had far-reaching international consequences that are still reverberating throughout Asia. One of its first results was the normalization of Sino-Japanese relations (in 1972), followed by the conclusion of a Treaty of Peace and Friendship (in 1978), events which may in the longer run eclipse in significance even the reorientation of America's China policy. The treaty has been described in China as well as in Japan as an historic event. Its implications are still being analyzed; but *Peking Review* has suggested the scope of the new relationship, and the terms on which the two parties agreed to cooperate, as well as Chinese hopes for the future:

> In short, though China and Japan have different social and political systems and face different circumstances, so long as both adhere to the principles set forth in the Peace and Friendship Treaty, *maintain the policy of seeking common ground on major issues while reserving differences in minor matters* and act on the basis of the friendly exchanges that have taken place down the long years, *much can be done through mutual cooperation, coordination, and joint efforts ... the conclusion of the treaty has opened up broader prospects for friendship between the two countries . . . .*[17]

Chinese policymakers have thus agreed to postpone the resolution of minor controversial matters pending between the two countries, such as the future of the Senkaku (Tiaoyu Tai) Islands, in order to facilitate cooperation on major issues including, from the Chinese viewpoint, a Sino-Japanese alignment against the Soviet Union as symbolized in Beijing's insistence on an "anti-hegemony" clause in the treaty. Subsequent comments by Chinese and Japanese leaders involved in the treaty negotiations indicate that both sides were keen enough on obtaining a mutually acceptable treaty to agree on a wording sufficiently ambiguous to allow for varying interpretations.

From statements made in Beijing, it is clear, if it wasn't already so, that in Chinese eyes the reference in Article II about the contracting parties opposing efforts by any other nation to seek hegemony in the Asia-Pacific region aims at the Soviet Union. In that sense the treaty can be said to have established an anti-Soviet alignment. That is, indeed, how it is interpreted in the Chinese and Soviet capitals. But in Tokyo it is pointed out that not only does Article II fail to mention a particular country, Article IV specifically states that "the present treaty shall not affect the position of either contracting party regarding its relations with third countries." This could be interpreted—and the Japanese government asserts that this is the proper interpretation—as underlining the unchanging Japanese desire to develop cordial relations with the Soviet Union.

Little credence is given in Moscow to such Japanese protestations of impartiality. Thus, the noted Soviet military commentator Colonel A. Leontyev has ridiculed Tokyo's attempt to describe the treaty as a harmless declaration of general principles committing Japan to nothing.[18] An earlier comment in the Soviet government newspaper *Izvestia* had already made the Soviet interpretation and anger crystal clear when it stated:

> Although the treaty is formally intended to settle bilateral relations, it actually extends beyond the framework established for documents of this

---

[17] *Peking Review*, October 20, 1978, p. 22 (emphasis added).
[18] *Krasnaia Zvezda* (Red Star), September 17, 1978.

kind . . . . The enshrinement of an anti-Soviet thrust in the text of the "Peace and Friendship Treaty" thereby transforms it into a document which extends beyond the framework of bilateral relations and which *lays a foundation for an alliance between Peking and Tokyo directed against the Soviet Union.*[19]

While patiently pursuing their goal of concluding a peace treaty with China, Japanese policymakers were careful not to provoke the Soviet Union unnecessarily, as evidenced by the Japanese handling of Chinese pressures to include an anti-Soviet clause in the treaty text. Even so, Soviet comments, warnings, and implicit threats of action against Japan suggested that relations between Moscow and Tokyo might be entering into an era of turbulence. This has not been the case, however. In fact, the Soviet response to the Sino-Japanese treaty has proved surprisingly mild and essentially confined to the realm of words. The Soviets apparently realize that their leverage over Japanese policy decisions is currently quite limited, that outright pressure applied against Japan would likely have the counterproductive effect of encouraging China and Japan to draw even closer together, and that more could be gained by patient and indirect efforts to undermine the Sino-Japanese rapprochement while adopting a wait-and-see strategy toward Japan. They may reckon that China's lure will gradually wane in the face of Chinese economic and political realities. Soviet patience might then reap more benefits than would be gained from any precipitate countermeasures that could be adopted now. (Whether Soviet calculations also include the hope that the impending Soviet negotiation with Beijing will reduce Chinese incentives to move closer to the United States and its Japanese ally is not clear, though this is not implausible.)

China and Japan, the two leading nations of East Asia, have formally opted for a cooperative relationship. The consequences of this momentous decision—should its implementation endure or be enhanced—will be felt not only in Beijing and Tokyo, but throughout the region and beyond. Soviet efforts to prevent a Sino-Japanese rapprochement have failed. What once could be described as an equilateral Moscow-Tokyo-Beijing triangle of tense relations has given way to a new structure in which Japan occupies a place alongside China. This political defeat for the Soviet Union may have wide-ranging strategic and diplomatic implications for the future of Soviet-Japanese relations and for Soviet behavior and policies in the region. Close economic cooperation between China and Japan, should it develop during the years ahead, would inevitably also tend to create conditions for closer political ties between Tokyo and Beijing—unless the Soviets can prevent or slow such a development through potent economic incentives to Japanese business and through concessions regarding the festering issue of the northern territories.

The Soviets themselves profess to view the new bonds between China and Japan as merely a prelude to a more advanced stage of Sino-Japanese cooperation, when the two nations will coordinate with the United States their strategy against the Soviet Union. Having concluded a treaty with China despite Soviet warnings, Japan must now be prepared to face Soviet attempts to slow and obstruct the further deepening of the Sino-Japanese entente. For the moment, however, Moscow is adopting a wait-and-see posture in its relations with Japan, putting Tokyo

[19] *Izvestia*, August 15, 1978 (emphasis added).

on notice that Soviet reaction to the Sino-Japanese treaty will be strictly a function of the actual behavior of the two parties.

In the past, Soviet strategy toward Tokyo has experimented unsuccessfully with both hard- and soft-line policies. Whether the Soviets were applying pressure on Japan or offering economic enticements, they have rather consistently underestimated what it would take to discourage the Japanese from eventually leaning toward China. They have failed to appreciate the powerful emotional appeal in Japan of a normalization of relations with China, and they have also misjudged the depth of resentment and nationalistic feeling aroused by their seizure of Japan's former island territories.

As late as the 1960s, a formula might have been found to defuse this territorial question through mutual compromise. For military as well as political considerations, the Soviet leaders decided against such a course, embittering the Japanese and making the northern islands a national issue in Japan, thereby restricting the Japanese government's freedom of action in seeking an acceptable solution to the territorial issue. It is questionable whether the military advantage gained by holding on to the contested islands will be worth the political price the Soviet Union is paying in its contest with China over the alignment of Japan. Similarly, even when Moscow held out economic incentives for Soviet-Japanese cooperation, it insisted on terms that made such cooperation unpalatable to Japan, especially after China offered more immediate and favorable opportunities to Japanese economic interest groups.

Viewed against this background of past Soviet-Japanese interaction, the questions for the 1980s are whether the Soviet Union retains sufficient means to threaten the development of Sino-Japanese cooperation, what Japan might do to reduce the likelihood and effect of Soviet threats or incentives, and how this new situation might affect the interests and policies of the United States.

In the past, Tokyo has shown no signs of succumbing to Soviet attempts to "Finlandize" Japan through implied threats and demonstrations of military power. As long as U.S. global policies and capabilities, especially as demonstrated in the Far East, retain credibility in Japanese eyes, direct Soviet military threats against Japan appear both unlikely and ineffective. This is not to say that the Soviet Union could not apply some form of indirect military pressure against Japan if concerted Sino-Japanese anti-Soviet policies should threaten Soviet interests in the region. The Soviet Union has the power to create uncomfortable situations for Japan by heightening tension in a wide zone from the Sino-Soviet border to the Korean Peninsula, in Southeast Asia, and in the sea lines of communication that carry Japanese energy resources and commerce to the seas around the Japanese islands. Such a policy would present the United States with difficult military decisions, which in turn could not fail to test the U.S.-Japanese alliance and the Japanese commitment to cooperation with China.

In light of Moscow's global interests and commitments and the Soviet Union's relatively limited military capabilities in the Far East, it is unlikely that Soviet leaders would want to risk a confrontation with the United States unless Sino-Japanese cooperation reached a point at which important Soviet interests were clearly at stake. This could be the case if the Sino-Japanese relationship should assume the character of a true alliance and cooperation should extend—as Beijing appears to desire—into the military sphere. In present circumstances, Chinese encouragement of a Japanese military buildup can only irritate the Soviet Union; but the creation of close Sino-Japanese military ties—improbable though this may seem at this point in time, at least from Tokyo's perspective[20]—could only be interpreted in Moscow as a reckless provocation inviting Soviet retaliatory action.

One conclusion that might be drawn from this situation concerns the parameters and mode of future Sino-Japanese cooperation. From both Japanese and American points of view, it would seem desirable to promote Sino-Japanese cooperation in a manner that is not likely to arouse deep-seated Soviet fears of a U.S.-Chinese-Japanese (anti-Soviet) tripartite security alliance. It appears important to avoid unnecessary and dangerous confrontations and not to foreclose Soviet options for policies facilitating accommodation. In turn, this suggests that it is in the interests of both the United States and Japan—though probably not of China—that Sino-Japanese policy coordination not go beyond informal consultation and that cooperative activities in the military or quasi-military spheres be avoided in the absence of serious Soviet provocations. To maintain a limited level of formal cooperation while sustaining the existing momentum toward a desirable Sino-Japanese rapprochement will be a difficult diplomatic task. It might be supplemented by indications of Japanese readiness to extend economic cooperation to the Soviet Union. In Japan at least, conditions are favorable for such an effort (which from Tokyo's perspective should also involve the United States). Influential circles in Tokyo are already looking soberly at the international political implications of cooperation with Beijing. They caution against leaning too far to one side, and would like their government to demonstrate more clearly that Japan continues to be interested in a more tension-free relationship with Moscow and wishes to play no part in the Sino-Soviet conflict.

There can be no question that since the early 1970s Japan has experienced a China "boom" and that this boom is not merely a response to the lure of economic opportunities that have now opened up for Japan. There has always existed something of a Japanese fixation on China (termed by some a "China syndrome")—an amalgam of historical legacies, war guilt, and ethnic-cultural affinity. China clearly enjoys a very special place in Japanese thinking and policies, relative to the Soviets and even to the United States; and the Japanese people have long desired friendly relations with China. That has now been achieved at long last.

Postwar Japan has been searching for some psychologically satisfying mission to define the country's place in the world. To some influential Japanese, that mission might be found in cooperation with China. This impulse, while potentially constructive, holds a potential danger for the United States in that too close a Sino-Japanese tie might develop at the expense of Japan's relations with the United States. While at the moment this sentiment is muted, in no small measure because Chinese leaders now stress to Japanese officials the primacy of good Japanese-American relations for Japan's security interests,[21] in time this situation could

---

[20] Japan's Prime Minister, the Foreign Minister, and the Director General of the Defense Agency have made it clear that no military tie with China is intended and that Japan will not give assistance to the development of Chinese military capabilities.

[21] Thus, Vice-Premier Deng Xiaoping (Teng Hsiao-p'ing), meeting with a group of Japanese editorial writers in Beijing, stated, "China attaches great significance to Japan-U.S. relations," and recalled that both the late Chairman Mao Zedong (Mao Tse-tung) and Premier Zhou Enlai (Chou En-lai) had said more than once that Japan-U.S. relations come first for Japan and Sino-Japanese relations second. *Tokyo Kyodo*, September 6, 1978, reproduced in Foreign Broadcast Information Service (FBIS), *Daily Report—People's Republic of China*, September 7, 1978, p. A1.

change. For the present, however, Japan—and China—are likely to emphasize the importance of Sino-Japanese relations for the economic development of the PRC. Japanese officials and the public at large see an inspiring national opportunity and a real challenge to Japanese dynamism in participating massively in the modernization of a neighboring nation that has loomed very large on the Japanese horizon for more than a thousand years and that is so vast. Such sentiments underlie a recent statement by one of Japan's most influential business leaders who, upon his return from the Chinese capital, urged the Japanese not to view the opening of China as a money-making proposition but rather as an opportunity to serve world stability by offering selfless assistance even if such assistance might not always prove economically profitable. Although a more sober appraisal of Chinese developments and opportunities for Sino-Japanese cooperation is beginning to become evident in Japan, conditions remain favorable for the establishment of a close working relationship between Japan and China which could eventually extend into areas beyond China itself.

What Beijing hopes to achieve through the broadening and strengthening of its ties with Tokyo emerges from a reading of statements made by the Chinese leadership: (1) to enlist Japan's impressive and demonstrably effective technological and organizational capabilities in the cause of China's modernization, assigning Japan a special place in that effort because of historical-cultural affinity, the proven success of Japanese economic-technological policies, and the close ties linking Japan to the United States; (2) to pull Japan, together with its American ally, to Beijing's side, thus facilitating Chinese attempts to constrain Soviet influence in Asia.

It is true that these new Chinese policies could benefit both Japan and the United States in a number of ways. An important benefit might be reaped from China's presumed willingness to assist in easing tensions in areas where the Soviet Union could otherwise inject itself. If the opening to China provides opportunities for both the United States and Japan, however, it also creates new problems, as demonstrated by China's punitive military action against Vietnam. The fact that Beijing and Tokyo—and for that matter the United States—do not view their interests and possible forms of cooperation in the same light cannot be ignored. Chinese leaders are eager to build ties with Japan, the United States, and other developed countries and to use them against the Soviet enemy. Hence, fundamental Japanese and U.S. policy considerations will tend to limit the scope of cooperation with Beijing insofar as the security aspects of such cooperation are concerned. But "security" is a broad term that can be interpreted in many ways.

As we move into the 1980s, there exists a clear need for the United States and Japan to arrive at agreements about the content of their respective assistance to China in the economic and technological spheres and about ways to effectively signal to the Soviet Union that cooperation with China is not meant to foreclose opportunities for an easing of tensions between the Soviet Union and the West. It is reasonable to assume that this message will at the same time convey to Soviet leaders that the nature of their response, i.e., their willingness to refrain from heightening their military involvement in Asia, will determine whether their fears of a U.S.-Japanese-Chinese tripartite alliance against the Soviet Union will eventually prove to have been justified.

SOME POLICY IMPLICATIONS

Improved Prospects for U.S.-Japanese Defense Cooperation. International developments of recent years, particularly changes in the perceived U.S.-Soviet balance, have had their impact on Japanese views of national security. Nevertheless, as indicated earlier, available evidence does not suggest the imminence of a fundamental reassessment of Japanese defense strategy. Rather, the effect in Japan has been to underline the importance of the American alliance, to increase public acceptance of the once highly controversial Self-Defense Forces, and to create a psychological and political climate facilitating the discussion of defense matters in a less ideologically charged and more realistic fashion. The significance of the more positive frame of mind in which the Japanese are now dealing with issues of national security lies in the opportunities it opens up for the Japanese and U.S. governments to translate the concept of defense cooperation into a functioning reality.

Need for Alleviating Japanese Concerns about U.S. Security Policies in the Pacific Region. The changing Japanese perspective on national security has removed certain obstacles to effective military cooperation with the United States so that more frank and public discussions of major defense issues are now possible. As a result, U.S.-Japanese military-strategic relations today seem better than ever before. In this context, one might easily be tempted to exaggerate the practical implications of what appears to be a new mood in Japan. As a corrective, one must remember on the one hand that the many serious obstacles to an enlarged Japanese defense effort—psychological, political, institutional, Constitutional, and strategic—have not disappeared overnight, and on the other hand that a serious blow to Japanese confidence in the U.S.-Japan security tie could impel Tokyo to embark on some new and more independent defense policy.

One must also keep in mind that in the longer run the climate of cooperation can be maintained only if U.S. policies are capable of alleviating Japanese concerns. The Japanese are wondering whether the economically hard-pressed United States is not shifting its attention to the defense of Europe while preparing to cut its military commitments and presence in the Pacific region. Such conclusions are generated by the thinning out of the American military presence in the Far East and the meaning that Japan is reading into U.S. pronouncements, particularly statements on defense contingencies in the NATO region and the need to draw down Pacific forces in such emergencies. It is only natural that the pronouncement of such a strategy causes concern in Japan, since its security is linked so closely to the continued deterrent presence of U.S. forces in the region.

Another source of doubt about U.S. intentions has been created by the heavy emphasis given recently to Sino-American normalization. While this development has now been welcomed in Tokyo, the Japanese at first asked themselves whether China would replace Japan as the preferred U.S. partner in Asia. Such doubts were to be expected, since U.S.-Japanese tensions over Japan's huge trade surplus held the possibility of developing into serious friction between the two allies.

Japanese security concerns have been allayed in large measure by understandings reached between the U.S. and Japanese governments during the visit of Prime Minister Ohira to Washington in the spring of 1979, by the conversations President Carter held with the Japanese Prime Minister prior to and during the economic summit of June 1979, and by subsequent developments such as the Carter Administration's decision to suspend further withdrawals of American ground forces from Korea.[22] The United States has made it explicit that Japan remains the cornerstone of American policy in the Far East and that a Sino-American rapprochement has by no means resulted in a downgrading of the long-standing U.S.-Japanese alliance.

Economic problems also appear to have moved a long way toward resolution, or at least serious efforts at management. The multibillion-dollar trade balance in favor of Japan has begun to dwindle during the first months of 1979, as the Japanese government has taken long-needed steps to open the country's domestic market more widely to American goods. The Tokyo economic summit conference of the major developed nations, the first such meeting held in Asia, has not only added to Japan's prestige but has made a start toward confronting the mounting energy problem in a concerted way. Nevertheless, it must be recognized that economic issues could easily again reach a state that would threaten the political and security relationship between Japan and the United States. As long as the United States is unable to bring its problems of inflation and declining productivity under control while Japan continues to operate successfully in the changed international economic environment, friction between the two nations is likely to reoccur and spill over into the spheres of political and defense relations.

Policy divergencies between the United States and Japan could also arise from the tightening of world energy supplies. With no substantial domestic energy resources of its own, Japan is heavily dependent on imported oil and is thus understandably leery of any political or military move by other powers that might reduce or endanger the flow of Middle East energy supplies. Now, as in the 1980s, Japan cannot solve its energy problem without the cooperation of the major oil-exporting nations of the Middle East. They therefore exercise critical leverage over the orientation of Japan's policies toward that region. In view of the heavy U.S. involvement in the Middle East, the confrontations that are splitting that region, and the destabilizing role the Soviets play in the area, ample opportunities for policy divergence exist that could strain the U.S.-Japanese political and security alliance. The reconciliation of these conflicting perspectives will remain a major task for the two governments in the 1980s.

An Increased Japanese Financial Contribution. It has become clear to the Japanese leadership that U.S. military commitments encompass so much of the globe and that efforts to meet them all effectively entail such high cost that America's allies will have to increase their contribution. If Japan is to continue to derive its security from the American guarantee and from the U.S. military presence in Japan, a larger share of the related cost must devolve on Japan. Legal and technical difficulties still hamper a rapid expansion of the Japanese financial contribution, but joint efforts to remove the existing difficulties over time seem promising in the present climate of Japanese opinion and deserve to be actively pursued.[23]

Strengthening Japan's Indigenous Self-Defense. For military as well as economic reasons, the United States has been urging the Japanese government to strengthen its defenses at a more rapid pace and in a more systematic fashion. Until quite recently, the ceiling for Japanese defense spending of 1 percent of GNP appeared sacrosanct, and actual defense budgets have been held somewhat below

[22] See p. 131 below.
[23] See p. 103 below for additional discussion of this point.

this modest limit. In line with the greater emphasis the Japanese government expects to be able to place on the qualitative buildup of Japan's defense potential, it no longer seems out of the question that the traditional barrier on defense spending will be breached. But in the absence of some security crisis, this is likely to happen only in small increments, the pace responding to changes in the situation around Japan. The major factors here will be the scale of any future Soviet military buildup in the Pacific and the degree of instability on the approaches to Japan. As a first step, Japanese defense planners hope to increase military expenditures from 0.9 percent to 1 percent in Japanese fiscal year (JFY) 1981, with a further modest percentage increase during the next several years. Even then, the ratio of Japanese defense spending, when measured in relative terms, will still be very low compared to that of other U.S. allies (whose ratios average 3 percent and more); but in absolute terms such an increase would not be insignificant—1 percent of Japan's GNP corresponds to about $10 billion. Thus, in 1978, Japan's defense expenditures were exceeded by only seven non-communist nations.[24]

An upward curve in Japanese defense spending during the years ahead could substantially enhance the quality of Japan's defense forces, thereby positively affecting U.S. military requirements in and around Japan, particularly those regarding air defense and anti-submarine warfare. The Japanese government has already made it clear that its defense planning does not include a numerical expansion of the SDF. Manpower costs in the volunteer Japanese defense system are extremely high, and as long as Japanese strategy does not require military forces to be dispatched overseas, a manpower buildup would make little sense militarily (quite apart from the fact that even existing SDF manpower targets have not been met in many years). The effort to heighten the effectiveness of Japan's SDF would bear primarily on air defense (since the BADGE system is now considered antiquated), including ground-to-air missiles (substituting new weaponry for the outmoded Nike and Hawk systems) and anti-submarine warfare, and would also involve the improvement of reconnaissance and intelligence facilities. This military modernization program would have to draw heavily on U.S.-designed advanced military equipment and technology. In that respect Japan can be expected to raise the issue of American restrictions on the transfer of advanced technology to Japan that appear to the Japanese to be discriminatory when compared to U.S. policy toward the NATO powers.

Joint Contingency Planning. Japanese defense planning has been hampered in the past by the long-standing political taboo on the development of concrete defense scenarios and joint studies with the U.S. military. The weakening of these inhibitions will now permit the joint consideration of potential emergencies and the elaboration of required countermeasures. The effect of this new development will not be limited to improvements in the flow of information between the two allies; in the longer run, it will create a Japanese defense system that is more suited to meet security contingencies. Thus, the possible Soviet interdiction of Japan's vital sea lanes of communication can be examined against the background of Soviet capabilities as demonstrated in the Okean II military exercise of 1975, among others. In this regard, U.S. experience, advice, and cooperation will, of course, be essential.

[24] See "Comparisons of Defense Expenditures 1975-1978," in *The Military Balance '78/'79*, Aerospace International, December 1978/January 1979, p. 104.

A first step toward facilitating the meshing of U.S. and Japanese military planning efforts was the adoption by the Japanese government, in late 1978, of the Guidelines for Japan-U.S. Defense Cooperation. This very important policy decision formally authorizes the U.S.-Japanese assessment of joint security requirements, joint defense planning and exercises for meeting contingencies, and coordination of required military countermeasures. Thus, U.S.-Japanese defense cooperation, which has long been hampered by Japanese political sensitivities, is now able to move gradually from concept to actuality.

Expansion of Japan's Defense Perimeter. Japanese plans to enlarge the SDF's capacity for reconnaissance and intelligence-gathering will result in a broadening of Japan's defense perimeter. By taking over some of the functions hitherto assigned to U.S. forces, Japan could ease the U.S. burden in the Pacific region while retaining for the SDF its traditional defensive mission. Such a move is in line with the Japanese decision to strengthen its self-defense capabilities and reduce its heavy reliance on U.S. protection. On the other hand, Japan's interests would not be served if the expansion of its defense perimeter simply resulted in an overall reduction of the American military presence in the Far East and the consequent weakening of the U.S. commitment to Japan's defense. Therefore, U.S. responses to this aspect of Japanese defense plans could be a factor in their implementation.

Broadening of the Japanese Concept of Security. As indicated earlier, a number of factors militate against the development of a large Japanese ground force. Similarly, Constitutional prohibitions against war potential and offensive weaponry will set limits to the qualitative improvement of the SDF. Moreover, there is no evidence of a weakening of the decision reconfirmed by successive Japanese governments not to develop nuclear weapons. Hence Japan's contributions to its own defense and to the security of the adjacent region will by necessity remain limited and will continue to impose a substantial financial burden on the United States. Yet Washington would like to see the Japanese make a contribution to the maintenance of security in the Far East that is more commensurate with the country's growing economic strength. This is increasingly being realized and accepted by the Japanese leadership.

A possible answer lies in the national security concept that Prime Minister Ohira has called "total security." This concept has emerged in the statements of other leaders of Japan's ruling political party, who have called it "overall security," "comprehensive security," and similar terms. The basic idea is simple, although its policy implications may present problems of implementation. It involves the broadening, conceptually and budgetarily, of national security to include not only military defense but the variety of economic and political measures that serve to strengthen Japan's security. This would include expenditures and programs aimed at buttressing the nation's capacity to survive an economic blockade (e.g., the stockpiling of food and energy supplies), and economic, technological, and even cultural-political activities contributing to the political stability of East Asia.[25] A case in point would be Japanese nonmilitary economic development assistance programs in Southeast Asia, an area which is not only a principal market for Japan but also the region through which virtually all imported oil for Japan's industries and other vital commodities must pass. Another would be Japanese assistance to

---

[25] See also pp. 107-108 below for comments on this concept by Takuya Kubo.

Indochinese refugees (given only reluctantly, and primarily through financial aid). By helping to stabilize these and other areas in which the Soviet Union might become involved, Japan would not only serve its own security interests but the common purpose of the American-Japanese alliance as well.

Advocates of this broadened concept of security argue that it will not be easy to raise Japan's spending on *military* defense much above 1 percent of GNP, but that this approach would make it possible to double or triple national security expenditures by redefining "national security" in a more comprehensive manner for budgetary action. It is obvious that depending on the manner of implementation, such a redefinition may simply amount to sleight of hand, concealing the fact that no real increase in security funding has taken place. However, U.S. and Japanese interests could be served if Japan were to carry out the planned qualitative improvement of its Self-Defense Force and simultaneously pursue economic and technological programs aimed at strengthening the region's security. Such a division of labor between Japan and the United States could have far-reaching consequences for both partners, for China, and for the other countries of the Far East. It would greatly enlarge the already dominant Japanese economic role in Southeast and Northeast Asia and would tend to create—whether Japan and the countries affected want it or not—a larger Japanese political stake in the region and conditions amounting to a Japanese zone of influence.

OUTLOOK FOR THE 1980s

Our analysis does not suggest that the Japanese are on the eve of a fundamental reassessment of their national security strategy. There is no indication that they are prepared to abandon the American alliance in favor of an independent course. Japanese policymakers view such a policy option as unrealistic and unprofitable, as well as lacking the necessary popular support. Moreover, a decision to build a military capability independent of the United States would almost surely require embarking on the road to nuclear weapons. Contrary to the predictions of some foreign experts, geopolitical and psychological conditions continue to militate strongly against such a choice. As long as the protection provided by American military power is perceived to be effective and reliable, the U.S. security tie will remain central to Japan's defense and international policies.

This is not to say that the solidity of the alliance might not be tested during the 1980s, even in the absence of any major change in the existing global and regional balance. In recent years, certain trends in the international environment have given rise to concern and uneasiness in Japan. Three related issues deserve special attention because in the long run they could have a damaging effect on U.S.-Japanese cooperation: (1) U.S. policies in the Far East that raise questions in the Japanese mind about the reliability of the American defense commitment; (2) the growth of the Soviet military and political role in Asia and its implications for Japan's national security; and (3) the tightening energy supply situation and the seeming inability of the United States to deal with it in a timely and effective fashion. These concerns could have an unsettling effect on Japanese perceptions of world trends and could lead to a gradual erosion of the U.S.-Japanese relationship during the 1980s. In the years ahead, the Japanese will certainly give very close attention to the global and regional evolution of the U.S.-Soviet political-military balance, to American policy decisions and behavior that reflect the strength of the U.S. commitment to the stability of conditions around Japan, and to the manner in which American policy copes with the energy resource issue, at home and internationally.

On the other hand, the Japanese are becoming increasingly aware of the need for an enlarged contribution to their joint national security effort with the United States. They no longer take the American alliance as much for granted as they have in the past. This new awareness should have a favorable effect in a number of policy areas where U.S. interests are at stake. As detailed earlier, we can expect a qualitative strengthening of Japan's self-defense capacity; greater Japanese efforts toward more effective defense cooperation with the United States; and an enlargement of non-military programs that will assist in stabilizing conditions in East Asia that are now threatened by political uncertainties and Soviet intervention. From the U.S. point of view, these are positive developments. As long as the American performance in the Far East does not raise new doubts in Japan about the U.S. commitment to the security of Asia, this favorable evolution in U.S.-Japanese cooperation for a common purpose can be expected to gather further momentum during the 1980s.

Even if the Japanese should devote no more than 1 percent of their GNP to a continuing defense buildup, they will possess a highly sophisticated military establishment by the end of the 1980s, making Japan one of the world's larger military powers in terms of defensive capacity. As discussed earlier, given the nature of modern weapons, the process of developing such enlarged defensive capabilities will tend to raise a number of key questions for Japanese defense planners.

The enlargement and modernization of Japan's defense programs will inevitably lead to some extension of the country's defense perimeter and, at the very least, to informal understandings with South Korea (and perhaps also with China). How far these trends will be allowed to carry Japan will very likely become a central issue in the Japanese defense debate of the coming decade. What we know about the mood of the Japanese public suggests that strong opposition to direct military association with powers other than the United States is not likely to disappear overnight. Japanese defense cooperation with South Korea is therefore likely to remain informal. Coordination will have to be accomplished largely by proxy, i.e., through the United States, which maintains bilateral security pacts with both nations. Resumption of the U.S. initiative toward withdrawing ground troops from the Korean Peninsula could stimulate the erosion of Japanese-Korean defense links, thereby weakening the security of both American alliance partners. And if any development were to provoke a Japanese reconsideration of its anti-proliferation policy, it would be South Korea's acquisition of nuclear weapons out of concern for an unreliable American defense commitment. American support for Korean security thus remains a vital element in the stability of the Japanese-American defense relationship and in the security of Northeast Asia.

Another issue that may arise from divergent U.S. and Japanese security perspectives relates to Japan's potential regional military role. A strengthening of Japan's defenses might encourage the United States to reduce military strength in the Pacific area correspondingly. Initially, such action could have the effect of discouraging broadened Japanese defense efforts. In the longer run, and in circumstances where Japanese faith in the American commitment had already been weakened, it could lead Japan to adopt a "go it alone" security strategy. Such a policy would inevitably generate adverse domestic and international repercussions and alter the power balance in Asia.

Also, the issue of Japan's future regional role could become troublesome in U.S.-Japanese relations in another regard. It is unlikely that Japan would wish to assume a regional military role in East Asia. Nor would such a role be welcomed by other Asian nations, especially if this should occur at the expense of America's involvement and commitment. Even if U.S. policies should therefore acquiesce in limiting the Japanese role to non-military support programs in East Asia, friction with Japan may arise over the desirable dimensions of such a Japanese effort, the allocation of the resources, and the potentially negative impact on U.S. economic interests. It will not be an easy task to arrive at a mutually acceptable strategy when the U.S. security mission will require the expensive maintenance of a quasi-permanent presence in East Asia while Japan stands to reap much of the economic benefits.

Finally, the 1980s are certain to confront Japan and the United States with the continued challenge of effectively coordinating their international strategies, especially with regard to the communist powers and to the nations of the Middle East controlling the flow of oil to the competing, energy-thirsty American and Japanese economies. Difficulties can be expected to arise from the dissimilar military, geopolitical, psychological, and resource situations of the two allies.

Given prevailing circumstances and the Japanese perspective on national security, Japan's policies during the next decade will predictably continue to emphasize an "omnidirectional" foreign policy orientation, albeit within the framework of the special relationship with the United States. In dealing with China and the Soviet Union, the Japanese have shown a strong preference for an equilibrium strategy that seeks to soften tensions through an enmeshing of economic interests—a strategy for which Japan is eminently well equipped. Considering the available evidence about Japanese postwar behavior, it is quite conceivable that during the 1980s the Sino-Japanese rapprochement will stop far short of concerted Sino-Japanese action in Asia and that Japan might return to a more evenhanded policy toward Moscow and Beijing. Any future intensification of the U.S.-Soviet confrontation would then create a dilemma for Japan.

Similarly, the American-Japanese alliance may be strained by the need for reconciling dissimilar energy resource situations in dealing with the oil-rich nations of the Middle East. It is the consensus in Japan and elsewhere that during the 1980s Japan will remain crucially dependent on the energy resources flowing from that region. Under these circumstances, the Japanese would be most reluctant to participate in any political or economic strategy or action engaging the United States and its allies in confrontation with these countries, much less in military conflict. Japan expects the United States to find a solution that would spare Japan politically disruptive deprivations. Depending on the course of developments in the Middle East, such a solution may not present itself.

In sum, Japan and the United States are entering the 1980s with reasonably good prospects for a continuing close working relationship. Yet, as indicated, this relationship could be threatened or at the very least seriously strained by international developments. The undeniable uneasiness that has been developing in Japan about American reliability and consistency of purpose, viewed against the background of a growing Soviet world role, could crystallize into a Japanese search for an alternative security strategy should the United States prove unsuccessful in coping with a series of exogenous events, from Korea to the Middle East. American failures might then be perceived by the Japanese as indicators of long-range, adverse shifts in the political-military balance compelling Japan to reassess its national policy stance during the years ahead. Such a reassessment could come about as the result of an accumulation of unsuccessful American attempts to solve international issues or else it might be the consequence of a single, dramatic international crisis having a powerful impact on Japan's interests. At a time of considerable flux in world affairs, the range of such conceivable crises has multiplied. They include but are not limited to a severe and lasting economic crisis with worldwide repercussions, the proliferation of nuclear weapons all around Japan, a sudden U.S. decision to withdraw from commitments in the Pacific region (such as the defense of South Korea), or a devastating military conflict in Asia or the Middle East.

None of these possibilities can be safely ruled out. But it seems much more likely that threats to the American-Japanese security relationship during the 1980s might come from less dramatic developments and in a slower and more insidious way. They could originate in the more mundane zone of economic relations, gaining an adverse momentum through a succession of frustrating interactions between the two allies. This is now recognized on both sides of the Pacific, and remedial actions have been under way for some time. But it is not clear whether more permanent solutions can be found so long as there is convincing evidence of a growing disparity in the economic performance of the two allies. Responsible Japanese recognize the need for further Japanese concessions and compromises in the economic sphere in order to remove a major source of friction in American-Japanese relations. At the same time, they cannot help but fear the repercussions in the national security sphere should the United States be unable to address effectively what are perceived as troubling weaknesses in the American social and political system.

PART II
REGIONAL CONFLICTS AND SECURITY PERSPECTIVES

Chapter 5
SECURITY IN NORTHEAST ASIA

Takuya Kubo[1]

CHARACTERISTICS OF SECURITY ISSUES IN NORTHEAST ASIA

Even though two patients may suffer from the same disease, the treatments to be prescribed must differ if the physiologies of the individuals differ. The same approach is required in international affairs; should regional or national characteristics differ, measures specifically adapted to such characteristics must be applied.

In this sense, any discussion of security in Northeast Asia demands first of all a common understanding of the characteristics peculiar to this part of Asia. I would like, therefore, to deal initially with a number of these characteristics that have a bearing on security issues. These may not be peculiar to Asia alone, but they do arise conspicuously in the region and combine to form a context which shapes the character of security issues in Northeast Asia.

Nationalism

Ebbing Japanese and European influence in Asia, coupled with rising demands for self-determination after World War II, led to the rise of nationalism in many countries. This nationalism moved in the direction of national independence and the eviction of foreign powers. At times, the trend was toward simple linkage with leftist or rightist elements. This should not be regarded as particularly dangerous so long as international cooperation for economic or security purposes remains unavoidable. On the contrary, it is desirable to encourage efforts for the fulfillment of international responsibility through support for healthy nationalisms in ways that enhance the independence of differing races and nations and contribute to regional stability and development.

In the process of national construction, a number of people were attracted to socialism, which they believed would be helpful in overcoming the constraints and inequities of existing social structures and in carrying out construction programs aimed at ending poverty and overcoming national weakness. The Soviet Union and China, declaring that national liberation struggles were just wars, offered aid to such movements. This led a number of people to draw even closer to socialism. In doing so, however, nationalism was seeking to make use of socialism as a system without necessarily resulting in its own captivity by the communism of the Soviet Union or the People's Republic of China (PRC).

If nationalism can be regarded as a fundamental movement of a people or a nation, then the diversified nature of socialism must be recognized. Accordingly,

[1] Takuya Kubo is Managing Director of the Research Institute for Peace and Security in Japan. From 1976 to 1978 he served as Director General of the National Defense Council, having previously been a Vice-Minister of Defense. His publications include "The Meaning of the U.S. Nuclear Umbrella for Japan," in Franklin B. Weinstein (ed.), *U.S.-Japan Relations and the Security of East Asia*, Westview Press, Boulder, Colorado, 1978.

even if the United States considers Soviet communism to be a potential enemy, it does not necessarily follow that socialism among other peoples should be similarly regarded.

In Northeast Asia also, nationalism progresses in forms that are not always readily visible. Particularly in Japan and the Republic of Korea (ROK), which have outstanding economic vitality and human resources, the ways in which nationalism progresses are bound to exert considerable influence on Asian stability.

Immaturity in Democracy and Human Rights

Contemporary democratic concepts and systems in Asia are not indigenous to the region but were imported in modern times from the United States and the Western nations. Even in Japan, true democracy was implanted under American guidance and spread through the self-awakening of the Japanese people after World War II.

It can thus be said that democracy in other Asian nations is still in a process of formation. This does not always mean an active process of development, however; depending on respective national conditions, democracy in some countries is presently stagnating after reaching a certain level.

For example, in both the ROK and Taiwan, where military and ideological challenges directly threaten independence and security, democratic processes have been inhibited in the interests of national defense. In a number of other lands, instability persists within the political systems. In such nations, there is the danger that totally democratic political movements might jeopardize national security and brew political and social anxiety. Conversely, of course, when democracy is unreasonably suppressed, political and social unrest will result. Many Asian nations today face such a contradiction.

It is certain, however, that a Euro-American yardstick should not be applied to democracy in Asian nations, with the possible exception of Japan. That is to say, the social and political values of different peoples and political systems in this area are quite diversified and do not always exactly reflect the values advocated by the American Congress.

This brings up the issue of human rights. President Carter of the United States has been strongly criticized for linking the human rights question—inherently a universal problem—with America's policy of granting military aid to various nations. It must be noted that every family has its own issues to deal with, and there are national circumstances that are not fully observable from faraway Washington. Accordingly, with regard to the issue of human rights, would it not be more appropriate to proclaim to a nation—or to the world in general—a definitive political principle, like the Five Principles of Peaceful Coexistence advocated by China, or to take up this issue at the United Nations?

Of course, if communists are utilizing Marxist ideology as an instrument of foreign policy, it is understandable that attention would be directed toward one of the major flaws of the communist system—the lack of freedom inherent in it—and that the question of human rights would be utilized as an instrument of strategic opposition to the communist bloc. Such an instrument, however, must be exercised with caution, and with appreciation of the basic concerns of the nation in question.

National Diversity

Asia contains no groups of regionally homogeneous nations such as are seen in Northern Europe, the European Economic Community (EEC) member nations, or the Arab world. Only the states of the Association of Southeast Asian Nations (ASEAN)[2]—whose ability to unite was initially considered problematical—have begun to possess a "regional sense" to a greater degree than was forecast at first. No concept of "Northeast Asian nations" yet exists, and each state in this area acts individually. Moreover, although there are many similarities among these countries, there is also a heterogeneity that makes them incompatible. Thus, while relations of mutual aid may be possible in this region, joint action relationships among the nations of Northeast Asia will be difficult to achieve.

It is necessary, therefore, for the United States to adopt individual bilateral policies with each of these nations. This is the reason why only bilateral security treaties are in force between the United States and the various countries of Northeast Asia. In reverse, this indicates that there is no foundation for a regional alliance—or a Japan-ROK alliance or a Japan-China alliance—to come into being. Rather, a loose organization for vaguely defined cooperation within the entire region, such as the Asian Collective Security system advocated by the Soviet Union, is a more logical concept.[3]

The Problem of Domestic Stability

The question of Asian security is essentially less one of conflicts between nations than one of the effects of domestic instability on peace and order. It is true that armed conflicts are taking place, for example, between Vietnam and Kampuchea (Cambodia) and between China and Vietnam. Also, armed confrontation is present between North and South Korea and between China and Taiwan. But speaking in broad terms, the major security problem facing each nation is that of achieving domestic stability.

On the Korean Peninsula, for example, it is more reasonable to envisage a scenario in which political, social, and economic problems cause instability in the ROK than it is to forecast a situation like the previous Korean War. Such conditions might lead to the instigation of widespread riots by anti-establishment elements within the country. Taking advantage of these conditions, North Korea might then attempt to intervene militarily. In the case of Taiwan, also, should similar instability lead to unrest among socialist or Taiwanese nationalist groups against the present administration, the potential for military intervention by China would exist.

Security discussions at present seem to center on the question of military balances between nations in confrontation. But more important to the maintenance of peace and stability in Northeast Asia is the prevention of this kind of political, social, and economic instability in the ROK or Taiwan. Although both nations are presently strengthening their stability, there is no absolute assurance that such

---

[2] Thailand, Malaysia, Singapore, the Philippines, and Indonesia.

[3] Reference is made here only to the nature of such a concept. I do not mean to imply that such a system has the potential for realization in the present international environment.

For a description of the Soviet-advocated "Asian Collective Security" system, which to date has not gained support among the states of Asia and which is roundly denounced by the PRC, see I. I. Kovalenko, *Sovetskii Soiuz v bor'be za mir i kollektivnuiu bezopasnost' v Azii* (The Soviet Union in the Struggle for Peace and Collective Security in Asia), "Nauka," Moscow, 1976.

contingencies as hypothesized above could not arise. It is necessary for the United States to take these factors into consideration, and this is an area in which Japan too should extend cooperation.

Democracy is becoming firmly rooted in Japan, and it is difficult to imagine any crumbling of the economic environment in the foreseeable future. In general, the Japanese people are conservative or moderate and do not favor communism. Thus the major problems of Japanese security are defense against threats from military powers and assurance of access to resources from overseas. In this sense, the question of Japan's security can be said to possess Euro-American rather than Asian characteristics.

Influence of the Confrontation of the Three Big Powers

Soviet-American confrontation and détente and Sino-Soviet confrontation are all major factors in Asian security, and the region most sharply affected by these factors is Northeast Asia. Indeed, tension in Indochina has been enhanced and Sino-Soviet confrontation has been directly brought to the region due to the conflicts between Vietnam and Kampuchea and between China and Vietnam. But the United States has no intention of intervening directly in the area as long as the conflicts remain between East and East. Therefore, Indochina is not at present directly influenced by U.S.-Soviet relations.

While the Sino-Soviet confrontation has certain aspects advantageous to the security of the United States and Japan, it is at the same time difficult to anticipate any settlement of the Korean problem as long as this confrontation continues. The ROK seems to wish to improve its relations with China and the Soviet Union, stimulated by the general trend of détente and Sino-American normalization. This attitude might be accelerated if the United States were to weaken its defense commitment to the ROK. On the other hand, I cannot support the view that Taiwan would approach the Soviets if the United States were to abandon any military commitment to the island's defense.

THE STRATEGIC BALANCE AND INTERNATIONAL RELATIONS IN NORTHEAST ASIA

Issues in the Asian Policies of the United States, the Soviet Union, and China

As long as areas of instability remain in Asia and military disequilibria exist between nations, the presence of American forces is mandatory for the maintenance of a strategic balance in this region. The U.S. government has declared that its policy, at least until the mid-1980s, is not only to maintain the present scale of military strength—excepting the uncertain prospect for withdrawal of American ground forces in the ROK—but also to plan for qualitative improvements. It seems that the United States is adjusting its commitments in Asia after the end of the Vietnam War so as to minimize the need for increases in military deployments to the region.

A number of events have given many people in Asia the impression (or a sense of anxiety, at least) that American interest in this region is dwindling, and that the

United States is withdrawing from Asia. Despite successive statements by concerned U.S. government officials, such impressions or anxieties have not faded away. Given this atmosphere, the normalization of U.S.-China relations was welcomed by most Asian people, as it implied a U.S. "return" to Asia. They expect the continuance of an American presence in the area to counterbalance the influence of the confrontation between the Soviet Union and China. If this presence decreases in the future, the confrontation between the communist powers will be brought in more distinct form into this region, and some countries may be forced to accommodate to the Soviets or to China. It will affect the strategic balance in Asia, and this cannot mean stabilization of power relationships in the region.

The Soviet Union steadily increased its military capabilities during the 1970s. Soviet military activity has become both more intense and broader in scope, and this trend will continue through the 1980s. Such developments are, at a minimum, intended by Moscow to defend the Soviet mainland from attacks by the United States or China and to attain the capability of breaking through any naval blockade; but it is also probable that against a background of military strength, the Soviet Union is attempting to expand its political influence in the region.

Nevertheless, the Soviets probably have no intention of turning Japan and the ROK—which are within the peripheral Soviet area—into socialist states, as has been done in Eastern Europe. More probable is a desire by the Soviet Union to exert influence over Japan and the ROK, as it does in Finland, rendering them friendly, or at least harmless. From such a viewpoint, the Soviet Union naturally opposes the Japan-U.S. and ROK-U.S. security treaties, but there is probably no need to view the Soviet Union as having military ambitions with regard to Japan or the ROK at the present time.

The Soviet Union is not necessarily strong in "exporting" ideology, nor is the Soviet capability for economic assistance very advanced. Thus, Moscow appears to be utilizing military strength as the basis for increasing its international political influence. These circumstances, however, in conjunction with the fact that Soviet intentions are not clear, are stirring unease and wariness among the people of Asia. America's military presence in the region, therefore, serves to counterbalance the threat posed by Soviet armed might. Nevertheless, regarding this type of "battle of military presences," the problem remains the total lack of East-West dialogue on arms-control issues in this region, despite negotiations regarding the Indian Ocean and Europe. It will be desirable for the stability of Asia to begin discussion about this problem in the 1980s among the big powers, including concerned regional states such as China and Japan.

Based on domestic activity within China—the efforts to promote modernization in four major fields[4]—it is believed that China is placing greater emphasis on domestic, rather than foreign, policy. Externally, China adopts an "anti-hegemony" strategy based on its "Theory of the Three Worlds"[5] and aims at isolating the Soviet Union. As a factor in this policy, China undoubtedly believes that through the conclusion of the Japan-China Treaty of Peace and Friendship in 1978 and normali-

---

[4] The present leadership in Beijing stresses a national development policy of the "four modernizations," that is, modernization of agriculture, industry, science and technology, and national defense.

[5] "Chairman Mao's Theory of the Differentiation of the Three Worlds Is a Major Contribution to Marxism-Leninism," Editorial Department of *Renmin Ribao*, in *Peking Review*, No. 45, November 4, 1977, pp. 10-41.

zation of relations with the United States, it has secured Japanese and American collaboration. Within the Sino-Soviet confrontation, the Korean Peninsula has more geopolitical importance to Chinese security than to that of the Soviet Union. China is thus likely to attempt to induce North Korea to move closer to the PRC. It will be difficult, to a corresponding extent, for China to become friendly with the ROK. In any case, China's comparatively long-range emphasis on domestic development is likely to facilitate maintenance of the strategic balance in Northeast Asia.

Superpower Relationships

As long as the United States and the Soviet Union continue to maintain their powerful military capabilities, including nuclear components, both sides will have a common interest in avoiding any military clash. To that end, mutual efforts toward détente are essential; and as a part of such efforts, the SALT talks should be continued, whatever the final results. Linkage between SALT and regional issues is undesirable. Such continuation of Soviet-American efforts toward détente will provide the background for assuring stability in Northeast Asia.

Because of the historical and geopolitical factors behind the Sino-Soviet split, there is no easy solution to that confrontation. While the possibility of some limited easing of tension between these two nations should be taken into consideration, fundamental improvement in Sino-Soviet relations is unlikely, possibly until China gains greater confidence in its own security—that is to say, until the 1990s, if even then. While this is useful for maintenance of the status quo in American and Japanese security policies, at the same time the Sino-Soviet confrontation influences Asia as a whole and has become a factor of instability. The military conflicts between "East and East" in Indochina in 1979 do not directly influence the security of Northeast Asia. But as the Sino-Soviet feud has been brought in direct and concrete form into Indochina, Northeast Asia may be more strongly affected by the confrontation.

Provided that no extraordinary situation occurs in Taiwan, that the Sino-Soviet confrontation continues, and that China maintains friendly relations with the United States on the basis of the Maoist Theory of the Three Worlds and the economic policies of the "four modernizations," it is unlikely that China will attempt to liberate Taiwan by armed force. Accordingly, the further normalization of Sino-American diplomatic relations will continue into the 1980s in a way that will not endanger the security of Japan or the ROK. Generally speaking, improved ties between Washington and Beijing (Peking) will contribute to the overall stability of Asia and to the United States maintaining the strategic balance. But China will seek to utilize it as the formation of an anti-Soviet bloc of three big powers. Because of this, the Soviet Union will react in many ways in the area surrounding China, and only the development of détente between the United States and the USSR will mitigate a Soviet overreaction.

The Korean Peninsula

The degree of security on the Korean Peninsula will vary as a function of relations between North and South Korea, East-West relations in general, and the status of the Sino-Soviet conflict. Without some overall improvement in these factors, security on the Korean Peninsula will be difficult to achieve. The peaceful

unification of the Korean Peninsula is desired not only by the two Koreas themselves, but by all nations concerned with the region. Is there, however, any realistic
policy likely to lead toward peaceful reunification?

Several measures have been proposed, including renewing the dialogue between North and South Korea; an international conference on Korea including
those most deeply concerned; cross-recognition of the two Korean states by the
nations concerned; and simultaneous admission of both Koreas to the United Nations under the premise of peaceful reunification. While the ROK has been favor-
ably disposed to such proposals, North Korea has consistently rejected them. Only
since the beginning of 1979 has North Korea begun to show a positive attitude
concerning renewal of the dialogue between North and South. But it is unthinkable
that the dialogue will proceed smoothly. Nor can the "confederation" approach to
reunification proposed by North Korea be regarded as realistic in present circumstances.

The intent of most nations concerned, therefore, despite hopes of eventual
peaceful reunification of the Korean Peninsula, is to maintain the status quo for the
immediate future. Measures are being taken toward this goal. Although the
present situation is somewhat akin to sitting on a keg of dynamite, it would seem
to serve to maintain the strategic balance in Northeast Asia.

The position of the Korean Peninsula as a contact point between East and West
exerts influence on Japanese domestic politics. Political beliefs among the Japanese
people range freely through the entire spectrum from right to left. There have long
been voices in Japan calling for the normalization of diplomatic relations with all
neighboring nations. One result of this was the normalization of diplomatic ties
with the PRC in 1972. Only North Korea at present remains outside normal diplomatic channels; and voices demanding the establishment of diplomatic relations
with Pyongyang and impartiality toward both Koreas will continue to be heard
within the Japanese political world and among some people well-versed in this
issue. In the present international environment, Japan might increase exchanges
with North Korea, but without carrying this to the extent of normalizing diplomatic
relations with Pyongyang.

The continued viability of South Korea is vital to Japan's security. Because of
the ROK's existence, it is possible to reduce multidirectional readiness requirements in defense planning. There are many Japanese who state that should Korea
be unified under a socialist state, the military threat to Japan would increase
greatly. While I myself do not subscribe to this theory, certainly such a development would make it necessary to restudy defense programs and to step up military
preparedness to a certain extent. An even greater problem under such circumstances would be a division of opinion among the Japanese people, who would be
surrounded by socialist nations. It is quite possible to predict political and social
instability in such a situation.

A Network of Bilateral U.S. Security Ties
   with Various Asian Nations

The strategic balance in East Asia reinforces the strategic balance in Europe.
This is an indispensable factor in America's global security strategy. The pillars
supporting U.S. strategy in East Asia are the security systems with Japan, the
ROK, and the Philippines. While it is widely understood that following Vietnam an

"island" strategy has been adopted in deploying American forces, if this should mean the future withdrawal of U.S. forces from present bases in Korea and Japan (Okinawa), it could not be called an advantageous choice for U.S. strategic purposes. Worse yet, the further withdrawal of front-line troops to the Marianas could only signify American abandonment of Asia.

For the nations of this region, bilateral security arrangements with the United States constitute the elemental factor in the American defense guarantee. Nevertheless, following the proclamation of the Nixon Doctrine in 1969,[6] the post-Vietnam American consolidation of its security commitments, and the trend toward reduction of U.S. forces in the region, the nations of East Asia have embarked on the improvement of their own defense capabilities. The Carter Administration's announced intention in 1977 to withdraw U.S. ground forces from the ROK was not welcomed by the people of either South Korea or Japan. Upon being confronted with this development, the ROK embarked on vigorous efforts to achieve a more self-reliant defense capability and establish a basis for greater self-confidence in handling its own security affairs.[7] In Japan's case, this could not happen to the same extent.

JAPANESE DEFENSE POLICY AND THE JAPAN-CHINA TREATY OF PEACE AND FRIENDSHIP

A Growing Japanese Public Defense Consciousness

The Japanese public has gradually heightened its understanding of defense issues in the past several years. Public opinion surveys commissioned through private institutions by the Prime Minister's Office in 1972, 1975, and 1978 have brought to light the following changes in opinion:

- Popular support for the Self-Defense Forces has been gradually increasing, from 73 percent in 1972, to 79 percent in 1975, to 86 percent in 1978.
- There is increasing public recognition that "Japan's defense should be carried out through a combination of the Self-Defense Forces and the Japan-U.S. Mutual Security Treaty." Forty-one percent supported this perspective in 1972, 54 percent in 1975, and 61 percent in 1978.
- There is a correspondingly sharp decline in support for abrogation of the Japan-U.S. Mutual Security Treaty and reduction or abolition of the Self-Defense Forces: 16 percent supported these actions in 1972, 9 percent in 1975, and 5 percent in 1978.

In contrast with years past, Japan's mass media are now dealing frequently with defense issues, not from an automatic position of opposing the Self-Defense Forces or the Japan-U.S. Security Treaty, but with serious content. At times, scenarios of "Japan's crisis" are presented. Since about 1975, the opposition parties have shown signs of less automatic and vehement opposition to the government's

---

[6] See *Public Papers of the Presidents of the United States, Richard Nixon, 1969,* U.S. Government Printing Office, Washington, D.C., 1971, pp. 544-557.

[7] The policy of withdrawing all American ground forces from the ROK was reversed following President Carter's visit to Seoul in June 1979. See p. 131 below.

defense policies and have become somewhat more flexible. Even so, the situation has not yet progressed to the point where a consensus can be reached between the government and opposition parties on defense issues.

Against this background, however, such issues as Japanese-American talks on defense cooperation, the study of emergency legislation, assumption of a larger share of the expenses for U.S. forces stationed in Japan, etc.—all of which would have been subjected to severe criticism several years ago within the National Diet, by the mass media, and by the general public—are currently being dealt with by the government under easier circumstances.

Such changes in public defense consciousness seem to have arisen through a combination of the following factors:

- The 1973 oil shock, which caused the public to consider the need for guaranteeing supplies of natural resources.
- Tension on the Korean Peninsula throughout 1975.
- The fall of three Indochinese nations to communist control in 1975, and the concurrent withdrawal of the United States from a direct role in Southeast Asian security affairs.
- China's favorable stance toward the Japan-U.S. Mutual Security Treaty and the Self-Defense Forces, following the normalization of Sino-Japanese diplomatic relations in 1972.
- Opposition party trends toward adopting more realistic policies in conjunction with the near-equilibrium in government-opposition power within the National Diet.
- Adoption of the National Defense Program Outline in 1976.
- The severe attitude of the Soviet Union during the 1977 Soviet-Japanese fishing negotiations and heightened Soviet military activities in Northeast Asia from 1976 onward.

National Defense Progam Outline

In 1976 the Japanese government first adopted a "National Defense Program Outline."[8] This forms the basis for improvements in defense strength being undertaken at the present time. The National Defense Program Outline aims at achieving a level of defense strength regarded as the minimum requirement for Japan as an independent nation within the international environment foreseeable in the future, and under the Japan-U.S. Mutual Security Treaty. Accordingly, while there will be no major quantitative increases from the present force levels, major improvements are being sought in both quality and functional capability.

In this regard, although not necessarily emphasized by the government at present, one of the aims of the National Defense Program Outline is, I think, to enhance the self-reliant nature of Japan's defense capability. The structure for a self-reliant defense capability is considered to be a force level equipped with the various functions required for defense of the nation: the capability to deploy ground, maritime, and air defense strength evenly through the Japanese main islands and periphery; and the capability to react instantly and single-handedly in

[8] See the *Defense of Japan* of 1976, 1977, and 1978, issued by the Japan Defense Agency in an English edition, for detailed explanation of the contents of the National Defense Program Outline for these years.

times of small-scale and limited aggression. This differs from past national defense strength buildup programs, which placed unlimited dependence on the United States, and which were based on the full expectation that U.S. forces would make up any gaps in Japan's defense capability.

Instead, the National Defense Program Outline directs that Japan should itself possess at a minimum the core of its own defense capability. By no means does this reduce the need for mutual security arrangements with the United States. On the contrary, by clarifying the scope of defense activities to be undertaken by Japan and the related capability that the country should possess to fulfill its role, the outline increases the functional efficiency of the Japan-U.S. security relationship.

A number of international circumstances provide the premises for the National Defense Program Outline, and one of these is the maintenance of the status quo on the Korean Peninsula. Compared to the period during which the outline was drafted, a new uncertainty has now arisen: the possible withdrawal of U.S. ground forces from the ROK. Nevertheless, since it is difficult at this time to forecast any outbreak of large-scale military conflict on the Korean Peninsula, the Japanese government does not consider any restudy of the outline to be necessary at present.

Another premise is continuation of the Sino-Soviet confrontation. There are many possible ways of viewing this issue, but the Japanese government, in proceeding with the outline, has been promoting the development of outline programs under the assumption that tensions between Moscow and Beijing will not be relaxed to the extent of dissolving the Sino-Soviet military confrontation.

As mentioned previously, consciousness of defense issues among the Japanese people is undoubtedly changing. However, under the peace Constitution, the people's feelings, directed toward peace and an anti-military ideology, remain deep-rooted. Therefore, while it can be said that changes have come about in public consciousness, the changes amount to an understanding of the present requirement for the Japan-U.S. Mutual Security Treaty and the Self-Defense Forces; they do not indicate any approval for further large-scale reinforcements of domestic defense strength.

This attitude exists at a time when no imminent military threat against Japan or sudden drastic change in the international environment appears likely. Under these circumstances, the goal for Japan's defense capability in the 1980s is to fully achieve the substance of the present National Defense Program Outline. It would be proper to predict that in the coming decade defense expenditures for this purpose will not significantly exceed 1 percent of the Gross National Product (GNP).

U.S.-Japan Defense Cooperation

Japan is seeking to enhance the self-reliant capability of its defense strength. At the same time, however, because of the position of the Japanese-American security system as the cornerstone of Japan's defense, improvement of defense capability from the standpoint of complementarity and cooperation with U.S. forces becomes vital. The U.S. government and military authorities have pointed out in the past that the emphasis of Japan's defense efforts should be placed on anti-submarine warfare, air defense, and logistics. It is not necessarily clear, however, what functions the United States wishes to see raised to what levels of capability, in light of American national interests and international strategy. It is desirable that such problems be studied within the Japan-U.S. Subcommittee on Security Cooperation.

One issue currently being considered by Japan and the United States concerns the allotment of expenses for the stationing of American forces in Japan. The fiscal burden on the United States forces stationed in Japan is believed to amount to $1.26 billion, including expenses for military personnel which totaled $536 million in fiscal year (FY) 1978. The Japanese government assumed a burden of $887 million of these costs in FY 1979, compared with $544 million in FY 1977. With respect to this sharing of expenses, according to the terms of the Agreement Regarding Facilities and Areas and the Status of United States Armed Forces in Japan, Japan's contribution cannot be increased without limit.[9]

The Japan-China Treaty Seen from the Standpoint of Security Cooperation

The conclusion of the Japan-China Treaty of Peace and Friendship in 1978 aroused criticism both inside and outside Japan on the grounds that it seemed to constitute the basis for a tripartite Sino-Japanese-American alliance, or that Japan, willingly or unwillingly, has been dragged into the international power game. The position on this issue taken by the Japanese government, elaborated as follows, seeks to minimize the impression of such an intention.

The Japan-China Treaty of Peace and Friendship, according to the Japanese government, expresses immutable principles of peaceful diplomacy such as the Five Principles of Peaceful Coexistence. As stipulated in Article IV, "The present treaty shall not affect the position of either contracting party regarding its relations with third countries" and thus does not affect Japan-Soviet relations. Accordingly, Japan hopes to maintain separate relationships of peace and friendship with both China and the Soviet Union. Thus, according to the official Japanese view, criticism of the treaty as the formation of a tripartite alliance involving Japan in an international power game is entirely groundless.

Nevertheless, it can be anticipated that China will use the "anti-hegemony" clause in the treaty as a lever in promoting its worldwide anti-Soviet strategy. This is, of course, disadvantageous for the Soviet Union. When viewed from the Soviet side, therefore, it is only natural to expect the Soviet Union to criticize China for the development of such a strategy. The Soviets will also criticize Japan for taking part in this Chinese maneuver through conclusion of the Japan-China treaty. The Soviets warn that they will carefully observe the practical policies toward the Soviet Union adopted by Japan if it asserts that Japan-Soviet relations will not be affected by the treaty.

From the standpoint of security, it is essential for a nation to possess its own defense capability and to have an ally capable of covering any gaps in that defense strength, while at the same time taking steps to reduce potential threats from surrounding nations. In this sense, any increase in tension with other nations is undesirable. Former Prime Minister Fukuda, who concluded the Treaty, advocated

[9] Article XXIV:
   1. It is agreed that the United States will bear for the duration of this Agreement without cost to Japan all expenditures incidental to the maintenance of the United States armed forces in Japan except those to be borne by Japan as provided in paragraph 2.
   2. It is agreed that Japan will furnish for the duration of this Agreement without cost to the United States and make compensation where appropriate to the owners and suppliers thereof all facilities and areas and rights of way, including facilities and areas jointly used such as those at airfields and ports, as provided in Articles II and III.

an "omnidirectional diplomacy of peace." This policy does not necessarily mean a foreign policy of "equal distance" from all countries. It expresses the concept that Japan should maintain friendly relationships with all countries, based on U.S.-Japan relations. Present Prime Minister Ohira does not use such words, but the basic foreign policy posture of the Japanese government has not been changed.

Speaking from such a position, there is a need for Japan to carry out, in the immediate future, positive diplomatic steps toward the Soviet Union. At present, the Japanese government adheres firmly to the attitude that conclusion of a Japan-Soviet Peace Treaty, which would resolve the territorial dispute over Japan's four northern islands, is a priority matter. But when considered from the point of Japan's peaceful diplomacy, I think, Japan should be positive about negotiating with the Soviet Union for a treaty of good neighborliness and cooperation, while sustaining the fundamental policy of demanding return of the four northern islands. However long it may take, negotiation itself is important.

With the exception of the strong opposition registered by the Soviet Union, the majority of Asian nations have given a positive evaluation of the Japan-China Treaty. But the reaction of the ROK has been somewhat negative, and there seems to be some anxiety in parts of Southeast Asia over possible future pressures being exerted by a cooperative Sino-Japanese relationship.

Both Koreas, with their mutual confrontation, must be experiencing complex feelings over seeing their respective allies or friendly nations joining hands with old antagonists. Nonetheless, China, having clarified its position in the Japan-China Treaty, will find it difficult to support any positive military action by North Korea against the ROK, provided there is no military aggression from the ROK side. It is also difficult to believe that the Soviet Union will increase assistance to North Korea or support some military action by Pyongyang in order to take advantage of the situation. Thus, regarding the stability of the Korean Peninsula, the Japan-China Treaty seems to be a definitely positive factor.

FUTURE PROSPECTS AND POLICIES AFFECTING SECURITY IN NORTHEAST ASIA

Adjustment of U.S.-Soviet and East-West Relations

Tensions in relations between the United States and the Soviet Union, and consequently East-West relations overall, inevitably cast shadows on Asian concerns. Because these relationships are global in nature, it will be difficult for certain Asian issues to be resolved without some worldwide improvement in relations between Moscow and Washington. Thus, progress in détente between the United States and the Soviet Union and in Europe, the Strategic Arms Limitation Treaty (SALT) talks and the Mutual and Balanced Force Reductions negotiations which back détente, and the achievement of peace and stability in the Middle East are of particular importance to Asian security.

The Chinese, however, are likely to be critical of any progress in East-West détente; and as long as the Sino-Soviet confrontation continues, an ultimate resolution of Asian problems remains in the distant future. Therefore, even while the fundamental confrontation between China and the Soviet Union continues, it is desirable that relations between these two nations improve to some extent and that Sino-Soviet discussions on Asian stability be held.

One topic of frequent discussion at present is the forecast of an energy shortage in the Soviet Union during the latter half of the 1980s; and in conjunction with this, the potential exists for an international crisis centering around the Middle East. There are, however, other opinions which dispute this scenario. In any case, from the standpoints of both international security and a stabilized supply of Middle East oil, it is undesirable for the Soviet Union to face an energy shortage. In this regard, it might be well for the United States, Japan, and the nations of Western Europe to study means of cooperating with the Soviet Union in the development of oil and natural gas resources in Siberia. The extending of cooperation to Soviet development of Siberia, rather than only assisting China in its "four modernizations," is unlikely to run counter to the security strategy and interests of the Free World nations.

Clarification of U.S. Policy on Asia

At the end of 1975, U.S. President Gerald Ford announced a new "Pacific Doctrine" in Hawaii. The Carter Administration, making its appearance one year later, made no mention of this doctrine, concentrating instead on human rights diplomacy and the withdrawal of U.S. ground forces from the ROK. These developments greatly puzzled the people of Asia. Subsequently, in order to allay anxiety and unease in the region regarding American intentions, the Carter Administration issued a succession of reassuring statements.[10]

These official pronouncements were generally passive in nature, however, and were received as mere explanations of such decisions as the withdrawal of U.S. ground troops from Korea. Nevertheless, people in Asia are undoubtedly expecting that the United States will carry out its overall commitments by continuing to express a long-term interest in the region and by taking appropriate defense, economic, and political measures.

The U.S. government has stated that current deployments of U.S. forces in Asia and the Pacific Ocean area will be maintained into the mid-1980s. The general situation will probably remain unchanged throughout the coming decade, but uncertainties remain. Because of its presidential and electoral system, America's policy viewpoints are inevitably limited to four-year or eight-year periods. In contrast, the Soviet Union and China are able to project extremely long-range strategies. Concerning Europe, considered the most vital region for U.S. interests, a major change in U.S. policy following a change in presidential administrations is hardly possible. There are no guarantees for other regions, however, and anxieties remain over the long-range prospects for American policy. Should some radical change in policy occur, various Asian nations will be perplexed as to how to respond, and anxiety will arise because of the great influence of China and the Soviet Union. Therefore, even if alterations occur in U.S. policy, it is preferable that the

---

[10] These include Secretary of Defense Brown's speech before the World Affairs Council in Los Angeles (February 20, 1978); President Carter's speech at Wake Forest University (March 17,1978); Presidential Adviser Brzezinski's speech before the Japan Society (April 27, 1978); Vice-President Mondale's speech at the East-West Center in Hawaii (March 10, 1978); and Assistant Secretary Holbrooke's speech before the Women's National Democratic Club in Washington, D.C. (November 27, 1978).

changes be carried out in a moderate manner, through moderate procedures, so that the regions concerned can conform properly in an orderly manner.

Stabilization of the Korean Peninsula

Should understanding increase between Japan and China on the basis of the Japan-China Treaty of Peace and Friendship, and between the United States and China through normalization of diplomatic relations, opportunities will increase for these nations to understand the true intentions of the two Koreas with the resulting possibility of their being able to play a role—albeit indirectly—in mitigating suspicions between North and South. This would support stability on the Korean Peninsula, where relative calm prevails for the time being.

Beginning with the two Koreas, all nations concerned desire the peaceful reunification of the Korean Peninsula. But no formula for achieving this objective has yet been found. Just as in the case of East and West Germany, racial unification is the earnest wish of the people, and it is well for this ideal and goal to be kept firmly in mind. North Korea and China seek reunification through the efforts of Koreans alone, however, without intervention by other countries. Consequently, the conception and procedure for reunification must be left up to South Korea and North Korea. It can only be hoped that time will solve the problem.

What concerned nations such as the United States, the Soviet Union, China, and Japan can do is to encourage restraint and self-control in every field, so that there will be no resort to arms by North or South Korea. Assistance and cooperation should be extended to enable both Koreas to maintain economic and social stability, so that internal insecurity will not lead to warfare.

The reduction and withdrawal of U.S. ground forces should be considered within the framework of the above line of thought. The Korean Peninsula has an immediate influence on the interests of Japan, China, and the Soviet Union. Since these relationships also affect the interests of the United States, reduction and withdrawal of U.S. forces should not be thought of only in connection with domestic American politics. Measures should be taken in ways appropriate to promoting stability on the Korean Peninsula.

Japan's International Responsibilities

With Japan's international influence increasing, and with relations of mutual dependence increasing throughout the world, it is no longer permissible for Japan to devote exclusive attention to domestic politics or economic development. Former Prime Minister Fukuda's tour of Southeast Asia in 1977 and his statement in Manila[11] at that time, the approach to the three nations of Indochina, the Prime Minister's visit to the Middle East in 1978, the economic cooperation pledged at the summit meeting of the leaders of the industrially advanced nations, and Japanese-American negotiations are all moves indicative of Japan's growing international role—though they are insufficient as yet.

[11] The following three points were the highlights of the Prime Minister's Manila statement: (1) Japan will adhere to peace and never seek to become a military power. (2) Japan will endeavor to deepen mutual understanding with the nations of Southeast Asia, placing importance on heart-to-heart contacts. (3) Japan will contribute to the peace and prosperity of Southeast Asia as a whole, including the ASEAN countries and the three nations of Indochina.

Japan's postwar diplomacy was mainly concerned with the United States until the 1960s, but with the normalization of Sino-Japanese diplomatic relations in 1972 and the conclusion of the Japan-China Treaty of Peace and Friendship in 1978, the spotlight has been turned onto Japanese policy toward China and the Soviet Union.

Together with policies toward Southeast Asia and Europe, an "omnidirectional"—as former Prime Minister Fukuda termed it—Japanese diplomatic effort is moving forward. Whether Japan likes it or not, it has become necessary to exert efforts to contribute to the stability and prosperity of the world.

When security is considered in this context, Japan is seen to be bound by its Constitution; and with the exception of the Japan-U.S. Mutual Security Treaty, no military relationship with another nation can be conceived of. The Japanese people, who desire peace and disarmament, will undoubtedly continue to place stricter inhibitions on the export of weapons than any other nation. Based on the same ideals, Japan exercises strong self-restraint in regard to defense expenditures and increases in defense capability.

Accordingly, in order for Japan to contribute to international security, such contributions should be founded on the following conception: Security expenditures to be borne by Japan should not be limited to defense funds alone but should be considered as including funding for economic cooperation and technical development. Under the premise that stability in Asian nations is based on internal peace, order, and economic development, a major increase in Japanese economic assistance expenditures to these nations will contribute to their stability and, in turn, to the stability of the region. Moreover, this will be useful in promoting Japan's own security.

At present, a number of Japanese industries are in competition with the indigenous industries of other Asian nations, which have developed considerably in the past decade. This is not a desirable situation. Japan's labor-intensive industries should be transferred to other Asian nations as much as possible. Japan should place emphasis on knowledge-intensive industries, competitive with those of Europe and the United States. In this manner, a relationship of productive coexistence can be developed with the other nations of Asia. In order to do this, however, there will be a need for increased investments in new technological development. If Japan comes to possess a higher level of technology, the dependence of the Soviet Union and China on Japan will increase, which in turn will enhance Japan's security. Again, Japan is acutely lacking in energy resources. Thus, huge investments will probably be essential for energy research and development because of the necessity of guaranteeing supplies of natural resources.[12]

When the aforementioned factors are seen as a part of overall government security expenditures, defense spending now stands at 0.9 percent of Japan's GNP, economic cooperation funding at 0.2 percent, and technical development funding at 0.5 percent—a total of 1.6 percent. Considering all of these expenditures as security-related, it is desirable to raise the total spending to a level of about 3 percent of Japan's GNP at a suitable time in the 1980s. The share of individual items within this figure can be decided according to the situation prevailing at the time, although it probably will be appropriate to maintain military expenditures at a low level.

[12] See the Agreement on Energy Research and Development in the Communique issued at the seven-nation Economic Summit Conference in Tokyo on June 29, 1979, *New York Times*, June 30, 1979.

European nations and the United States spend from 3 to 5 percent of their GNPs on defense. Since Japan's circumstances differ both domestically and internationally, the above system of an overall consideration of security-related funding is appropriate. Such a concept has also been proposed by Japanese research institutions[13] and by Yasuhiro Nakasone.[14] These proposals have advocated that the above-mentioned items be expanded to include funds for food and oil stockpiling and for international cultural exchanges. This would bring the total up to the 3 to 3.5 percent level.

Although such proposals are as yet limited in scope, the fact that they are beginning to appear indicates a growing body of opinion in Japan which views security as extending far beyond military aspects alone. This can be regarded as a concept resulting from the growing recognition in Japan of the country's international responsibilities.

[13] *The Search for Japan's Comprehensive Policy Guideline in the Changing World—National Priorities for the 21st Century*, National Institute for Research Advancement and Nomura Research Institute.

[14] Yasuhiro Nakasone referred to this point in several public addresses in 1978 and in his book, *The Logic of a New Conservative*, Kodan-sha, Tokyo, 1978. He has served successively as Director General of the Science and Technology Agency, Minister of Transportation, Director General of the Defense Agency, Minister of International Trade and Industry, Secretary General of the Liberal Democratic Party, and Chairman of the LDP Executive Council. He is regarded as a promising future candidate for the Prime Minister's chair.

Chapter 6

PROSPECTS FOR KOREAN SECURITY

Richard L. Sneider[1]

The border between South and North Korea is one of the most dangerous in the world, with a high potential for all-out conflict and the ever-present danger of military incidents. Conflict could arise in the form of a calculated attack across the demilitarized zone (DMZ) dividing the South and North or from a miscalculation in escalatory responses to incidents along the DMZ or in the coastal waters around Korea, particularly near the small islands held by the South adjacent to the northwest coast of North Korea and within North Korean territorial waters. The greatest risk derives from possible North Korean miscalculation regarding the political stability and the depth of political dissent in the South, or from a perception that the United States, weary of involvement in Asian wars, would not intervene to fulfill its commitment to the defense of the Republic of Korea (ROK).

Since the Korean Armistice Agreement came into effect in 1953, the danger of renewed hostilities has been a dominant factor in the policies of both Korean states as well as in the policies of the outside powers toward the Peninsula. The frequency of military incidents along the DMZ has been very high, although it has declined notably in recent years. The last major incident occurred in August 1976, when the North Koreans killed two Americans who had attempted to cut down a tree within the American Sector of the Joint Security Area at Panmunjom. The dangers of conflict have increased with the growing militarization of the DMZ, more frequent patrols within it, the strengthening of the military capabilities of both sides, the offensive deployment of more and more North Korean forces in areas adjacent to the DMZ, and the avowed objective of the North to achieve unification on its own terms. The shaky peace that has been maintained for more than twenty-five years testifies not only to the restraint exercised by the United Nations (U.N.) and South Korean forces in response to repeated provocations, but also to the balance of forces on the Peninsula, the stake of the four major outside powers—the United States, Japan, the Soviet Union, and the People's Republic of China (PRC)—in preventing renewed hostilities in Korea, and the incalculable costs of another Korean War.

This paper examines the principal factors that have provided security for the ROK and have deterred a renewal of hostilities. It first examines the principal elements in the deterrence equation—the North-South military balance, the U.S. presence and commitment, the role of Japan, the influence of the PRC and the USSR, the role of the U.N. peace-keeping machinery, and the interrelationship of these elements. It then considers the prospects for security in the 1980s. It finally examines the prospects for negotiating a reduction of tensions in Korea, taking into

---

[1] Richard L. Sneider, fomerly American Ambassador to the Republic of Korea, currently is a consultant on Asian affars, adjunct professor at Columbia University, and member of the Board of Trustees of The Asia Society. During thirty years of service as a foreign service officer he was stationed in Japan and Pakistan, served as a senior staff member of the National Security Council in 1969, was Minister in Charge of the Okinawa Reversion Negotiations, and was Deputy Assistant Secretary of State for East Asian Affairs (1972-74).

account the factors underlying past failures, the peace-keeping potential of different negotiating scenarios, and incentives for agreements.

The analysis assumes that the four major powers will continue to view Korea as an area of significant national interest. It is also assumed that no fundamental changes will take place in the international environment and power relationships in the foreseeable future; that is, a "straight-line," no-disaster context is assumed. Clearly, such basic changes in the international environment as a Sino-Soviet war (or rapprochement), the remilitarization of Japan, heightened U.S.-Soviet tensions, or a return to U.S. neo-isolationist policies would have a major impact on Korea and would necessitate a full reevaluation of current and prospective security arrangements.

THE STAKE OF THE OUTSIDE POWERS IN KOREA

Korea historically has been a country of strategic importance to its neighboring states. Throughout the centuries, Japan and China have vied for influence and control over the Peninsula, which has served as the land bridge between them. Korea's strategic importance has greatly increased in this century, particularly as a result of the Soviet Union's growing role in Asia. The interests of the various key players in Korea are summarized below.

The Communist Powers

Both the Soviet Union and the PRC would consider control over the northern portion of Korea by a unified, non-communist Korea allied to the West to be inimical to their interests. Their concern over such a development was amply demonstrated by Chinese intervention in the Korean War in 1950, and there have been no subsequent indications that this concern has decreased. The economic and military strength and the future capabilities of South Korea have undoubtedly enhanced their uneasiness. Both the Soviet Union and the PRC avow a preference for a unified Korea, although each would be threatened by a Korea unified under a communist regime allied to the other.

The Soviets and the PRC would both consider any effort to unify Korea, particularly by military force, as highly risky, for a number of reasons. First, any conflict in Korea would carry the implicit risk of a broader confrontation involving the great powers. Second, the anticipated Japanese reaction is of great concern, particularly to the PRC, since a major rearmament effort would probably result. Third, both of the communist powers would prefer to avoid hostilities in the region, since the United States would be likely to intervene or, at a minimum, would find such action unacceptable in terms of its global interests. Neither country is willing to risk its relationship to the United States for the sake of a unified Korea at the present time. Fourth, both powers would almost certainly be concerned about the potential for independent action which a unified, highly nationalistic (non-communist or communist) Korean regime might exert in the region.

Sino-Soviet interests are not, however, wholly parallel. The Soviets would be concerned that a unified Korea might tip the Sino-Soviet balance toward the Chinese, given the North's bias toward China. On the other hand, Moscow may, in the longer term, be tempted to support an effort at unification, assuming that the North could only win with Soviet support and the USSR could then exercise the predominant influence over a unified communist Korea. Moscow would also have to assume that the United States would avoid involvement. A unified communist Korea could tip the balance against Japanese influence in Asia, although the trend toward a U.S.-Japan-PRC entente in Asia might be strengthened, unless Japanese confidence in the United States had been totally compromised by America's failure to defend South Korea.

Given the PRC's plans for modernization, it is unlikely that Beijing (Peking) would be similarly tempted to support a reunification effort through military action because of its likely impact on regional security and thus China's own defense requirements.

Japan

While Japan historically has sought control over Korea, its objective today is to keep the Peninsula neutralized as a direct threat to Japanese security. Tokyo's minimum objective is to maintain a state of peace in Korea, given the risks of renewed hostilities and Japan's probable indirect involvement in them. Second, Japan seeks to prevent communist control over a unified Korea, which would represent a major threat to its own security and economic interests. A communist Korea would likely have far greater military forces than Japan now has and would force a reassessment of Japan's military posture as well as raise internal security problems with its Korean minority. Moreover, a communist victory in Korea would cast grave doubts upon the credibility of the U.S. security commitment to Japan, likewise forcing a reassessment of its military posture and increasing the likelihood of a major rearmament effort. Japan would prefer a unified non-communist Korea, but not at the risk of conflict or of arousing Sino-Soviet countermeasures. Japan might even have qualms about a unified Korea with far more powerful military forces than it now possesses.

The United States

America's security interest in Korea is largely derivative, rather than direct. It derives, first, from U.S. postwar involvement with the ROK, including the Korean War, and from the recognition that disengagement from this involvement is apt to be construed in Asia as another major step toward total disengagement from the security affairs of the region. The Asian reaction to the Carter Administration's announcement in early 1977 of its intention to withdraw all U.S. ground forces from Korea demonstrated this point most forcefully. Second, the U.S. commitment to Korea derives from American interest in establishing a more stable, peaceful regime in East Asia and the recognition that communist control over Korea would fundamentally and adversely affect the balance of power in the region and would be destabilizing both in the immediate future and in the long term.

While the United States accepts the reunification of Korea as an ultimate goal, it has no present interest in pressing for a non-communist unified Korea at the cost of hostilities or in a manner that would be construed by the Soviet Union and the PRC as a direct threat to their interests. The American stake in Korea is destined to expand beyond these security interests during the 1980s, when Korea will emerge as a significant middle-rank power with the largest military force and the second largest economy in non-communist East Asia.

Finally, U.S. interests in Korea are derived from the treaty commitment to preserve the security of Japan. In fact, the security of the ROK and that of Japan are virtually inseparable; indeed, the security interests of the two countries should be viewed from a broader regional Northeast Asian perspective, rather than as separate issues.

Thus, the major outside powers share a common recognition of the importance of the Korean Peninsula to their interests and tacitly support the common, minimum objective of maintaining the status quo and preventing a reoccurrence of hostilities in Korea. Any change in the status quo would be disadvantageous to two of the outside powers (China and the Soviet Union) and would pose unacceptable risks to the other two (the United States and Japan). Any reoccurrence of open hostilities would potentially involve all four powers, particularly if the hostilities appeared to be leading to a significant change in the status quo in Korea and the Asian power balance.

The communist powers, however, as a result of the Sino-Soviet rivalry, have been unwilling to translate this congruence of interest into joint action to reduce tension. The Soviet Union might support reunification of Korea under communist control in the unlikely circumstance that such a policy involved no serious risks or costs to the USSR in terms of either relations with the United States or influence over North Korea. The United States and Japan, conversely, share the goal of a unified non-communist Korea, but they too would support this development only if it could be achieved without risk or other costs.

NORTH-SOUTH OBJECTIVES

To a much greater degree than the outside powers, both South and North Koreans prefer a unified country, for obvious nationalistic reasons. The prospects for unification as a result of a peaceful process of compromise and agreement, however, are apparently nil for the foreseeable future, given the fundamental ideological differences between the two sides, the impossibility of breaching the leadership gap, and the bitter memories of the Korean War, particularly in the South.

Neither North nor South Korea can be expected to give up its hopes for ultimate unification. The operative question is their relative willingness to accept the status quo—the continued division of Korea—for the indefinite future. Related issues concern whether either state is willing to pay the price of attempting to alter the status quo, and whether either is willing to live with the status quo and contribute to its stabilization by reducing tensions on the Korean Peninsula.

At the present time, the ROK is prepared to accept and stabilize the status quo as an interim step toward unification. Military adventures would be extremely costly to the ROK, given its exposed military position. The Seoul industrial complex is only 30 miles from the DMZ, and the North Koreans are so firmly entrenched in their sector of the zone that an attack on the North is well beyond South Korea's military capabilities.

The North, on the other hand, continues to profess ambitions for unification on its own terms and continues to reject any suggestions for developments that would reinforce the status quo. Its military posture is essentially offensive and expansive. It has built up its mobile armored forces, increased its firepower, and stationed larger forces in hardened positions closer to the DMZ. On the other hand, the North does have inhibitions about renewing aggression, and it seems to have calculated that the costs of an offensive are too great to incur. At the same time, it disdains any serious efforts to stabilize the status quo by reducing tensions on the Peninsula. The North has forcefully rejected a two-Korea approach, denouncing it as a plot of "splitists" and contrasting the very "different" situations of Germany and Korea. The North is the only power actively seeking to revise the status quo.

Under these circumstances, the prospects for Korean security will depend at a minimum on deterring North Korea from reinitiating hostilities on the Peninsula. A risk of hostilities will still prevail, however, and any improvement in Korean security will depend on reducing tensions and stabilizing the division, both of which require a basic change in North Korean policy. In terms of U.S., Japanese, and ROK interests, these optimum goals are desirable, although it must be noted that the ROK might find that reduced tension poses a new set of problems in maintaining the degree of discipline and unity necessary to support a large and continuing defense effort. The Soviet Union and the PRC would probably not be averse, in principle, to a reduction of Korean tensions in the short term, but both are willing to support a policy dictated by North Korea opposing any step that might stabilize the division of Korea. Neither country has been willing to exert pressures to effect a change in the North Korean position. For the present, deterrence of hostilities is the only alternative.

THE DETERRENCE EQUATION

The Major Components

The deterrence equation consists of several major components which are inherently interrelated: (1) the relative strength of the South Korean forces measured against those of the North; (2) the strength of U.S. forces stationed in Korea or available for action there; (3) the supplementary role of Japan; (4) the weight and direction of Soviet and Chinese influence over the North; and (5) the U.N. peace-keeping machinery. Additionally, the anticipated costs of a conflict deter all parties from initiating one. The first two factors, South Korean and U.S. military strengths as well as the role of Japan, are susceptible to direct control by the major powers. The latter two are subject to only a degree of outside influence and are therefore less dependable elements of the deterrence eqution. Thus U.S. and ROK decisions concerning force levels must be made without reference to the other powers involved. On the other hand, efforts to increase the deterrent effect of the Sino-Soviet balance or of the U.N. peace-keeping machinery hinge upon a reciprocal action on the part of the communist powers.

The critical question in evaluating deterrence in Korea is, in fact, how large a deterrent force is necessary and how much risk a given level of deterrence incurs. Deterrence does not consist only of the war-fighting capabilities of the U.S. and ROK forces; it also involves the countermeasures being developed in the North (which are not easy to calculate) and, more importantly, the perceptions of the

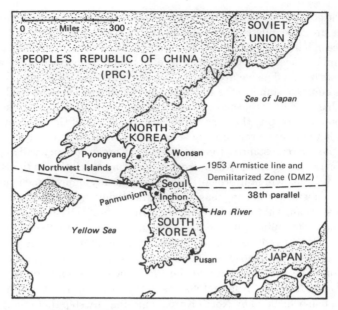

Map 1—The Korean peninsula and environs

communist powers, particularly the North, regarding the deterrent forces and their credibility. Deterrence may be achieved at low levels of military strength if the North considers these levels sufficiently strong to make the costs of aggression too great. A crucial component in the North's perception must therefore be the will or intention of the status quo powers to use their forces in the case of aggression.

The assessment of intent to use force is particularly relevant to U.S. military capabilities. The North has a distinct advantage in that its major population and industrial centers are located almost 200 miles from the North-South boundary, whereas the Seoul industrial and political center is only 30 miles from the DMZ. The willingness of the United States to commit its forces to compensate for this advantage is a crucial element in the North's assessment of the risks of aggression. Likewise, South Korean concerns about the U.S. will to fight have led some to advocate an independent South Korean retaliatory capacity which would include nuclear weapons.

The North undoubtedly assumes that the ROK will use every capability at its command, but it may assume that those capabilities are limited by internal weaknesses. The North constantly conjures up a vision of broad internal dissent in the South, which could lead to dangerous miscalculation and misadventure. By the same token, the North may recognize the inherent military strength of the United States, but it may assume that U.S. forces will avoid engagement in a conflict situation, or will not be reinforced by American military assets stationed outside Korea, or will find that Japanese support for U.S. military operations in the area is sufficiently circumscribed as to weaken the response to aggression. Thus, any evaluation of deterrence by force must consider not only actual military strength but also the perception of this strength in the minds of the North Koreans whose isolation and ideological bent could lead to gross miscalculation—although it should be noted that that has not been the case since the armistice in 1953.

The North-South Balance

Military Strength. Modernization of the North Korean forces commenced in the mid-1960s, approximately five years before similar steps were taken in the South. In addition, the resources devoted to the military buildup in the North have been consistently greater than those in the South: 15 to 20 percent of the North's Gross National Product (GNP) has been devoted to direct defense support, compared to 6.5 percent or less in the South.

The North-South military balance in 1977 was as follows:[2]

Republic of Korea (South Korea)	Democratic Republic of Korea (North Korea)
Population 34,410,000	Population: 15,940,000
Military Service: Army and Marines 2½ years Navy and Air Force 3 years	Military Service: Army 5 years, Navy and Air Force 3-4 years
Total armed forces: 625,000	Total armed forces: 467,000
Estimated GNP (1974): $17.5 bn	Estimated GNP (1972): $3.5 bn
Defense expenditure (1975): 353.1 bn won ($719 m.) $1 = 491 won (1975), 397 won (1974)	Defense expenditure (1974): 1,578 m won ($770m.) $1 = 2.05 won

Army 560,000
23 infantry divisions
2 armored brigades
40 artillery battalions
1 SSM battalion with *Honest John*
2 SAM bns each with 2 *Hawk* and 2 *Nike Hercules* btys
1,000 M-47, M-4S and M-60 med tks; 400 M-113 and M-577 APC; 2,000 105 mm, 155 mm and 203 mm guns and how; 107 mm mor; 57 mm, 75 mm and 106 mm RCL, *Honest John* SSM; *Hawk* and *Nike Hercules* SAM

Reserves: 1,000,000

Navy: 20,000
7 destroyers
9 destroyer escorts (6 escort transports)
15 coastal escorts
22 patrol boats (less than 100 tons)
10 coastal minesweepers
20 landing ships (8 tank, 12 medium)
60 amphibious craft

Reserves: 33,000

Marines: 20,000
1 division
Reserves: 60,000

Air Force: 25,000, 216 combat aircraft
11 FB sqns: 2 with 36 F-4C/D, 5 with 100 F-86F, 4 with 70 F-5A
1 recce sqn with 10 RF-5A

4 tpt sqns with 20 C-46, 12 C-54 and 12 C-123
15 hel, including 6 UH-19, 7 UH-1D/N
Trainers incl 20 T-28, 20 T-33, 20 T-41, 14 F-5B

Reserves: 35,000

Para-Military Forces: A local defense militia, 2,000,000 Homeland Defense Reserve Force

Army: 410,000
1 tank division
3 motorized divisions
20 infantry divisions
3 independent infantry brigades
3 SAM brigades with 180 SA-2
300 T-34, 700 T-54/-55 and T-59 med tks; 80 PT-76 and 50 T-62 lt tks; 200 BA-64, BTR-40/-60/-152 APC; 200 SU-76 and SU-100 SP guns; 3,000 guns and how up to 152 mm; 1,800 RI and 2,500 120 mm, 160 mm and 240 mm mor; 82 mm, 106 mm RCL; 45 mm, 57 mm, 100 mm ATK guns; 12 *FROG-5/-7* SSM; 2,500 AA guns, incl. 37mm, 57mm, ZSU-57, 85mm; SA-2 SAM

Reserves: 250,000

Navy: 17,000
8 submarines (4 ex-Soviet W-class, 4 ex-Chinese R-class)
15 submarine chasers (ex-Soviet *SO*/-class).
10 *Komar* and 8 *Osa*-class FPB with *Styx* SSM
54 MGB (15 *Shanghai*, 8 *Swatow*-class, 20 inshore)
90 torpedo boats (45 P-4, 30 P-6 class, ex-Soviet)

Air Force: 40,000; 588 combat aircraft
2 light bomber squadrons with 60 Il 28
13 FGA sqns with 28 Su-7 and 300 MiG-15/-17
16 fighter sqns with 150 MiG-21 and 40 MiG-19
1 recce sqn with 10 Il-28 *Beagle*
1 tpt regt with 150 An-2
1 tpt regt with 30 Mi-4 and 10 Mi-8 hel
70 Yak-18 and 59 MiG-15 and MiG-17 trainers

Reserves: 40,000

Para-Military Forces: 50,000 security forces and border guards; a civilian militia of 1,500,000 with small arms and some AA artillery

[2] International Institute for Strategic Studies, *The Military Balance, 1978/79,* 1979.

The shift in the military balance from 1970 to 1977 is shown in Table 1.

When measured by firepower alone, the balance has shifted from rough parity in 1970 to a definite advantage for the North in 1977. Even before recent new intelligence studies, it was estimated that North Korea enjoyed a two-to-one advantage in both total mobile assault weapons (tanks, APCs, assault guns) and shelling capability (artillery, rocket launchers, and mortars). The North also enjoyed a two-to-one advantage in combat jet aircraft (although this is somewhat offset by qualitative inferiority) and a more than four-to-one advantage in anti-aircraft guns and navy combat vessels. A further breakdown of military strength made in 1978 is given in Table 2.

In addition, North Korea had almost nullified South Korea's active duty manpower advantage by 1978. This trend is apparently planned to continue, since the North Korean draft age has just been lowered to 16.

According to a report of the Pacific Study Group to the Senate Armed Forces Committee in January 1979, these data in fact underestimate the North Korean advantage. The report states that an intelligence reassessment "postulates a substantially larger and more offensively oriented North Korean military posture than heretofore assumed." Press reports based on new assessments credit the North

Table 1

MILITARY FORCE BALANCE COMPARISON

	1970		1977	
	Republic of Korea	North Korea	Republic of Korea	North Korea
Personnel				
Active forces	634,000	400,000	600,000	520,000
Reserve forces	1,000,000	1,200,000	3,000,000	2,000,000
Maneuver divisions	19	20	19	25
Ground balance				
Tanks	900	600	1,100[a]	2,000
APC	300	120	400[a]	750[a]
Assault guns	0	300	0	105[a]
Anti-tank	NA[b]	NA	NA	24,000
Shelling capability				
Artillery/multiple rocket launchers	1,750	3,300	2,000[a]	4,335[a]
Surface to surface missiles (battalions)	NA	NA	1	2-3
Mortars	NA	NA	NA	9,000
Air balance				
Jet combat aircraft	230	555	320[a]	600
Other military aircraft	35[a]	130	200	400
AAA guns	850	2,000	2,000[a]	5,500[a]
SAMs (battalions/sites)	NA	NA	2	40-45
Navy Combat vessels	60	190	90-100	450-475

Source: Senate Committee on Foreign Relations, *U.S. Troop Withdrawal from the Republic of Korea, January 9, 1978*, U.S. Government Printing Office, Washington, D.C., 1978.

[a]These are approximations; actual figures may be greater.

[b]NA = not available.

Table 2

COMPARISON OF GROUND AND NAVAL FORCES, 1978

Component Ground Forces	North Korea	Republic of Korea
Active duty personnel	440,000	520,000
Combat divisions	25	20
Infantry	20	19
Motorized	3	0
Armor	2	1
Separate infantry brigades	4	2
Separate armor regiments	5	2
Light infantry brigades	6-8	0
Paramilitary/militia	2,500,000	2,800.000
Medium tanks	1,850	840
Light/amphibious tanks	100	0
Assault guns	100	0
APCs	750	500
Field artillery pieces	3,000	2,000
Multiple rocket launchers	1,800	0
Mortars	9,000	5,300
Infantry anti-tank weapons	24,000	11,000
AAA weapons	5,500	700
SAM sites	38-40	33
Naval Forces		
Personnel	27,000	46,000
Bases	18	8
Total combatant ships	425-450	104
Patrol frigates	6-7	9
Missile attack boats	17-19	68
Coastal patrol	300	. . .
Amphibious craft	90	18
Submarines	10-12	0

Source. Senate Committee on Foreign Relations, *U.S. Troop Withdrawal from the Republic of Korea, January 9, 1978*, U.S. Government Printing Office, Washington, D.C., 1978.

with an army of 550,000 to 600,000 men and from 37 to 41 divisions, with a significantly larger and stronger armored force (more than 2,600 tanks and over 1,000 APCs), greater firepower (3,500 artillery pieces and 1,600 multiple rocket launchers), and substantially larger reserves capable of exploiting a "blitzkrieg" deep into the ROK.[3]

The North's superiority is not quite as pronounced as the numbers indicate, however, if assessed from the perspective of the respective missions of the two forces. The North Korean forces are configured largely for offensive operations and therefore must be assumed to require a distinct superiority. North Korea has developed highly mobile armed forces, supported by airborne elements. The element of surprise gives the North a distinct advantage, along with the advantage of geography. The South, on the other hand, is unable to trade distance for stronger defensive positions; it must defend all the major corridors of attack very close to

[3] Sam Jameson, "U.S. Believes N. Korean Troops Outnumber the South's," *Los Angeles Times*, July 16, 1979, Sec. 1-A, p. 1-2.

the DMZ, which requires it to spread its defense forces. The North's emphasis on airborne operations and tunnel-digging is apparently designed to strengthen its capabilities for a surprise attack that would neutralize the DMZ defenses of the South.

The Humphrey-Glenn Senate Report summarized the respective military advantages of North and South Korea as follows:[4]

North Korea (generally offensive deployment)	South Korea (generally defensive deployment)
More ground combat divisions	Advantage of terrain and defensive positions
Greater ground firepower	More modern air assets
More armor assets	Better educated military leadership
Superior naval forces	Vietnam combat experience
More air assets	Better transportation network
Better air defense system	Continued U.S. deterrence
Larger logistics production	
Greater military production	
Capability of surprise	
Ability to concentrate attacking forces	
Distance to Seoul	
More commando-type forces	
Proximity of major allies	

Weighed against the ROK forces, the North has a clear military superiority which would be most effective in a short conflict aimed at controlling a limited area of the South extending down into the Seoul industrial belt. In a longer conflict, the South might be able to counterbalance this advantage, but at the probable cost of the destruction of major industrial and urban areas, a very high price.

The military advantages enjoyed by the South must also be weighed. The Northern armored forces have only limited corridors of attack open to them, affording the South terrain that is advantageous for defense. The South can focus its military effort on defensive capabilities designed to exploit favorable terrains and strong points. It also has superior aircraft with better trained manpower. Moreover, the South is backed by American deterrent forces, particularly air and naval forces that are far superior to comparable North Korean elements.

Prospective Balance. Both the South and the North are engaged in strengthening their military forces. While it is difficult to make projections of the North Korean buildup, the pattern of recent years indicates a continued strengthening of armored forces, increased artillery and other firepower, greater airborne strength, greater ammunition reserves, and a continued buildup of naval strength, particularly submarines. This buildup is almost entirely within the capability of the current North Korean defense industry. Additional strengthening of Northern forces would depend upon the Soviet Union for more technologically sophisticated weapons and upon the PRC and the Soviet Union for additional aircraft.

The North Korean forces have three potential vulnerabilities. First, their air

---

[4] U.S. Senate Committee on Foreign Relations, *U.S. Troop Withdrawal from the Republic of Korea,* January 9, 1978, U.S. Government Printing Office, Washington, D.C., 1978, p. 28.

force is equipped with aging jet aircraft, the most modern being MiG-21s and SU-7s. Second, North Korea has a manpower shortage, and the drafting of 16-year-olds is apparently affecting its industrial manpower pool. Finally, North Korea may not have enough trained technicians, which puts it at a disadvantage in the utilization of more sophisticated military technology.

The buildup of South Korean forces is likely to increase in the near future with the delivery of weapons systems ordered under the Force Improvement Plan (FIP), the transfer of equipment associated with the partial drawdown of U.S. Second Division forces, and the decision of the ROK to increase its defense expenditures as a result of the new estimates of North Korean military strength.

The FIP projects a five-year (1976-80) expenditure of about $5.5 billion, with foreign exchange costs of $3.5 billion. The equipment to be provided to ROK armed forces under the FIP includes the following:[5]

Army
Air defense equipment
Armor/antiarmor
Air mobility
Small arms/equipment improvement
Artillery
Communications
Surveillance equipment
Reserve projects

Navy
Vessels
Missiles and munitions
ASW aircraft
Communications
Base improvement
Equipment improvement
Reserve projects

Air Force
Aircraft
Early warning radar
Other radar
War reserve materiel and electronics
Communications and electronics
Air Force base/tactical construction
Other
Reserve projects

General
Equipment replacement

The present imbalances between the North and the South are likely to be reduced in the next five years. During this time, South Korea will substantially

[5] Ibid., p. 45.

modernize its tank, anti-tank, and helicopter capabilities; its Air Force will benefit from both quantitative and qualitative improvements; and its firepower should be considerably enhanced by the additional artillery now projected. Nevertheless, the South will remain militarily inferior to the North.

The package of arms designed to compensate South Korea for the withdrawal of U.S. ground forces, estimated at a value of $800 million, would have provided South Korea with additional mobility in the form of helicopters, APCs, and self-propelled mortar carriers; firepower in the form of new M-48A5 tanks, converted older M-48s, TOW launchers, Cobras, and howitzers; and anti-aircraft weapons, I-HAWK battalions, and Vulcan guns. The suspension of the Second Division's withdrawal will probably require the ROK to acquire many of these weapons by direct purchase, instead of at no cost.

The buildup plans will allow the ROK Army to assume a greater share of its own defense but will not provide sufficient offensive assets for the ROK to success-fully attack North Korea.

Even if North Korea acquires only enough equipment to modernize its current inventory, it will still have a numerical advantage over South Korea in all key categories except APCs and SAM launchers by 1982. But U.S. analysts do not expect North Korean armament levels to stabilize. Rather, they anticipate a con-tinuing buildup in all major categories except fighter aircraft and anti-aircraft guns. The prospect, therefore, is that the North will maintain its numerical advantage well into the 1980s, but the South can develop the capability to match that numeri-cal advantage if it so chooses.

Defense Industry. At the present time, the North has clear advantages in the scale of its defense industry. It has the capacity to equip its ground and naval forces with all but the most sophisticated equipment and can produce massive numbers of tanks, APCs, mobile artillery, and smaller ground force weapons, as well as sufficient ammunition. Its submarine and gunboat output is increasing. It also has invested heavily in hardening and putting underground not only military but also industrial facilities.

The South, despite its stronger industrial base, has devoted far less of its GNP to developing an indigenous defense industry, and only in recent years has that industry expanded. At the present time, the ROK defense industry can meet only part of the requirements of its ground forces, and South Korea still imports almost all of its heavy equipment. It produces 105mm and 155mm artillery, mortars, M-16s, and smaller weapons; it has recently started a tank rebuilding program and is developing indigenous tank production; it has capabilities for maintenance of Hawk and Hercules missile systems and F-4 engines; it is engaged in coassembly of light helicopters; it produces a light manned armored vehicle; and it is increasing its capacity for ammunition production. It is now projecting co-production of F-5 arcraft. It has only a limited ability to support its naval forces, producing patrol craft that are equipped with imported weapons, electronics, and engines. It must depend upon external resources for all sophisticated equipment, as well as for aircraft (until the F-5 program is in production) and electronic gear. By the mid or early 1980s, however, South Korea should be able to produce a far larger percent-age of its ground force weapons, including tanks and helicopters. Nevertheless, it will depend upon external sources for sophisticated fire control and other electronic equipment for many years. The South also plans to develop a capacity for building and constructing its own frigates, but these will have to be equipped with imported weapons and other gear.

Projecting current and planned capacity, the North is likely to maintain its defense industry advantage, although it will be far less pronounced in the 1980s than it is at present. The South does have a capacity for considerably upgrading its defense industry, but only at the cost of decreased investment in the non-military industrial sector, which would have consequent effects on its economy. Furthermore, any investment in defense industry must always be weighed against the cost of such equipment purchased abroad. Assuming that the United States continues to be a reliable supplier, it is questionable whether the South should invest heavily in much of the more sophisticated equiment its forces will require. However, its defense industry could be expanded in less sophisticated areas of technology which would be economical and would improve the South's indigenous base of support.

External Support. Both South and North Korea are dependent on external support for their defense forces, but the South is considerably more dependent than the North. The North Korean Air Force has received MiG-21s, helicopters, and light transport aircraft (primarily from the PRC), and the Soviet Union is apparently supplying the more sophisticated electronic and surface-to-air equipment, although the flow of Soviet materiel has probably decreased considerably in recent years.

South Korea receives large amounts of equipment for all its armed forces, and its air and naval forces are almost completely dependent upon external sources. Sophisticated ground force equipment, including armored vehicles, tank parts, anti-tank guns, longer-range artillery, electronic equipment, and communication equipment, is supplied almost totally from U.S. sources. Foreign exchange expenditures for ROK defense forces have increased to about $600 million to $750 million annually. Furthermore, the South depends upon U.S.-funded ammunition reserves stockpiled in the ROK. It has voiced complaints regarding U.S. failures to deliver highly sophisticated equipment, such as the Lance missile, but the South's access problem is not as serious as that faced by the North.

It is likely that the 1980s will see increasing pressures from both North and South Korea on their respective allies to supply more sophisticated equipment. The North is likely to increase pressure on the Soviet Union for the delivery of MiG-23s, and Soviet restraint about delivery of more sophisticated aircraft might not continue under these circumstances. The motivations for Soviet restraint are not entirely clear, but it appears that the Soviet Union is prepared to support only North Korea's defensive capabilities, although it will not inhibit the development of offensive capabilities on the ground. Some have conjectured that Soviet constraints reflect a desire to avoid an arms race in Korea. However, the pace of the North Korean military buildup and the support it has received from both the Soviet Union and the PRC would indicate that neither was acting with consistent restraint or in response to U.S. levels of support for the ROK. In fact, there is good reason to presume that Soviet constraints are essentially politically motivated and that a more evenhanded North Korean policy vis-à-vis the two communist powers may be the price of MiG-23s or other advanced equipment. It is likely that at some point within the next five years North Korea will be equipped with more advanced aircraft supplied by the Soviet Union, while its numerical advantages will be maintained by replacement of the MiG-15/17s with MiG-21s from the PRC.

South Korea is likely to continue to have more extensive external support, presumably from the United States. However, Seoul has tried to diversify its sources of military supply, in a limited way and with mixed success. American military equipment is preferred because such equipment is interchangeable with that held by the U.S. forces in Korea, and U.S. logistic backstopping, including spare parts, is considered far superior to that of other suppliers. Furthermore, the South Korean armed forces are familiar with U.S. military equipment and have found it reliable over the years. On the other hand, if a superior weapon system is available from another Western supplier, or if the United States decides to deny certain systems, other sources—particularly the French, British, and Germans—are available and in fact anxious to meet Korean needs. The ROK no longer has serious foreign exchange problems inhibiting purchases of equipment from other sources, and those sources have proved willing to provide generous financing; thus foreign exchange shortages will not be a constraint for Seoul.

The United States may find that its major problems in supporting the South Korean force buildup will involve decisions about providing more sophisticated weapon systems, particularly missiles and advanced aircraft. Denial of these systems to South Korea would increase reliance on U.S. armed forces and could also result in the ROK seeking other sources of supply or developing domestic industries. On the other hand, there are strong arguments for maintaining a ceiling on the level of sophistication to avoid unnecessarily escalating the arms race on the Peninsula. Current U.S. arms sales policies also establish constraints on the overall level of equipment that can be sold to Korea within each year. Although the arms sales policy is to be applied on a case-by-case basis with some exceptions granted, its application to South Korea is questionable. A strong case can be made to except Korea from the policy, just as NATO, Japan, and ANZUS are excepted.

Economic Factors. Comparisons of the relative strength of South and North Korea often ignore fundamental economic and political considerations. The military inferiority of the South is clearly not reflected in the relative strengths of the two economies. The South Korean economy is far stronger than the North's, and this advantage is likely to increase as South Korea's industrial base—its steel, heavy machinery, petrochemical, and electronic industries—expands rapidly. Its shipbuilding capacity is also much greater than that of the North and is likely to expand. Furthermore, its current account balance and its high credit rating provide sufficient foreign exchange to support the development of both its economy and its defense infrastructure.

The North, on the other hand, faces increasingly serious economic problems, with major deficits in its current account balance and a heavy external debt not only to its communist supporters but also to the West. Moreover, the economic growth potential of the North is limited, as is its flexibility in terms of independent choices for the purchase of weapons systems.

Some indication of the relative growth potential of the two economies can be found in Figs. 1 through 4. They demonstrate the major shift in economic capability and development from the North to the South during the 1970s and the contrast between the relatively static North Korean projections for the years ahead and the continued high level of growth anticipated in the South. Given the inadequacy of reliable data on the North, and according to reports of observers in North Korea, these charts may overestimate North Korean Gross National Product (GNP), per capita GNP in particular.

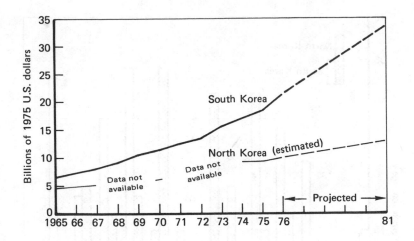

Fig. 1—Gross National Product

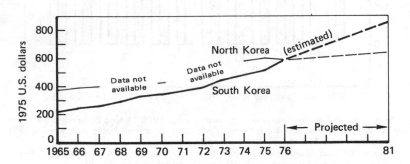

Fig. 2—Per capita Gross National Product

Source: Central Intelligence Agency, National Foreign Assessment Center, *Korea: The Economic Race Between the North and the South*, January 1978.

124

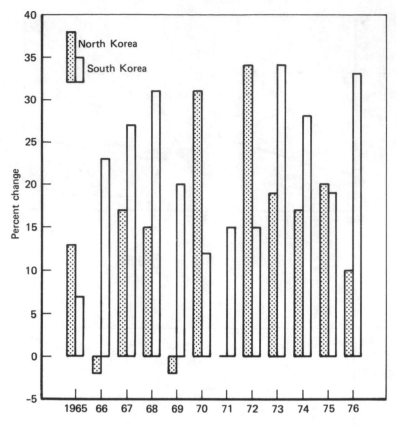

Note: The average annual rate of growth during 1966-76 was 14 percent for North Korea and 23 percent for South Korea. The industrial output index numbers for 1976 (1965 = 100) were 422 and 975, respectively.

Source: Central Intelligence Agency, National Foreign Assessment Center, *Korea: The Economic Race Between the North and the South*, January 1978.

Fig. 3—Industrial growth

Comparisons of the two economies can be deceptive, however. The North has demonstrated a willingness to allocate a far larger percentage of its resources to defense than has the South. While accurate figures are lacking, it is likely that North Korea's real military expenditures remain equal to, if not greater than, those of the South. North Korea spends upwards of 20 percent of its GNP on defense, compared with an average of a little over 6 percent for the South in recent years. Twelve percent of the North Korean working-age male population is in the regular armed forces, as compared with only 6 percent in the South; and the relative proportion of the North's work force in the defense industry is even higher. The North has made a total commitment and has given absolute priority to its military effort; and so far it has been able to deprive its civilian economy without serious internal problems.

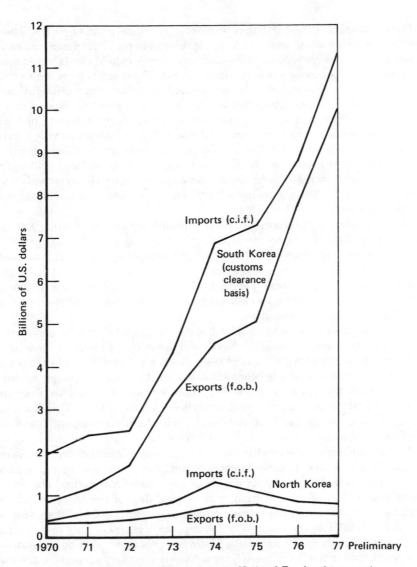

Source: Central Intelligence Agency, National Foreign Assessment Center, *Korea: The Economic Race Between the North and the South*, January 1978.

Fig. 4—Trade

On the other hand, the North may be reaching a critical point where it will have to reallocate both financial and manpower resources to the civilian sector in order to prevent a serious breakdown in its economy. Heavy capital inputs would seem to be required if the economy is to continue to grow. These inputs must come either from external sources—particularly the Soviet Union—or from a reallocation of internal resources. One critical factor will be the willingness of the Soviets to bail out the North Korean economy in the near term, and whether the Soviet Union will call for a reallocation of resources from defense to the civilian economy in return. Such a reallocation would have very important implications for the prospects of tension-reduction measures on the Korean Peninsula. Another factor will be the North's capacity to increase its foreign exchange earnings, which has recently been improving. That the North is selling military equipment overseas is a measure of its economic problems.

An alternative for the North is to move militarily against the South before the combination of its declining economic strength and the growing military potential of the South preclude such an option. An early offensive, even if only partially successful, could destroy much of the South's industry and overcome the North's growing economic disadvantage. Yet North Korea's industrial structure is vulnerable to U.S. air attacks, making its assessment of America's will to defend the South critical in the deterrence equation.

None of the choices faced by the North are inviting, and all require the revision of its current economic policies. The North will probably seek to defer its decision as long as possible, but within the next few years it must decide whether to reallocate resources from military to economic investment and/or seek major external assistance (probably only from the Soviet Union), or face a declining economy and a growing Southern military potential, or strike against the South. Paradoxically, at this juncture, the risk of hostilities could increase while the opportunity for achieving a reduction of tension was also improving.

Political Balance. The two Korean states have significantly different political systems. The North Korean government is totalitarian, exerting perhaps the most rigid controls over the lives of its people of any communist nation. The South Korean government is authoritarian, with a good deal of freedom granted the population, particularly in the economic and social aspects of life. Both governments are able to command the loyalty and support of their citizenry in support of their defense and other military efforts. There is no reason to question this support in the North; and in the South there is considerable voluntary support for defense, not only because of the material benefits accruing to the average South Korean from the economic sector and the relative equity of the income distribution, but also because of the bitter memories of North Korean outrages during its occupation of a large sector of the South. A 20 percent defense surtax, for example, was imposed in 1975 without complaint in the South.

There are some doubts as to whether both governments will be able to generate the same level of discipline and support for high defense expenditures and for universal military service in the next decade. The problem could be more pronounced in the South, especially as per capita income rapidly expands. The Korean Development Institute projects an increase in per capita income to over $4,000, and popular interest in more consumer goods over the next decade will increase the difficulty of levying the same level of sacrifice for defense as in the past. In the

North, very little is known about public attitudes, since the government makes every effort to suppress dissent. But one can conjecture that the failure of the civilian economy to improve living standards might lead to widespread dissent.

Perhaps the critical unknown is the effect that changes in leadership in North as well as South Korea will have in the 1980s. Active opposition and continued student problems in the South resulting from the assassination of President Park could affect stability and support for defense, while the North may have even more serious problems should a family succession be imposed by Kim Il-sung.

Kim's efforts to establish a clearcut line of family succession have apparently not succeeded. A leadership fight or the emergence of a collegial leadership could force the North to turn inward and revise both its economic and external policies. One possibility could be an effort to allocate greater resources to the economy, making a reduction of tension—even a temporary reduction—more desirable. A shift in the North's position regarding the two-Koreas issue and other tension-reduction measures could result. Another possibility might be a heightening of tensions and the utilization of this threat to unify the North while it is experiencing leadership problems. The one relatively certain factor is that the succession in the North is likely to introduce new fluidity into the Korean situation.

The politics of the South are likely to become more complicated and less prone to tight central control in the 1980s, given the almost revolutionary changes that are occurring in the economic and social structure of the country. Nevertheless, the present broad public support for effective defense measures against the North is not likely to be seriously diluted. Succession in the South will likewise add an element of fluidity and uncertainty. There is clear evidence that the North believes it missed its golden opportunity to move against the South during the period in 1960 when President Syngman Rhee was overthrown by student demonstrators. There is always the danger that it may strike against the South if it perceives the levels of dissent to be greater than they really are, especially if Kim Il-sung feels he has little to lose in a "now or never" situation.

Thus, both North and South Korea are likely to face leadership problems in the 1980s. Neither has a clear line of succession, and the likelihood of increased political instability at leadership levels until a new political equilibrium is established will result in increased temptation to both North and South to provoke a conflict.

Both Koreas will be under strong pressure to consolidate a new leadership rapidly, if only to forestall any temptation to intervene on the part of the adversary. New leadership, particularly in the North, would also open opportunities for a relaxation of past pressures and negotiation of a two-Korea accommodation. Kim Il-sung's departure could open the way for a reassessment of economic policies, if not already undertaken, to give the new leadership time to consolidate and seek popular support. The South is less likely to experience any change in basic policy, but new leadership will likewise be able to move away from past rigidities in policy.

Conclusion. North Korea is clearly superior to South Korea in purely military strength, while South Korea has by far the stronger economy. The potential of the South to upgrade its defense effort is greater than that of the North, although to do so would entail allocating greater resources to defense, with consequent economic costs. The North, with its limited resources, its smaller population, and its weaker economy, has nonetheless mobilized a greater defense effort, but its military advantage is likely to decline in the future. Furthermore, the North, while having a larger defense industry, is less certain about external support than the

South and has less financial resources to increase this support. The North's military superiority provides it with a capability to achieve an initial thrust to the Han River and, with the capture of the Seoul area, to control a high percentage of the population and industrial capacity of the South. The North Korean threat is real, ever-present, potentially growing, and certainly not a "paper tiger."

However, the North has vulnerabilities that could become more pronounced in the 1980s. Its domestic economy may be reaching the outer limits of support for the military effort, and its dependence on external support is therefore likely to increase. The Soviet Union will be at an advantage in such a situation, since its resources—both economic and technological—are far greater than those of China. The Soviet Union, therefore, could conceivably play the more critical role in the evolution of North Korean policy toward the Korean Peninsula in the 1980s.

The probability of leadership changes in both North and South will increase in the coming decade, opening up the possibility of political instability in both and a major policy reassessment in the North. The North could be faced with choices of seeking a relaxation of tensions to permit reallocation of resources to civilian economic development, watching the South gain military superiority, or even attacking the South to nullify its growing economic and technological advantages.

The possibility of nuclear proliferation, particularly on the part of the South, also cannot be ignored, even though the ROK adheres today to a policy of non-proliferation. South Korea, with its expanding nuclear energy production, will have a growing potential for nuclear warhead development.[6] Furthermore, research and development in missiles will provide the basis for a nuclear weapons delivery system. The North so far lacks a similar potential. An effort by either side to acquire a nuclear weapons system would have the most destabilizing effect on the North-South equation of any development in the 1980s. It could easily work to the advantage of the non-nuclear state, since it could lead to preemptive action by the major powers. For example, the Soviet Union and China might act if the South reversed its non-proliferation policy; and in addition, the South would jeopardize American support. Since it is virtually impossible to develop nuclear weapons secretly, the proliferating state would be faced with punitive countermeasures even before its weapons program was completed. Thus the prospect of a destabilizing nuclear weapons program by either North or South Korea during the 1980s is slim, but it still cannot be totally ignored.

U.S. Force Levels

Current Levels. At the present time, there are approximately 40,000 American troops stationed in Korea. The major elements of these forces are the Second Infantry Division, less one battalion withdrawn at the end of 1978; the 314th Air Division, with 72 combat aircraft; Army missile and air defense commands; and associated logistic, intelligence, communications, and support units. Reinforcements for these military units in nearby areas are Marine ground and air assets, an Air Force Wing in Japan, B-52s in Guam, and the Seventh Fleet, which provides for the naval defense of Korea, and additional airpower. Finally, U.S. capabilities to bring air forces quickly from the United States provide another important deterrent.

[6] See discussion of this issue by Leslie Gelb, especially pp. 263, and 227 below.

The major U.S. forces have three missions: (1) to compensate for the deficiencies and vulnerabilities of the ROK forces; (2) to provide a major deterrent to North Korean attack and an incentive for the USSR and the PRC to counsel restraint; and (3) through the U.N. command, to provide an overall command structure and supervision of the peace-keeping machinery provided for in the Armistice Agreement.

The more specific war-fighting capabilities of the U.S. forces include (1) a highly mobile reserve armor and anti-armor capability which offsets South Korean deficiencies and reinforces its defense lines; (2) airpower capable of gaining air superiority and providing vital tactical air support; (3) experienced air controllers who can direct air strikes; (4) intelligence gathering and analysis to maximize the prospects for early warning; (5) a base of operations for reinforcement of ground, naval, and air forces from outside South Korea as well as an ability to call in these forces on an emergency basis; (6) effective communication and logistic support, including the availability of war reserve ammunition held by the U.S. forces; (7) training for the ROK; and (8) a source of key equipment transfers. These capabilities not only make up for deficiencies in the ROK forces relative to those of the North, they also make possible a forward defense strategy designed to keep the military action as far from Seoul as possible.

The deterrent mission of U.S. forces is performed in various ways. The presence of American troops on the Korean Peninsula provides a "tripwire," warning the North Koreans that an attack against South Korea would involve not only South Korean forces but U.S. military power as well. The Second Division, even though in reserve posture, would undoubtedly be involved in fighting very shortly after the outset of conflict and thus serves as one form of "tripwire." The 314th Air Division is likely to be even more quickly involved due to the central command role played by the U.S. Air Commander in the air defense of Korea and the necessity of defending U.S. airbases near the DMZ at the outset of any conflict. Furthermore, the U.S. commander, by virtue of his role as both U.N. commander and commander of combined U.S. and ROK forces, would be immediately involved.

Deterrence, however, constitutes more than the prospective reaction of U.S. forces to a North Korean attack. Deterrence, in the last analysis, rests on North Korea's *perception* of that reaction. The North Koreans have shown great respect for American military power and have reacted with evident concern to exercises in which U.S. air and naval forces have been brought in from outside Korea. The U.S. nuclear capability is particularly feared by the North and serves as a deterrent, whether based in South Korea or not. These perceptions, however, can change, both as a function of North Korean views and as a function of the perceptions of South Korea, Japan, and the rest of Asia concerning the reliability of the American commitment. Should these countries perceive the U.S. commitment as wavering, the judgment of the North will inevitably be affected. Uncertainty regarding the American commitment thus both encourages North Korean offensive proclivities and discourages South Korean dependence upon the United States.

When the case for ground force withdrawal is based upon limiting U.S. involvement in a future conflict and leaving open the option of non-involvement, it impacts upon the North Korean assessment of America's will, not its capability, to defend Korea. It potentially encourages North Korean aggressive tendencies and paradoxically could increase the risk that the U.S. forces remaining in Korea could be involved in conflict.

The third role of the U.S. forces, maintaining the Armistice and commanding the joint forces, is more significant than is readily apparent. While many of the provisions of the Armistice Agreement have been violated or are unenforceable, the truce-keeping machinery under the U.S. commander does maintain an internationally recognized border between the North and the South, making any move by either force across the DMZ readily apparent. Moreover, it provides machinery for negotiations with the North relating to major incidents, as was the case, for example, with the Pueblo incident of 1968 and the more recent tree-cutting incident in the Joint Security Area, when new provisions for controlling that area were negotiated. Finally, the U.S. command role provides a means of controlling reactions to North Korean incidents in a manner that can be both firm and non-provocative, as was the case in the tree-cutting incident and in the North Korean attack on a U.S. helicopter that strayed over the DMZ in 1977. The U.S. command and presence provides an additional safeguard against an (unlikely) attack by South Korea as well as a basis for expanding the peace-keeping machinery should the North be prepared to do so.

Reduction of U.S. Forces. In 1977, withdrawal of American ground forces from South Korea was projected to take place in three phases. Initially, one brigade of the Second Division and some other support units totaling 6,000 men were to be withdrawn in 1978-79. In the second phase, in 1980, logistic and other support units including the surface-to-air defense command, totaling 9,000 men, were to be withdrawn. In the final phase, in 1981-82, the remaining two brigades and the division headquarters would be withdrawn. The United States planned to maintain augmented air, intelligence, and communications units in Korea indefinitely.

These plans for the withdrawal were made with a view to minimizing its potential adverse effect on the U.S. commitment to Korea. The transfer of some $800 million worth of American equipment now largely held by the withdrawing forces, in combination with preexisting ROK plans for its own force improvement, were to assure that the military deficiencies and vulnerabilities now compensated for by U.S. forces would be filled by the reinforced Korean military. As the prior analysis pointed out, however, North Korea is likely to retain its military superiority, particularly with anticipated North Korean force improvements.

Larger questions, however, remained concerning the potential effect of withdrawal on the U.S. deterrent power. The perceptions of North Korea and of the other Asian countries have an important bearing on whether U.S. deterrence is respected; thus a very unstable situation could be created if the ground force withdrawal were perceived to reduce the risk of U.S. involvement in a new Korean conflict. Concerns throughout Asia regarding a greatly reduced U.S. deterrent were in fact moderated by subsequent developments, including the attenuation of the withdrawal, the decision to leave two-thirds of the Second Division in Korea at least until 1981-82, the augmentation of the air elements, the establishment of the U.S.-ROK Combined Force Command, and the increase in the scale and frequency of joint exercises. But those concerns remained at least until the withdrawal was suspended.

Finally, maintaining the U.S.-commanded joint structure would be more difficult in the absence of U.S. ground forces. The withdrawal would also raise doubts about the future of the Armistice machinery and the U.S. capability for moderating reactions to violent incidents in the DMZ and elsewhere.

Reacting to Asian concerns, particularly those of the ROK and Japan, and Congressional pressures, the Carter Administration committed itself initially to a review of the ground force withdrawal in two specific contexts. That review began in the spring of 1979. The joint statement of the Tenth U.S.-ROK Security Consultative Meeting in July 1977 contains a commitment for continuing consultations with South Korea on the development of Korean capabilities, the military balance, and other factors affecting peace and security in the region to assure that "the deterrent to North Korean aggression remains strong." In addition, the Congress, in providing authorization for the transfer of military equipment, established a requirement for assuring that withdrawal can be accomplished with minimum risk. Specifically, the Congressional authorization stated:

(d) The President should also transmit to the Congress, 120 days prior to each phase of troop withdrawal, a report on the viability of the withdrawal. This report should include assessments of the military balance on the Korean Peninsula, the impact of withdrawal on the military balance, the adequacy of United States military assistance to the Republic of Korea command structure, Republic of Korea defensive fortifications and defense industry development, the United States reinforcement capability and the progress of diplomatic efforts to reduce tension in the area.

(e) (1) It is the sense of the Congress that further withdrawal of ground forces of the United States from the Republic of Korea may seriously risk upsetting the military balance in that region and requires full advance consultation with the Congress.

(2) Prior to any further withdrawal, the President shall report to the Congress on the effect of any proposed withdrawal plan on preserving deterrence in Korea, the reaction anticipated from North Korea, the effect of the plan on increasing incentives for the Republic of Korea to develop an independent nuclear deterrent, the effect of any withdrawal on our long-term military and economic partnership with Japan, the effect of any proposed withdrawal on the United States-Chinese and United States-Soviet military balance, and the possible implications of any proposed withdrawal on the Soviet-Chinese military situation.[7]

On July 20, 1979, after President Carter had visited Korea, the combination of local Asian concerns, increasing Congressional pressures, and the new assessment of larger North Korean military strength led President Carter to reverse his ground force withdrawal decision. The July 20 Presidential announcement stated that the further withdrawal of the Second Division is "to remain in abeyance," and that some support units, including the I-Hawk Air Defense Battalion, will depart Korea, but further withdrawal will be examined in 1981 taking into account not only the North-South military balance but progress toward a reduction of tensions on the Korean Peninsula. Three considerations were cited as the basis for the decision: (1) the new estimates of North Korean military strength; (2) U.S.-ROK plans to seek negotiations with the North announced during the Carter visit; and (3) the need to reassure American allies in Asia, given the growth of Soviet military power and "conflict and new uncertainties in Southeast Asia."

The announcement suspending the troop withdrawals is significant in two respects: for recognizing the psychological aspects of deterrence, specifically the need

---

[7] *Conference Report on International Security Assistance Act of 1978*, U.S. House of Representatives Report No. 95-1546, Sec. 23, September 7, 1978.

to avoid conveying misleading impressions to the North, and for linking further reduction not only to the military balance but also to "a reduction of tensions" on the Peninsula. The critical U.S. role in the deterrence equation is not only preserved but strengthened by the July 1979 decision; and hopefully the process of erosion of Asian confidence in the U.S. security commitment will be reversed.

Japan

Japan's role in the deterrence equation is far less direct than that of either the United States or South Korea, but not much less vital. The Japanese do not contribute military forces to the defense of Korea and should not be expected to do so in the foreseeable future. The memories of the past are still too vivid for Korea to welcome a direct Japanese military role, even if Japan were prepared to undertake such a mission. On the other hand, Japan not only has an important stake in continuing stability on the Korean Peninsula, it also has by its policies the means to undermine the deterrence equation. Japan has several positive roles to play in Korean security. First and foremost, it provides a base structure (for air, naval, and logistics forces) that is essential to the support of the U.S. military forces in Korea. Various understandings provide for this support; and Prime Minister Sato, in the Okinawa Reversion Settlement, accepted the vital importance of Korea to Japan's security and affirmed Japan's preparedness to respond promptly and positively when consulted on use of bases in defense of Korea. Second, Japan can provide positive intelligence and logistic support to South Korean forces. Third, Japan's ability to control its communist-leaning Korean population is potentially critical. Finally, Japan's economic support for and relationship with the ROK plays a positive role in South Korea's overall security position.

For the future, Japan's continuing political support for the ROK will be required, particularly in avoidance of the temptation to succumb to North Korean lures. Also, trade issues between South Korea and Japan are likely to become more complex and potentially disruptive. Finally, Japan might take a larger and more direct role in deterrence throught the provision of weapons or defense-related equipment if its own defense inhibitions soften. But the fundamental factor will be Japan's willingness to provide all support short of military forces to the broad deterrence equation.

Other Deterrent Factors

As has been noted, while the United States can exercise a large measure of positive control over both its own and ROK capabilities, it has no such control over the roles of the PRC and the USSR and the effectiveness of the truce-keeping machinery. These factors can be influenced by U.S. actions, but the decisions rest basically in the hands of the North Koreans, the Soviets, and the Chinese.

Over the years, both the PRC and the USSR have exercised restraint over North Korea's aggressive tendencies for reasons of their own national interest. Particularly at the present time, renewed conflict in Korea would greatly disrupt China's plans for economic modernization. Chinese relations with the West and the United States have priority over support for North Korean goals, and stability in East Asia generally serves Chinese interests. Vice-Premier Deng Xiaoping (Teng Hsiao-p'ing) made this goal abundantly clear in his travels to Japan and Southeast

Asia in late 1978. Similarly, the Soviet Union has no apparent wish to undermine the SALT talks or prospects for détente with the United States which would likely result from active support for North Korean aggressiveness. Furthermore, neither the Soviet Union nor the PRC wishes to devote the major resources necessary to support a conflict in Korea, given their concerns about each other and competing resource demands from their own economies and military establishments. Their willingness to cooperate and support North Korea in a conflict would be at most minimal.

As a consequence, both the Soviet Union and the PRC exercise a degree of restraint upon the North. Following the shooting down of an American EC-121 aircraft in the spring of 1969, the Soviets sent a high-level delegation to Pyongyang with very clear indications that its mission was to warn the North Koreans not to attempt further tests of America's willingness to fulfill its commitment to the ROK, despite its preoccupation with the Vietnam War. The Chinese exercised similar restraint in April 1975 when Kim Il-sung visited Beijing. Kim arrived in the Chinese capital trumpeting the call for unification without qualifications, apparently looking for support for military action against South Korea and a United States that was weak and divided by the Vietnam War. The Chinese responded by pointedly emphasizing *peaceful* unification and encouraging Kim to focus his effects on broadening support in the non-aligned bloc where Beijing presumably expected him to be discouraged from a military adventure. The only concession made by the Chinese was the acceptance of the North as the sole legitimate government of Korea, an honor previously reserved for the South in successive U.N. resolutions.

More recently, Deng Xiaoping, during visits to Tokyo in the fall of 1978 and Washington in January 1979, sought to alleviate any anxiety regarding North Korean intentions. The Soviets have shown their restraint by repeatedly failing to parrot the North Korean line and by stressing the need for *peaceful* unification. During the 1976 tree-cutting incident, both the Soviet Union and the PRC were very careful not to endorse in any way the North Korean action. During the negotiations of the Military Armistice Commission (MAC) regarding the new arrangements for the Joint Security Area, the Chinese raised the level of their representation on the MAC and made apparent their interest in a quick settlement of the issue.

The United States has a limited capability for influencing Beijing and Moscow by emphasizing its concerns over potential conflict on the Korean Peninsula and its intention to fulfill its commitment to the South. Efforts by the United States to maintain a significant and visible deterrent also provide the USSR and the PRC with the necessary rationale to warn North Korea not to challenge or test the United States. Both possess the intelligence capabilities that the North lacks to provide information on the actual and potential retaliatory power of the United States, reinforcing Pyongyang's concerns. By the same token, plans for U.S. force withdrawals could have worked negatively in terms of the capability of the communist powers to restrain the North.

Both Moscow and Beijing have, however, established the fact that their influence over the North is limited. While they have been active in restraining Kim Il-sung's proclivities for offensive actions, they have clearly made no effort to pressure him to adopt measures that would reduce tensions and stabilize North-South relations. The Chinese could, for example, play a more active role in supervising the Armistice. Kim Il-sung would undoubtedly resist such pressures to the point of turning his back on whichever of his allies exercised them. Neither Moscow nor Beijing seems willing to risk such alienation at the present time.

The weakest link in the deterrence equation is the current U.N. peace-keeping machinery under the Armistice Agreement. Most of the provisions of the Armistice Agreement are either inoperative, violated, or ignored. The DMZ is impregnated by major military installations on both sides, including hardened fortifications; joint inspection of incidents is rejected by the North; even the military demarcation line is poorly marked, raising the danger of patrols from both sides drifting across the boundary. The Chinese have adopted an inactive, observer role in this area.

The Final Balance on Deterrence

The prospects for Korean peace in the 1980s depend upon maintaining the deterrence equation and calculating the variables in it. For example, a further withdrawal of American ground forces would have reduced the capacity of the USSR and the PRC to restrain the North and necessitated the strengthening of ROK forces. On the other hand, plans for a major buildup of South Korean forces could likewise unbalance the equation, providing the North with a rationale for seeking far greater support from its allies, particularly in the form advanced weapons systems for defense, if not for a preemptive strike against the South.

Should South Korea decide to develop its own damage-inflicting deterrent force with advanced missiles and nuclear warheads, the deterrence equation would very likely be destabilized. The North might choose to launch a preemptive strike at the very moment when U.S.-ROK relations would have deteriorated over the proliferation issue and before the South had fully developed its own deterrent capability.

The interrelationships between the domestic defense industries of both North and South Korea and external sources of military support are another key element in the equation. Denial of weapons systems to the South places greater obligation on the United States to maintain such systems in the ROK under its unilateral control, thus potentially constraining the U.S. capability to reduce its forces.

With the many uncertainties in the deterrence equation, stability in the military balance between North and South in the 1980s is by no means assured. The equation is bound to change, if only as a result of South Korean military modernization, the continued North Korean buildup, and anticipated pressures from both Koreas on their allies for more sophisticated weaponry. The United States will face a series of critical decisions whose implications for other factors in the deterrence equation will need careful evaluation. The most basic decision, as discussed earlier, concerns the plans for withdrawing all or part of the remaining elements of the Second Division, which are now held in abeyance until 1981. A failure of the North to negotiate any reduction in tensions, which must be assumed for the present, will raise questions as to whether the United States should give up a negotiating card by withdrawing even if a military balance between North and South is attained.

Other key decisions relate to the transfer of more sophisticated military equipment: the level of total U.S. sales, given present overall global limits, and the degree of support for the South's defense industry. Just as important will be decisions relating to the priority Korea is given in overall U.S. relationships with the PRC and the USSR; and to how much emphasis the United States should place on the need for Sino-Soviet measures, taken separately, to restrain North Korea and to pressure it to accept measures that would stabilize North-South relations. In this connection, the prospects for increasing South Korean economic and military strength might convince the communist powers that it would be to their advantage to maintain Korean security in the 1980s by greater restraint on the North and by new steps to reduce tensions. Or those powers might consider their interests sufficiently threatened by the South Korean buildup to give the North more leeway for action.

Perhaps the greatest uncertainty in the deterrence equation is North Korea's reaction to its economic and technological deficiences. While the North has the capacity to improve its defense capabilities in the short term and maintain a clear military superiority over the South, its longer-term prospects are far less favorable. During the 1980s, the greater and growing economic power of the South and its technological advantages provide the basis for gradually developing military superiority over the North. The crossover point could occur by the mid to late 1980s. The closer the crossover point gets, the less latitude the North has to defer a decision on its course of action.

Thus, U.S. decisions on force reduction and arms supply must take full account of the uncertainty regarding long-term North Korean policy. The deferral of withdrawal plans and a judicious strengthening of South Korean military capabilities without tipping the deterrence equation too rapidly in favor of the South are likely to force an earlier decision by the North and render unacceptably costly the option of a preemptive strike. The prospects for a reduction in tensions should likewise increase if Soviet support were made conditional upon a reallocation of domestic North Korean resources from military to economic goals. The 1980s, therefore, are likely to see significant changes in the deterrence equation, resulting from the strengthening of the South and from new policy decisions forced upon the North. The United States has within its capability the power to influence these changes and to increase the prospects for a more stable and secure situation in Korea.

BEYOND DETERRENCE: THE NEGOTIATING ALTERNATIVE

Past Efforts at Negotiation

The choice in Korea lies essentially between preserving the military balance in a manner that deters conflict or seeking to stabilize the current division of the country via political measures in a manner that reduces tensions between North and South. When the Armistice Agreement was signed in 1953, it provided that a political conference would be arranged to negotiate a final settlement endorsed by the U.N. General Assembly. The goals of the conference were to be negotiation of a final peace treaty and unification of Korea. Neither objective has been achieved, and over the years a wide variety of negotiating efforts have proved fruitless.

The history of international negotiating efforts on Korea dates from the Geneva Conference in 1954. The Geneva Conference was called as a result of an agreement between the Big Four foreign ministers reached at Berlin on February 18, 1954, to convene a meeting of the participants in the Korean War, including representatives of both the Soviet Union and the PRC. The conference broke down when it became clear that there was no basis for consensus on either unification of Korea or a peaceful settlement of the Korean question.

Negotiations subsequently took place at the Mixed Armistice Commission and at the United Nations. The Armistice Commission sought to enforce the terms of the Armistice Agreement, including control over the introduction of weapons into Korea and monitoring the DMZ. It failed to implement most of the provisions of the Agreement, although it did prove useful in settling a few major disputes.

Negotiations relating to unification of Korea took place at the United Nations, where the Korean item was a major Cold War issue in successive General Assembly sessions for many years. Prior to 1975, a resolution favoring South Korea was able to achieve majority support, but that majority gradually shrank. In 1975, two resolutions were passed, one supporting the South and the other supporting the North's position. Until the early 1970s, the General Assembly supported the position that South Korea was the sole legitimate government on the Peninsula and would not recognize the existence of two Koreas. Efforts to bring the ROK alone into the United Nations were frustrated by the Soviet veto, while earlier Soviet efforts to bring in the two Koreas were frustrated by the United States, under pressure from the ROK. In 1971, however, the ROK switched its position and accepted the temporary existence of two Koreas and dual admission into the United Nations. But by this time, the Soviet Union, the PRC, and North Korea refused to accept the admission of both Koreas.

The U.N. experience was an exercise in frustration, requiring increasing amounts of diplomatic pressure on the part of the United States, the ROK, and the West to maintain even a bare majority in support of the South. It proved largely unsuccessful in advancing the prospects for peace and unification, and was largely a divisive Cold War exercise, with the sole exception of a consensus resolution introduced with Chinese support in 1973 abolishing UNCURK[8] and urging various steps to reduce tension.

The Korean issue has been dropped by the General Assembly for the past three years, relieving some nations of the need to press for votes and others of the need to make choices they wished to avoid. Abstention was clearly welcomed by the neutral nations.

In 1975, the United States proposed a four-power conference of the two Koreas, the PRC, and the United States as a forum for resolution of the Korean issue and a step toward stabilizing the status quo and reducing tensions on the Peninsula. This proposal was summarily rejected by North Korea and the PRC.

Various intermediaries have since sought to arrange talks in Korea, as well as trying to convince North Korea to look to the German formula as a model for Korea. Former Prime Minister Bhutto of Pakistan and Prime Minister Ceaucescu of Romania pushed for a two-power, U.S.-North Korean conference in talks with the United States. President Tito of Yugoslavia tried to advance a three-power meeting, which the North never accepted. East German Chairman Honnecker during a visit to Pyongyang suggested trying the two-Germany formula, but this concept was rejected by Pyongyang. The North, in turn, has been pushing its own proposal for bilateral U.S.-North Korean talks that would not include the ROK. All of these efforts to resolve the Korean issue, however, have failed.

The most recent international negotiating initiative was launched during President Carter's visit to Seoul, when the United States and the ROK proposed trilateral talks among senior officials of the United States and both Koreas "to seek means

---

[8] The United Nations Commission on the Unification and Rehabilitation of Korea.

to promote dialogue and reduce tensions in the area." Trilateral talks had been opposed in the past by the South. Despite some optimism in Washington, based in part on U.N. Secretary-General Waldheim's talks in Pyongyang during the late spring, North Korea rejected the proposal as "utterly infeasible," sticking to its refusal to accept the South as an equal participant in negotiations on a peace agreement.

The other major negotiating approach has been direct talks between the two Koreas. In 1971, negotiations commenced at the Red Cross level and then moved on to the political level, resulting in the July 4, 1972, joint declaration. This joint statement sought a basis for reunifying Korea by peaceful means, without outside interference. It also established the North-South coordinating committee at a senior level, set up a "hot line" between Seoul and Pyongyang, and promoted Red Cross talks between the two sides. A series of meetings through 1972, 1973, and 1974, however, made it clear that a basis for agreement on substantive issues was lacking in a direct North-South forum. The South proposed moving ahead with small, limited steps that would build confidence and lead to a broader basis for unification; the North sought to establish a political framework that would create opportunities for influencing South Korean politics and undermining the status of the Seoul government. At the present time, the "hot line" is closed, but North-South talks have been resumed at the initiative of the late President Park. No evident results have emerged to date.

North Korea has exerted continuing pressure for reunification on terms that would greatly advance its own interests, while the South has been willing to accept, for the present, a division of the two Koreas. The South has proposed humanitarian measures for exchanging information on families and for developing some minor forms of social contact between North and South; the North has rejected these— probably to maintain its population's isolation from and ignorance of the South. The North-South talks seemed to arouse defensive reactions in both Pyongyang and Seoul. Apparently the Northern representatives were shocked by the relative material advancement of the South and were concerned that their people would become aware of the higher standard of livng achieved in the ROK. The South apparently was concerned about the higher degree of discipline and control found in the North and feared that dissidence and disunity in the South might create opportunities for manipulation and subversive actions by Pyongyang. The ROK Yushin Constitutional Revision of 1972, which strengthened the authority of the President, may have been influenced by this concern.

The frustrations resulting from both international negotiating efforts and the bilateral North-South talks have brought virtually all negotiating efforts to a halt for the moment. Given the slim prospects for meaningful negotiations and the wide gap between the two Koreas, none of the larger powers accords a very high priority to Korean negotiations, although both Pyongyang and Seoul are apparently willing to sustain bilateral exchanges in order to avoid being accused of opposing negotiations. The United States has left the door open for a change in the North's position on trilateral talks but apparently is not pushing its proposal.

Future Prospects for Negotiations

The failure over the past twenty-five years to reach a stable basis for peace and to reduce tensions on the Korean Peninsula leaves scant cause for optimism about the future. The inherent potential for renewed conflict produces a constant search for a military balance sufficient to deter hostilities, but South Korea is increasingly dynamic and productive in terms of military capabilities. The arms race will continue, with new prospects for employment of weapons with sophisticated technology and increasing strength of both the North and South armed forces, with the United States continuing to play the crucial balancing role in local deterrence. Unless agreements are negotiated, the DMZ will remain one of the most dangerous borders on the globe, with the increasing risk that renewed conflict will be difficult to localize, given the important national interests of the four major powers in Korea; however, the maintenance of Korean peace may be enhanced by the very fear that a local conflict would inevitably enmesh the concerned outside powers. The framework for future negotiations needs to be considered from various viewpoints: appropriate negotiating channels; the substantive issues involved; and possible incentives for agreement.

Negotiating Channels. Almost every possible forum for negotiations between North and South Korea has been attempted or proposed. In fact, recent proposals for negotiations have focused too much on the negotiating channels and too little on the substantive issues involved. If the political conditions for negotiations are favorable, the type of forum selected for discussions is of only secondary importance as long as the parties concerned, particularly the two Koreas, have confidence that the negotiating channel is not designed to undermine their interests.

There are three major substantive issues for negotiation: (1) negotiations relating to the reduction of North-South military tensions and the balance of forces on the Peninsula; (2) negotiations relating to North-South social contact and interrelationships; and (3) negotiations relating to the role of the outside powers in the affairs of Korea. Different forums are appropriate for each of these issues.

Negotiations on military tensions must involve at least those powers having military forces on the Korean Peninsula now or in the past. The logical forum is the MAC, in which all are represented. Beyond its role in pacifying incidents, the MAC is largely ignored except for initiatives for tension reduction generated by the U.S. (U.N.) Commander, with no supporting diplomatic efforts. Yet the MAC's role in developing and enforcing measures to reduce military tension along the DMZ will be critical. A serious initiative to reduce tensions, however, will need not only formal negotiations by the MAC but a full panoply of other diplomatic actions to buttress these negotiations in the capitals of the major powers, as well as steps to develop broad international support, including support within the Third World. The U.N. Command has in fact made a number of proposals in the MAC, including proposals to make more effective use of the Neutral Nations Supervisory Commission (NNSC), which would ease the potential for conflict in Korea. Such MAC-originated proposals are likely to have no effect unless they are part of a broader negotiating effort and unless the North is prepared to participate seriously, under pressure from the PRC and the Soviet Union.

The second substantive area for negotiation, North-South bilateral relations, logically should continue to be left to the two parties concerned. The North-South Coordinating Committee and Red Cross talks are still in effect, and other private channels are also available. Nevertheless, impetus and support for effective negotiations on the part of the North depend on Beijing and Moscow. The South has demonstrated its willingness to keep open the bilateral Korean channel and to probe for meaningful North-South negotiations, so future prospects rest with the North. In September 1978 Kim Il-sung left the door open to a resumption of a North-South dialogue, but he still attaches political conditions amounting to acceptance of his premises for unification. He is currently demanding talks between representatives of political parties rather than of governments, in an effort to buttress his policy of reunification through an all-party structure—a policy loading the dice in the North's favor.

The final negotiating area relates to the future roles of the outside powers in Korean security. Any agreements effecting a reduction of tensions will necessarily involve the outside powers, either directly or indirectly; and a whole range of issues—cross-recognition, admission of the two Koreas to the U.N., and new arrangements replacing the Armistice Agreement—will require direct participation by the outside powers.

Under present circumstances, any formal negotiations involving the interested powers look infeasible. The Chinese are likely to continue to reject a four-power proposal, since it would put them at a disadvantage vis-à-vis the Soviet Union with respect to North Korea. Five- or six-power talks including both the PRC and the USSR also seem unlikely, given the present state of Sino-Soviet relations. Even more unpromising is any revival of the U.N. General Assembly debate on Korea, given its past record and the membership's disinclination to become involved with Cold War issues. Finally, revival of the Geneva Conference is not likely to be an acceptable forum for dealing with Korean issues.

North Korea has proposed a negotiating format involving North-South talks on matters relating to the internal affairs of Korea and U.S.-North Korean bilateral negotiations on external matters, e.g., a peace treaty and withdrawal of U.S. forces. The proposal has some superficial attraction for the United States; for example, it might permit an extensive probing of the North's position, affording an avenue for influencing the North to negotiate seriously and change its basic stance on unification. But there is no evidence to support this view, and clear evidence exists that the North sees bilateral talks as a propaganda move according it greater prestige, placing the South at a disadvantage and adding a significant new divisive element to U.S.-ROK relations. Such talks would, moreover, justify the North's claims to sole legitimacy and arouse not-too-latent Southern fears of an American sell-out of its interests. The memory of U.S.-North Vietnamese negotiations is still fresh in ROK minds, and under these circumstances, whatever advantages might accrue from bilateral U.S.-North Korean talks are heavily outweighed by the disadvantages.

Assuming a desire on the part of North Korea to negotiate, the U.N. Security Council may be the more feasible channel. Chinese and Soviet membership in the Security Council provides a convenient cover for discussions with both, and private talks could be initiated under a Security Council guise. In the last analysis, however, any engagement of the outside powers in Korean negotiations must commence with private bilateral talks between the United States and the USSR and the United States and the PRC. Given the involvement of both communist powers in Korea and the unlikelihood of drawing them into joint discussions, parallel discussions with both the PRC and the USSR on measures to reduce Korean tensions are an essential starting point, even if negotiations and agreements should later be formalized in a broader forum such as the Security Council. The role of

Japan is likely to be peripheral, although Tokyo may be helpful in fostering an atmosphere favorable to negotiation.

Substance of Negotiations and Agreements. The range of issues open for negotiation is very wide, given the broad differences now prevalent, but the substantive issues can be broken down into three categories: (1) measures to reduce the level of military tension between North and South; (2) measures to stabilize a temporary two-Korea arrangement; (3) agreement on wider measures, such as a peace treaty or steps to unify Korea.

Measures for reducing military tension. The risks of conflict, whether calculated or accidental, are greatly increased by the close proximity of the two opposing forces within and along the DMZ. Measures to lessen this risk could start with demarcation of the line dividing the two zones, since patrols move constantly within the DMZ. Other measures could include firm agreements on procedures for investigating incidents and for direct and immediate communications at the outbreak of incidents, and on use of the NNSC in the control and investigation of incidents. A measure of greater significance would be the demilitarization of the DMZ, lessening the risk of incidents and providing a measure of deterrence against surprise attack. Even greater security would be attained by broadening the DMZ and establishing an international force within it, in the pattern of the Sinai peace force. Even the enforcement of Armistice Agreement provisions for the DMZ, however, would be a major step toward tension reduction.

Serious efforts to reduce tension would require participation of the political leadership of the outside powers, even though negotiation *per se* would be by the Armistice Commission. The problem in reaching agreement on these measures lies in their inherent disadvantage to the potential agressor and in past North Korean opposition. But the South is also likely to resist steps to demilitarize the DMZ, in view of past North Korean disregard of agreements on the DMZ and the greater difficulty the South faces in reciprocating Northern actions in violation of agreements.

Another potential area for reducing military tension is control over arms transfers. The Armistice Agreement provides for such control, including supervision by the NNSC. These provisions were flagrantly violated by the Soviet Union in the years immediately following the Korean War, and there is consequently little basis for attempting to reinstate them. The North Koreans are unlikely to give the NNSC the freedom of movement necessary to effect proper supervision of arms imported into Korea.

On the other hand, there have been *de facto* limitations on both sides regarding arms importations. The North Koreans have received an ample supply of ground weapons, including FROG 7 missiles, air defense systems, and technology for submarine and high-speed attack boats, but they have not received any advanced aircraft and have reportedly complained bitterly of Soviet refusal to provide MiG-23s. The United States has also limited the flow of high-technology weapons such as Lance missiles and other longer-range attack missile systems. Moreover, both Koreas have been clearly warned against efforts to develop nuclear weapons systems. These limitations have led to suspicions that an implicit agreement is already in effect to limit the flow of high-technology weapons to either Korea, but the evidence is far from convincing inasmuch as both the Soviet Union and the PRC have provided North Korea with the weaponry to constitute a viable offensive capacity, and South Korea has developed the scientific manpower and industrial base to develop nuclear and other high-technology weapons.

The question for the future is whether the current unilateral limitations can be expanded upon, either through an explicit agreement or through implicit arrangements clearly understood by the outside powers and developed through a process of discussion that falls short of specific agreement. Conventional arms control measures are now being discussed by the United States and the USSR, and these could conceivably include Korea.

Any arms control agreements would have several shortcomings. First, such agreements have tended in the past to be more binding on the United States than on the USSR or the PRC, and violations are far easier to detect in South Korea. Second, an agreement—implicit or explicit—to limit certain types of weapons, such as advanced aircraft, might not necessarily stabilize the North-South military balance. The Koreans, in fact, place too much emphasis on "mirror imaging"—i.e., if the North has submarines, the South feels it must duplicate this force. As stated earlier, the structure of the two forces is not comparable, since the North focuses on an offensive ground attack capability and air defense, while the South Korean mission is defense supplemented by the U.S. deterrent. Different weapons systems are required to match these missions, and parallel restrictions on weapons imports might conceivably lead the South to focus on an offensive mission. Third, both Koreas have domestic defense industries capable of expansion, but the North Korean industry now is far advanced and can only be balanced by arms imports to the South. In the longer term, the balance could shift to the South, with its industrial and technology advantages. Finally, a U.S.-Soviet agreement fails to take account of other arms suppliers. South Korea has both the requisite foreign exchange and the access to other suppliers who are anxious to gain markets there; North Korea indeed may have indirect access through the sale of Western arms to the PRC. A U.S.-Soviet arms control arrangement would not be feasible or reliable among such a large group of suppliers, and there is even more doubt whether an explicit arrangement including both the PRC and the USSR would be possible.

Nevertheless, the problem of arms control is likely to become acute as both sides move to more technologically sophisticated weapons. The only feasible approach may be the present one, in which both Koreas and their international backers exercise restraint, bearing in mind the different missions of the two forces.

Measures for stabilizing the two-Korea division. While any steps to reduce military tension on the Korean Peninsula will have the inherent effect of stabilizing the current status quo, there are a variety of non-military measures that could achieve the same objective.

One means might be revival of the "hot line" and reactivation of the North-South Coordinating Committee and the Red Cross committees. Further efforts would include establishing preliminary contacts that would involve exchanges of information on locations of families, exchanges of mail, and, perhaps at a later date, limited movement between the two Koreas. The July 4, 1972, agreement also called for a moratorium on propaganda, which could be revived. More extensive relations would involve trade between the two Koreas, and possibly some form of mutual representation at their capitals, as well as more extensive movement between them. Clearly, the broader the interrelationship, the more likely it will be resisted by North Korea, and quite possibly by the ROK, given the growing differences in the economic growth and prosperity of the two zones and the mutual suspicion that exists between them. The South Korean policy of inviting members of the pro-North Korean group in Japan for "family visits" is aimed at the North's concern with exposure to the South. But by the same token, South Korea has found the mutual ability of both sides to utilize any contact to infiltrate and influence their respective populaces unbalanced in favor of the North.

Given the problem of mutual suspicion, the conflicting ideological bases of the two regimes, and the growing gap in living standards, North-South interrelationships can probably develop only very slowly and step by step. The South has offered economic assistance to the North, but acceptance of this aid would constitute a concession of defeat in economic competition, which the North is not likely to agree to. By the same token, exchanges that would expose too much of the North's population to the progress of the South are likely to be resisted by the North because of their potentially discordant effects. The South would likewise be hesitant to permit many North Koreans into its area for fear of subversive activities. Yet such steps might be acceptable as part of a broader effort to reduce tensions and achieve a two-Korea accommodation.

The outside powers can substantially influence the stabilization of the status quo by their willingness to act in parallel, if independently, to provide either formal or *de facto* recognition of the two Koreas, and by their mutual willingness to enter into direct relationships with both sides. North Korea, through its observer delegation to the United Nations, already has a base of operations within the United States. South Korea has no comparable situation within the communist orbit, but the Soviet Union has recently become more liberal in permitting South Korean delegations to participate in international conferences and events within its borders. The first visit by a South Korean cabinet minister to a communist country was that of the Minister of Health, who attended a World Health Organization conference in the Soviet Union in 1978. The 1980 Olympics will require the Soviet Union to permit a much larger group of South Koreans to visit, unless the Soviets violate the rules of the game. South Korean contacts with representatives of the PRC have been reported on a very informal basis, but the PRC is much more circumspect, given its preferred position with the North and its determination not to give Moscow an opening in Pyongyang. At the present time, neither the PRC nor the Soviet Union is prepared for any more extensive contacts.

Should the Soviet Union and the PRC choose to move into broader contact with the South or accept a process of cross-recognition, in which they would recognize South Korea and the United States and Japan would recognize the North, there is very little the North Koreans could do to inhibit them. The critical factor would be the willingness of both the PRC and the USSR to move in parallel courses so that neither would feel that the other had any advantage in terms of its position in Pyongyang. At present, Soviet moves in this direction seem designed to warn the North that the Soviet Union may have other options, rather than to serve as a considered process of cross-recognition. Formal recognition could also conceivably be preceded by an opening of commercial relationships, perhaps on a triangular basis to avoid direct trade (as is possible now), then later permitting direct bilateral trade.

Membership of the two Koreas in the United Nations may be a more remote goal, although it could flow directly from a process of formal cross-recognition. The two Germanys have established a precedent for such action, of which North Korea is now painfully aware. Kim Il-sung has gone out of his way, in fact, to reject this formula for Korea. During a visit by East German Prime Minister Honnecker to Pyongyang in early 1978 (which may well have been prompted by the Soviet Union in order to encourage adoption of the two-Germany formula), Kim forcefully rejected any parallelism between Germany and Korea, calling advocates of two Koreas "splitists." It is conceivable but not likely that membership of two Koreas in the United Nations, if approved by the Security Council, could precede cross-recognition, since it would ensure the type of parallelism that seems important in terms of Soviet and Chinese moves with respect to Korea.

In sum, the potential for progress toward stabilization of the two Koreas may lie more in developing arrangements among the outside powers than through a process of North-South talks.

More permanent solutions to the Korean problem. Prospects for unification of Korea or arrangements that would give a degree of permanence to the division between North and South are presently remote. The replacement of the Armistice Agreement by a peace treaty between the two Koreas along with a non-aggression pact and guarantees of security would seem to require a willingness to accept an indefinite division, and North Korea does not have that willingness. The goal of unification must be kept alive. South Korea has proposed a non-aggression agreement between the two Koreas, but this is likewise unlikely to come into effect because it gives a sense of permanence to the division, which is presently unacceptable to Pyongyang.

On the other hand, the North has pressed for unification through political measures, which would have the effect of legitimizing North Korean-sponsored opposition within the South without any reciprocity or hopes of a fair vote in the North. Efforts have been made by the United Nations to unify the area on terms essentially advantageous to the South, but these seem to hold very little promise of being acceptable to the North either now or in the indefinite future.

In sum, efforts that go beyond stabilizing the status quo seem unlikely to be acceptable at the present time. Neither unification nor permanent division is a viable negotiating objective.

Incentives for Negotiation. At the present time, the principal obstacle to any negotiating strategy is North Korea, which professes concern regarding South Korea, given the South's economic potential. Some of this concern may be legitimate, although the argument conveniently serves North Korean propaganda interests. North Korea sees any steps that would stabilize and solidify the division as a threat to its ambitions to achieve the downfall of the Seoul government and the unification of Korea on its own political terms—in effect, absorption within the communist system.

Neither the Soviet Union nor the PRC is prepared to press North Korea to accept any changes in the current situation, but both have indicated that they are prepared to discourage the North from military efforts to change the status quo in its favor. Neither wishes to further advantage the other, although the Soviet Union has moved to the point of developing limited contacts with South Korea.

The PRC presently has the predominant position of influence in the North, and it now has an even greater incentive to preserve that position, because of the close ties between the USSR and Vietnam and the hostility of the surrounding communist states (Laos and the People's Republic of Mongolia), with the exception of North Korea. The North clearly feels more comfortable with the Chinese than with the Soviets, if only on racial grounds, but it has also pointedly preserved its independence even from Chinese influence. The Soviet Union, on the other hand, has more freedom to maneuver and has done so. But neither power has sufficient incentive to pressure the North to adopt a fundamental revision of its policies, and both see unacceptable risks to their interests from doing so.

The political problem, therefore, is how to create a structure of incentives for both North Korea and its supporters to negotiate.

Recent history has demonstrated that crisis situations tend to force countries to face the need for a more solid basis for their security. A renewed Korean crisis that threatened resumption of hostilities might provide just the incentive necessary for the Soviet Union, the PRC, and North Korea to stabilize the situation. There are, in fact, a number of possible sources of crisis in Korea—for example, a North Korean-inspired incident to test the U.S. defense commitment, leadership succession problems in both the North and the South, or mischief-making by the Soviet Union. Continued adverse economic trends could also create a crisis in North Korean leadership.

There are distinct, and unacceptable, risks to developing and provoking a crisis scenario that is sufficiently alarming to motivate a change in communist policies. The major risk is obviously that the crisis situation might not be contained and hostilities would break out. On the other hand, if a crisis situation did arise as a result of an escalation of incidents along the DMZ or in Korean waters, the outside powers might have sufficient motivation to reduce tensions in the region. The tree-cutting incident of 1976 mentioned earlier had such a limited effect and produced arrangements reducing the risk of incidents within the Joint Security Area at Panmunjom.

Internal developments within North Korea may give the Soviet Union and the PRC increased leverage over North Korean policies. It is evident that North Korea has strained its resources to the limit in order to support its military establishment and at the same time keep its civilian economy going. It faces heavy external debt, with virtually no resources to invest in economic development. It also has serious internal problems, including shortages of power, transportation, and manpower; and its capabilities for domestic production of military equipment may be increasingly constrained by its lack of access to advanced technologies. In effect, North Korea, which has prided itself on its ability to maintain its independence, is likely to become more dependent upon its outside supporters, both for economic assistance and for higher levels of military and industrial technology. The North Korean dilemma will be further aggravated by the South's growing economic and military strength, as discussed above.

These prospective developments could provide both the communist powers and the United States with leverage over North Korean policy. On the communist side, the Soviet Union is likely to have the predominant leverage, since it has both the greater economic resources and the advanced technology required by the North, and it has less to lose by an initiative, given its subordinate position in the North. The PRC could influence Pyongyang through its provision of economic assistance, petroleum, and weapons, but it is far less likely to take any initiative.

American leverage in this situation can work in two directions. First, the ease with which the South can acquire new technology could influence the North, forcing it into a more dependent relationship with the PRC and the USSR. This situation would provide North Korea with a greater incentive to seek to reduce the potential South Korean threat and improve its own relative position. In this context, stabilizing the status quo might be viewed as an advantage to the North, rather than to the South. Paradoxically, this scenario would probably result in North Korean pressures on the United States to retain ground forces in the South as a control against aggressive tendencies emanating from Seoul.

Major U.S. leverage is also likely to rest with the priority it attaches to the Korean situation, particularly should the bailout of North Korea become an imminent prospect for both the PRC and the USSR. If both Moscow and Beijing believed that their overall relationship with the United States would be affected by their actions with respect to North Korea, and if both also viewed the growing relative strength of the South as an increasing threat to the North, they could be motivated to stabilize the division.

Another potential incentive for the North to alter its policies rests with the level and status of U.S. forces in South Korea, and their effect on tensions in the region. There is no doubt that the North attaches the highest priority to the withdrawal of all U.S. forces, not only ground forces but also air assets, which have recently been strengthened. North Korea has exhibited great sensitivity to the nuclear potential of the U.S. forces in Korea. The Carter Administration has been criticized for not exacting a reciprocal price from the North for its initial decision to withdraw U.S. ground troops, given the North's urgent desire for that action. The linkage to North Korea's actions established in the July 1979 decision to suspend troop withdrawal opens the way to use this leverage.

Finally, a broader and more intangible incentive for Moscow and Beijing lies in the effect of tension reduction in Korea on the broader international environment, particularly in the Asian region. Both powers have a stake in maintaining peace and stability in Korea, if only in terms of their competitive and conflicting interests. Both likewise have a stake in improving their relations with the United States. Up to the present time, the United States has not accorded a very high priority to Korea in its broader relationships with either the Soviet Union or the PRC, but according a higher priority to Korea's role in East Asian stability might give the communist powers increased incentive to modify their North Korean policies. The linkage between Korean stabilization and normalization of U.S. relations with the PRC is an important consideration. While the Chinese have limited flexibility in pressuring the North to reduce tensions, they must also understand that an expected dividend from U.S. support of China's modernization plans is the creation of stability in East Asia, with Korea being an initial test.

CONCLUSION

At the present time, the prospects for reducing tensions on the Korean Peninsula through a negotiating process cannot be considered promising. Neither North Korea nor its Soviet and Chinese allies have reached the point where a reversal of policy seems dictated. Pyongyang remains adamant in opposing a two-Korea accommodation, and its allies are not prepared to press for a change in its policy. But the balance in Korea during the 1980s will increasingly shift toward the South, and even the current prospects for North Korean military superiority may vanish. The growing economic and technological superiority of the South will present the North with even slimmer prospects for achieving unification on its own terms. In fact, a role reversal, with the South pressing for unification and the North supporting a divided status quo, is not inconceivable.

Sooner or later, Pyongyang must face up to the changing situation on the Korean Peninsula and recognize the need to change its policy of unification, priority for military investment over civilian economic development, and continued independence from its communist supporters.

The United States can play a decisive role in influencing North Korean decision-making when the North finally reacts to its declining prospects. The objective of U.S. policy clearly must be to exploit this decisive moment, to steer the North Koreans away from a preemptive military strike against the South and toward a reduction of Pyongyang's military effort, combined with specific agreements to reduce the level of tension in Korea and to gain communist acceptance of a two-Korea accommodation.

The United States has both military and diplomatic tools at its disposal to achieve this objective. Reduction of U.S. troop strength provides an incentive if it continues to be linked to demonstrable steps to reduce tension. The North must be aware that there is a clear-cut price attached to troop reduction. Second, the United States can alter the military balance through the flow of technology and weapons to the South. Both the pace and scope of the expansion of South Korea's defense industry will be influenced by U.S. and ROK decisions, and both can conceivably be linked to tension-reduction measures. Finally, any measure to reinforce the U.S. defense commitment and emphasize its capability and determination to react with overwhelming military power to North Korean aggression will strengthen the deterrence equation and discourage North Korean preemptive tendencies. These military measures should have the further favorable effect of dampening Seoul's anxiety regarding the U.S. commitment and its tendencies to seek a unilateral deterrent.

Political stability in the South could also be a vital factor affecting North Korean decisions during the next few years. The North, in its search for alternatives, could mislead itself into deferring a change in policy or even into aggression by misreading signs of dissidence in the South. While the United States is not in a position to assure political stability in the ROK, its human rights policies could encourage the North to wait for and depend upon dissidence and dissention in the South to weaken the U.S. commitment. Succession problems in both the North and the South add a further element of uncertainty into the equation. One must anticipate unpredictable developments in the 1980s which the United States has very little capability to influence, unless it tries to intervene in the domestic politics of the South.

Finally, the "crossover" in the North-South balance during the 1980s and the consequent policy dilemma facing the North should offer an opportunity for diplomatic initiatives on the part of the United States and the ROK. The objective of the diplomacy should be to offer a combination of incentives and pressures to the North and its Soviet and Chinese allies to accept a reduction of tension and a two-Korea accommodation. A diplomatic initiative will need to exploit the increased leverage afforded Moscow and Beijing when the North turns to them, as it must one day, for increased economic and technological support. At this stage, the United States must establish the high priority accorded to a Korean settlement in its overall relationship with both communist powers. On the other hand, positive incentives in terms of the dividends the North will enjoy from accommodation will also be required.

There will be a need to move in a parallel fashion, but separately, with the Soviet Union and the PRC. Neither will act if such action works to the advantage of the other in terms of relations with Pyongyang.

China is unlikely to take any initiative to exert further pressures on the North, at least until it is clear that the Soviet Union is willing to play in the same ballpark. Furthermore, Moscow's greater economic and technological resources give it the prospect for greater leverage with Pyongyang. An effort to negotiate reduction of tensions in Korea therefore should logically begin with an initiative toward the Soviet Union; only later can serious discussions with the PRC be expected to have any prospect for success. But developing a scenario for parallel Sino-Soviet action with respect to Korea depends to a large extent on the priority accorded Korea in the overall U.S. relationship with these powers.

Finally, the negotiating process will need refurbishing. In the past, the tendency has been to rely upon a single set of negotiations—a U.N. conference, or four-power talks, or North-South talks—and to emphasize the *forum* for negotiation rather than the *substance* of the negotiations, a mistake repeated with the trilateral talks proposal this year. The Korean situation will require a more sophisticated and multidimensional approach. It will require a combination of measures designed to reduce the level of military tensions along the DMZ, to improve the climate of direct North-South negotiations, and to stabilize the North-South status quo for the indefinite future through a process of cross-recognition. To achieve these objectives will in turn necessitate a series of parallel negotiations on different fronts, largely using existing mechanisms.

The Armistice Commission offers the best prospect for dealing with strictly military measures; revival of the North-South Coordinating Committee offers the best prospect for development of elementary intercourse between the two Koreas; and the U.N. Security Council may offer the best prospects for developing parallel approaches to the USSR and the PRC regarding steps toward cross-recognition. A negotiating effort moving in tandem on all three fronts will require careful coordination, confidence in the negotiating process on the part of South Korea, and elevation of priority in the level of U.S. representation in such talks. The critical element will of necessity be direct diplomatic approaches to the USSR and the PRC setting the stage for this multiple negotiating effort. Armistice Commission negotiations seeming to emanate from local levels, for example, are unlikely to attract any real response. On the other hand, Armistice Commission negotiations with clear support from Washington and coordinated efforts to renew the North-South talks, along with separate outside power discussions, could have an entirely different character in communist eyes. They are less likely to be ignored and more likely to attract broader Third World support, putting pressure on the North Koreans to respond or face the onus of being resistant to peace. In short, a piecemeal, low-key negotiating effort has far poorer prospects for success than a multiple-track, high-priority approach. Maximizing these prospects will require a sophisticated, concerted, and high-level negotiating strategy and a calculated sense of timing linked to increasing North Korean economic and military vulnerabilities and dependence on its communist supporters and the policy dilemmas posed by its increasing inferiority relative to the South.

Chapter 7

VIETNAM AND BIG-POWER RIVALRY

Goh Keng Swee[1]

World War II ended in August 1945 with the capitulation of Japan, but peace did not come to the Asian mainland. In China, fighting continued for another four years, ending in the overthrow of the Kuomintang or Nationalist government by the Communists. In Indochina, fighting began in late 1946 as an anti-colonial revolt against the French and increased in scale and intensity. Eventually, it drew the United States into its largest and longest postwar military involvement to contain communist expansion. The decades-long conflict also brought the Soviet Union and the People's Republic of China (PRC) into the contest; although neither of them sent combat troops, both provided weapons, food, and other materiel to North Vietnam.

The American military forces were withdrawn from Indochina following the Paris Accords of January 1973, but this did not at long last bring peace to Indochina, nor did the conquest of South Vietnam by the North. Fighting has continued on the Peninsula in different forms and between different adversaries, and former allies in the fight against American power and the U.S.-backed regime in South Vietnam are now at each others' throats.

How and why has Indochina been plagued by such conflicts? What is the likely outcome of the current period of hostilities? What will be the effect on the states of Southeast Asia in the 1980s? Can the United States play any role in bringing peace and stability to Indochina? What adjustments have to be made by the states of the region, particularly the five ASEAN countries (Thailand, Malaysia, Singapore, Indonesia, and the Philippines)? This paper presents some tentative answers to these questions and traces the origins of the recent conflicts between the Socialist Republic of Vietnam (SRV) and the PRC.

RENEWED CONFLICT IN INDOCHINA

It was clear toward the end of November 1978, when the rainy season in Vietnam ended, that an invasion of Kampuchea (Cambodia) by the Vietnamese army was imminent. It was also clear that this conflict would not be a local one

[1] Dr. Goh Keng Swee, currently Deputy Prime Minister and Minister of Education of the Republic of Singapore, served as Minister of Defense from 1965 to 1967 and 1970 to 1979.

This paper is an updated version of a draft prepared in November 1978. The original paper correctly predicted the Vietnamese invasion of Kampuchea (Cambodia), but not the manner in which the military action was carried out. It assumed prudent action on the part of the parties concerned (China, Vietnam, and the Soviet Union). Lack of Vietnamese prudence, however, eventually stimulated a Chinese military response, though a limited one, in February 1979. This paper has been updated to discuss the potential consequences of these military operations on regional security in the coming decade, particularly their impact on the ASEAN states.

Mr. H. K. Heng, Desk Officer, Ministry of Defense of the Republic of Singapore, assembled much of the material on which this paper is based.

The views expressed here are the author's and do not represent the position of the Government of Singapore.

149

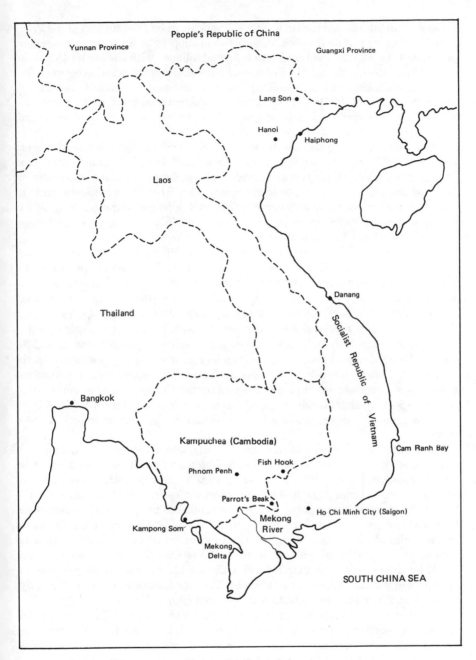

Map 1—Southeast Asia

between Kampuchea and the SRV. The Kampucheans had the support of the PRC, which had made repeated public statements in support of Kampuchean independence; and the SRV had entered into a formal alliance with the Soviet Union on November 3, 1978. Although the Treaty of Friendship and Cooperation between the Soviets and the SRV did not explicitly require the Soviet Union to take military action in support of the SRV if the latter were threatened or attacked, there was an obligation to consult and "take appropriate and effective measures to safeguard the peace and security of the two countries."

The Chinese had no defense treaty with Kampuchea, but following its open quarrel with Vietnam (which will be discussed later), the PRC began to send substantial amounts of military supplies and large numbers of military instructors to Kampuchea, using the sea route to Kampong Som. The Chinese leaders made it clear that they would not send combat troops to Kampuchea if it were attacked by Vietnam; however, their statements remained ambiguous about a possible Chinese response to a major invasion of Kampuchean territory.

Up to the end of November, the manner in which the Vietnamese Army would carry out its invasion of Kampuchea was uncertain. For several months, there had been a substantial reinforcement of Vietnamese troops along certain sectors of the Vietnam-Kampuchea border. There also had been a methodical accumulation of combat supplies in field dumps. Military observers believed that some fourteen divisions had been deployed along the border, with large concentrations in the Parrot's Beak and Fish Hook areas. Opposing them were some 40,000 to 60,000 Khmer Rouge soldiers, lightly equipped and lacking in either heavy weapons (such as tanks and medium artillery) or adequate means of line and radio communications. Major supplies rushed to Kampuchea by the Chinese included tanks, anti-tank weapons, medium artillery pieces, and even a few fighter aircraft. These weapons probably arrived too late for the Khmer Rouge soldiers to learn to use them.

The question of how the Vietnamese Army would conduct its campaign in Kampuchea was a crucial one. Despite the absence of a military commitment to protect Kampuchea, the PRC could hardly view a full-scale Vietnamese invasion with equanimity. Chinese pledges of support would lose credibility if they were not backed by an adequate response. Since geography did not permit Chinese troops to move by an overland route to Kampuchea, Beijing (Peking) might be obliged to initiate military operations along the China-Vietnam border. If such operations took on the proportion of a major invasion of Vietnam, the Soviet Union in turn would be obliged—likewise to avoid losing the credibility of its treaty pledges—to open a third front on the Sino-Soviet border. The four nations, as one observer aptly put it, found themselves caught in a three-sided game of chicken.

What were the options open to the three major contestants? The intentions of the Vietnamese were crucial, for it was they who would initiate the first action, the invasion of Kampuchea. It was within their control to determine the level of forces used, the extent of penetration, and the objectives of the military campaign.

There were two courses of action open to Hanoi. The first was an all-out invasion, leading to the capture of Phnom Penh and the occupation of Kampuchea. We must assume that the Vietnamese were aware that an all-out invasion could provoke a major Chinese military response, despite their recently concluded defense treaty with the Soviet Union. Nobody knew whether the Chinese would be deterred by this treaty from going further than a token military action on the border, and it is doubtful that the Vietnamese could be sure of the consequences of their actions.

Furthermore, an all-out Vietnamese invasion of Kampuchea would very likely damage Hanoi's standing in the Third World. The ASEAN states, in particular, would regard such action as naked aggression. Japan and the West would be greatly disturbed and would be less inclined to extend aid.

Vietnam also had a more prudent military option, with which it could still achieve certain political objectives in Kampuchea. If its goal was *not* to occupy the whole of Kampuchea through military force and convert the country into a province of Vietnam, it could pursue the military objective of closing in on the Khmer Rouge troops deployed along the border and destroying or dispersing them without occupying the whole of the country. The Pol Pot regime governed by the free use of terror, the instrument of its rule being the Khmer Rouge army. The destruction of this army would enable pro-Vietnamese Kampuchean armed forces to occupy Kampuchean territory with relative ease while Pol Pot's troops were engaged by the Vietnamese Army. In a sense, this would be a replay of what happened in 1970 after the overthrow of Sihanouk by Lon Nol. The Khmer Rouge forces then numbered only 2,000 or 3,000 armed guerrillas deployed in small, isolated pockets in the northeast, southwest, and southeast of Kampuchea. They were not a serious threat to the government forces, which consisted of some 75,000 troops.

In 1971 it was the North Vietnamese army that engaged Lon Nol's forces in major operations, first in a sweep across the northern part of Kampuchea, and second in several major engagements in which Lon Nol's troops along Highway 6 were disastrously defeated. By 1972 the North Vietnamese army had cleared virtually half the country of government forces. This enabled the Khmer Rouge to follow in its trail and set up large *de facto* liberated areas that were safe from government harassment. By the middle of 1972, when most of the North Vietnamese troops were withdrawn from operations in South Vietnam, the Khmer Rouge army had increased to between 40,000 and 50,000 troops.

For some time following Pol Pot's unwise tangling with the North Vietnamese Army along their common border during 1977-78, the Vietnamese had been building up on the territory of the SRV an insurgent Kampuchean military force consisting of deserters from the Khmer Rouge army, civilian Kampuchean refugees, and Khmer Krom (South Vietnamese residents of Khmer ethnic origin). The size of this force was estimated at between 10,000 and 30,000 troops.

The Vietnamese also had been harboring a number of high-ranking Kampuchean leaders who had defected from Pol Pot's regime. Their names had been broadcast by Hanoi radio from time to time, and they included So Phim, the former first Vice-Chairman of the State Presidium, Som Rin, the former Secretary of the Eastern Region Committee and Commander of the Force Division, and Chia Xim, an ex-member of the People's Assembly. These men were to constitute the nucleus of the new regime which the Vietnamese intended to install in Phnom Penh.

The options open to Pol Pot were not attractive. He could stand up and fight along the border, but this would mean the rapid destruction of his army; or he could break his army into small groups and retreat into terrain favorable for the conduct of guerrilla warfare, but this would mean that Phnom Penh could be easily occupied by the Kampuchean protégés of the Vietnamese. The operation could then be presented to the world as a Kampuchean civil war—the overthrow of an unpopular regime and the assumption to power of successful revolutionaries as the new legitimate authority.

Neither were the options open to the Chinese attractive. The PRC had stated that it would not dispatch soldiers to fight in Kampuchea. It was unlikely that the Chinese could prevent the installation of a pro-Vietnamese government in Phnom Penh by direct military action on the China-Vietnam border without risking more than a minor dust-up on the border with the Soviet Union. The expulsion of Pol Pot's regime from Phnom Penh, even if the Khmer Rouge could continue a guerrilla war, would represent a serious setback for Beijing and a major triumph for the Soviet Union.

ESCALATION OF THE CONFLICT

These consequences could have been foreseen when, early in 1978, the open political quarrel between Vietnam and the PRC was allowed to escalate beyond the point of no return toward military conflict. Were there some compelling reasons that moved the PRC to this course of action? The open quarrel had first erupted in the spring of 1978 over the flight into China of large numbers of Vietnamese of ethnic Chinese origin. Even before this, however, the relationship between the two had had some difficult moments.

Historically, there was little love lost between the Vietnamese and the Chinese. Vietnam had been subject to Chinese invasion or punitive military expeditions several times in past centuries when a strong emperor sat on the dragon throne. Even when China and the Soviet Union were supporting Vietnam with considerable military supplies in its war against the Americans, the relationship was a fractious one. For example, the Vietnamese have since revealed that during the height of China's Cultural Revolution, Beijing withheld some Soviet military supplies that were on transit by rail through China.

The Chinese expressed public disapproval of Vietnam's decision to commence negotiations with the United States in Paris in 1968 and reminded the Vietnamese that "the Vietnam question can be solved only by completely defeating the U.S. aggressor on the battlefield and driving it out of South Vietnam."[2] President Nixon's visit to China in 1972, while the war was still on, was strongly resented by the Vietnamese. The bombing of North Vietnam and the blockade of Haiphong harbor, in fact, took place not long after the release of the Sino-American Shanghai Communique. And Hanoi must have viewed China's military takeover of the Paracel Islands from South Vietnamese forces in January 1974 as the forceful acquisition of Vietnamese territory.

Bad blood had thus existed between the two governments long before the open quarrel broke out between them in 1978. The political part of this quarrel can be conveniently divided into three phases, the first extending from April 30 to July 3, 1978. It began with the expression of concern by the PRC's Director of the Office of Overseas Chinese Affairs over the influx of large numbers of ethnic Chinese fleeing from Vietnam, and it ended with the termination of all aid projects and the recall of all Chinese technicians. The second phase started on July 4 and ended on

[2] "U.S. Imperialist Chieftain Johnson Tries New Fraud," *Peking Review*, No. 15, April 12, 1968, pp. 14-15.

September 26, 1978, when the Chinese suspended talks at the Vice-Ministerial level. The third phase lasted from September 27 to November 3.

On April 30, 1978, the Director of Beijing's Overseas Chinese Association addressed a large gathering of Overseas Chinese at a tea party in Beijing. His reference to refugees from Vietnam was almost an aside to his main statement of welcome.[3] The Vietnamese response on May 4 was conciliatory, attributing the exodus to unfounded rumors of impending war between Vietnam and China over Kampuchea. It contained a strong expression of desire for continued friendship between the two countries.

Eight days later, China unilaterally stopped aid on twenty-one economic construction projects in Vietnam, and on May 25, Beijing issued a strong statement accusing Vietnam of persecuting Chinese residents. Two days later, the Vietnamese issued a spirited denial of the PRC's charges. From then until the end of the first phase, the public charges and countercharges in the official media of the two countries increased in virulence. On May 30, the PRC announced the termination of another fifty-one aid projects. On June 28, Vietnam applied to join the Soviet-dominated COMECON,[4] and its application was accepted the following day in an unprecedented display of speed (it normally takes two to three years to process an application).

Refugees constituted the central issue in the first stage. The PRC claimed that Vietnamese discrimination and bad treatment of ethnic Chinese—termed "Overseas Chinese" by Beijing—caused the exodus; the Vietnamese retorted that the exodus was engineered by the PRC with the object of disrupting social order and economic progress in Vietnam. Low-level discussions to solve the problem began on June 19 when arrangements were set in motion for the evacuation of refugees, but these came to naught after sixteen meetings.

In the second phase, recriminations centered around border incidents. On July 12, the Chinese refused to receive any more refugees and sealed the border. Some 2,500 refugees were stranded, ironically, on the Vietnamese side of the "Friendship Gate." On July 22, agreement was reached on continuing talks at the Vice-Ministerial level, and on August 8, the Chinese negotiators arrived in Hanoi. Eight rounds of talks proved fruitless, and the Chinese Foreign Minister returned home on September 26. We do not know what transpired in these talks. From media announcements by both sides, it seems to have been a point of honor for each to reject out of hand any proposal made by the other toward reaching a settlement. Near the end of September there were mutual accusations of territorial violations and large-scale troop deployments along the common border.

In the third phase, the Vietnamese news media increased their denunciations of the PRC, alleging massive troop deployments and serious border intrusions. Hardly a day passed without Nhan Dan or Radio Hanoi making such charges. In contrast, the Chinese media remained relatively quiet. They paid little attention to alleged border incidents, preferring to concentrate on the charge that the Vietnamese intended to invade Kampuchea. On November 3, Vietnam and the Soviet Union signed the Treaty of Friendship and Cooperation. The shrill charges of

---

[3] Liao Chengzhi's (Liao Ch'eng-chih's) address; translated in Foreign Broadcast Information Service (FBIS), *Daily Report—People's Republic of China*, May 1, 1978, pp. A1-A3.

[4] The Moscow-based Council for Mutual Economic Assistance, composed of the Soviet Union, Bulgaria, Cuba, Czechoslovakia, East Germany, Hungary, Mongolia, Poland, and Romania.

China's aggressive intentions on the border, broadcast during the previous six weeks, had obviously been orchestrated to prepare domestic opinion for this fateful move.

What can we make out of this strange affair? Although the quarrel began over the flood of refugees streaming into China, this was not the real source of conflict. The Vietnamese alleged that the Chinese had started the outflow by organizing a rumor campaign over the imminence of war along the border, but this accusation lacks plausibility. China stood to lose, not gain, by the inflow of refugees. The refugee problem, in fact, grew out of certain measures carried out in South Vietnam by the SRV government.

In March 1978, the SRV government announced its decision to nationalize small private enterprises. This measure, together with an announced plan to transfer some of the unproductive urban population in Ho Chi Minh City (formerly Saigon) to the New Economic Zones to grow food, had a tremendous impact on Vietnamese residents of ethnic Chinese origin. Most of these people were small traders, and they had no desire for pioneering farm work, especially in the border region where they would be subject to Khmer Rouge depredations. The result of these policies was predictable. Evidence of a considerable outflow of South Vietnamese of Chinese ethnic origin accumulated, with refugees arriving at the PRC border by train, in buses, and even in motor cars. Since travel in communist countries is under strict control, such population movements could not have taken place without the approval of SRV authorities.

Was the refugee problem an unforeseen outcome of Vietnamese policy, or was it intended? We shall never know for certain, but there are reasons for believing that Hanoi deliberately created the refugee problem in the full knowledge that it would bring Vietnam onto a collision course with China. Events prior to and after the refugee outflow began suggest that the Vietnamese had decided that it was not possible to maintain good relations with both Beijing and Moscow and that if a choice had to be made, they would be better off by having closer ties with the Soviet Union even at the expense of an open rupture with the PRC.

The SRV had already reduced Laos to the status of a client state. However, it faced an unfriendly regime in Pol Pot's Kampuchea. Whether or not one believes that the Vietnamese leaders have long cherished the dream of an Indochinese Federation of Vietnam, Laos, and Kampuchea under Hanoi's control, it is clear that they found the Pol Pot regime intolerable and decided that it should be replaced by one more amenable to their influence. It was also obvious that the replacement of Pol Pot's regime could be achieved only through military means, and that in such circumstances a hostile reaction from Beijing could not be avoided. However, Soviet support for such an undertaking, which was necessary to deter the Chinese from taking military counteraction against Vietnam, was expected to be readily forthcoming.

The speed with which Vietnam was accepted into COMECON and the signing of the Treaty of Friendship and Cooperation indicate that these steps were not taken in response to events as and when they occurred. There are strong implications of planning and collusion between the two parties. Vietnamese military preparations had reached an advanced stage by this time, and the launching of the offensive was timed most advantageously to begin with the end of the rainy season.

UNCERTAIN CHINESE MOTIVES

If the mistreatment of some 150,000 ethnic Chinese residents of Vietnam was not the real reason for the conflict between the PRC and the SRV, what was China's objective in pressing that quarrel to the point where Vietnam had no option but total dependence on the Soviet Union? We have seen that in the third phase of the dispute the subject of ethnic Chinese in Vietnam faded out of the picture. The official PRC explanation given was their opposition to the establishment of the Indochinese Federation, which they accused Hanoi of planning.

What is the Indochinese Federation? The matter goes as far back as 1930, when the Indochinese Communist Party (ICP) was formed under the direction of the Comintern, with Ho Chi Minh as its agent. This action formalized for the first time a political movement to fight for the independence of the whole of what was then French Indochina. The area embraced Laos and Cambodia as well as Vietnam, but the members of the ICP were almost entirely Vietnamese. In 1951, acting on the Comintern's orders to struggle under the banner of "nationalism" rather than "communism," the ICP dissolved itself and broke into three separate parties, one each for Vietnam, Laos, and Cambodia. The trouble was that the ICP had no Laotian or Cambodian members of any stature, so both these parties were dominated by Vietnamese. The Cambodian Communist Party did not achieve independent status until 1960, when Pol Pot captured power after the murder of suspected pro-Vietnamese protégés in the Central Committee.

The Vietnamese claimed, in an official statement by their Foreign Ministry on April 7, 1978, that the dissolution of the ICP in 1951 was a final renunciation of the Indochinese Federation as their political goal. The statement referred to the Geneva Agreement of 1954, which affirmed the separate sovereignty and independence of Cambodia, Laos, and Vietnam. Moreover, we can find no reference to the consolidation of the three countries in Ho Chi Minh's testament to the Federation, although during his lifetime he was believed to be in favor of federating the three states along the lines of the autonomous republics of the USSR, under the control of one political party.[5]

Whether or not the Vietnamese have any intention of forming an Indochinese Federation along these lines, the Pol Pot regime's aggressive behavior and irrational claims to Vietnamese portions of the Mekong Delta area gave Hanoi ample reason to initiate military counteraction against the Kampuchean government. The puzzle is this: How did the Chinese come to find themselves committed to supporting Kampuchea in her confrontation with Vietnam? If the PRC's objective was to frustrate formation of the Indochinese Federation, it had chosen the wrong place to thwart Vietnamese ambitions. Without a common border with Kampuchea, and with the necessity of a long sea line of communication, China is limited in its ability to assist the Pol Pot forces in their fight with Vietnam. The logical place to frustrate the Vietnamese would have been Laos, with which China has a common border. Yet the Chinese appear to have done very little there during the Indochina war, apart from building a network of roads in Northern Laos and stationing engineering troops, most of which were later withdrawn.

We therefore conclude that the Chinese had no compelling reason to save the Pol Pot regime from destruction by the Vietnamese. Perhaps they were drawn into

[5] Dennis Duncanson, "Limited Sovereignty in Indochina," *The World Today*, July 1978, p. 263.

supporting Kampuchea in stages, beginning with Sihanouk's exile in Beijing in 1970. When the conflict between Kampuchea and Vietnam escalated, it could have been argued among Beijing policymakers that the abandonment of a friend in trouble would diminish China's credibility throughout the world and especially in Southeast Asia. This was precisely the kind of argument that was advanced to justify increased American military commitment to South Vietnam in the 1960s. Advocates of involvement conceded that the area was of no vital strategic importance to the United States, but they asserted that abandoning Vietnam would damage American credibility among Asian and NATO allies.

The last question to be answered, then, is why China chose to escalate the quarrel with Vietnam to the point where Vietnam was obligated to seek Soviet protection. There are no convincing and simple answers. Perhaps it was an accumulation of minor and major grievances over the years. What appeared to have riled Beijing in this quarrel was the persistent Vietnamese rejection of two Chinese requests: a review of former President Diem's conferment of Vietnamese nationality on all Chinese residents of South Vietnam, and the establishment of a PRC Consulate in Ho Chi Minh City.

These were minor irritations that could have been contained. However, sometime in May or June of 1978, it must have become clear to the Chinese that the Vietnamese were determined to proceed with their attack on Kampuchea. Once this conclusion was drawn, the logical consequences followed. Vietnam had no choice but to depend solely on the Soviet Union. It was no longer feasible for China to match Soviet aid, since that would not deflect the Vietnamese from their purpose, nor would it keep them out of the Soviet camp. China then faced the problem squarely and withdrew its aid, thereby compelling Vietnam to join COMECON and thus be identified as a Soviet client state.

Let us consider this situation from the point of view of the Vietnamese. If Hanoi could achieve its objective of overthrowing the Pol Pot regime and installing a pro-Vietnamese regime in Phnom Penh, Vietnam would have gained a singular victory over the PRC. Chinese support for Kampuchea would have been revealed as ineffective, and China would have been challenged successfully. But these gains would have been achieved at some cost. Vietnam would have to assist the new regime in Phnom Penh in quelling what could be a troublesome insurgency campaign. Vietnam would be totally dependent on Soviet power for protection against Chinese retribution. The industrial states of the West and Japan would be disenchanted and hesitant to extend the aid Vietnam badly needed to reconstruct its economy. After three and a half years of peace, the Vietnamese economy remained in poor shape, and this fact must have given some pause to the leaders in Hanoi who were considering what were potentially very costly actions against Kampuchea.

VIETNAM'S INVASION OF KAMPUCHEA
AND ITS CONSEQUENCES

We now know that the Vietnamese leaders discarded the more prudent course of action that was open to them, i.e., the use of the SRV's regular divisions to engage Pol Pot's troops wherever they could be found and destroy or disperse them in piecemeal fashion. The occupation of major towns, undefended by the Khmer

Rouge army, could have been left to the forces of their protégé Heng Samrin, and the operation could have been presented with some plausibility as a Kampuchean civil war.

In any event, the SRV decided to launch a full-scale offensive against Kampuchea on December 25, 1978. They used 14 divisions, totaling 120,000 combat troops, which poured down the main highways between Vietnam and Kampuchea. Forward units were sent to encircle Phnom Penh, which fell on January 7, 1979.

The main Khmer Rouge forces were bypassed as the Vietnamese forces swept through undefended towns without meeting significant resistance along the way. The occupation of territory was the primary military objective, and as a result the Khmer Rouge army was left largely intact. It retreated to the difficult terrain of the Dangrek Mountains in the north and the Cardamom and Elephant Mountains in the southwest.

Why did the Vietnamese leaders discard the more prudent option and decide on an all-out offensive, using all the means of modern combat, including armored formations and air strikes? We shall never know the answer to that question. Perhaps they decided to give the generals their head; if so, this was a reversal of the policy they pursued while fighting the Americans and the Thieu regime in South Vietnam. At that time, they realized that political objectives were supreme and military operations were a means of attaining them. But perhaps they were overconfident of their military power and placed too much reliance on their treaty with the Soviet Union, failing to anticipate a Chinese military response.

Whatever the reasons for Vietnam's lack of prudence, it did result in Chinese military action in the border provinces within a month of Hanoi's occupation of all Kampuchean territory other than the mountainous jungle areas to which the Khmer Rouge had retreated. On February 17, 1979, China launched an attack along the entire Sino-Vietnamese border, covering six Vietnamese provinces. By the following day, Chinese troops had advanced six miles inside the border at some points. By February 27, Chinese forces had reached the vicinity of the provincial capital of Lang Son. The Battle of Lang Son began in the early morning of March 1, and the town was captured on March 2 or 3. Lang Son was the final objective of the Chinese operation. On March 5, Vietnam ordered a general mobilization throughout the country, and China announced the beginning of its troop withdrawal from Vietnam and asked for negotiations with Hanoi to begin. On March 15, 1979—one week after Chinese troops had withdrawn from Vietnam—the Vietnamese Foreign Ministry proposed that Vice-Ministerial-level talks be held at a site on the Sino-Vietnamese border. The following day, PRC Foreign Minister Huang Hua announced the completion of the Chinese withdrawal and welcomed the Vietnamese government's agreement to negotiate.

The details of the fight and the casualties suffered by each side remain uncertain, but casualties were certainly high, and the level of fighting was intense. What is known is that an exceptionally high volume of artillery fire was used by the Chinese troops. A large fleet of fighter aircraft and bombers that could be used in the conflict had been assembled by the Chinese at airbases in the border provinces of Guangxi (Kuanghsi) and Yunnan; some intelligence estimates placed the number at approximately 500. The Chinese, however, did not resort to air strikes.

Perhaps the airpower was kept in reserve in case the heavy volume of artillery fire proved insufficient to break Vietnamese resistance. It could also be that this was a means of signaling to the outside world, and especially to the Soviet Union, that the military operations were intended to be limited in scope, both in terms of area and method of fighting. On February 19, two days after the offensive was launched, Vice-Premier Deng Xiaoping (Teng Hsiao-p'ing) announced that the action would be a limited one. Throughout the fighting, similar announcements were regularly made by various Chinese leaders.

The Soviet Union did not initiate military operations along the Sino-Soviet border. The Soviets had read the Chinese signals correctly and saw no advantage in starting a fight. The restraint shown by the Kremlin was noted around the world with relief, and with some acclamation. However, certain observers believe that the Soviet Union suffered a loss of credibility as a consequence. This is a mistaken view. The fact that Chinese armies did not venture further than a few miles inside the border was ample testimony to the credibility of Soviet deterrence. In accordance with their treaty obligations, the Soviets sent military aid to the Vietnamese, the details of which are not fully known. The aid included the supply of transport aircraft and tank landing ships. In addition, the Soviets were in a position to provide—and doubtless did provide—up-to-date intelligence on Chinese troop movements. They also took advantage of the occasion to dispatch several types of warships to the area, calling at Danang and Cam Ranh Bay. This caused concern in Washington and Tokyo, but the Soviets had an ironclad case to justify their presence.

Let us review the consequences of the incident for the four contestants. The Pol Pot regime has been ousted from power. The remnants of the Khmer Rouge army are now fighting desperately in the mountain areas of the Kampuchean-Thai border. Large numbers of troops and civilians fled into Thailand before the Vietnamese onslaught, which began in March. Some of the troops, probably a substantial proportion, were allowed by the Thais to reenter Kampuchea. This worsened the relationship between Thailand and Vietnam.

Nobody knows how long the Khmer Rouge army can keep on fighting. Since they are unlikely to get the voluntary support of Kampuchean farmers for their supplies, they either have to get food by force or have it delivered from outside sources. Either way, the logistical difficulties are enormous and could be the major cause of the final collapse of organized Khmer Rouge resistance.

The Vietnamese have attained their objective of installing a client regime in Phnom Penh. They are, however, faced with the task of crushing resistance mounted by the remnants of the Pol Pot regime. If they cannot accomplish this quickly, the Heng Samrin regime will not receive international recognition. Vietnam's standing among Third World countries, particularly among the nonaligned nations, has suffered.

More serious than this is the deep enmity on the part of China that Hanoi incurred by the attack. The all-out assault provoked China's counterattack in the border provinces of Vietnam, which can hardly be called a punitive expedition, as it has not brought about the submission of Hanoi to Beijing's will. To attain this end, it would be necessary for Chinese troops to occupy Hanoi. Obviously, any attempt to bring down the Hanoi regime would very likely bring about a strong Soviet response. It is therefore not feasible for the Chinese to achieve this through either military means or economic or political measures.

The continuing negotiations between Beijing and Hanoi following the withdrawal of Chinese troops show that Chinese hostility toward Vietnam will continue for a long time. It is clear that the gap between the two sides is too wide to be settled by the normal processes of negotiation. While the Vietnamese are prepared to treat the border dispute as such and defuse the situation by technical means, e.g., through the establishment of demilitarized zones, this is not acceptable to the Chinese. Beijing has put forward eight demands which are unacceptable to Hanoi and are likely to remain so for the foreseeable future.[6] To settle the border dispute in a manner acceptable to the Chinese, the Vietnamese will have to withdraw their military forces from Kampuchea and Laos, and this is too much of a concession to expect from a government which does not regard itself as having been vanquished on the battlefield.

As a result, the Chinese can be expected to continue to exert pressure on the Vietnamese through a variety of means, including occasional military sorties, support of insurgent groups, and economic and diplomatic measures designed to bleed the Vietnamese. The Chinese have calculated that the total aid given to Vietnam by the Soviet Union and its other COMECON partners, amounting to some $800 million (U.S.) per year, will be grossly insufficient even in peacetime. The military burden on Hanoi of maintaining large military forces in combat or at a high state of alert will impose severe and continuing burdens on the beleaguered Vietnamese economy. Only a people long inured to hardship can bear such a burden. In short, the Vietnamese face a bleak future. Soviet protection will safeguard the country against large-scale Chinese attacks, but Soviet economic aid will not provide the means whereby Vietnam can rise above its impoverished condition. Was this one of Beijing's objectives in attacking Vietnam?

Chinese involvement in the conflict in Indochina has yielded mixed results for PRC interests. Although it did not save the Pol Pot regime, the limited Chinese military operation, which was aimed at "teaching Vietnam a lesson," prevented the PRC from being written off as a paper tiger. The willingness of the PRC to take enormous risks to retain the credibility of its word will no doubt be taken into account in future calculations of Chinese intentions.

But China's credibility has not been sustained without cost. The direct effects on the PRC's program of economic development—the four modernizations—are calculable and, most likely, sustainable. But the other effects are more difficult to assess. First, China has been drawn, intentionally or otherwise, into involvement in Thailand's security. It has expressed public support for the security of Thailand against Vietnamese aggression, and this could lead to future tests of Chinese credibility and further risks. Moreover, the PRC must face these risks in a situation in which it does not hold the initiative. It is Hanoi that will decide whether or not Vietnamese armies will move across the Thai border, and if so, how, where, and when. Since the Vietnamese cannot make major moves without the concurrence of the Soviet Union, it is the Soviets who will determine in what manner Chinese resolve will again be tested.

[6] For a detailed description of PRC terms for resolution of the conflict, of which withdrawal of SRV troops from Laos and Kampuchea and settlement of certain territorial issues are the most important elements, see the speech by Vice-Foreign Minister Han Nianlong (Han Nien-lung) in *Beijing Review*, No. 18, May 4, 1979, pp. 10-17.

SOVIET GAINS

The Soviet Union has turned out to be the sole winner in the Sino-Vietnamese conflict. Moscow has gained a valuable ally on the southern flank of China, a vigorous people enjoying a closely knit leadership and possessing demonstrated military prowess—in contrast to some of the unstable regimes supported by the Soviet Union in Africa and the Middle East. No doubt, there will be great demands on Soviet economic resources for development assistance to Vietnam; but this, as well as military assistance, will be readily forthcoming.

What does the Soviet Union want in return? Undoubtedly, one of the most coveted rewards would be the use of the naval facilities at Cam Ranh Bay. Initially, this could take the form of refueling and victualing support for the Soviet Pacific fleet. Later, it could be extended to minor repair and maintenance services, and finally to the establishment of full base services. It is unlikely that these facilities would be willingly granted. Hanoi is aware of the alarm that would be created in Japan and in the United States[7] should it accede to Soviet demands. But it is not in a good position to resist these pressures, which are likely to be strong and persistent.

The Soviet Pacific fleet is large, consisting of 755 ships, with a total displacement of 1.33 million tons.[8] The fleet has approximately 10 cruisers, close to 30 destroyers, and more than 100 submarines of all varieties, including ballistic missile submarines deployed in the Pacific.[9] In the last five or six years, the presence of the Soviet fleet in the Indian Ocean, in terms of ship days, exceeded its presence in the Pacific. Logistics support for these operations is conducted by underway transfers of fuel, spare parts, and other supplies through special supply ships and even commercial freighters. It is a costly and inefficient way of maintaining a fleet at sea during peacetime and it would be highly impractical in war. But it is unavoidable, since the Soviet bases are far away in Vladivostok and Petropavlovsk on the Kamchatka Peninsula. A naval base at Cam Ranh Bay would solve many of these logistic problems.

The political and psychological impact of a Soviet naval base in the South China Sea would certainly be enormous, not only on major powers such as Japan, the PRC, and the United States, but also on the five ASEAN countries. To the ASEAN states, Soviet power would no longer be a remote and almost abstract matter for strategists to discuss in conferences. It would be a tangible presence at the front door.

It is unlikely that the Soviets can be denied the use of Cam Ranh Bay and other major facilities in Vietnam. It is difficult to see how Moscow will be deflected from this purpose by expressions of American disapproval, if those expressions are not backed by an ability to apply sanctions. As far as the PRC is concerned, a Soviet military presence at Cam Ranh Bay will not constitute a *casus belli*. On the con-

[7] According to news reports, President Carter expressed concern about the development of Soviet military bases at Cam Ranh Bay and Danang to Leonid Brezhnev at the Vienna summit meeting in mid-June 1979. Brezhnev was reported to have given assurances that the USSR would not develop such bases. See "Carter Says Brezhnev Ruled Out S. Viet Bases," *Los Angeles Times*, June 24, 1979.

[8] The information on force strength and deployment of the Soviet Pacific Fleet was obtained from papers submitted by Donald Daniel and Makoto Momoi to the International Symposium on the Sea, sponsored by the Brookings Institution and the International Institute of Strategic Studies, held in Tokyo in October 1978.

[9] *Jane's Fighting Ships, 1978-1979*, John Moore (ed.), Franklin Watts, Inc., New York, 1978, p. 484.

trary, it could be—in part—a welcome development for Beijing. The PRC Navy is not in the superpower class and would not feel threatened; but the Chinese would regard the effect of the Soviet presence on American and Japanese attitudes toward regional and global security to be a salutory one.

Partly for this reason, Soviet use of base facilities is likely to increase in gradual stages so that all concerned will get accustomed to the new naval presence. In this way, the Soviet Union will try to avoid unduly provoking Washington or Tokyo while gaining Vietnam as a military ally and developing access to its base facilities —achievements that will represent a major triumph of Soviet power against both China and the United States. Did this come about fortuitously as the end result of a series of events that began with the outflow of refugees across the China-Vietnam border in the spring of 1978? Or, going back to the question posed earlier, was the exodus contrived? If so, was it an independent action undertaken by the Vietnamese? What reason would the Vietnamese have to carry out an action that could only enrage their giant neighbor to the north?

These questions lead one to speculate that the Soviet Union thought out and masterminded the whole series of events, inducing the Vietnamese to create the refugee problem as a means of disrupting Vietnam's ties with the PRC. In return for this, Vietnam received the military guarantee it needed to be able to proceed with the conquest of Kampuchea. There is no doubt that the Vietnamese needed little encouragement. What is open to doubt is whether the SRV leadership foresaw the consequences that their reckless invasion of Kampuchea has brought upon Vietnam—the enmity of China and total dependence on the Sovet Union. Vietnam once again has become a pawn in the power game of the great powers.

The Russians are now sitting pretty. They are in a position to decide what initiatives to take. The other powers are only able to react to whatever moves the Soviet Union may decide to make. However, in the long term, a number of difficulties will arise that Moscow may well find intractable. It is beyond Soviet means to put the Vietnamese economy in order, even with the assistance of its COMECON allies. Not only are the economies of Vietnam, Laos, and Kampuchea in a shambles, Chinese military and other pressures will ensure that Vietnam will have to devote a disproportionate share of its scarce resources to defense and security. The Vietnamese seem to have overlooked an important difference between having America as its enemy and having China in that role. When hostilities with the United States ended, American troops went home, a long way from Vietnam. Chinese troops will also go home, but home is next door and the troops will always be there.

The Chinese believe that the partnership between Vietnam and the Soviet Union is an unnatural and incompatible one. This belief is based on Chinese perceptions of the character of the Vietnamese people and the way the Soviet Union administers aid to Third World countries. In the Chinese view, the Vietnamese suffer from both arrogance and xenophobia: arrogance born of successes against two of the most powerful nations in the world in two Indochina wars; and xenophobia arising from conflicts with China over the centuries and from experiences in the years following World War II.

The system of Soviet aid to Third World countries has shown itself to be ponderous, inflexible, and insensitive. This is partly a result of the nature of the communist system, which requires centralized decisionmaking; it is partly inherent in the nature of aid extended by rich countries to poor countries. The Soviet practice has been to station an army of planning, management, and technical personnel in a recipient country to construct and manage big projects, whether those projects are for development of the economic infrastructure, e.g., power, transport, and communication facilities, or for the construction of industrial plants.

While this approach is inescapable under the communist system, it is not without advantages. It ensures that projects will be completed and that the nationals of aid-receiving countries will be trained to manage them. But its greatest advantage is that it ensures that aid funds and resources will be properly spent and not diverted into the pockets of politicians and officials, an outcome that occurs with distressing frequency in the case of aid provided by Western governments. It must also be pointed out that the Soviet Union has not been able to propel a single Third World country into the stage of self-sustaining growth. The Americans, on the other hand, can point to South Korea and Taiwan as remarkable examples of successful economic transformation under the free-enterprise system.

The Soviets labor under another severe handicap, which could bring about their undoing in Vietnam. That handicap arises from delicate problems of cultural interaction between peoples of different backgrounds. Since the standard of living in the Soviet Union is much higher than that in the recipient countries, Soviet citizens working in these countries must be supplied with special consumer goods and services that are not generally available to the local population. This is bound to be a source of resentment and friction at the numerous points of contact between the aid givers and the aid recipients; and sensitivities are aggravated when the two parties have different ethnic and racial backgrounds.

It is an irony of history that while the Vietnamese, by the exercise of outstanding tenacity, valor, and skill in battle, succeeded in expelling two groups of Caucasians from the Indochina Peninsula in long and bloody wars, they now find themselves in the grip of a third Caucasian power. The relationship is one of client and patron, rather than one of adversaries, and it is not a position that a proud people like the Vietnamese can relish or can long tolerate.

One final observation must be made. Events on the Indochina Peninsula since World War II have repeatedly managed to confound all predictions, and this essay may fare no better than other attempts at crystal-ball gazing. Yet there is one constant factor that runs through all the vicissitudes of big-power rivalry on the Peninsula. The French, the Americans, and now the Chinese have, in their turn, come to grief mainly because their local friends and allies were unreliable and ultimately let them down. The Chinese believe that the Soviet enterprise will meet the same fate. The PRC leaders expect the Soviet enterprise in Vietnam to come to grief in about eight to ten years.

THE IMPACT ON ASEAN OF THE NEW INDOCHINA CONFLICT

Events on the Indochina Peninsula, particularly the conflict between China and Vietnam following the latter's invasion of Kampuchea, are matters of concern to the governments of the ASEAN states.[10] ASEAN's concern is based on two factors. First, a member of the Association, Thailand, shares a long common border with

---

[10] The views discussed in this section of this chapter are the author's personal views, not those of the Government of Singapore or the government of any of the other ASEAN states.

Laos and Kampuchea and can hardly escape the consequences of conflicts in these two countries. Second, all five ASEAN states have had the problem of coping with large numbers of refugees, particularly those fleeing from Vietnam.

The dominant feature in the relationship between the Indochinese and ASEAN states is the superiority of the armed forces of the SRV over those of ASEAN, singly or collectively. Vietnamese military superiority prevails in almost every aspect of the military equation: number of troops, combat experience, quality of command, firepower, and sophistication of weapons. In any military contest between the two sides—assuming there is no third-power intervention—the outcome could be quick and decisive.

In such circumstances, alarm and despondency might be expected to prevail in the ASEAN capitals, leading to a decision to build up national military forces and a desire to form a defensive military alliance. Yet none of these things are happening. Only in Thailand and Malaysia have military budgets been increased, and even those increases have been modest. In the other countries, although the conflict on the Indochina Peninsula is a subject of close attention in the foreign ministries, there is no evident feeling of urgency that something needs to be done. This may seem to be an extraordinary situation to students of military and geopolitical strategy; it does call for some explanation.

The explanation can be found in the nature of the Association and of the individual states themselves. Without exception, each of the five states accords top priority in government policies to economic development. These governments have long realized that unless they can improve the living standards of the people and offer some hope for a better life to the growing numbers of educated young men and women, their tenure in office will be brief. This holds true even when tenure depends on the support of generals rather than of the electorate.

The main concern of the ASEAN governments is to achieve a high rate of economic growth and to spread the benefits of such growth through all sections of the population. They have been remarkably successful in achieving the first objective. Since the oil crisis of 1973-74, when economic growth in most countries—including the Western industrial powers—declined significantly, the ASEAN states have regularly achieved real annual growth rates of their Gross National Product (GNP) of between 6 and 9 percent.

This economic success has been due principally to two factors. First, economic policies have been designed to induce capital investment; and second, the terms of trade for the export of primary products have remained generally good. The growth strategies of the ASEAN states depend on access to the capital markets of the United States, Japan, and Western Europe, as well as to their commodity and consumer markets. Except for exports of rubber to the USSR and the PRC, economic dependence on communist countries is slight.

The pursuit of economic growth induces an inward orientation in the policy thinking of government leaders. This tendency has been reinforced by the fact that except for Thailand, the ASEAN countries are new states with no tradition of a geopolitical outlook on global affairs. (An exception can be made for the brief Sukarno interlude of extravagant performance on the world stage.) In this respect, the ASEAN countries differ profoundly from the European states. Europe, both Eastern and Western, has had a long history of dynastic rivalries between kingdoms and states. The long peace after World War II might have blurred but did not erase memories of past interstate rivalries. In Eastern Europe, particularly where the Soviet Union is concerned, the long peace has not produced any noticeable softening of attitudes. The political commissars may have removed the Romanoffs from power, but the urge of the Soviet state to expand its influence remains. If there is any difference between the commissars and the tsars, it is that the commissars have proved to be more systematic and effective in their use of power.

The third point to note about the ASEAN states is the way they work as a group. Although the Association has a central Secretariat in Jakarta, it does not possess the enormous bureaucracy that grew out of the Treaty of Rome. Decisions are made at meetings of ASEAN Foreign Ministers, and common positions on fundamental matters are taken at occasional meetings of the heads of state. This process of decisionmaking has a number of consequences that have left their imprint on ASEAN.

First, in the absence of an elaborate and skilled bureaucracy working according to complex legal procedures, ASEAN is not able to handle complicated problems. This is the principal reason for the slow progress that has been made in various schemes of economic cooperation between the states. As ASEAN is a loose association of independent sovereign states, its important decisions are reached by consensus. The natural desire to avoid contentious problems therefore limits the range of issues that ASEAN ministers are willing to discuss.

Given these limitations, the Association has been remarkably successful in the areas to which it has devoted attention: the adoption of common positions in international forums such as the United Nations and its agencies, GATT, the group of nonaligned nations, and the group of 77. The ASEAN nations have submitted common proposals to the United States, the European Economic Community (the EEC), and Japan for a commodity price stabilization system, and they have taken a common position in negotiations with the EEC on trade matters. The ASEAN foreign ministers or heads of state have never held formal sessions on security and defense matters. There is, however, active bilateral cooperation among the intelligence services of the five states. Arrangements have also been made for bilateral military operations between Malaysia and Indonesia, and between Malaysia and Thailand. The targets of these operations are communist guerrilla units operating along their common borders.

Given this background, it is not really surprising that the ASEAN governments do not feel any urgency about making defense preparations to meet contingencies which may arise out of the conflicts on the Indochina Peninsula. That was the position in the spring of 1975 when South Vietnam fell to Hanoi's troops and Kampuchea succumbed to the Khmer Rouge. It still holds true today, although the readiness of communist armies to cross international frontiers under one pretext or another is causing some unease in the minds of ASEAN leaders.

While we cannot forecast the future direction of thinking on defense cooperation among the ASEAN states, there are two important matters that will affect this thinking: (1) differences in perceptions by the various ASEAN states of the threat arising out of the military conflicts in Indochina; and (2) future changes in the attitude of the U.S. government. The differences in the perception of potential threat are influenced by two factors—the distance between the ASEAN states and the trouble spot, and the position of the ethnic Chinese minority in relation to the indigenous majority (except in Singapore, where the Chinese form the majority). The Chinese in Southeast Asia have shown a capacity for business enterprise and management which has helped these countries to achieve high rates of economic growth; but this has resulted in strains and stresses in race relations. These are always delicate and, in times of crisis, potentially explosive. Business success brings with it visible affluence. Even when the Chinese are not particularly rich, they are visible, especially in the towns, where they own most of the retail shops. In contrast, the majority of the indigenous people remain in their traditional occupations as peasant cultivators or laborers of one kind or another. The subject of race relations in Southeast Asia has been studied extensively, and it is not necessary here to go beyond stating that these problems exist and that they influence the attitudes of the governments concerned toward the Indochina conflict.

Where resentment against the ethnic Chinese minority is widespread and distance from the trouble spot is great, the Vietnamese Army is not seen as an imminent threat. On the contrary, Vietnam is regarded as a buffer against the expansion of China's influence in Southeast Asia. There is ample opportunity for Vietnamese diplomacy to exploit the situation. It could be argued that Vietnam, having no ethnic presence in the ASEAN states, would have no cause to create friction. On the other hand, the Chinese minority could be presented as a potential "Trojan horse" for the extension of PRC influence. Statements by Beijing on its Overseas Chinese policy, particularly the one issued on January 4, 1978, gave the Vietnamese (and the Soviets) free and valuable propaganda ammunition. Liao Chengzhi, a member of the Central Committee of the Chinese Communist Party, pointed out in that statement:

> Most of the Overseas Chinese are ... working people ... , the masses forming the base of the patriotic united front among Overseas Chinese and are a force we should rely on .... The majority of them are patriotic and eagerly wish to see a strong motherland with a higher international status. They have also made contributions to economic and cultural development in the countries where they live and are part of the motive force for combatting imperialism, hegemonism, and colonialism, and winning national and economic independence in these countries .... We should work energetically among them ... and strive to form the broadest patriotic united front among the Overseas Chinese ...."[11]

Where these two elements—ethnic resentment and distance—are missing, the perception of threat is completely different. For instance, Thailand is nearest to the trouble spot and has most successfully absorbed its resident ethnic Chinese into its domestic social and political system. There is no temptation here to regard the Vietnamese as a buffer against the Chinese. On the contrary, the Chinese are regarded by the Thais as potential protectors against the Vietnamese, who have a number of scores to settle with them because of Thai support for the United States in the war in Vietnam. Thai leaders greeted the news of Chinese military incursions into the border provinces of Vietnam with great relief. It was clear to them, even though their declared public position is one of neutrality in the Sino-Vietnamese conflict, that the one dependable deterrent against further Vietnamese military

---

[11] Liao Chengzhi, "A Critique of the Reactionary Theory of the 'Gang of Four' About So-Called 'Overseas Relations,'" *People's Daily*, January 4, 1978; translated in FBIS, *Daily Report—People's Republic of China*, January 5, 1978, p. E16.

adventures—of which Thailand can be the only immediate target—is the force of Chinese arms.

With these differences of threat perception, it is improbable that the ASEAN states will move quickly toward a military alliance. The reluctance to do so is strengthened by the current belief that they cannot depend on the intervention of American sea and air power if Vietnam should invade Thailand. In these circumstances, the stationing of ASEAN troops in Thailand would serve little purpose. It might even provoke the Vietnamese into a military response that the combined forces of ASEAN could not counter.

The present situation is therefore unstable. There is nothing to prevent the southward march of the Vietnamese Army all the way to Singapore, except the deterrence of another communist army, the People's Liberation Army of the PRC. This deterrence can be reduced by the Soviet Union if it so desires, given Soviet superiority in both conventional and strategic arms. It is therefore well within the capabilities of the USSR and the SRV to conquer mainland Southeast Asia. There is no adequate countervailing power that can prevent such an outcome, given the evident unwillingness of the United States to apply its military power on the Asian mainland.

The scenario is horrendous—if not inconceivable—to residents of the region. It is so horrendous that few believe that it will actually happen. Some argue that a grand slam bid of this kind is contrary to Soviet policy in recent years. Expansion of Soviet influence in Africa and in the Middle East has taken the form of prudent, low-risk actions resulting in incremental rather than massive gains. Still, the possibility exists; and unless the Americans recover their will to use military power to deter overt aggression, the danger will remain.

Let us finally discuss the American role in the Southeast Asian strategic balance. Again, the perception of an American role differs in each of the ASEAN countries. The Philippines, which has a defense treaty with the United States and which provides major naval and air bases, is militarily the most secure from the expansion of communist power, whether by the PRC or the SRV. Indonesia does not feel directly threatened by the prospect of invasion by any of the communist powers and believes that with its large population and rich resources it can look after itself. It is less certain, however, of the situation on peninsular Malaysia and in Singapore. In both of these countries, the underground Communist Party of Malaya, which is Beijing-oriented, has been carrying out armed revolution for the last thirty years. Although this insurgency has failed to produce results, it still goes on, and no one can predict what would happen if the Malayan Communist Party were to receive substantial assistance from outside sources in the form of weapons, training, and money.

None of the ASEAN states believes it can depend on military intervention by the United States should a communist power mount aggression either directly or by proxy, first in Thailand and later against peninsular Malaysia and Singapore. The United States does not appear to have recovered from the trauma of Vietnam. Although the Seventh Fleet possesses the strongest conventional sea and air power in the area, ASEAN leaders do not believe that this power will be exercised when it is most needed. It is therefore not regarded as a credible deterrent against Vietnamese military expansion.

The ASEAN leaders are not moved by the official expressions of American strategic interest in the area that are made from time to time by important leaders in Washington. Nobody doubts that the United States has such an interest and wants to maintain the status quo. What is in doubt is the political will to exercise the enormous power that the United States possesses. ASEAN leaders do not form their opinions solely on the basis of statements by American leaders. They also watch events in Africa and in Iran. The apparent ease with which the Shah was brought down and current changes in the attitudes of pro-American Middle East countries such as Saudi Arabia are taken as disturbing signs of America's continuing lack of will to be assertive in matters of regional security.

The situation is a disturbing one for the ASEAN countries, since their future prosperity depends on continuing economic access to the United States, Western Europe, and Japan. These economic relationships have brought about enormous benefits in the last decade, and there is no way in which all the communist countries combined—even if concerted action of this kind were possible—could make up for the severance of these ties. The result of a cutoff in relations with the advanced industrial states would be an immediate and calamitous fall in the standard of living. That is why the ASEAN countries fear the expansion of communist influence, either by direct military aggression or by the more subtle means of subversion and externally assisted guerrilla insurgency.

Perhaps the ASEAN leaders have been both unfair and wrong in their assessment of America's commitment to maintaining peace and stability in the region. But if the U.S. government is firmly resolved not to allow the expansion of communist power in Southeast Asia through military conquests, American leaders have not made their intentions credible.

ASEAN leaders, however, are not as depressed as this analysis might suggest. They realize that under the American system of government, policy changes do take place, especially in times of trouble, and the present phase of indifference to Southeast Asia may not last. America's preoccupation with its own current domestic economic difficulties may give way in the future to greater concern and involvement in world problems, especially when informed public opinion comes to understand the extent of the loss of American prestige in the international community which current U.S. foreign policies have brought about.

One hopes that this realization in the United States will not be too far off. Such a change in attitude could come more quickly if the loss of prestige could be shown to have a tangible effect on the American standard of living—for example, if it could have influenced the oil squeeze which a friendly Saudi Arabia could have prevented but did not. Until then, the Southeast Asian states will depend for their security on the antagonism between the PRC and the SRV generated by Vietnam's invasion of Kampuchea, and the rivalry between China and the Soviet Union for influence in Southeast Asia. But this is a fragile balance which may not last very long.

The parlous nature of the power balance in East Asia will slowly but surely affect the thinking of ASEAN leaders. Attitudes could change rapidly should there be a collision between Vietnamese and Thai forces (which could happen, for instance, if Vietnamese army units intruded into Thailand in hot pursuit of Pol Pot's forces, or under the pretext of such action). The present feeling of unease could congeal into something more coherent. We cannot predict the courses of action the ASEAN countries might take in the interest of their collective security. A formal military alliance is a long way off and is unlikely to come about except under the most compelling circumstances, which cannot now be foreseen. These problems are compounded by the realization, never publicly acknowledged, that no combination of ASEAN ground forces can provide a credible deterrent to the Vietnamese.

The intelligence communities of the ASEAN governments are likely to address their minds more systematically to the question of collective security than will public opinion. The logic of the situation presents them with some disturbing and immediate problems. The first is that Thailand, as a frontline state, depends for its security on one communist power to protect it against aggression by another.

As long as the Vietnamese live up to the public pledges they have given to the ASEAN states of their peaceful intentions, Thailand's vulnerability will be a matter of concern but not of sufficient gravity to stimulate a move toward concerted action.

The situation could change, however, if the SRV were to adopt a belligerent attitude toward Thailand. In such circumstances, the ASEAN states are likely to show more overt and common responses to problems of collective security. Nevertheless, unless there is a change in the political climate in Washington favorable to the use of American sea and air power as a means of checking overt communist aggression, the efficacy of the ASEAN response will remain in doubt.

Chapter 8

AN INDONESIAN PERSPECTIVE ON SECURITY TRENDS IN EAST ASIA

Soedjatmoko[1]

In assessing Asian and American perspectives on regional security issues in the 1980s, I sense deep differences in views of the future. Asian specialists on security affairs seem to share a sense of the fragility of the situation in the Western Pacific, in rather sharp contrast with the American attitude of optimism—sometimes bordering on self-satisfaction—with regard to the U.S. position in the Asia-Pacific region. Although both American and Asian specialists are sensitive to a broad range of problems which will shape regional security issues in the coming decade, their attention at present seems to be focused rather narrowly on events in the Indochina region, on conflicting perceptions of who is encircling whom, and on how much leverage one major power might have over the local contending parties for use in contending with other major powers.

Fears seem to play a continuing role in building self-fulfilling prophesies of the future. Much of the current tension in Indochina seems to result from China's fear of continuing major power involvement south of its borders and from the reciprocal Vietnamese fear of Chinese hegemony. These concerns have produced what is now clearly, at least at one level of analysis, a struggle for a mutually acceptable power mix in two countries doomed to be buffer states, Kampuchea (Cambodia) and Laos. The outcome of the current conflict will determine whether it is possible for Vietnam, China, and Thailand to coexist in some viable equilibrium.

The tortured history of conflict in Indochina since World War II seems to me to emphasize, given the fervent patriotism of the Vietnamese, how limited foreign influence on the Peninsula has been. This history also shows how constrained is the effective long-distance projection of military power, unless it is supported by a broad complex of economic and political factors. Thus, future projections of Soviet influence over events in Asia must give due consideration to the factors that will limit Moscow's leverage over current developments. We must not be prisoners of the present situation—much less the past—in assessing regional security issues, policy choices, and dilemmas that the United States and the countries of East Asia will have to face in the coming decade.

FUTURE PROSPECTS FOR SOVIET INFLUENCE IN ASIA

In this presentation I propose to point out without extensive elaboration a

[1] Dr. Soedjatmoko currently serves as adviser to Indonesia's National Development Planning Agency (Bappenas), having previously held many posts in the Indonesian foreign service. He was Indonesia's ambassador to the United States from 1968 to 1971.

The personal views expressed in this paper, which are based on the author's presentation to the *Conference on East Asian Security in the 1980s*, do not necessarily reflect those of the National Development Planning Agency.

number of issues that I believe must be given due weight in any proper assessment of likely security problems in the Asia-Pacific region for the 1980s. First, there is the Soviet Union. It is of course quite possible to argue about the capacity of the Soviet Union to project its military or political power much beyond present limits— provided, of course, that the Vietnamese perception of the Chinese threat remains at its present level. The current degree of Soviet influence need not constitute a major threat to the equilibrium of forces within the region, although to say this does not exhaust the subject. After all, there is the likelihood that in the 1980s the Soviet Union will experience a change of leadership. A new team in Moscow is initially bound to be an uncertain and much less prestigious one than the present leadership. It might, for instance, feel compelled to assert itself rather aggressively in order to establish its own credibility; and this, in turn, could affect Moscow's response to a number of problems. How would this affect Moscow's policies toward the Middle East? Would an American willingness to provide the Soviet Union technology that would speed up domestic oil exploration and exploitation affect Soviet behavior toward the Middle East? In this connection, it will make a great deal of difference how this new leadership perceives the United States—its strengths, its weaknesses, and ultimately its political resolve. The next decade is bound to be a period of great uncertainty which will have its reflection in the Asia-Pacific region.

In addition, population trends in the Soviet Union suggest that an increasingly large proportion of the Soviet draft-age population will come from the Muslim and/or Turkic nationalities in Soviet Central Asia, Kazakhstan, and the Caucasus rather than from the dominant Slavic populations (Russians, Ukrainians, and Belorussians).[2] A major proportion of these Asians will be Moslem. Even though religious expression has not been encouraged in the Soviet Union, it is inconceivable that these Soviet Asians with Moslem roots will remain insensitive to developments in the Islamic world south of the USSR.

Also, the relationship between the Soviet Union and the Eastern European countries is certain to change in the next decade as a result of several anticipated economic and political developments. These changes, while far removed from the Asia-Pacific region, will affect power balances and perceptions of Soviet power in that region as well.

TRENDS IN JAPAN'S REGIONAL ROLE

These balances and perceptions would be far more directly affected by a conclusion on the part of the Soviet Union that improved relations with Japan would facilitate rather than hinder the attainment of its goal of strengthening the Soviet naval presence in the Pacific in order to achieve some degree of parity in the balance of superpower naval capabilities. Such a conclusion, at the right time and under the right conditions, might lead to a very attractive Soviet offer of mutual cooperation that Tokyo would find difficult to reject. Such an offer might involve

[2] See Jeremy Azrael, *Emergent Nationality Problems in the USSR*, The Rand Corporation, R-2172-AF, September 1977, pp. 16-22; and Murray Feshbach and Stephen Rapawy, "Soviet Population and Manpower Trends and Policies," in *Soviet Economy in a New Perspective*, Joint Economic Committee, U.S. Congress, Washington, D.C., October 14, 1976, pp. 143-154.

the four northern islands[3] and some share in the economic development of Siberian resources. At that time Tokyo might be much more interested in entertaining such an offer than it would be right now, given Japan's current desire to develop an evenhanded approach in its relations with China and the Soviet Union[4] and the need to secure energy supplies.

The chapters in this volume by Takuya Kubo and Paul Langer provide some very significant insights into possible changes in Japanese defense policy; but once we reach the comforting conclusion that in the 1980s Japan will most likely remain under the protection of the defense treaty with the United States, we tend to minimize the potential for future problems. I believe we underestimate the longer-term impact of what, in my view, are the unreasonable pressures the U.S. government and the Congress have been putting on Japan with regard to its trade surplus with the United States. The continuing hectoring and monitoring of Japanese performance in reducing the trade surplus—which, as Harald Malmgren notes, is a manifestation of structural problems not only on the Japanese side but also on the American side of the relationship[5]—must be deeply humiliating to the Japanese nation as a whole. This is bound to provide a psychological impetus to the growing Japanese desire to gradually assume a more independent stance in foreign policy.

However glacially slow, a shift in Japanese psychology and in Japan's perception of the world toward the development of the kind of international environment that will better suit its own resource requirements and trading needs is quite likely to manifest itself in the 1980s. Rising energy prices, recession, and slower economic growth rates in the global economy as well as in Japan may speed up this process. This shift is certain to be reflected in changes in Japan's domestic political constellation, with an end to the power monopoly of the Liberal Democratic Party (LDP).

Given the growing Japanese perception that protectionist trends in the United States and Western Europe are closing it out of very important industrial markets (markets that are essential to keeping the population fed and maintaining the economic growth rate to which Japan's social and political system has become adjusted), and given the additional insecurity of access to energy supplies, Japan may move much closer to China and to the Third World in the 1980s, and to the Soviet Union as well. Whether we will see such a confluence of developments in Northeast Asia may depend to a large extent on the willingness and the capacity of the United States to forgo short-term satisfactions in dealings with Japan in favor of a longer-range understanding of the mutuality of interests of the two countries as they both move into their post-industrial phase. A repositioning of Japan toward the communist powers would profoundly affect the distribution of economic and political power in the Asia-Pacific region. It would also raise questions about whether the revival of Japanese nationalism associated with such a shift would be accompanied by a new militarism as opposed to a continuing commitment to democracy. The course of these potential developments is certain to have a profound impact on the region as a whole in the coming decade.

[3] See pp. 48, 80, and 104 above for further discussion of this issue.
[4] This point is discussed by Takuya Kubo, pp. 103-104 above.
[5] See pp. 206-207 and 212-213 below.

CHINA'S MODERNIZATION EFFORT

While most current discussion on the question of China focuses on the international impact of China's modernization efforts, and in particular on the effect of closer Chinese-U.S. contacts on the Soviet-American relationship, an equally important question is the likely impact of rapid change on China itself. The speed with which Deng Xiaoping (Teng Hsiao-p'ing) has moved to institutionalize the "four modernizations"[6] is of course understandable. In the limited time he still has in a position of national leadership, he obviously wants to make the process of economic and social development irreversible. But one wonders whether he is aware of the political and social costs of rapid modernization—the dislocations, disparities, and tensions that inevitably develop as part of such an effort (quite apart from the remaining strength of his opposition in the Politburo, the Army, and the Air Force).

It seems to me only realistic to assume that even if the modernization goals are consistently pursued, the process itself will be a halting one with many sudden stops and starts, zigs and zags. There is also the question of what pattern of industrialization the present Chinese leadership envisages, and what kind of political economy. In any event, China will have to develop a great deal of its resources for export purposes in order to be able to pay for the import requirements of the "four modernizations."

Beyond this issue lies another question. Will China develop an export-oriented, outward-looking, growth economy, or an inward-looking one, aimed at increasing the efficiency and capacity of its local industry? In the first case, the domestic impact of economic growth would be profound in terms of patterns of income distribution and consumption, the distribution of power among the various regions of China, and the level of popular expectations. If the Chinese opt for an export economy, no market in the world will remain unaffected by its entry. In particular, the economies of the low-income countries of the Asia-Pacific region would feel the negative impact of cheap Chinese manufactured goods on their own industrialization efforts. In the case of an inward-looking pattern of growth, China's claim on global resources would very substantially affect existing patterns of resource supply simply because of the size of its claim on those resources.[7] Whatever the choice, patterns of trade and resource flow within the Asia-Pacific region in the next ten years will inevitably be substantially altered by China's participation in the world economy, with important, but as yet unclear, strategic implications.

There is another aspect of Beijing's (Peking's) modernization program that deserves consideration. In their efforts to mobilize resources in the West, the Chinese have shown an interest in involving American and European citizens of Chinese ancestry—what Beijing calls "Overseas Chinese"—in their projects. They are also discovering that in the Southeast Asian region the Overseas Chinese constitute an immeasurable fund of skilled manpower in a variety of fields. Undoubtedly, these skilled workers will be increasingly drawn into the modernization effort. Contrary to our expectations of ten or twenty years ago, China's appeal to the Overseas Chinese will not be primarily political, but economic. Nonetheless, this process will seriously affect popular perceptions and feelings in those countries of Southeast Asia where the Overseas Chinese are a minority. How these perceptions

[6] See pp. 216-220 below.
[7] See the analysis of this issue by Guy J. Pauker, pp. 225, 228-229, and 239-240 below.

and attitudes will be affected is still unclear, but the changes that result from China's modernization effort will create political problems relating to questions of assimilation, integration, national cohesion, and ethnic harmony in the region.

Before leaving the subject of China, I would like to add one comment on the question of Taiwan's future. Much current speculation centers on the possibility of a "Hong Kong" formula for the island's status in relation to the mainland; but we should keep in mind that a reverse scenario might turn out to be the case. It is not inconceivable that once Beijing and Taipei have worked out some acceptable solution to the Taiwan problem, China might find such a formula rather attractive in determining its future relationship with Hong Kong and Macao as well. Whether or not this situation will develop in the next decade, the perception itself is not without strategic implications for the Asia-Pacific region.

Finally, as China moves forward in its modernization process, it can be expected to try to develop closer ties with the Third World. As it encounters the complexities and the perplexing contradictions that accompany economic development, both internally and in its dealings with the outside world, it may become interested in the various lessons that can be drawn from the developmental experience of a number of Third World countries. While it has continued to give aid to a small number of countries, often on rather generous terms, China so far has not shown any particular interest in involving itself significantly in the problems of the Third World (this may be related to the disastrous role that China tried to play internationally in the course of the Cultural Revolution), except as a function of its adversary relationship with the Soviet Union. To the extent that China experiences the frustrations of the modernization and industrialization process, it is quite likely to share in the growing bitterness with which a large part of the Third World now views the development of North-South relations.

THE FUTURE OF NORTH-SOUTH RELATIONS

It is rather revealing that none of the contributors to this volume deal with the North-South issue. We should not underestimate, however, the impact of North-South tensions on the Asia-Pacific region. It is true, of course, that the ASEAN countries have been rather moderate members in the Third World's dialogue with the North. Nevertheless, they are undeniably part of that world, sharing the perceptions, aspirations, and emotions that characterize this loose conglomeration of nations. And finally, we should not forget that the countries of Indochina are also part of that world.

In late 1978 I had the opportunity of attending a "South-South" conference in Arusha, Tanzania. It was the first time an effort was made at the non-governmental level to bring together "negotiators and thinkers" of the Third World to assess the state of the North-South dialogue. The meeting turned out to be an exercise in relentless self-examination. Discussion was quite frank and searching about the weaknesses and the mistakes of the Third World in this dialogue in terms of negotiating strategy, selection of negotiating focus and agenda, and solidarity in the face of growing disparities among and within the Third World countries. At the same time, anger and bitterness were expressed toward the North for its by then obvious unwillingness to try to accommodate the essential development requirements of the Third World. There was a strong sense among the participants, in varying degrees, that "the Third World has been had."

The signs of a North increasingly immersed in its own problems closing itself off from the industrialization of the South have since become only clearer. The slogan "no more Japans" is another indication of this trend. The Third World's capacity to counter this mood or to retaliate effectively, except to a small extent with its oil resources, is obviously very limited. But there was already an awareness at the Arusha conference that the breakdown of a meaningful North-South dialogue had become a real possibility as a result of the inability of both the North and the South to come to grips with the need for structural changes at a national level in tandem with international structural reforms.[8]

Such a breakdown would mean the end of the hopes and visions, however vague and tentative, of a collective and carefully managed series of steps toward the establishment of a viable, more equitable international system. The 1980s would then become a decade of continued drift and fragmentation at the international level, with radicalization of the Third World, growing instability and unpredictability, and armed conflicts complicated by East-West or intra-Eastbloc tensions and rivalries. It should also be said, parenthetically, that such a situation would doom to failure any "Northern grand design," any alternative fallback plan, or even any new international monetary system.

In such circumstances, it would be highly unrealistic to expect that a rapid deterioration in North-South relations would not have a serious effect on the Asia-Pacific region, despite the optimistic mood and favorable projections of the region's economic development prospects made by some observers.

Quite apart from the likelihood that high energy prices and slowing growth rates in the OECD countries will also exacerbate North-South tensions in general, I might point to two specific developments that are also bound to have a bearing on these relationships. One is referred to in the analysis by Mr. Malmgren, i.e., the role of the international capital market in development.[9] The other is the religious revival of the Islamic world.

As to the first, there is no doubt that the private capital market is playing an important role in resource transfers from the industrialized world to the developing countries, including those of the Asia-Pacific region. While this transfer has greatly assisted the attainment of relatively high growth rates in a number of the developing countries, we should not be unaware of its broader implications. One is the increasing dependency of the developing countries on the private banking system. In some countries the effort to maintain at almost any cost creditworthiness in the eyes of the international banking system has led, and will continue to lead, to distortions in the development effort. Inevitably, the emphasis given to bankable, modern sector development projects will lead to a reduction of resources available for social development and for the creation of preconditions for greater social equity. Within the next decade there may well be a political backlash against this kind of dependency and distortion.

Neither should we close our eyes to the utter fragility of the role capital markets are now playing in relation to the developing countries. The reason for making

[8] This issue is discussed in more detail by Harald Malmgren on pp.206-208 below.
[9] See pp. 210-211 below.

this point is that private resource flows are often used as an argument for the reduction of government aid. The fact is, of course, that aid will remain an important resource for the creation of employment opportunities and social development projects, especially in the low-income, populous countries. Such aid will be very important for keeping the inevitable inequities that are part of the economic growth process within politically sustainable limits.

In this regard, we should not close our eyes to the fact that we know very little about how to create productive jobs in the rural areas of populous Asian nations on the massive scale that is required. The empirical data base and the state of theory that could help us do this are sadly deficient, and no large and populous developing country has thus far solved the problem satisfactorily. It would be a grave mistake to underestimate the impact of the rate of population increase on the security of the region over the next ten years. This issue will have its domestic impact in terms of pressures on resources, on job opportunities, and on the political system as a whole, but it will have a transnational impact as well. It is quite likely that the 1980s will see large population movements within and across national boundaries as people search for work, food, and physical safety. The current Indochina refugee problem is just one manifestation of this problem. Given growing income disparities and the limited capacity of governments to manage structural social change in a humane way, this problem is likely to become more acute in the next ten years. And inevitably, such developments will have security as well as social and economic implications.

THE REVIVAL OF ISLAM

With regard to the phenomenon of the religious revival in the Moslem world, we should be aware that this development constitutes, in part, a moral backlash against the excessive materialism, greed, and corruption that always seems to accompany rapid modernization and industrialization. The revulsion against these trends in the Islamic world has been dressed in a religious garb covering a complex set of reactions, in part a regressive fundamentalism and in part a more open, progressive response somewhat similar to the European counterreformation of the sixteenth century

We should remember that all countries in the ASEAN region have important Moslem populations. In the coming decade the region is bound to be affected by developments in the Islamic world in the Middle East and South Asia. It is of course impossible to foresee the shape of the problems this might create in the ASEAN region. But it would be foolhardy to ignore the likelihood of their arising in the not too distant future.

ASEAN AND REGIONAL SECURITY

The future of ASEAN is now a matter of particular interest, given the renewed turbulence in Indochina. Some observers are raising the question of whether ASEAN should not gradually assume security functions in addition to its political and economic roles. In my view, the greatest mistake ASEAN could make would be to abandon the primacy of economic development as the mainstay of stability in the region. The ASEAN states do not have the resources to both arm themselves and successfully pursue economic development plans. An armed ASEAN without adequate economic development would be self-defeating. I am quite confident that the China-Vietnam conflict and the pressure that is now being put on Thailand by the Vietnamese incursion into Kampuchea will not break ASEAN solidarity. This, of course, may not be the only test that ASEAN will have to face in the next ten years. There is the likelihood that all countries of the Association will have to go through problems of leadership succession in the 1980s. They will also have to deal with problems arising out of rapid economic development and its uneven impact on delicate social and ethnic balances.

Another test of ASEAN solidarity might be the impending independence of Brunei. And finally there is the problem of the great disparity in growth rates between, let us say, Singapore and the other countries of the Association, especially those with large populations. The demonstration effect of Singapore's high consumption patterns may lead to expectations in the other countries that will seriously strain their political systems. This problem is, of course, only part of the more general need to develop new and mutually beneficial, and therefore non-exploitative, relationships between the newly industrialized countries in the Asia-Pacific region and the low-income, populous latecomers to the development process. I have no doubt, however, that ASEAN will pass these tests.

THE CREDIBILITY OF AMERICA'S REGIONAL SECURITY ROLE

Before concluding this brief *tour d'horizon*, I would like to refer to the particularly troublesome issue of nuclear proliferation. The pursuit of an autonomous deterrent capacity by any country in the Asia-Pacific region would have profound consequences for the region as a whole. South Korea is not the only country that is thinking, if not talking, about the development of an autonomous nuclear deterrent capacity. The critical factor here obviously is not the rational calculus pertaining to nuclear weapons, but the credibility of America's political will, the perceptions of Asian countries regarding the American political capacity to act according to its security commitments, as distinct from verbal assurances and policy statements. Where does the United States think it is going, and where is it perceived to be going by the other countries in the region? There are deep uncertainties in Asia about America's political will and about its capacity to get on top of its domestic problems and subsequently to provide international leadership. These uncertainties lie at the heart of the anxieties that exist within the region regarding security prospects for the 1980s.

This brief enumeration of the profound changes that can be expected in East Asia in the 1980s, and some of the problems these may pose, highlights my view that regional security in the coming decade will not be primarily a military problem but will be more economic and geopolitical in character. Nor will these social changes and economic processes be amenable to manipulation by external forces through the application of military power—either by the United States or by the Soviet Union. We should also realize that we are at the beginning of an historical process, one that is long in duration and conflict-laden, that will eventually see the emergence of new, non-Western civilizations alongside those of the West: a Sinitic civilization, a Hindu, a Moslem, and possibly others. This is not an unlikely development, especially in light of the continuing reduction of American power relative to the rest of the world. Undoubtedly, for a long time the United States will continue to be the strongest political, military, and economic power on the globe, but in terms of its capacity to shape the international order and to influence the course of history, that power is going to be increasingly limited.

What are the implications of such trends for the United States? There is in the first place a need for the United States to realize that under present world conditions, its security can no longer be unilaterally defined and safeguarded. It will have to learn to live—with some degree of equanimity and self-confidence—in an international environment that will be increasingly uncertain and vulnerable. It will also have to realize that these uncertainties and this sense of vulnerability will not be overcome by the development of military strength alone. Of course, nobody denies the need for the United States to sustain adequate military strength as an essential element in the strategic balance and in contributing to the viability of the international system, such as it is. But I believe it is very important for the United States to accept the limits to its capacity to influence the very deeply rooted social and political processes now transforming various parts of the world, and to resist the temptation to use its military power for political purposes in the mode of earlier decades and historical periods.

At the same time, the nature of the changes that are likely to take place in the various countries of East Asia, affecting the security of the region as a whole, suggests the need for the United States to enlarge the range of available instrumentalities that would enable it to interact wisely and effectively with these countries while these processes of change are going on. This means, first, a more effective structure for continuous and intensive communication. The transformations of the 1980s will entail changes in interests, shifts in perception, and also new uncertainties, new fears, new aspirations, and new tensions. To deal with them will require much more intensive and frequent communications across the board, bilaterally and multilaterally. One necessity for effective communication is a research institution like the OECD for the Asia-Pacific region, an institution capable of articulating the broader implications of specific national policies. In the course of the next ten years, it might be possible as well as desirable to establish an Asia-Pacific forum encompassing all the countries in the region, irrespective of ideological orientation, as an indispensable instrument for tension management.[10] Japan may be the only nation that will be in a position to take the initiative for the establishment of such a forum, although one might be started on a subregional basis—a Northwest Pacific Forum, or a Southeast Asia Forum encompassing ASEAN as well as the countries of Indochina.

America's capacity to deal with the security implications of the changes that can be anticipated for the 1980s will also require greater emphasis on education that relates to the Asia-Pacific region. The recession in the United States in the past decade has led to the partial dismantling of its infrastructure for listening to and interacting with other cultures. There have been significant cutbacks in the opportunity for people from Asia, both civilian and military, to study in the United

[10] See further discussion of this concept on p. 214 below.

States. It is important to reverse this trend. Likewise, foreign-area studies in the United States have been drastically cut back.[11] It is very important to enlarge the number of experts and the quality of expertise on the various countries in the Asia-Pacific region available to the United States. There is also a need to combine expertise on the Soviet Union and the Pacific region. And in view of the crucial importance of developments in the Islamic world for America's security interests, the number of centers for Islamic studies in the United States is sadly inadequate.

Finally, there is the matter of cultural policy. Given the rapid pace of developments in East Asia, it is of the greatest importance that within the region there be a greater sharing of perceptions of the nature and the direction of changes that are taking place in Asia as well as in the world at large. If there is any validity to my surmise that we will see the emergence of a number of modern non-Western civilizations in the world, there will likewise be a variety of non-Western forms of modernization. It is important that the United States develop the capacity to understand these different processes and paths of modernization and, if possible, to maintain contact with them in order to share certain basic values. Cultural policies, by themselves, will not solve political conflicts, but they could help to change perceptions of social and political trends and conflict situations and could thus exert a positive influence on the terms by which tensions will be managed or conflicts resolved.

[11] A detailed analysis of the current state of foreign-area training and research in the United States is given in Sue E. Berryman, Paul F. Langer, John Pincus, and Richard H. Solomon, *Foreign Language and International Studies Specialists: The Marketplace and National Policy*, The Rand Corporation, R-2501-NEH, September 1979.

PART III

ECONOMIC TRENDS AND REGIONAL SECURITY

Chapter 9

THE HISTORICAL AND WORLD CONTEXT OF EAST ASIAN DEVELOPMENT[1]

Herman Kahn[2]

INTRODUCTION

Let me begin by giving a metaphor on much of the historical and world context. The metaphor is based upon a cartoon that has been much circulated in the Pentagon. The cartoon shows a log drifting down a river. There are about 10,000 ants on the log, and they are well organized. They have study groups, briefings, conferences; they make decisions; and so on. Each of these ants thinks that he is steering the log or helping the organization or individual doing the steering. In fact, about 98 percent of the time, the log moves pretty much as wind, weather, and current drive it. Once in a while it comes too close to a rock, sandbar, or shore. Then, by heroic efforts, the ants can avoid or lessen the danger—or help dislodge the log if it gets stuck. Once in an even greater while, there is a fork in the river. The ants can look down each branch of the fork and make a decision as to which branch they would like to take. They always base this decision on some combination of self-interest, national interest, and ideology. In any case, they choose the branch that appears to be best as far as they can see. They cannot know, of course, that just around the turn, there is a waterfall or something equally disastrous. They tend to pick the branch that looks more attractive in the short run, unless they have a theory or ideology of the right or of the left, in which case they tend to pick the right and left alternatives more or less blindly.

DEGREES OF BELIEF

There is an ancient Chinese proverb, attributed to Confucius, that observes, "To know what you know, and to know what you don't know, is the characteristic of one who knows." This seems a most useful insight; but, fortunately or unfortunately, we ourselves in many cases are in an in-between state. We may know a good deal about a subject, without knowing enough—or even knowing how much we know. Or we may know that some theories do not hold, but not know what theories do hold. Thus, the context set forth in this chapter often involves, implicitly or explicitly, theories of cause and effect, or at least a theory as to why certain events

[1] I have drawn freely from my book, *World Economic Development: 1979 and Beyond*, Westview Press, Boulder, Colorado, 1979. The interested reader can find there an elaboration of many of the following arguments.
[2] Herman Kahn is a specialist in public policy analysis, notably defense and foreign policy and economic, technological, and social trends. After working at The Rand Corporation, he founded the Hudson Institute in 1961. He is now the Director and Chairman of the Institute. In addition to numerous articles, Mr. Kahn has published many books, including *On Thermonuclear War, The Year 2000,* and, most recently, *The Japanese Challenge* and *World Economic Development*.

tend to be correlated even if we are not quite sure of the causal relations involved. Some of the theories or correlations are widely accepted, but many will be conjectural or controversial. To aid in distinguishing among the degrees of belief various groups have in these theories and conditions, we have found it helpful to have an explicit scale of distinctions, as set forth below:

1. *Atheism.* Complete rejection of a theory; this can be friendly or hostile in approach.
2. *Agnosticism.* Simply not knowing. One may or may not believe the knowledge is obtainable. This position can be very important but is seldom expressed or acknowledged explicitly.
3. *Skepticism.* One is prepared to believe but wants more data or argumentation.
4. *Deism.* There is something in the idea, but one is not sure exactly what.
5. *Scotch verdict.* In Scotland, a jury can come up with three verdicts in a criminal case: guilty, not guilty, or unproven. The "unproven" decision implies that the jury believes that the individual is guilty but that the guilt has not been "proven beyond a reasonable doubt." This is very similar to the requirement in a commercial case in the United States in which all that is required for a decision is "a reasonable preponderance of the evidence." This concept of a reasonable preponderance of the evidence applies to many practical decisions by business and government, and we use it freely here.
6. *Acceptance.* This is always, of course, in relationship to a group. It can simply reflect what is often thought of as "conventional wisdom" or conventional standards of proof. Thus, what is sufficient for a physicist is often insufficient for a mathematician.
7. *Divine revelation.* A claim to total validity or unquestioning belief, perhaps because the proponent feels the information or position came from divine revelation or some other unchallengeable source.

It is interesting to note that in most academic discussions, one must generally have attained level-six belief in order to use an idea, while in practical affairs there is rarely enough time or data to advance beyond some lower level before it is necessary to act—i.e., to accept or reject a notion, at least for the time being and to a degree. This is one reason why it is difficult to bring the academic and the practical worlds together.

The above seven levels of belief (or distinctions) turn out to be much more useful than a simple dichotomy of true or false, or even a trichotomy of true, uncertain, and false.

THE LIMITS-TO-GROWTH CONTROVERSY

The question of whether—and how much—economic growth is desirable and feasible is a basic issue for affluent, developed nations and, in principle, for all countries. The two opposing sides of this debate are often presented in a somewhat exaggerated but common form, as shown in Table 1.

Table 1

TWO CHARACTERISTIC CURRENT VIEWS ON TECHNOLOGICAL AND ECONOMIC GROWTH

	Issue	Neo-Malthusian View	Post-Industrial View
1.	Basic model	World is a "fixed pie" with very limited and non-renewable resources.	"Growing pie" is more appropriate metaphor (the more one produces, the more one can produce—within limits).
2.	More technology and more capital	New technology and additional capital investment are more likely than not to exacerbate current problems.	Necessary to increase production to desirable levels and to protect the environment.
3.	Management and economic decision-making	Likely failure of effective management of resources and control of pollution.	Probable success; with some exceptions, level of management required not remarkably high.
4.	Resources	Will soon run into absolute limits on food, energy, other resources, space for waste disposal.	Possible to support world population of 20 to 30 billion living in relative affluence.
5.	Current growth	Uncontrolled and exponential—will accelerate dramatically the approaching exhaustion of resources.	Plausible case can be made for world "stabilizing" in 21st century at 10 billion people, $200 trillion GWP, $20,000/capita.
6.	Innovation and discovery	May postpone eventual collapse, but likely to make it more severe when it occurs.	Will often produce new problems but will also solve many, improve efficiency, and upgrade quality of life.
7.	Income gaps	Rising rapidly, making imminent a worldwide "class war" or a series of desperate crises between rich and poor.	Next century will likely see worldwide abolition of most absolute poverty.
8.	Industrial	Full industrialization of Third World would be disastrous; further growth of developed world worse.	Industrialization of Third World will (and should) continue.
9.	Quality of life	Continued economic or population growth means further deterioration of environment, endangering quality of life.	Adequate internalizing of appropriate external costs can mean high quality of life for almost all.
.0.	Long-range outlook	Unless revolutionary changes soon made, late 20th or early 21st century will see greatest catastrophe since black plague.	This period is likely to make the historical transition to a materially abundant life for almost all.

In a book published in 1976,[3] my colleagues and I presented a thorough discussion of four positions on world economic growth: Convinced Neo-Malthusian, Guarded Pessimist, Guarded Optimist, and Technology and Growth Enthusiast. The issues are much better presented if regarded as being among four choices, and the interested reader is referred to the book for a complete discussion of these concepts. We believe it is unnecessary to discuss the matter as fully here. As far as we are concerned, this particular debate has been effectively settled, at least if the discussion is restricted to the four positions. The Guarded Optimist position clearly earned at least a Scotch verdict in its favor and probably cannot, in the nature of things, achieve a higher level of confidence for any sober group. (This Guarded Optimist position is quite close to the Post-Industrial view described in Table 1). The Guarded Pessimist position could not be ruled out. The pure (or convinced) Neo-Malthusian view is not acceptable except as a relatively remote possibility (associated with bad luck or very bad management) or as a pure hypothesis. Yet in the mid-1970s this view was predominant. Many shared the view expressed by French President Valery Giscard d'Estaing at a press conference in 1974: "We can see that practically all these curves are leading us to disaster."

Or consider the U.S. Harris survey, which reported as follows in December 1975:

> A solid 61–23 percent majority of the American people feels it is "morally wrong" that Americans, who comprise only 6 percent of the world's population, consume 40 percent of the world's production of energy and raw materials. A 55-30 percent majority feels that this disparity between population and consumption "hurts the well-being of the rest of the world." Consequently, a 50-31 percent plurality is worried that a continuation of this consumption of the world's resources by Americans "will turn the rest of the people of the world against us."

However, Neo-Malthusian views are still widely accepted by many people in advanced affluent nations, even though they are no longer accepted by most experts and specialists, at least in their original form. This syndrome of attitudes is still very influential throughout the developed world, especially in Western Europe and Japan, in the sense that such views often dominate intellectual and policy discussions.

Thus, a reasonably distinguished English economist, E. J. Mishan, has stated in a recent book what he calls the third dismal theorem, "The more science, technology, and the gross national product grow, the more nasty, brutish, violent, and precarious become human existence." One interesting thing about this quotation is that it was repeated approvingly in a review by Leonard J. Silk, the business economist of the *New York Times;* similarly, *Business Week*, in reviewing a perfectly reasonable book by Ben F. Wattenberg explaining how well things were actually going in many aspects of the United States, was bitterly denunciatory of a simple pro-industrialization ideology.

One reason for such wide acceptance of these beliefs among upper-middle-class elites in affluent nations (even ones oriented to business) is that, to some extent, one's approach to economic growth is influenced—or even conditioned—by one's class interest (often even more than by one's occupational or other, more narrow

---

[3] Herman Kahn, William Brown, and Leon Martel, *The Next 200 Years*, Morrow, New York, 1976.

interests). Many aspects of the quality of life of the upper middle class do tend to decline as average per capita annual income in the society increases; in particular, it is not as much fun to receive a relatively high income if everybody else seems to have money also. In part, this is because to some degree wealth, like poverty, is relative. More importantly, the rising middle and working class crowd the upper middle class in traffic, recreation areas, perquisites, and so on. Their children compete with upper-middle-class children for educational, vocational, and recreational opportunities. Further, inexpensive high-quality services (e.g., maids) become less available or disappear. It is clear that the upper middle class today is spending more and enjoying it less. This helps to explain their eagerness to accept the limits-to-growth theory, and it helps to show why extensive debate is needed to promote an eventual consensus on the desirability of, and real possibilities for, economic growth to meet national needs and the interests of the rising middle and lower classes. It is still fun for people in these classes to join the upper middle class, even if it is not as much so (in some ways) as it was for those who made it earlier.

To summarize, the expressed Neo-Malthusian view of growth is a case of a great deal of smoke emerging from almost no fire at all, the smoke in this case being the notion that limited physical resources, pollution, and managerial inadequacies are almost certain to limit much further economic growth. The authors of *The Next 200 Years* are open-minded about how much economic growth is desirable, but not open-minded as to whether economic growth is likely to be halted or slowed because of such limits. The separate question of the degree to which economic growth should or will be limited by social (not physical) considerations is discussed briefly below.

FIVE BASIC TRENDS

I find it very useful, in presenting a broad context for the kind of discussion in this paper, to explicate some basic trends or forces that may affect the future and that are likely to be key elements in understanding one aspect or another of the present or the future. Five basic trends or events that we think will characterize the 1980s and the 1990s and that thus might supply important ingredients for our scenarios are listed below. Actually, the first point below can be thought of as a kind of 1,000-year background to our considerations; the second point gives part of a 10-year context; and only the last three points refer specifically to the next decade or two:

1. *The Millennial Background.* Emergence of a dramatically new period of history. There has already been a peaking in the percentage rates of growth of both world population and gross world product. Furthermore, what we call the Long-Term Multifold Trend of Western Culture—a complex concept that includes a 1,000-year movement from the sacred to the secular, and from traditional to modern—also begins to top out and in effect culminates in a 400-year period that we call the Great Transition. In this 400-year period, we expect to see a worldwide evolution from a poor and traditional world to a rich and modern one.
2. *The Long Cycle Background.* *L'Epoque de Malaise* for advanced developed nations, but continued dynamism for middle-income nations.

3. *Much Technological and Economic Progress* (e.g., in energy, in space, in various hyphenated sciences (such as bio-chemistry), and above all, in information generation, processing, and distribution). Full emergence of a problem-prone, super-industrial world economy[4]; early post-industrial economies begin to emerge in many advanced capitalist nations (ACNs).

4. *A Much More Multipolar and "Normalized" World, at Least Relatively.* The first planetwide economic and technological ecumène since *La Première Belle Epoque* (1886-1913).

5. *Continued Intense Confrontation Between Reformation and Counter-reformation in Values, Politics, and Attitudes.* Initially at least, a more or less worldwide "conservative renaissance." A full emergence of the Neo-Confucian culture accompanied by the rise of the Pacific Basin as a center of economic and cultural dynamism. A partial modern renaissance.

The above list uses some special vocabulary, or even jargon. As a result, it may cause some initial annoyance in some readers; yet it is often most useful to have such a simplified context, with a relatively simple but precise language that summarizes a lot of useful concepts and information. The *World Economic Development* book elaborates on all of the above even more than does the text below.

THE GREAT TRANSITION

I would now like to turn to the most important metaphor (or, if you will, concept or theory) of this overview, the Great Transition—the change in world society from traditional to modern, from pre-industrial to post-industrial, from primitive to technical and scientific, from poor to affluent, and so on. We can summarize the Great Transition as follows:

Two hundred years ago, mankind was almost everywhere scarce, everywhere poor, everywhere powerless before the forces of nature. Two hundred years from now, barring bad luck or very bad management (an essential caveat), mankind should be almost everywhere numerous, almost everywhere rich, and almost everywhere in control of the forces of nature.

I must concede that usually when a speaker refers to "a great transition," he is referring to more of the same—i.e., referring to a period of time between two other transitions. But I mean this quite differently. I am told that when Adam and Eve left the Garden of Eden, Adam turned to Eve and said, "We are living in an age of transition." Things are really going to be quite different—before and after.

Because this Great Transition is so important, I would like to set forth some of the major issues and the contexts in which it is occurring. I will make most of my remarks from the perspective of Western culture because, until recently, it is this culture more than any other that was responsible for what I often call the Progress Trinity: sustained economic growth; sustained increases in affluence; and sustained advancements in technology. No other culture did it before. However, I also feel, as discussed later, that Western culture is losing its preeminence in this process and that this preeminence will probably pass to what I call the Neo-Confucian culture (or cultures).

[4] Which, hopefully, will be largely problem-controlled by the early 21st century.

Probably the dominating phenomenon of Western culture is that it is now entering the last century of a 1,000-year trend from the sacred to the secular, from what Sorokin called an ideational culture to a sensate culture. We will describe later how some of the more recent manifestations of this trend have aroused the greatest concern in the Neo-Confucian cultures and in the Soviet Union, which think of the West in general and the United States in particular as a source of trends that they view as eroding important values, if not decadent.

Whether or not one accepts this perspective, one can recognize that almost all macro-historians have felt that such a trend to a "late sensate" culture is often associated with a permanent loss of vitality and dynamism or at least a loss until some crisis occurs and a drastic change is made in the society—a change that, still using Sorokin's terminology, is from "sensate" to either "ideational" or "idealistic." In any case, almost all the macro-historians seem to feel that it is very difficult to maintain a late sensate society in a state of high morale, dynamism, and general strength and creativity. It is also generally agreed, however, that the early sensate period is usually one of maximum brilliance, glitter, and apparent vitality.

Whether or not there has been any validity to these concepts for past civilizations, we argue that the history of Western culture is likely to have a very different end from the common picture of the decline of Rome. We feel that because of what we call the multifold trend (described below), many other things are happening in addition to the change from the sacred to the secular. As a result of these other things, the likely end of the story is more probably something more like the Great Transition than a Decline and Fall, though this is by no means assured.

I would also like to note that even though Western culture is relatively sensate, the middle class in the United States is probably less sensate than almost all other Western subcultures—that is, despite the shifting values of the high culture (i.e., of the more visible culture), the middle-class American seems to have held on to "square" values quite well. This holding on can be illustrated by the fact that during all of the turmoil of the late 1960s, a man like George Wallace was admired by something like four out of five Americans because he was defending square values —or, as it was said, he was "speaking out" on the issues. True, Eric Hoffer, in observing this phenomenon, remarked, "There's something sick about a society in which only a Southern racist cracker is speaking out on the major issues."[5] But even if this was true, the majority of Americans did not share this "sickness." It must be remembered that they did not admire Wallace's racism or his being a Southerner; they largely restricted their admiration to his defense of square values against the onslaughts of intellectuals and radicals.

I would also note that from 1969 through 1974 the U.S. population, when polled by Gallup as to what living person they admired most in the world, repeatedly gave one man second place:[6] The man was Billy Graham; and his startling prominence is again a testimony to the pervasiveness of square values in the United States. It should also be noted that neither Billy Graham nor George Wallace is a media hero. They both have been able to use the media, but the common idea that the values of the literate media dominate American thought and discussion is simply wrong when one is looking at the majority of the population.

[5] Quotation is from memory. H.K.

[6] The President of the United States always came out first, except during Watergate, when Henry Kissinger was first.

These observations, and some related trends, are especially relevant when considering the willingness of the American people to support some square or "traditional" policy which the President also supports as being in the national interest but the media or the Congress do not go along with. The possibilities for either creating such support or getting along without it are much greater than most discussion today would suggest.

Let us turn back to what I term a multifold trend which heavily emphasizes economic growth, technological advancement, and increasing affluence. Despite the above discussion on square values, one important aspect of this multifold trend is the emergence of the upper middle class as an increasingly visible and influential group in American society. The leading edge of this upper middle class is the intelligentsia, particularly the educated specialists of various sorts who operate the system, and the increasing number of relatively pure intellectuals (we sometimes call them the New Class or the Symbolist Class) who dominate the media and other professions devoted to manipulation and use of symbols, policy analysis, and the ideology of "the information society" generally. While neither the specialists nor the pure intellectuals are monolithic as a group—indeed, there is a spectrum of positions within both—each exhibits a very different distribution of attitudes and values than occurs among the general population. In particular, there has been a relatively general turning away from the Progress Trinity of economic growth, technological advancement, and increasing affluence as the major foci of people's lives, and a turning toward new emphases of various sorts—i.e., new priorities and new values. It is this turning away and the new emphases that accompany it[7] that made the limits-to-growth position so acceptable and that seems likely, eventually, to put a stop to rapid economic growth. (The stoppage will not result from shortages of resources, increasing pollution, or overwhelming problems of management, as is asserted in so much popular literature today.) This is terribly important for our prognosis. If there were a genuine likelihood of permanent and worldwide shortages of resources, one could expect desperate attempts to intervene in and control the resources of the Middle East or Southeast Asia. But it seems likely that under all but extreme circumstances, most resources will remain commercially available commodities at reasonable prices, even though there will be some specific examples of quasi-crises in availability.

THE MULTIFOLD TREND

Let us now look at what we call the multifold trend of Western culture. While much of this trend goes back 1,000 years or so, it can also be viewed as a quick summary of many of the major trends of the second half of the 20th century, those that have attained the most prominence or importance:

1. Increasingly sensate culture (empirical, this-worldly, secular, humanistic, pragmatic, manipulative, explicitly rational, utilitarian, contractual, epicurean, hedonistic, etc.). More recently, we see an almost complete

---

[7] See Chap. 3 of Kahn, *World Economic Development*, op. cit., or almost any publication on the New Class or on the social limits to growth for a discussion of these issues.

decline of the sacred and of "irrational" taboos, charismas, and authority structures.

2. Accumulation of scientific and technological knowledge. We are now witnessing the emergence of a genuine theoretical framework for the biological sciences; but social sciences are still in an early, largely empirical, and idealistic state.

3. Institutionalization of technological change (especially research, development, innovation, and diffusion). There is a conscious emphasis on finding and creating synergisms and serendipities.

4. Increasing role of bourgeois, bureaucratic, "meritocratic" elites. This trend is characterized by the emergence of intellectual and technocratic elites as a class; increasing literacy and education for everyone; the "knowledge industry" and the "triumph" of theoretical knowledge.

5. Increasing military capability of Western cultures. Issues of mass destruction, terrorism, and diffusion of advanced military technologies (both nuclear and conventional) are increasingly salient to both Western and non-Western cultures.

6. Increasing area of the world dominated or greatly influenced by Western culture. Of late, the West has become more reticent in asserting its values, with a consequent emphasis on synthesis with indigenous cultures and various "ethnic" revivals.

7. Increasing affluence. And, recently, more stress on egalitarianism.

8. Increasing rate of world population growth (until recently). This rate has probably passed its zenith, or soon will.

9. Urbanization. This trend is now characterized by suburbanization and "urban sprawl." Soon it will evolve to the growth of megalopoli, "sun belts," and rural areas with urban infrastructure and amenities.

10. Increasing recent attention to macro-environmental issues (e.g., constraints set by finiteness of earth and limited capacity of various local and global reservoirs to accept pollution).

11. Decreasing importance of primary and, of late, secondary occupations. Soon a similar decline in tertiary occupations and an increasing emphasis on advanced, honorific, or desirable quaternary occupations and activities.

12. Emphasis on "progress" and future-oriented thinking, discussion, and planning. Currently we see some retrogression in the technical quality of such activities. Conscious and planned innovation and manipulative rationality (e.g., social engineering) is increasingly applied to social, political, cultural, and economic worlds, as well as to shaping and exploiting the material world. There is some interest in ritualistic, incomplete, or pseudo-rational styles of things.

13. Increasing universality of the multifold trend.

14. Increasing tempo of change in all the above (which may, however, soon peak in many areas, or already has).

To illustrate what we mean by saying that the multifold trend has exhibited great dynamism during the 20th century, we will discuss Item 8, the rate of growth of world population. As shown in Fig. 1, we expect to see an extraordinary spike in the rate of population growth. These three curves illustrate a 50-year perspective, a 400-year perspective, and then a 20,000-year perspective. The last curve (c)

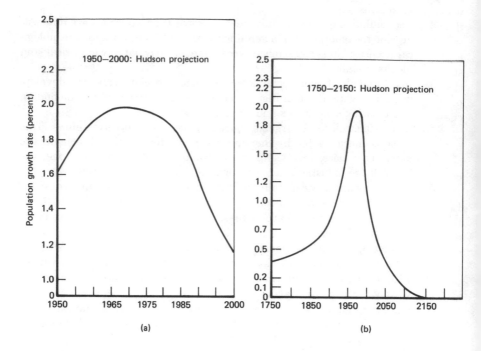

(a)

(b)

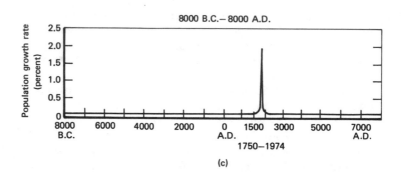

(c)

Fig. 1—Three historic perspectives on rate of growth
of world population

SOURCE: Ronald Freeman and Bernard Berelson, "The Human Population," *Scientific American*,
September 1974, pp. 36-37.

is taken from a 1974 issue of *Scientific American*. The first two curves use somewhat later data. Almost all the studies during the last five years or so tend to agree that the rate of population growth went through an incredibly rapid transition—a spike which peaked (probably in the early 1960s) at a little less than 2 percent and is about 100 years wide at the 1 percent point. If it is true that this extraordinary spike is unique in the 20,000-year period of history that started 10,000 years ago, then this is indeed a very special and unique period in human society. But the population spike is in many ways no more unique or dramatic than the rate of change of other aspects of the multifold trend described above.

In other words, we believe that the rate of change of almost every aspect of this multifold trend will go through a real or metaphoric spike at some point in the second half of the 20th century. To give another example of this rate of change, consider the state of Christianity in Western Europe. Immediately after World War II, a large number of Christian Democratic Parties were started in continental Europe. In almost all of these parties, there was a widely and deeply held concept that the purpose of the party was to subject politics to Christian principles as exposited in the Bible. This position has just about disappeared. Christian Democratic Parties are now simply thought of as parties that are slightly to the right of center. There is an almost equally dramatic change in the character of Christianity in most of Latin America. There have been in the last two decades (and will be in the next two) equally great rates of change in other value and belief systems. Further, these do not seem to be simply cyclical phenomena, even in the sense that the peaks of the cycles tend to be much lower with each peaking; rather, they represent a genuine rapid change for a short period of time, even if they are not as spectacularly spikelike as in population growth. It is these real and metaphoric spikes which lead us to believe that history is going to be so different from now on. However, we also believe that there are more continuities than discontinuities, i.e., that although this may be one of the most dramatic periods of change in world history—if not *the* most dramatic—the best way to consider specific issues is usually to look first at their historical roots and contexts, not to think of them as isolated events occurring as if the world had stated *de novo* in 1970 or so.

THE PACE OF ECONOMIC DEVELOPMENT

Let us turn now from these grand, almost cosmic trends to some more mundane and current issues. The concepts that follow are almost clearly at the "acceptable" level of belief—at least from a descriptive point of view. I would argue that the interpretations I will present deserve at least a Scotch verdict. However, some of my interpretations, all of which I elaborate in *World Economic Development*, may be more at the Deist level—but this, of course, the reader must judge for himself. These concepts are summarized in Fig. 2, where the growth of the gross domestic product of 16 advanced capitalist nations (ACNs) is set forth. These purely economic curves are used to define a set of periods characteristic of the world as a whole, or at least of the affluent societies.

It seems quite clear that the ACNs, along with the Soviet Union, are entering a much more confused and troubling economic situation in the 1980s than was characteristic of the first two or three decades of the postwar period. We all know now, although many did not recognize it at the time, that from the viewpoint of

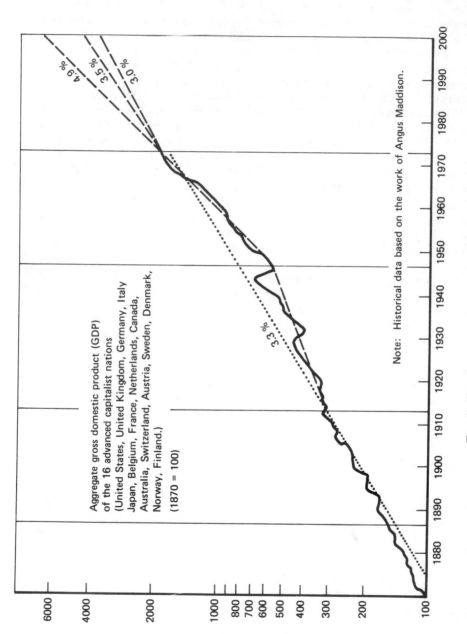

Aggregate gross domestic product (GDP)
of the 16 advanced capitalist nations
(United States, United Kingdom, Germany, Italy
Japan, Belgium, France, Netherlands, Canada,
Australia, Switzerland, Austria, Sweden, Denmark,
Norway, Finland.)

(1870 = 100)

Note: Historical data based on the work of Angus Maddison.

Fig. 2—The four periods of the 20th century

Source: The Economist, June 1979, p. 205.

economic growth, the world passed through an extraordinarily creative and productive period in the 26 years from 1948 through 1973. During this period, the growth rates of the ACNs averaged about 5 percent per year. This was the first time in history that such high sustained growth rates had been achieved. Furthermore, and even more extraordinary, the rest of the world, again for the first time in history, began to industrialize rapidly. It actually averaged slightly more than 5 percent per year. We feel that this 26-year period may go down in history as *La Deuxième Belle Epoque* (much in the same way that the period from 1886 to 1913 is already known throughout most of Europe as *La Belle Epoque).*[8]

It should be noted that, while the ACNs grew unprecedentedly rapidly in *La Première Belle Epoque*, the actual achieved growth rate averaged only 3.3 percent per year, or only two-thirds the average growth rate achieved in *La Deuxième Belle Epoque*. Furthermore, except in the Soviet Union, the growth rate in the rest of the world at that time was almost negligible, often not even keeping up with the population growth rate.

The use of such a phrase as "Belle Epoque" does not, of course, imply that there were no problems in the ACNs, not to mention the rest of the world, during either of these two periods; nor does it imply that the timing of this epoque was the same for all countries. In fact, in many of the ACNs, and particularly in the United States, a deterioration in the economic (and social) situation started in the early 1960s rather than the early or mid-1970s. As explained below, we refer to the period 1974-2000 or so as a time that will probably be characterized as *L'Epoque de Malaise* (at least for the ACNs and the Soviet Union).

Perhaps the most characteristic phenomenon of *L'Epoque de Malaise* will be an extraordinary combination of relatively high unemployment, excess industrial capacity, and inflation—a combination that afflicts most of the ACNs today, or that threatens to afflict them. The term "stagflation" has been coined to denote this condition, which increasingly is anticipated to be a persistent condition for almost all the ACNs for the foreseeable future. A decade or so ago, many economists and others would have denied the very possibility of such a widespread and persistent phenomenon. We blame the persistent stagflation partly on structural[9] (including institutional) problems, but mostly on unwise fiscal and monetary policies. We believe that even if these fiscal and monetary policies had been much improved, there would still have been some persistent malaise, though it might not have included such widespread and persistent stagflation. A good many of our scenarios reflect various prognostications of how this stagflation phenomenon may evolve.

SOME CULTURAL AND POLITICAL ISSUES

Again, continuing with our emphasis on the world context, we note first that there is an almost worldwide conservative renaissance, at least if we choose to interpret the word "conservative" in appropriate ways in various parts of the

---

[8] We shall refer to that period as La *Première* Belle Epoque in order to distinguish it from La *Deuxième* Belle Epoque.

[9] We define a structural problem as any economic problem that cannot generally be fixed by short-run (year or two) monetary or fiscal policies (though such problems are often strongly affected by these policies). Structural problems can involve institutional and value issues as well as structural imbalances in industries or in the labor force.

world. I need not comment here on the political aspects of this movement in the advanced capitalist nations, in particular in the United States, England, France, Australia, and Canada, and—to some degree—in most of the rest of the ACNs, except to note that this seems likely to arrest certain tendencies that grew up during La Deuxième Belle Epoque. It may also help to restore the credibility of the U.S. government to its own people and, in particular, it is likely to influence the next election in the United States.

On the other hand, it is important to note that this conservative renaissance in the United States (and in some other areas) is more a return to traditional values than a return to traditional classical liberal economics. (However, there is an important movement among younger U.S. economists toward "rational expectations" and "supply-oriented" models which do include a good deal of revisionist thinking.) Furthermore, to the extent that the popular movement does involve a return to certain principles of classical liberal economics, it is, often to a remarkable degree, anti-business in a way which of course would not be characteristic of most current advocates of classical liberal economics. (However, Adam Smith once observed that when two businessmen get together, even on a social occasion, they usually plot restraint of trade. It should be noted that a large proportion of the American public fears that something like this—or other "bad" things—is happening.) I do not wish to comment on but only note here the program of the "four modernizations" now going on in the People's Republic of China (PRC). To some degree, this too is a movement toward conservative economic policies and away from the politics of radical extremism. It is also, to a remarkable extent, a return to more classical liberal economics.

I would also like to comment on the rise of Islamic fundamentalism, or what one might call a Moslem renaissance. This is a worldwide movement and has not yet had a great impact in Asia, but it seems likely to. In particular, it could lead to severe problems in Malaysia and the Philippines and could change some of the current trends in Indonesia. This renaissance is greatly enhanced and intensified by the increased importance of the oil-exporting Arab countries, but the oil situation is not the only reason for it. It is not particularly a pan-Moslem movement and does not seem to have led to much increase in Moslem unity. Rather, there is a growing consciousness of what it means to be Moslem and a movement toward greater militancy, and occasionally, extraordinary ambitions. Some observers have taken this to be a kind of nativist movement which involves a major rejection of Western technology. Others just assume that it is part of the worldwide anti-technology movement without giving it any particular nativist overtones.

Actually, it does not seem to involve either of these elements to any great extent. In fact, with regard to modern technology, it is more of what is often called a "synthesis movement" (sometimes violent, sometimes peaceful)—an attempt to synthesize more satisfactorily the tenets of the Moslem religion with economic development and political power. The case of Iran is a good example. The Ayatollah Khomeini has nothing against electricity, cars, refineries, airplanes, etc. In fact, he likes these things. But he wants to combine them with deeper, more traditional, religious attitudes and behavior—in a context involving much greater adherence, both real and nominal, to the Islamic faith and Moslem rituals. He may yet succeed, at least to a degree. It is not impossible to have some degree of synthesis between these seemingly disparate and often contradictory cultures. Indeed, it is important to realize that almost all of this Moslem revival is, in its own way, more a modernizing movement than a rejection of modernization, even though it attempts to revive a traditional faith and social forms.

There is also a great deal of what might be called self-confident nationalism in the area. This is particularly true in the ASEAN states, and to a lesser degree in Vietnam. The self-confidence of ASEAN, as much as anything else, has grown from the economic success of its members and the lack of "dominoes" outside of Indochina after the U.S. defeat in Vietnam. This self-confident nationalism seems to be remarkably resilient and, on the whole, very constructive. It is true, however, that anxiety has increased recently in these areas because of the Vietnamese invasion of Kampuchea (Cambodia); and Hanoi's great self-confidence has been weakened to some degree by its lack of economic progress.

One pressing question that remains is what will happen to Indochina and what the foreign and defense policies of Hanoi will be. One of Hanoi's policies is responsible for the most important current crisis, the growing refugee problem—the boat people generally, and the Kampucheans in Thailand in particular. The more or less forced expulsion from Vietnam of the Chinese minority represents an approach to genocide that is startling in its moral and political implications.

TWO PERSPECTIVES ON THE ECONOMIC DEVELOPMENT OF THE PACIFIC REGION

The title of this conference volume is "East Asian Security in the 1980s." It almost equally well could have been entitled "Security Problems of the Pacific Basin" (including the fringes of the Indian Ocean in this concept). Such an emphasis on the geographical concept of the Pacific Basin is useful. It highlights the interaction between the four superpowers, or supercountries, of the Pacific Basin (the United States, the Soviet Union, Japan, and the PRC) and the new industrial countries of the area (Taiwan, South Korea, Hong Kong, Singapore, and to a lesser extent Malaysia, Thailand, and the Philippines).[10]

Both of these perspectives—the Pacific Basin and new industrialization—provide important insights into what is happening in the region. Let us examine the second one first.

As we noted earlier, for about 175 years industrialization was more or less a monopoly of the ACNs and the Soviet Union. However, in *La Deuxième Belle Epoque* (the period from 1948 to 1973), for the first time what we now term the middle-income nations, and particularly the new industrial countries, began to modernize quite rapidly and quite effectively. At the present time the star performer is, of course, South Korea, which managed sustained growth of about 10 percent from 1963 to 1973. Since then, South Korea has done even better during a depressed era; that is, in 1974 it grew over 10 percent; in 1975, about the same; 1976, 15 percent; 1977, 10 percent; 1978, around 11 percent. The growth rate this year is expected to be about 10 percent. This outstanding record is the result of good management, energy, intensity, skill, and cultural adaptability—qualities also found in many of the smaller countries in the region. The degree to which these qualities are present, of course, varies.

[10] With luck and skill, the latter three may also become "new industrial countries."

The cultures of most of the countries in the region are largely derived from Chinese culture or have been strongly influenced by having a large element of ethnic Chinese who have been there a long time and are relatively well integrated (e.g., in Thailand) or who immigrated more recently and are less well integrated (e.g., in the Philippines, Malaysia, and Indonesia). All of these national cultures or ethnic enclaves are members of various Neo-Confucian cultures (or subcultures). The use of the plural emphasizes that these cultures differ significantly among themselves. But they contain certain common elements.

I argued in *World Economic Development* that, under current conditions, these Neo-Confucian cultures are better adapted to economic growth than are Western cultures and that what might be called the "Confucian ethic" is playing a similar, but more spectacular role in the modernization of East Asia than the Protestant ethic played in Europe. Thus, in much the same way that the United States passed England in its rate of economic growth and later was passed (at least for a while) by West Germany and France, almost all of these Neo-Confucian countries now outperform the West. The continued relatively rapid growth of Japan, the possibly rapid growth of China, and a continued rapid growth rate in the smaller Neo-Confucian cultures seem likely to be the dominant trend of the next decade or two. This trend might also lead to a kind of culturism (i.e., conflicts between cultures) that could cause all kinds of new and old issues to arise.

Another related perspective is the emergence of the Pacific Ocean as one of the greatest "connectors" in the world. This is rather paradoxical because, historically, the Pacific has been one of the greatest geographical "separators." The extent to which the largest of all oceans becomes an efficient connector rather than a barrier greatly affects our prognosis for the East Asian region. If the Pacific is emerging as the great connector, the countries of the Pacific Basin (including countries like Brazil, which is technically not part of the Pacific Ocean but whose commerce and foreign investment increasingly involve nations that are geographically in the Basin) will surely come to form a relatively tight trading and investment community.

In any case, the Pacific Ocean is now becoming a great connecting force. It is now cheaper for the Japanese to ship cars to Los Angeles or sometimes even to New York than it is for Detroit to do so. Indeed, because of modern developments in shipping, communications, transportation of individuals, the use of the computer, and so on, this ease of interaction is increasingly pervasive. This development may represent a new stage in the march of (Western) history, which focused first on the Mediterranean and then on the North Atlantic. I also believe that a remarkable amalgam of Western, Chinese, and Indian cultures will be created around the Pacific Basin "connector." In some ways, Singapore is a prototype of the new culture, since it mixes Western (mainly American and British) with Sinic (Chinese and Japanese) roots and adds a significant Indian influence.

The likelihood that the Pacific Ocean will increasingly become a connector of nations and peoples does not, of course, depend simply on shipping. For the Pacific to work effectively in this way, new telecommunications systems are needed that can tie organizations together almost as tightly as if they were in the same building. These are being created (e.g., the current General Electric Mark III time-sharing computer system). Supersonic aircraft seem likely, eventually, to facilitate the movement of key personnel and goods and thus further stimulate the interconnectedness of the Basin.

The single most important ingredient for drawing this huge region together would be a continuation, even at a slightly slower rate, of the extremely vigorous economic growth that has been occurring there since World War II. This seems likely for the next decade or two, at least for the middle-income nations. As a result, it seems most likely that our area of interest will grow quite rapidly—a growth that will appear even more rapid in contrast with the relatively lackadaisical economic performance of most of the rest of the world.

OPTIMISTIC AND PESSIMISTIC PERSPECTIVES

Let us start with an optimistic view of what is happening in the Pacific Basin. One way to begin is by looking at the area from the viewpoint of our major opponents—the Soviet Union, and sometimes China—and to argue that if the competitive situation looks bad from their point of view, it is likely to look good from the non-communist point of view. This, of course, is not always true. We are not engaging in what mathematicians call a zero-sum game. Thus, if there were a huge thermonuclear war, it would be bad from almost all points of view; but, to some degree, much that is good for the Soviets is bad for us, and vice versa. To a much lesser degree, we can say the same of the PRC.

First and foremost, the Soviets worry about what seems to be a developing entente between China, Japan, and the United States. From the Soviet point of view, it looks as if this developing entente was created because the Chinese played their American and Japanese cards, not because the Americans played their Chinese card. As a result, recent events leading to "normalization" and economic cooperation probably look that much more threatening to the Soviets. But this threat seems more likely to lead to caution and prudence on the part of the Soviets than to risky adventurist moves that could easily be counterproductive, i.e., could increase the scope or intensity of U.S.-Sino-Japanese cooperation.

Further, the Soviet tie with Vietnam has recently led them into what most observers consider a very humiliating situation. Soon after the Vietnamese signed a treaty of friendship with the Soviets and joined COMECON,[11] Vietnam was invaded by China. The Soviets did absolutely nothing about this invasion. Even though some people now believe that the Vietnamese humiliated the Chinese almost as much as the Chinese humiliated the Vietnamese, the political pressure on the Soviets to do something was nevertheless intense. In any case, it is quite clear that the Soviets did not distinguish themselves as a protector or leader. Of course, some argue that the Soviets showed a commendable and responsible level of prudence and caution by their inaction. But even those who applaud and admire this self-restraint and prudence usually concede that most allies do not want a leader and protector who is so "responsible, cautious, and prudent" that their interests may be injured or left unprotected.

It is just because inaction leads to such high political and other costs that restraint and prudence in the face of provocation are so difficult to pursue. Indeed, these costs can be so high that, from a long-term perspective, short-term prudence and self-restraint may turn out to be imprudent. Further, except for Vietnam (and

---

[11] The Council for Mutual Economic Assistance, which also includes the Soviet Union, Bulgaria, Cuba, Czechoslovakia, East Germany, Hungary, Mongolia, Poland, and Romania.

perhaps even there), the Soviets are almost universally detested, feared, or suspect in the Pacific region. Indeed, it can be argued that there are few regions in the world that are less influenced by Soviet tactics and capabilities.

It is not that the Soviets do not have a great deal of potential in the region; they do. But the potential is based almost completely on the threat of raw power and to a lesser extent on the flow of Soviet aid; and any attempt to exercise this potential power could backfire. Of course, Eastern Siberia has enormous economic potential and therefore, eventually, the potential for the expansion of Soviet economic as well as military influence into Asia. But the enormous cost and technical and administrative[12] difficulties that handicap the economic development of Eastern Siberia seem likely to leave the area relatively dormant for the next decade or so.

Dropping the Soviet issue (except as it relates to an area of genuine tension and uncertainty involving Indochina and its interaction with its immediate neighbors), the entire area we are looking at seems likely to be characterized by relatively high levels of stability and economic progress probably for the next decade or so and almost certainly in the immediate future. Very interestingly, with the possible exception of the valuable time bought by the American effort in Vietnam, this relatively positive prognosis has come about almost despite American policies and efforts, not because of them.

In some ways, the most important potential development involves mainland China, the PRC. From this point of view, the rapid growth of the PRC, as long as it is combined with policies that will promote stability in its border regions, is probably a good thing for the West and for the area we are discussing. However, if these Chinese policies happen to fail or backfire, or, conversely, if they result in too strong a China, then a very difficult prognosis for the area could emerge. In any case, various policies that the Chinese could adopt will create very different kinds of local national security problems, particularly in the Indochina area.

Another set of pessimistic possibilities would arise from examining the nature of many of the relatively undemocratic, not completely legitimate, and disorderly aspects of many of the regimes in the area. These regimes tend to have some dangerous vulnerabilities and instabilities, likely points of crisis, and many unattractive aspects that could contribute to disabling external pressures as well as regional conflict in the coming decade.

It is often said that the United States has lost a good deal in the region because of the moral, political, and other ambiguities that accompanied the Vietnam War. Some would also point to an unnecessarily callous American treatment of Taiwan—or at least too weak a public and private position in the normalization negotiations with Beijing. This is probably correct. It is also a commonplace that the United States still represents the leading power in the world, from the economic and even the military point of view (though the latter is increasingly eroding in reality and in reputation), and in general there continues to be great admiration for American institutions, notably our record as a leading industrial and democratic nation. But this too is eroding.

It is seldom understood that for many of the countries of Asia, the United States also represents a kind of decadence and even a cultural and social threat to some

---

[12] In many ways, the Soviet bureaucracy has been less than effective in negotiating with the Japanese and Americans on a number of crucial projects, and these bureaucratic problems seem likely to continue.

of their most deeply held values. This is particularly true in Japan, the Soviet Union, and some of the authoritarian countries of the Neo-Confucian cultural area. In order to understand this phenomenon, one need only think of what the likely attitudes would have been some twenty years ago to any of the following phenomena: (1) the news that cocaine or marijuana was readily and rather openly available at many White House functions and other parties attended by the great and near great (and also in the National Football League); (2) reports that 5 to 10 percent of the U.S. Army in Europe may not be available for duty at any given time because of being on a marijuana high; (3) the open hard-core pornography on the American newsstand (I am referring here to *Hustler* magazine and publications which emerged from the underground press, not to *Playboy*, though the latter is also censored in much of East and Southeast Asia); (4) the rock 'n roll music and now the disco music which is thought of as a kind of anarchic, nihilistic, pornographic, drug-encouraging propaganda (or movement) against establishment values, particularly in terms of influencing the young;[13] (5) the general lack of discipline and order among the younger generation; (6) the law-and-order problems in the streets of many American cities; (7) the declining quality (at least until recently) of the American school system; (8) the almost complete inability to deal with such problems as energy, stagflation, New York City finances, etc.

Most Americans would be surprised to learn how threatening contemporary U.S. culture looks to many of the people we are trying to influence and help. Those people often want to learn to use the good aspects of our way of life, but they do not want to increase contacts that might raise the risks of "cultural contamination."

It is also possible that highly protectionist policies in the West or a general and relatively deep recession could cause a pronounced slowdown in the economic growth of the Pacific Basin. And even in those countries with high economic growth rates, one can write all too plausible scenarios for explosive events; for example: internal strains between the Moslem and Chinese communities in Malaysia; ongoing insurgencies in several countries; renewed problems between Vietnam and China, or Taiwan and China, or South Korea and North Korea; three-way disputes about rights in offshore areas, or over disputed frontiers; etc. Further, history often turns out to be more cunning than the imagination of the scenario writer. Under these circumstances, complacency of any kind would be misplaced. Nevertheless, it is easier to write scenarios for relative stability, dynamic economic growth, and peaceful evolution in the Pacific Basin during the 1980s than to anticipate major violent conflict, crippling stagnation, or other disasters.

---

[13] It is true that rock 'n roll and disco are universally popular and are performed even in the Soviet Union by state-paid orchestras, despite the fact that the official position of the state is very hostile to this kind of music; but this is typical of a tactical policy and does not contradict the basic attitude of the older and squarer social elements.

Chapter 10

AN ECONOMIC PERSPECTIVE ON THE EAST ASIA REGION

H. B. Malmgren[1]

Any assessment of the prospects for political and economic security in East Asia, or in the Asia-Pacific region, must include an evaluation of regional economic patterns and trends from a global perspective. The nature of economic growth in this area of the world is so interactive with the global economy that focusing exclusively on the region by itself barely gives a blurred image of what is happening.

THE GLOBAL ENVIRONMENT

From World War II to the beginning of the 1970s, the world economy experienced a period of unprecedented growth and structural change. Global output grew almost 5 percent per year, while world trade grew at a rate nearly double that. This process brought about increasing interdependence of national markets, as the growth of sales to and supplies from international markets greatly outpaced national growth. Facilitating global growth and the acceleration of trade was a remarkable expansion of capital flows, combined with intensified technology transfers, vastly improved communications and transportation systems, and a rapid increase in the movement of people.

It became increasingly difficult in the latter part of the 1960s for governments to separate the functioning of national economies, and the policies which were intended to guide them, from international market developments. In the monetary field, the buildup of large U.S. balance-of-payments deficits in the 1960s and an array of controls to cope with them led to the cumulation of a huge dollar pool held in various financial centers around the world. This in turn resulted in the creation of new types of capital markets which transcended national monetary systems, as part of the dollar pool was used for lending to borrowers everywhere. (The privately held part of this dollar pool came to be known as the Eurodollar market.)

By the early 1970s, the scene had been set for a fundamental shift in the interaction of national economies. Business cycles in various nations, rather than counterbalancing each other, moved into synchronization, to the point where a worldwide boom developed in the early 1970s. This greatly enhanced inflationary forces, and in 1971-72, world markets experienced soaring prices for virtually all tradable resources and commodities. Accidental events such as the bold Soviet entry into world grain markets, droughts and cutbacks in cereal production in

---

[1] H. B. Malmgren served as Deputy Special Representative for Trade Negotiations and Chief Trade Negotiator for the United States during the years 1972-75, having previously been a high U.S. trade official from 1964 to 1969. A frequent author of articles and books on international economic problems, and a past professor of economics at several universities, he now heads his own international economics consulting firm.

Australia and Canada, and the vanishing of supplies of Peruvian fish meal led to an explosion of prices.

At the same time, the postwar currency system strained and cracked, and a new movable exchange-rate system emerged in the 1970s that created new types of financial uncertainties. Managers of assets and enterprises shifted from currencies to commodities and gold and then back to currencies, in a search for stability and protection of assets against erosion. The oil embargo of 1973 and the subsequent quadrupling of energy prices was superimposed on this already explosive situation, creating massive discontinuities in markets and abruptly devaluating existing industrial capital. The subsequent plunge into the deepest global recession in the post-World War II period was an inevitable consequence.

The recovery from this deep recession, in the latter 1970s, was weak. Capital spending in the industrialized economies of the West in particular fell far short, in terms of real growth, of levels experienced in previous economic recoveries since World War II. Real investment in 1977 was below the level of 1973, except in Canada. Structural adjustments to the new circumstances were therefore not made, or at least not on the scale necessary to meet the new economic requirements. Existing capacity was not modernized, nor was it even replaced at traditional rates. Throughout the recovery of the 1970s, inflation continued to plague the entire world market, and unemployment rose to unprecedented levels in Europe, even when the partial recovery was at its strongest. Few nations succeeded in controlling inflation, and those that did found their currencies appreciating at rates that seemed to threaten their domestic economic policies.

Concurrent with the massive changes in the functioning of world trading and financial markets were the emergence of industrialization and accelerated economic growth rates in many countries that heretofore had been relatively undeveloped. Among these, the Mediterranean countries, certain nations in Eastern, Southeastern, and South Asia, Latin America, and more recently the oil-producing nations of the Middle East, developed rapidly. They even became significant buyers and sellers in world trade, as well as significant recipients of direct investment and significant borrowers on world commercial capital markets.

As the traditional growth of the countries of the Organization for Economic Cooperation and Development (OECD)[2] slowed from average real rates of growth of 5 percent per year or better to rates of 4 percent or less, a large number of developing countries in the 1960s and 1970s raised their rates of growth to 6 percent or better. Gross National Product (GNP) growth for about 35 to 40 of the less-developed countries (LDCs), other than the Middle East oil producers, has been growing at 6 percent or better for the last fifteen years. Indeed, for the two decades up to the oil crisis of 1973, GNP growth for the developing countries as a whole averaged 6 percent, as compared with an average of 5 percent for the industrialized Western countries.

The non-market economies of Eastern Europe also expanded in step with the OECD countries. However, because of growing external requirements for capital goods and technology, they found themselves needing to greatly expand borrowing and also to construct complex trade arrangements which required those enterprises that sold to them to buy back goods from those countries, helping to offset the trade deficits of Eastern Europe.

---

[2] See footnote 4, p. 216 below, for a listing of these countries.

Imbalances in payments among the largest trading nations, together with recycling of oil revenue surpluses, have led to vastly expanded international capital flows. This in turn has facilitated the rapid emergence of the developing nations in world markets, as they were able to borrow to expand their economies. This has led to expanded trade, but also to intensified global competition for markets. The fast growth areas of trade have focused pressures for adjustment in a series of specific markets, beginning with textiles, apparel, and footwear, and now broadening to many areas of manufacturing and even shipbuilding and engineering services. These new and growing pressures create additional needs for structural adjustment of the existing industrial capacity of the economically most advanced nations, at a time when such adjustments have become increasingly difficult because of the slowness of capital spending, inflation, and relatively high unemployment.

The renewed oil crisis of 1979 has intensified the long-term squeeze on all countries other than the major oil producers. In these new circumstances, the economic growth of the developed countries of the West in the 1980s is uncertain. Growth might stabilize at a new trend level of 3 percent or so, or there could be a rebound back to the higher average rate of the two decades leading up to the oil crisis. Which avenue will be taken depends primarily upon official policies and upon the expectations for capital spending. But in either case, the pace of growth of this group of countries is likely to continue to lag behind that of the developing world (the LDCs). The differential in aggregate growth is likely to be on the order of one to two percentage points. In the case of advanced developing countries such as South Korea, the differential in aggregate growth is likely to be even one or two percentage points higher than that average for developing countries.

The rearrangement of world production and trade patterns which has been taking place will continue to change the relative competitiveness of countries and of sectors within each country. With slow capital spending, restructuring will be difficult, and the governments of the advanced industrialized countries are likely to step up intervention to assist troubled sectors. This will take many forms, ranging from increased protectionism to direct aids to industries and regions, with an array of policy instruments including government purchasing policies, assistance to research and development programs, participation in equity through state holding companies, and the like. This process of intervention will tend to operate as "adjustment resistance," slowing down the transformation of national economic structures to meet changing world circumstances, inasmuch as aid will tend to go to the weaker sectors rather than to the stronger sectors, which are better positioned to make appropriate adjustments.

THE DEVELOPING COUNTRIES AS AN ENGINE OF GROWTH

Until recently, the share of world exports accounted for by the non-oil-producing LDCs has been declining. This trend, however, masks some fundamental shifts in the pattern of export production that are now taking place worldwide. In particular, the competitive position of the LDCs is undergoing a major transformation as a number of them shift emphasis from reliance on primary products to trade in manufactures, concurrently with their progress in industrialization and with the general rise in the share of manufactures and the decline in the share of primary products in world trade. (Between 1955 and 1976, the constant dollar share of manufactures rose from 45 to 57 percent, while the primary products' share dropped from 42 to 21 percent, excluding fuels.) The pressures on primary products stem from a variety of sources, including substitution of synthetic materials, conservation of materials in production and use, lower income elasticity of demand for foodstuffs and certain raw materials, and supply problems in exporting countries.

Because of the very rapid rise in manufacturing production in the LDCs, their share of world trade *in manufactures* has been rising. In 1976, the position of the non-oil-producing LDCs as exporters of manufactures had risen to about 10 percent. Overall, manufacturing production in the LDCs has increased at a rate of growth of about 6.7 percent between 1960 and 1976, while the growth rate for manufacturing production in the developed countries (DCs) has averaged 4.9 percent per year for the same period. As the industrial sector grows in importance in most of these economies, exports of manufactures will also grow, with the result that the secular decline of LDC shares in general world trade will be reversed.[3]

Perhaps a better illustration of the nature of this fundamental change is to be found in the relative performance of the DCs and the LDCs in employment and capital formation. The rate of growth of employment and capital formation in the LDCs in recent years has moved well ahead of that in the DCs, a trend which began to become obvious in the mid to late 1960s. Employment in manufacturing in the DCs grew by 1.8 percent per year from 1960 to 1969 and by 0.2 percent per year from 1969 to 1973; it *declined* by 2 percent per year in 1973-76. In the LDCs, for the period 1960-69, the growth rate was 3.6 percent; for 1969-73, 5.5 percent; and for 1973-76, at least 3 percent. Capital investment was weakened in the DCs, decelerating since the 1960s and running negatively in 1973-76, whereas it has been accelerating in the LDCs (from a 6.4 percent growth rate in the 1960s to about 9 percent per year in the latter 1970s).[4]

In conjunction with the rapid growth of capital formation and manufacturing production in these countries, there has been an acceleration of their imports of manufactures, especially from the DCs. They have, in fact, become the new growth markets for DC exports of manufactures, and their share of total world demand for trade in manufactures has already reached impressive levels that are not yet widely recognized. In 1974-75, for example, when the world economy went into the most serious downturn since the 1930s, world trade actually contracted. However, exports from the DCs to the LDCs continued to rise, providing a major cushion to the downturn. In 1975, roughly one-quarter of the total exports of the DCs—about $135 billion (U.S.)—went to LDCs. Of DC-manufactured exports alone, 30 percent went to LDCs. If intra-EEC trade is not counted, then 44 percent of all DC exports went to LDCs in 1975.

The United States and Japan are among the major suppliers in this newly emerging market, with more than one-third of U.S.-manufactured exports and 45

[3] For general analyses of these structural changes, see R. Blackhurst, N. Marian, and J. Tumlir, *Adjustment, Trade and Growth in Developed and Developing Countries*, GATT, Studies in International Trade, No. 6, September 1978; The World Bank, *World Development Report, 1978*, Washington, D.C., August 1978; and *The Impact of the Newly Industrialising Countries on Production and Trade in Manufactures*, Report by the Secretary-General, OECD, Paris, 1979.

[4] R. Blackhurst, N. Marian, and J. Tumlir, *Trade Liberalization, Protectionism, and Interdependence*, GATT, Studies in International Trade, No. 5, November 1977, Table 7, p. 45.

percent of Japanese-manufactured exports going to the LDCs. The ratio of exports of DC manufactures to LDCs to exports of LDCs manufactures to DCs is a little less than 5 to 1. This is not solely or even mainly a matter of OPEC purchases. On the contrary, the non-oil-producing LDCs accounted for about two-thirds of the demand for total exports destined for the oil-producing and non-oil-producing nations taken together.

The rapid growth of LDC exports of manufactures, especially from East Asia, has already created adjustment problems in certain industries in the DCs, most notably textiles and apparel. However, it has now become clear that those LDCs that experienced the fastest growth of total exports also became the fastest-growing markets for manufactures exported from the DCs. Thus the prospect for some degree of disruption to traditional industries in the DCs is considerable, but the offsetting effect of more than proportionate exports to the LDCs mitigates the impact on the DC economies, when taken as a whole. Another important element of this structural change in world trade is the fact that the ratio of exports to national production in the LDCs is still much less than that in the DCs. This means that in most areas of manufacturing in these LDCs, the economies of scale to be derived from trade are only beginning to be exploited.

The composition of manufacturing production and exports of manufactures is also changing rapidly, as might be expected. Until 1955, food processing, textiles, and clothing dominated the manufacturing output in the oil-importing LDCs, while textiles were the major manufactured exports. Since 1955, engineering products (including industrial machinery; office, telecommunications, and other electrical equipment; and transport equipment) have been the most dynamic sector, comprising 29 percent of the manufacturing output in 1976 for the oil-importing LDCs. This internal change has been accompanied by diversification of exports, especially in East Asia. The well-known examples are, of course, Korean shipbuilding and the production of electrical and electronics products in East and Southeast Asia. The diversification is spreading into many fields, and the pace is accelerating (the share grew from 13 percent in 1963 to 29 percent in 1976).[5]

The vigorous expansion of manufactured exports from these countries until recently has been concentrated among a relatively small number of countries, with the top 10 or 11 exporters responsible for over four-fifths of all the manufactured exports of this group. Korea, Taiwan, and Hong Kong alone accounted for over 40 percent in 1975 and nearly half in 1976. However, the base of this export performance is broadening. For example, the number of LDCs with exports of manufactures in excess of $100 million (U.S.), measured in terms of constant dollars, grew from 14 to 30 between 1965 and 1974. In the DCs, most of the concern expressed about the potentially disruptive effects of LDC exports centers on trade in manufactures. Yet, on the whole, DC exports of manufactures to the world have had more growth than imports of manufactures in the 1960s and, especially, in the 1970s.

So far, the specific impact of LDC exports of manufactures on DC markets is very small. One GATT report puts the ratio of imports from LDCs to DC overall consumption at 2 percent in 1975 (as compared with 1.2 percent in 1959-60).[6] The only sectors experiencing greater relative impact are textiles (8.6 percent in 1975) and clothing (3.2 percent in 1975). Thus the general impact is now small, but it is

[5] Blackhurst, Marian, and Tumlir, *Studies in International Trade*, No. 6, op.cit., p. 16, Table 7.

[6] Blackhurst, Marian, and Tumlir, ibid., p. 34, Table 22.

growing slowly. On the other hand, the potential for major progress on the part of the LDCs in particular product areas is amply demonstrated by the success of exports of shipbuilding, electrical, and electronics products from East and Southeast Asia. Moreover, the export efforts of the LDCs are sometimes concentrated within particular product areas, or particular countries, giving rise to competitive pressures of a very fundamental character, with national import-consumption ratios running at well over 50 percent in the DCs for certain items produced solely or mainly in LDCs (e.g., radios, certain types of footwear, and textiles).

The East Asian region's outlook can also be better understood in relation to changes in other regions of the world economy. The outlook for the Mediterranean LDCs that are would-be members of the European Economic Community (EEC)—Spain, Portugal, Greece, and Turkey—is very much tied up with the pace at which they become members of that Community. They will gradually evolve as the new cheap-labor, direct-investment havens for EEC-oriented production of manufactures. But this means that outsiders, including exporters in Japan and East Asia, will face intensified competitive pressures and protectionism in trying to sell to the EEC.

The group of oil-exporting countries includes great disparities in income, per capita income, and prospects for industrialization and agricultural development. Prominent among the forces at work shaping the economic development of these countries are (1) a rapid decline in the share of active population in agriculture; (2) serious shortages of labor in some, and shortages of skilled labor in all oil-exporting LDCs; (3) escalating costs of industrialization and of energy and resource projects, causing budgetary pain and a tendency for imports to drain off, or even exceed, oil revenues in some cases; and (4) aversion to holdings of foreign currencies, especially the U.S. dollar, and increasing interest in investment overseas. The interaction of these forces, combined with political uncertainties, is acting as a brake on the industrialization process and will probably retard the growth of imports of manufactures into these countries.

The Eastern trading area (or the centrally planned economies of Eastern Europe plus China) has been expanding faster than world trade averages, but this tendency has recently decelerated. Future growth depends very much upon financing from Western DCs. This in turn will depend increasingly on their ability to sell in world markets. What they can sell will be an array of products similar to the exports of the LDCs, thus intensifying in coming years the competition among cheaper or emergent suppliers. China is a special case in this context, for many reasons, including the current sluggishness in the rest of the world market and the strong desire of Western economies to boost exports of equipment and big projects wherever possible, at a time when demand for capital goods is weak everywhere. China's recent economic development policy shift away from "self-reliance" to large-scale importation of foreign capital looked heaven-sent to many Western companies and banks, in the context of weak world markets at the end of the 1970s.

Trade among the DCs themselves is still enormous, and they still trade with each other more than with the rest of the world. But the share of intra-DC trade in world trade will decline in the 1980s. Slow growth and slow capital spending will mean slowness in adjusting to change, setting the scene for more government intervention to assist troubled sectors, and probably more protectionism.

Trade among the LDCs themselves has been more or less steady as a share of world trade recently, except in the case of oil. But because of the rapid rise in their manufacturing production, it might be expected that there would be an increase in intra-LDC trade in manufactures relative to primary products. This in fact has been happening recently, with the share of engineering products in intra-LDC trade growing from 37 percent in 1973 to 43 percent in 1976. Intra-LDC trade in iron and steel, textiles, clothing, and other finished goods is declining. This reflects the rising protectionism of many of the LDCs, especially as regards traditional labor-intensive industries.

Taking these reservations into account, trade among the LDCs themselves is now moving into a phase of rapid growth, albeit at a slower aggregate pace than trade with the DCs. In the 1965-74 decade, LDC exports of manufactures to DCs grew at a rate of over 16 percent per year, and exports to other LDCs grew at nearly 14 percent per year. By comparison, for the same period, intra-Western European trade in manufactures grew about 11 percent per year, while U.S.-Canadian trade grew about 10.4 percent per year.

The various LDC regions differ markedly in their interaction with the DCs. East Asia is oriented primarily toward the industrialized market economies, and the expanding East Asian exports have been responsible for a large part of the total LDC exports of manufactures. On the other hand, about half of Latin America's exports of manufactures go to LDCs; and about one-third of such exports from African countries go to LDCs.

PROTECTIONISM AS A THREAT TO THE EAST ASIAN REGION

In theory, the Geneva Multilateral Trade Negotiations (MTN) that were completed in the spring of 1979 should result in a further easing of the official impediments and distortions to trade worldwide. This, in theory, should lead to trade expansion and, with that, a step-up in global economic growth.

In practice, the results of the MTN trade talks were scaled back from the initial objectives set in 1973, when the global negotiations were formally initiated. Tariffs will be cut by about one-third on the average, but over an eight-year period. This means a 0.43 percent annual reduction in existing tariffs, an amount that will often tend to be overrun by exchange-rate adjustments. New codes of conduct have been drafted which are designed to limit the freedom of governments to apply temporary import restrictions or anti-dumping and countervailing duties, to subsidize, "buy national," set exclusive standards, manipulate customs valuation, and otherwise intervene to favor home over foreign producers. In practice, the new codes call for limitations on sovereignty, which parliaments are unlikely to live by in every case. There will be a tendency to push for national solutions to trade problems and to test the new rules. Many LDCs are unclear about whether they should participate in the new codes; and how the codes will work in practice remains to be seen. For example, spokesmen of the EEC said in the Geneva MTN meetings that the EEC expected to be forced to discriminate in some cases in the application of import restrictions in coming years.

In the meantime, there is a clearly growing protectionist trend in virtually all of the Western DCs. Governments are being called upon to intervene more and more to assist troubled sectors or regions by shielding them from international competitive pressures. In the United States and the EEC, governments are reacting sympathetically with new policies and practices that give greater attention to domestic interests. Although the United States has introduced a number of specific new restrictions (on steel, TV sets, footwear, and textiles), the EEC countries have actually gone further. Individual EEC countries have maintained old restrictions and worked out new ones on products ranging from steel to ball bearings, from bicycles to TV sets, from ships to cars. Production restraint cartels have been under active consideration in the EEC in recent years. As noted above, the variety of instruments of intervention is limited only by the imagination of the officials concerned. This trend could also develop in Japan, which in 1978 announced a program to nationalize the aluminium industry, a program that included increased import barriers. Much, if not most, of the new protectionism, insofar as it concerns manufactures, is focused on exports from Japan and other exporters in East Asia.

As the LDCs and Eastern Europe, and perhaps even China, become active in more and more areas of exports, or of import substitution, the problem of adjustment to imports will be magnified for the DCs. It will be difficult for individual sectors in DC economies to adjust fast enough without more rapid capital spending than has taken place in the 1970s. Moreover, "sunset industries" cannot be phased out easily without high social costs unless "sunrise industries" somehow take their place, which also entails rapid capital spending. In other words, it will be difficult for the DCs to maintain a liberal trade posture in the face of slow capital spending. Unless the outlook for capital spending in the 1980s were to change markedly, this could act as a slowly tightening constraint on the potential growth of LDCs and Eastern Europe.

So far, the new protectionism has been an irritant but not a major impediment for exporters in East Asia. The fastest-growing exporters, including Taiwan, Hong Kong, and Korea, have been the ones primarily targeted by the DCs for new import restrictions. Yet they have maintained exceptionally high levels of export performance, through continuous diversification. Behind these leaders are a rising number of emerging LDC exporters, each of which will enter traditional export industries, such as textiles, apparel, and footwear, and drive out the more advanced LDCs, which in turn will have to move up the ladder to electronics and engineering products. This historic process of "rolling adjustment" has already been clearly demonstrated in textiles and apparel, where Japan has faded from its once dominant export position in world trade and is now suffering from imports from LDCs while it rapidly winds down its own industry. In addition, some fast-growing LDCs are already being deposed as export leaders by new LDC competitors.

EAST ASIA IN A TURBULENT GLOBAL ECONOMIC ENVIRONMENT

From this global perspective, the continued dynamism of the East Asian LDCs in the 1960s and 1970s is remarkable. The rate of growth of this region clearly puts it ahead of the rest of the world, except for the major oil producers of the Middle East, and even they have decelerated lately. The continuity in Japan's active growth—in excess of that of the rest of the industrialized world (see Table 1)—exerts a strong "pull" on the entire region. But trade for countries like Hong Kong,

Table 1

REAL RATE OF GROWTH OF TOTAL GNP

Region	Average Annual Growth Rate (percent)					
	1961-65[a]	1966-73[a]	1974	1975	1976	1977
Industrialized countries[b]	5.6	4.9	-0.1	-0.6	4.6	3.9
More advanced Mediterranean countries	7.6	7.1	6.3	2.2	4.7	5.2
East Asia and the Pacific[c]	7.6	7.9	5.5	5.3	9.8	7.8
Latin America and the Caribbean	5.3	6.7	7.7	3.3	5.0	5.3
South Asia	4.0	3.5	1.4	7.8	2.1	4.5
North Africa and Middle East	7.3	8.3	1.7	11.0	11.9	6.1
Africa South of the Sahara	3.8	4.5	8.6	3.0	5.2	3.0
All developing countries	5.9	6.6	5.5	5.0	6.4	5.4

[a]Yearly average for the period.

[b]Includes Australia, New Zealand, Japan, and 18 others.

[c]Includes Taiwan (Republic of China), Fiji, Indonesia, Republic of Korea, Malaysia, Papua-New Guinea, the Philippines, Singapore, Thailand, Cambodia, Lao People's Democratic Republic, Western Samoa, Solomon Islands, and Vietnam.

Source: World Bank, *Annual Report 1978*, Table 1, pp. 118-119.

Taiwan, South Korea, Malaysia, and Singapore is also strong outside the region and beyond the Japanese relationship (see Table 2).

The protectionist trends in North America and Western Europe will, in my opinion, intensify, although they focus more on specific trade-adjustment problems. The future for agricultural trade will be clouded by a continuing tendency for governments to intervene heavily in markets, with continuing export subsidies to get rid of unwanted surpluses, and with commensurate protectionism in importing countries. Primary product trade is likely to be weak in minerals as well as in agricultural products, except for precious metals, as long as world growth stays in a slow growth mode. Steel imports are already subject to tight official management, and chemicals are also becoming a troubled sector, with the capacity for production of petrochemicals growing rapidly beyond near-term market demand.

Manufactures appear to offer the most room for stepping up exports, and special efforts are consequently being made by the DCs and Eastern European countries, as well as by the LDCs, to promote this area of exports. Conversely, protectionism has expanded in manufactures trade to the point where almost any fast-growth trade item becomes subject to complaints from domestic producers in importing countries.

But protectionism has ironic twists. Trade restrictions in the United States and in Europe that have limited Japan's exports increasingly have stimulated the development of new export industries in the LDCs. In the 1960s, restrictions on Japan's textile exports to North America and Western Europe spawned new suppliers throughout East Asia. Demand for similar products from Hong Kong, the Republic of Korea, and others increased sharply, accelerating Japan's adjustment to the new conditions of world competition. Today, after years of friction with the United States, Canada, and the EEC over Japanese textile exports, Japan is itself experiencing intense textile import pressures, especially from the East Asian region.

Table 2

FOREIGN TRADE OF EAST ASIAN LDCs

Country	Imports 1977 (millions of $U.S., c.i.f.)	Change Over Previous Year (%)				Exports 1977 (millions of $U.S., f.o.b.)	Change Over Previous Year (%)			
		74	75	76	77		74	75	76	77
ASEAN countries	30,050	61	2	11	15	31,766	70	- 8	25	23
Indonesia	6,230	41	24	19	10	10,853	131	- 4	20	27
Malaysia	4,468	65	-13	9	14	6,085	39	-10	38	15
Philippines	4,267	93	8	5	8	3,094	49	-17	11	23
Singapore	10,471	63	- 3	12	15	8,241	58	- 7	22	25
Thailand	614	53	4	9	29	3,493	56	-10	35	17
Hong Kong	10,540	19	1	32	18	9,630	17	2	45	13
Republic of Korea	10,811	62	6	21	23	10,047	38	14	52	30
Total	51,311					51,443				

Source: GATT, *International Trade, 1977-78*, Geneva, 1978, Table 24, p. 117.

A similar example is emerging in the production and trade of color TV sets. Japanese exports captured a large portion of the U.S. market in 1976 and 1977 and appeared to threaten EEC producers. Export restraint agreements were worked out by governments, but now production in Taiwan and South Korea is rapidly building up, to the point where the United States finds itself needing to negotiate restraint agreements with Taiwan and South Korea to limit their export success in filling the gap left by limitations on Japan. In the meantime, Japan has been taking a production position inside the United States, through purchase of existing American production facilities and erection of new production plants. Ironically, Taiwanese and South Korean exports may well put into jeopardy these new Japanese TV production facilities.

As noted earlier, the East Asian countries have continued to show remarkable export performance, even though they have been the targets of import restrictions in North America and Europe. The twists and turns opened up by selective protection against Japan, and eventually against the strongest performers (Hong Kong, Taiwan, and South Korea), will simply open the way for other nations of the region, particularly if there is continued movement up the ladder of industrial sophistication. Indeed, it would appear that DC restrictions on these countries have often simply served to accelerate their diversification. Since other LDCs and Eastern Europe are rapidly coming to participate in the export of traditional manufactures, the increased diversification of certain East Asian countries has boosted their industrial growth even more.

South Korea's recent great successes in steel and shipbuilding are one example, and the major South Korean inroads into world engineering services are an even better example. Expansion of the manufacturing sector of this region is thus no longer dependent on traditional manufactures like shoes and textiles. Ultramodern technology is at the heart of South Korean steel production. World trends in technology should spur even more progress in the region as integrated circuits and memory chips are made available for wider and wider application in both producers' equipment and consumer end-products. Both production processes and the products themselves can be expected to reach the most advanced world standards in many areas of manufacturing in the region.

The consolidation of major industries in the United States and Europe, in the face of slow capital formation, is also forcing world standardization on a scale never seriously contemplated even ten years ago. A "world car" concept is now taking hold, as an answer to forced adjustment in the auto industry, calling for standardization of basic elements of automobiles, cutting across brand and make-of-car lines. The dynamism of the region will put South Korea in a better position than most other countries to participate in the changes in sourcing that are likely to take place. The losers will be producers in the DCs, especially where unit labor costs are high and capital spending is weak (e.g., Canada).

A few other developing countries, particularly Mexico, will be similarly positioned, but the number of LDCs able to move quickly will be small. Intensified manufactures competition from Eastern Europe and other LDCs will be a modest factor in the early 1980s but a much more important influence on world markets later, as those countries eventually also move up the ladder of sophistication.

FINANCIAL MARKET SUPPORT FOR THE REGION

Gross investment in the LDCs of East Asia and the Pacific has been running at a rate higher than in any other part of the LDC world, with the exception of North Africa and the Middle East in 1974 and 1975; and, of course, investment in the region has been growing much faster than in the industrialized world. I estimate that the trend growth rate of gross investment has averaged a little over 11 percent per year since 1961. This consistently strong performance is a major factor in what I have called the rolling adjustment of the region, especially during the recent period of international economic turbulence.

Japanese investment in the region has recently become even stronger than it was in the past. For example, of a little less than $3 billion (U.S.) in overseas investment in FY 1977, Japan placed $636 million in ASEAN alone—of which $425 million went to Indonesia. This is no longer solely a matter of resource acquisition to satisfy Japan's voracious appetite for raw materials. Japanese investment now involves production of such diverse manufactured items as electronic products, engines, auto parts, compressors, medical equipment, and copper tubing. Some of these investments are aimed at supplying Japan, but others are oriented toward the region's demand, and yet others are designed for exporting to North America, Europe, and elsewhere.

By comparison, American investment in East Asia has been somewhat less, although it is growing. Most U.S. overseas investment still takes place in Europe, although significant growth (often energy-related) is also taking place in Africa and Latin America. Nonetheless, U.S. capital expenditures for the Asia-Pacific region rose almost 15 percent in 1978, to over $3 billion, of which a little over $800 million was spent in Japan (about the same as in 1977), $1.1 billion in Australia/New Zealand, and $1.1 billion in the Asia-Pacific LDCs (a large proportion of this—almost a third—was in Indonesia, primarily in the petroleum sector).

While information on the profitability of foreign investments is somewhat shaky, U.S. official data are moderately reliable. According to Commerce Department figures and *Business Asia*, the rate of return on U.S. direct foreign investment worldwide in 1977 was about 13.9 percent.[7] The rate of return for the Asia-Pacific region as a whole was about 15.7 percent. This was higher than for Canada (9.4 percent), Europe (11.8 percent), and Latin America (14.1 pereent), although less than Africa (17.1 percent) and the Middle East (high but not easily estimated).[8] If manufacturing is viewed separately, the Asia-Pacific rate of return was higher than any in the world, with the main strength coming from Japan, Indonesia, the Philippines, and other LDCs of the region.

The ability of the LDCs of this region to borrow commercially is an important part of the outlook. Although Indonesia continues to make bankers uneasy, most of the countries exhibit such dynamism in the face of unfavorable world markets that they look stronger than most other parts of the world. The debt level of many LDCs is high, and the energy price squeeze is hurting many of them at the close of the 1970s. On the other hand, Eurodollar and Eurocurrency markets are glutted with lendable funds, and these days it is a borrower's market so long as the borrower looks relatively sound, with increasingly favorable margins from the borrower's point of view as competition to lend is growing among commercial banks. Until the rate of capital investment within the advanced industrialized economies picks up dramatically, this condition of excess funds available to be lent internationally will continue, and East Asian countries will look like relatively sound borrowers.

The rapid development of the Asian Currency Market (Asian Currency Unit, or ACU), the Asian version of the Eurodollar market, has not itself provided major stimulation to the growth of the Asia-Pacific region.[9] Its size relative to the Eurodollar and Eurocurrency market (about 5 to 6 percent of the net Eurodollar market) is far too small to make it a viable alternative for sourcing new capital requirements on a large scale. Petrodollars and reserve holdings of other countries have not yet become significant in this market; nor have multinational corporations utilized this market extensively. Bond issues have been infrequent and small, while Asian bond issues have usually been placed in Europe. Most of the ACU market in practice is an interbank market.

On the other hand, the existence and rapid growth of the ACU is a symptom of the vigor of the region. Even though New York and the Eurocurrency markets were already well established, the ACU came into being. With over 80 percent of ACU funds absorbed by the Asia-Pacific region, the market is a net receiver of funds. It has brought into an active role in the region many banks from throughout the world. This has probably made the securing of Eurocurrency loans far easier, so that the small size of the ACU market has in a way been subject to a kind of institutional Eurocurrency multiplier.

[7] Ralph Kozlow, John Rutter, and Patricia Walker, "U.S. Direct Investment Abroad in 1977," *Survey of Current Business*, Vol. 50, No. 8, August 1978, p. 22.

[8] "U.S. Profitability in Asia: Europe and Latin America Outpaced Eighth Time," *Business Asia*, Vol. X, No. 47, November 24, 1978, p. 373.

[9] A.K.B. Hattacharya, *The Asian Dollar Market: International Offshore Financing*, Praeger, New York, 1977.

ASEAN'S FUTURE

The favorable growth prospects for Hong Kong, Korea, and Taiwan require little comment. The position of the weaker ASEAN group is another matter, although the outlook for ASEAN is perhaps finally changing. For years a concept with little practical meaning in trade terms, intra-ASEAN trade seems finally to be picking up (increasing from under 15 percent of the total trade of the group in 1975 to over 16 percent in 1977). As intra-LDC trade, especially of manufactures, grows in other parts of the world, the economic logic of this grouping should be more compelling as these countries move out on the tracks laid by Japan, Taiwan, South Korea, and Hong Kong in manufactured-goods trade. Thus, the tariff cuts within ASEAN are likely to accelerate intragroup trade, even though the so-called complementation projects, or regionally coordinated investments, are moving slowly.

ASEAN is also likely to benefit from treatment by DCs as a single entity for purposes of assessing value-added content, for qualification for GSP treatment (Japan and the EEC were the first to do this for ASEAN). As intragroup trade grows, it will be more and more easy for products to qualify, and this in turn will tend to draw in more DC investment to create new production facilities within ASEAN.

ASEAN political leaders and officials were busy in the late 1970s promoting increased group contacts in Washington, Brussels, and Tokyo. These contacts did not appear to be aimed at quick trade results, but rather seemed oriented toward improving the longer-term posture of the DCs toward ASEAN, as well as encouraging increased investment in the group. These trips of ASEAN leaders have spun off various ideas, some of which have taken root, in Japan at least. For example, Japanese officials have recently been trying to develop special proposals to assist countries in the region whose commodity export earnings have fallen off due to world market fluctuations. These are modest beginnings, but global political and economic turbulence and regional vigor may work in favor of significant progress.

NEW POLITICAL INITIATIVES

During the 1970s, the persistent Japanese global trade and current account surpluses have become sources of acute embarrassment to Japan and a target for protectionist sentiments in North America and Europe. At the close of the 1970s, official Japanese target figures suggested a sharp decline in the account surplus in FY 1979, to about $7 billion (U.S.), but this is questionable. In fact, Japanese exports seemed to be regaining some forward momentum in mid-1979, and Japanese imports looked as though they would not rise as fast as forecasters had expected. This happened partly because the real growth rate of Japan was falling well below the official targets. Also, the increase in Japan's 1979 official budget under the new Prime Minister was far less than it had been in previous years, so public expenditure stimulus was much less than had been anticipated by other governments or by the press.

Faced with a continuing strong current account surplus, the Japanese government looked for something new and different to do in the spring of 1979. Promotion of LDC development and investment in China seemed to be logical initiatives, especially in view of the tremendous share of Japan's total exports now going to

LDCs and the promise of China as a market. This would also fit in politically with the need to respond to the changed circumstances in China and the uncertainties in North and South Korea and Southeast Asia, since any new LDC effort by Japan would naturally tend to emphasize the Asia-Pacific region.

In this context, some kind of new political-economic initiatives for LDCs in general, and for the Asia-Pacific region in particular, should have a compelling logic for the Japanese leadership. The June 1979 Tokyo economic summit would have been a logical place at which to raise this issue, and Prime Minister Ohira seemed to be interested in doing so. However, U.S. and European leaders were not really focused on the region, and the 1979 oil price crisis diverted all attention to the global energy problem. In any event, Japan's official development assistance is still so meager that Japanese initiatives are likely to be viewed by other DCs with caution and even skepticism.

Politically, Japan appears to be in a position of special status in relation to global economic and political security. American and European leaders often refer to Japan's "free ride" in relation to military-political security. This resentment factor in politics should not be underestimated. Moreover, there is a widespread feeling among economic experts that Japan benefits substantially from the stability and liberal thrust of the multilateral trading rules established under the GATT, and supported by the IMF, and yet does little to compensate in other ways for its favorable position. The announcements of doubling of Japanese overseas aid by Prime Ministers Fukuda and Ohira in 1978 and 1979 were not embraced with enthusiasm by other nations. Much of the "doubling" was perceived as yen appreciation, and the rest was seen as a step in the direction of catching up with levels of other industrialized nations.

Japan's official development assistance performance is now considered to be so poor as to constitute in itself a cause for bad political feeling. As Takuya Kubo has suggested,[10] Japan needs to be perceived in a different context, with its performance in the international political-economic-security arena measured by its total international commitments, combining aid and defense expenditures. Mr. Kubo suggests that the combined figure ought to be around 3 percent of GNP, which would require a substantial expansion of aid.

This type of approach is often discussed within governmental circles in Washington, and it has considerable merit. But even that would not satisfy Japan's critics, who complain about Japan's participation in the whole multilateral economic system, where it always takes a stance of reaction to the initiatives of other nations but rarely develops new proposals itself. In a general way, Japan needs to develop a new posture and program of action that will convey to other nations an image of active and effective participation—and of equivalence in economic and political "burden-sharing." This is not easy in the Japanese decisionmaking system; it even goes against the nature of Japan's cultural and social history. Yet it is a mode of behavior that can legitimately be expected of an economic superpower, which Japan has become.

The other industrialized nations need to find a way of reorienting the international discussions on the management of the Western market economy system. Economic summits to date have been notably unproductive. A new concept of

---

[10] See pp. 107-108 above.

Western economic-political security is needed which asks each nation to share in the burden of managing the system, i.e., to share the political and economic effort in a variety of fields. Thus, Japan could well be expected to lend more vigorous support to economic crisis operations aimed at securing the stability of individual countries that come into troubled times (e.g., Turkey and Egypt in 1979), even if these nations are not in Japan's area of immediate interest.

In the East Asian region, an expanded Japanese economic role must be handled delicately, given historic sensitivities about Japan's position in the region. There is need for a broader context, involving other nations, with diffusion of responsibility and political influence, even though Japan might be expected to be in the lead. A few years ago, I endorsed the idea of creating some new institution for the Pacific Basin, along the lines of the OECD, with the objective of providing a better basis for trade and investment liberalization, coordination of development assistance and industrial development efforts, and relations between the region and the rest of the world.[11]

The formation of such a new group would inevitably be a complex undertaking, given such sensitivities as the role of Vietnam, the role of the People's Republic of China (PRC), and the relationship of the two Koreas. But a new context could provide a framework for developing an interaction among these problem countries, and it could establish the basis for developing an economic framework for the long-term political security of the Asia-Pacific region. In essence, the U.S. policy posture, which became known in 1969 and 1970 as the Guam Doctrine, left more issues unanswered than it clarified. President Nixon's articulation of a policy of withdrawing from military leadership in the area and instead supporting Asian initiatives left serious questions as to who was to make initiatives and how, and what support could be expected from the United States. The "other half" of the Guam Doctrine is long overdue. From an American perspective, a transitional arrangement for dealing with Vietnam and North Korea in a diffused, regional context might be more realistic than a continued freeze in all contacts.

As the East Asian region continues to grow, the exports of the United States, Japan, and even Europe to this region will no doubt grow. Charity and security motivations for foreign policy may be overtaken and blended with commercial self-interest, in selling to and investing in the region and in dealing with the imports from it.

As for the ASEAN countries and the rest of the LDCs in the region, there is some doubt whether all of them can anticipate the kinds of policy difficulties that lie ahead and carry out coherent strategies for dealing with global economic turbulence in the 1980s. They need a mutually accepted strategy, and they need a more sophisticated understanding of the world political and economic forces that affect their destiny. The educative role of the United Nations ECAFE organization, the Asian Development Bank, and regional institutions could be developed further. Teams of experts, particularly trade experts, from the United States, the EEC, and Canada could be called upon.

Structural adjustment pains in Japan, Canada, and the EEC will often be

---

[11] H. B. Malmgren, "Japan, the United States and the Pacific Economy," *Pacific Community*, Vol. 4, No. 3, 1973, pp. 321-322; also, H. B. Malmgren, "Trade Liberalization and the Economic Development of the Pacific Basin: The Need for Cooperation," in H. E. English and K. A. Jay (eds.), *Obstacles to Trade in the Pacific Area, Proceedings of the Fourth Pacific Trade and Development Conference*, Carleton University, Ottawa, 1972.

politically severe in the 1980s. To thwart a lurch into heavy protectionism, the industrialization and trade strategies of the East Asian region will have to be thought through with great care in the next decade. The LDCs of the region will also need to think carefully about their relationships to the GATT as well as their bilateral relationships with the major trading nations.

As for the political and economic roles of China and the Soviet Union, much uncertainty will remain. If the PRC can maintain a steady course toward industrialization, based on interaction with the Western market economies, this will generate economic tensions for the LDCs in the region, as well as for Japan. The PRC will tend to export similar goods and therefore will constitute a strong competitive element in both regional and world markets. The desperate need to finance imports of capital goods into the PRC will give impetus to export programs that may well prove disruptive to the other nations in the region, both in their own markets and in their competitive position in selling to Japan, North America, and Europe.

An expanded Soviet role in the region is also conceivable, perhaps beginning with a greater deployment of sea power and the gradual development of more intimate relations with Vietnam. This could well cause some countries of East Asia to be more accommodating to the Soviets, especially in the absence of a strong American security presence in the region. How Japan will deal with the Soviet Union in the 1980s is an open question, but if the United States is increasingly hostile to Japan in trade policy and political rhetoric, this could well drive Japan toward warmer relations with the Soviets. This too could have an impact on the economies of the region. Competition over resources in the latter 1980s cannot be entirely excluded, although the world market for most resources will be in an oversupply situation for at least the early part of the decade. How the energy resources of the region are to be developed is perhaps the most potentially contentious resource question. Here, the evolution of offshore development offers prospects for either cooperation or conflict.[12]

In conclusion, then, we can expect continued economic dynamism in East Asia in the 1980s but growing tensions between the region and the markets of the advanced industrialized nations. We can anticipate a time of economic turbulence in the global marketplace, with intensified international competition and difficulties in making structural adjustments in the industrialized market economies of the West. There is a need for new policies within the region, and toward the region, to secure continued growth and improvement in the economic well-being of the East Asian peoples, but there is some uncertainty about whether this will take place—especially in the absence of effective multilateral mechanisms for discussing and planning for measures of economic adjustment on a regional and global basis.

[12] See the detailed analysis of this issue by Guy J. Pauker, pp. 231-247 below.

Chapter 11

THE SECURITY IMPLICATIONS OF REGIONAL ENERGY AND NATURAL RESOURCE EXPLOITATION

Guy J. Pauker[1]

THE LONG-RANGE IMPLICATIONS OF CHINA'S MODERNIZATION PROGRAM

About 1,500 million people now live in East and Southeast Asia.[2] By the year 2000 there will be some 600 million more. In its most recent demographic estimates for mid-1977 and projections of world population to the 21st century, the U.S. Bureau of the Census concluded that world population will increase from 4.2 billion in 1977 to between 5.9 and 6.7 billion in 2000. It also underscored "the increasing demands that can be expected to be made on the world's natural resources, its habitable land and its economic structure in coming decades."[3]

Most countries in Asia actively seek rapid economic growth and modernization. Obviously, as more people achieve higher standards of living, the demand for food, industrial raw materials, and sources of energy will increase. A quantitative expression of the magnitude of the task facing the developing countries indicates the pressure on natural resources and other factors of production that will be generated by the successful economic growth of East Asia's developing countries.

China's recent decision to abandon Maoist economic policies and become part of the international economic system is particularly significant because of the size of its population and the low base from which its economic expansion has to proceed. The North-South conflict, which involves the terms under which advanced industrial societies, especially the countries of the Organization for Economic Cooperation and Development (OECD),[4] are to assist the development of the Third World, is bound to be further exacerbated by the claims of an additional billion people, the Chinese, who previously were not an integral part of that bargaining process.[5]

---

[1] Guy J. Pauker has been with The Rand Corporation since 1960 as a Senior Staff Member in the Social Science Department, having previously taught political science at Harvard University and the University of California, Berkeley. His most recent publications are *Diversity and Development in Southeast Asia—The Coming Decade*, published in 1977 by the 1980s Project of the Council on Foreign Relations, and *Military Implications of a Possible World Order Crisis in the 1980s*, The Rand Corporation, R-2003-AF, November 1977.

[2] U.S. Department of Commerce, Bureau of the Census, *World Population 1977, Recent Demographic Estimates for the Countries and Regions of the World*, Washington, D.C., October 1978, Table B-1, p. 141.

[3] Robert Reinhold, "50 Percent Rise in World Population Forecast by Year 2000," *New York Times*, February 26, 1979.

[4] Australia, Austria, Belgium, Britain, Canada, Denmark, Finland, France, Germany, Greece, Iceland, Ireland, Italy, Japan, Luxembourg, the Netherlands, New Zealand, Norway, Portugal, Spain, Sweden, Switzerland, Turkey, the United States, and Yugoslavia (special status).

[5] The *Communique of the State Statistical Bureau of the People's Republic of China on Fulfillment of China's 1978 National Economic Plan*, released on June 27, 1979, stated that "at the end of 1978 China had a population of 975,23,000. Natural population growth rate stood at 12 per thousand." Xinhua News Agency, News Bulletin No. 11122, June 28, 1979.

China's recent commitment to what its leaders call the "four modernizations"[6] is an historic turning point in contemporary Asian history, with far-reaching implications for the world order and for the security interests of the United States in the Pacific region.

This paper raises the question of whether the future exploitation of energy and other natural resources in the Pacific region is likely to create significant conflict situations and, if so, what policies the United States could adopt to minimize, contain, or resolve such conflicts.

In principle, technology should be able to satisfy any amount of growing demand for natural resources if commodity prices were such as to make the exploitation of previously marginal deposits economical. In practice, it is questionable whether the present structure of the world economy and the internal social and political processes of the less-developed countries will make it possible for them to pay for such marginal resources and industrialize smoothly. It is also doubtful whether the currently proposed New International Economic Order, if it were to be realized, could overcome widespread economic and technological backwardness merely by resource transfers from rich to poor countries.

The constraints developing countries are bound to encounter in the 1980s are not difficult to imagine, but remedies are not easy to formulate. The search for solutions has to start with some basic questions: How will competition for natural resources affect the economic and political life of East Asian countries and their international relations? How can the United States and its OECD partners use their economic, political, and military influence to limit or avoid, in the 1980s, a destructive pattern of resource competition in East Asia?

In 1916, Lenin described the "struggle for the sources of raw materials, for the export of capital, for "spheres of influence," i.e., for spheres of profitable deals, concessions, monopolist profits and so on; in fine for economic territory"[7] as a characteristic manifestation of "monopoly capitalism."

Lenin was misled by ideological blinders and the lack of historical precedents, as only capitalist states were industrializing at that time. He failed to anticipate that competition for external sources of raw materials and for foreign markets was inherent in the process of global industrialization, rather than peculiar to capitalist economic systems. Expanding production was bound to increase the competitive demand for natural resources. The possibility of political and military conflicts was inherent in a setting of separate sovereign states.

It was not their "high stage of capitalism" but bad political judgment that prompted Japan and Germany to seek raw materials and markets by the forcible creation of a "Greater East Asian Co-Prosperity Sphere" or by conquering *Lebensraum*. A generation later, both countries discovered that good economic management was a vastly superior road to national power and prosperity. But whether the latecomers to the Industrial Revolution will be able to emulate the German and Japanese "economic miracles," as China's present leaders seem to believe, is not clear, despite the successes of Taiwan, South Korea, Singapore, and Hong Kong.

In East and Southeast Asia, the problems confronting the People's Republic of China (PRC), which has 65 percent of the region's total population, raise some

[6] See pp. 218-219 below.
[7] E. Varga and L. Mendelsohn (eds.), *New Data for V. I. Lenin's Imperialism—The Highest Stage of Capitalism*, International Publishers, New York, 1940, p. 254.

218

particularly vexing questions, not only because of China's dominant position in the region, but also because of the recent drastic reversal of Beijing's (Peking's) economic policies. The shift from a posture of stringent self-reliance to eager cooperation with advanced capitalist countries, if sustained, could have a profound impact on the international economic environment in which all the other countries of the region operate.

China's new economic policies are an historical development with immense implications. Twenty-three percent of the world's present population,[8] previously living in quasi-isolation, are now becoming claimants on the world's resources and markets. The full implications of this development for the international economic system will unfold only gradually, over an extended period of time.

The basic principles of China's new economic policies were incorporated in the "Outline of the Ten-Year Plan for the Development of the National Economy 1976-1985," endorsed by the First Session of the Fifth National People's Congress on March 5, 1978. On behalf of the State Council, Premier Hua Guofeng (Hua Kuo-feng) appealed to the nation to accomplish before the end of the century "the four modernizations," namely the development of agriculture, industry, national defense, and science and technology.[9]

With the assistance of Japan, the United States, and Western Europe, the Beijing government hopes to turn China into a developed country by the year 2000. Foreign exponents of "Maoist economics," such as the World Bank's Mahbul ul Haq[10] are being left out in the cold while Vice-Premier Deng Xiaoping (Teng Hsiao-p'ing) and his supporters seek new ways of speeding up economic growth, breaking with the past and adopting highly unorthodox methods. For instance, Deng told the Ninth National Congress of Chinese Trade Unions on October 11, 1978, "The working class should go all out to master modern technology and managerial skills so as to make outstanding contributions to the four modernizations. It is only right and proper that whoever makes more contributions to the four modernizations be accorded greater honor and more awards by the state."[11]

Less than two weeks later, the dynamic Vice-Premier was in Tokyo bringing into effect the Treaty of Peace and Friendship with Japan signed in Beijing on August 12, 1978, which will give China increased access to Japanese technology and managerial skills. Conceding, at a press conference for Japanese journalists, that China's target date for modernization by the year 2000 will be hard to meet, Deng was amazingly frank about his country's present backwardness: "If you have an ugly face, it is no use pretending that you are handsome," he told his Japanese audience.[12]

The initial goals of the Ten Year Plan elicited considerable skepticism among foreign experts, who doubted that China could reach production targets of 60

[8] The U.S. Bureau of the Census estimated China's population in mid-1977 at 982 million, out of a global total of 4,257 million. The World Bank used the figure of 836 million for mid-1976, which is much too low, as we now know from the figure released by the State Statistical Bureau in Beijing in June 1979. That figure is only slightly lower than the previous estimate of the U.S. Bureau of the Census.

[9] Hua Guofeng, "Unite and Strive to Build a Modern, Powerful Socialist Country!" report on the Work of the Government delivered at the First Session of the Fifth National People's Congress on February 26, 1978, *Peking Review*, No. 10, March 10, 1978.

[10] Mahbul ul Haq, *The Poverty Curtain: Choices for the Third World*, Columbia University Press, New York, 1976.

[11] "Greeting the Great Task," Deng Xiaoping's speech at the 9th National Trade Union Congress, *Beijing Review*, No. 42, October 20, 1978, pp. 5-6.

[12] "China and Japan Hug and Make Up," *Time*, November 6, 1978, p. 66.

million tons of steel and 400 million tons of food grains by 1985. China's pragmatic leaders seem to have reached the same conclusion within a year after the March 1978 commitment to the four modernizations. Heralded by several editorials in the *People's Daily* in late February 1979, a more cautious approach to development was announced by Premier Hua Guofeng at the Second Session of the Fifth National People's Congress on June 18, 1979. He informed the Chinese people that the State Council had concluded that "the country should devote the three years beginning from 1979 to readjusting, restructuring, consolidating and improving the national economy in order to bring it, step by step, onto the path of sustained, proportionate and high-speed development."[13] Referring to the Ten-Year Plan he had submitted fifteen months earlier, Premier Hua explained, ". . . some of the measures we adopted were not sufficiently prudent. The main problem now facing us is that our agricultural expansion cannot as yet keep up with the needs of industrial development, and at times cannot even keep up with the demands of a growing population. Many important products of the light and textile industries are insufficient in quantity, poor in quality and limited in variety, so there are not enough marketable goods. Although the coal, petroleum, and power industries and the transport and communications services have grown at a relatively swift pace, they still lag behind what is required by our expanding economy. Co-ordination within and between industrial departments is lacking in many respects. In capital construction, far too many projects are being undertaken at the same time and many will not contribute to our production capacity for years. . . ."[14]

After spelling out the meaning of readjustment, restructuring, consolidation, and improvement—which seem to be derived from sound management principles—Premier Hua responded to the comments elicited abroad when the revised three-year program had been announced through Chinese press editorials: "Along with this policy—Premier Hua said—we shall carry out the policy already adopted of actively importing advanced technology and making use of funds from abroad. The view that this policy of readjustment is a negative retreat and the view that its implementation will lead to a termination of the importation of advanced technology are both wrong through and through."[15]

1. Uphold the guiding idea of taking agriculture as the foundation of our economy and concentrate efforts on raising agricultural production.
2. Adopt resolute and effective measures to speed up the growth of light and textile industries.
3. Effectively overcome the weak links in our economy: the coal, petroleum, and power industries, transport and communications services, and building-material industry.
4. Resolutely curtail capital construction and try to get the best results from investments.
5. Vigorously develop science, education, and culture and speed up the training of personnel for construction.

[13] Hua Guofeng, *Report on the Work of the Government,* June 18, 1979, Xinhua News Agency, News Bulletin No. 11120, June 26, 1979, p. 12.
[14] Hua Guofeng, loc. cit., p. 12.
[15] Ibid., p. 17.

6. Continue to do a good job in importing technology, make active use of funds from abroad, and strive to expand exports.
7. Adopt a resolute attitude and take active and steady steps to reform the structure of economic management.
8. Preserve basic price stability, readjust those prices that are irrational, while strengthening price control.
9. Raise the living standards of the people step by step as production rises.
10. Continue to do a good job of family planning and effectively control population growth.[16]

The implications of these policy guidelines with regard to specific production targets were spelled out three days later, on June 21, by Vice-Premier Yu Qiuli (Yu Ch'iu-li). He announced that for grain production the target for 1979 was 312 million tons, an increase of only 2.5 percent over the 1978 total. Even more significant was the statement that "in order to reduce the pressure on fuel and power supplies and give more of both to the light and textile industries, it is planned to turn out no more than 32 million tons of steel this year."[17] According to official Chinese figures, steel production had reached 31.79 million tons in 1978.[18] Clearly, the development of heavy industry is being postponed in favor of the consumer, a policy diametrically opposed to Stalinist economics. Ironically, the larger-than-life portrait of the late Soviet dictator is still on display in Tian An Men Square.

Vice-Premier Yu Qiuli also disclosed that existing power-generating plants using oil will be converted to coal, or in some instances *back* to coal, and that an energy law will be drafted at an early date, which will stipulate "criteria for the rational exploitation, comprehensive utilization and the saving of energy."[18] The purpose of these new measures is obviously to conserve more oil for foreign-exchange generating exports, but it also betrays a growing consciousness of the resource constraints facing China's modernization plans.

But even if Beijing moves cautiously, the PRC will have a profound impact on the world economy, as a buyer of capital goods, an exporter of oil and other natural resources, and a client of the international financial market. The normalization of relations between Washington and Beijing, announced on December 15, 1978, and implemented on January 1, 1979, is creating interesting prospects for American business in China. It is also facing Japan and Western Europe with strong American competition in the newly opening Chinese markets, unless the industrial democracies work out cooperative arrangements among themselves. The impact of Beijing's new foreign economic policy was described in these words by a senior Japanese official, Nobuhiko Ushiba, at a symposium on trade issues held in Washington, D.C., on February 8-9, 1979:

Conclusion of the Sino-Japanese Treaty of Peace and Friendship in October, and normalization of diplomatic ties between the United States and China

---

[16] Ibid., pp. 18-32.

[17] Yu Qiuli, *Report on the Draft of the 1979 National Economic Plan*, June 21, 1979, Xinhua News Agency, News Bulletin No. 11123, June 29, 1979, p. 13.

[18] Communique of the State Statistical Bureau of the People's Republic of China on *Fulfillment of China's 1978 National Economic Plan*, Xinhua News Agency, News Bulletin No. 11122, June 27, 1979, p. 2.

in December, have totally transformed China's relations with the industrial democracies. The implications are earth-shaking, and it is no wonder that much of the world has been seized by a kind of China fever. What we are seeing is a nation of nearly 1 billion people, one quarter of the earth's population, suddenly emerging from nearly three decades of ideological isolation, and turning to the great democracies for the capital, technology and managerial skills to help transform China into a modern state by the year 2000.[19]

Competition between the industrial democracies for shares of the Chinese market could become the source of international conflicts and even of new power alignments in the coming decade, worsening the North-South confrontation amid the growing competition among the most successful developing countries. Short-term gains by one industrial competitor against the others may prove costly if they contribute to a further weakening of the existing world order.

With or without cooperative arrangements between exporting countries, China is an obviously welcome newcomer to the world market, and trade with the industrial democracies will certainly increase.[20] The difficult question is whether China will be able to produce and export the natural resources and manufactured goods that are needed to pay for the imports required by its modernization plans.

China is well endowed with sources of energy, oil, natural gas, coal, and hydropower, but specialists in the West claim that it lacks high-grade iron ore and non-ferrous metals, particularly aluminum and copper.[21] But in June 1979 the State Statistical Bureau in Beijing announced that "geological prospecting advanced relatively quickly in 1978 with new discoveries. The newly found reserves of iron, coal, copper, aluminum, phosphorus, pyrite and 15 other major minerals all surpassed the planned targets. Among these resources, those for iron ore increased by 2,200 million tons, and for coal by 8,800 million tons."[22] Nevertheless, in the immediate future Beijing will have to import iron ore until new domestic mines are developed.

Neither China's resource base nor the present structure of the international economic system seem adequate for the full modernization of 23 percent of the world's population. Will Deng Xiaoping's pragmatism bring about a Chinese "economic miracle" in the next two decades? Will current policies be carried out long enough to show results? Modern technology and managerial skills can indeed be learned, especially by a nation with China's great cultural tradition. But will adequate amounts of natural resources and capital goods be available to the PRC to sustain rapid economic modernization? Will Beijing be able to export enough oil, coal, and manufactured goods to finance its development program? What are the security implications of China's competition with other countries facing similar requirements?

The problem of integration into the world market is by no means peculiar to China or even to East and Southeast Asia as a whole. The countries along the rim

[19] Nobuhiko Ushiba, "Toward Stronger and More Effective Partnership," *Wall Street Journal*, March 23, 1979, p. 11.

[20] According to the *Los Angeles Times*, February 23, 1979, "the Commerce Department has said that U.S. trade with China, now less than $1 billion a year, could double in 1979."

[21] K. P. Wang, "China's Mineral Economy," in Joint Economic Committee, Congress of the United States, *Chinese Economy Post-Mao*, Washington, D.C., 1978, Vol. I, Table on p. 378.

[22] State Statistical Bureau of the People's Republic of China, op. cit., p. 9.

of the Western Pacific are not different from the rest of the world with respect to their growing demand for natural resources and capital goods. These will have to be acquired in part through international trade and in part by domestic production requiring major inputs of capital. The economic expansion of industrial societies enhances their interdependence and thus also their vulnerability to external economic and political forces beyond the control of individual nation-states.

The more successful East Asian countries become economically, the more interdependent they will be with the rest of the world. The constraints on their economic growth, in the immediate future, will be primarily the result of the present structure of the international economic system and of their own backwardness. Scarcity of natural resources will make itself felt only later, as the process of modernization becomes successful and requirements for imported natural resources increase without corresponding growth in the value of exports.

These constraints must be distinguished from those anticipated by the Club of Rome. In *The Limits of Growth*, we were warned that "the basic behavior mode of the world system is exponential growth of population and capital, followed by collapse."[23] Our present concern is that long before the world has tested the proposition that "the limits to growth on this planet will be reached sometime within the next hundred years,"[24] the latecomers to the Industrial Revolution, including China, may be engaged in fierce competition for available resources and markets in order to sustain their economic modernization.

MINERAL RESOURCE CONSTRAINTS ON ECONOMIC GROWTH

Japan is a good illustration of a highly developed economic system, devoid of natural resources, which became the second largest industrial power in the world by accepting the risks inherent in a high degree of dependence on foreign trade. In 1977, for instance, when Japan's Gross National Product (GNP) exceeded $500 billion, its imports amounted to more than $70 billion, 80 percent of which consisted of foodstuffs, raw materials, and mineral fuels. Japan's exports of over $80 billion consisted almost exclusively of manufactured goods.[25]

This outstanding success in achieving a highly favorable balance of trade has created considerable difficulties for Japan in the international community. Tokyo is currently under great pressure to reduce the surpluses of its trade balance. South Korea, Taiwan, Hong Kong, and Singapore are now achieving comparable successes as exporters of manufactured goods. Growing protectionism will make it increasingly difficult for other countries to attain their development goals in the setting of the present international economic system.

If the five economically most successful countries of East and Southeast Asia are already threatened by protectionist responses to the dynamism of their export drives, what is going to happen when economic growth generates in the other countries of the region, including China, very large requirements for imports of natural resources and capital goods, to be paid for by exporting other natural resources and manufactured goods? Will the present international economic sys-

[23] Donella H. Meadows, et al., *The Limits to Growth*, Universe Books, New York, 1972, p. 142.
[24] Op. cit., p. 23.
[25] The Oriental Economist, *Japan Economic Yearbook 1978/79*, Tokyo, 1978, pp. 19, 38.

tem be able to cope with these expanding requirements for a free flow of goods in international trade?

Japan, South Korea, Taiwan, Hong Kong, and Singapore, with a total population of about 168 million people, constitute at most one-eighth of the total population of East and Southeast Asia. Table 1, which is based on the World Bank's *World Development Report, 1978*, shows that the rest of the region still has a long way to go before it becomes an integral part of the modern industrialized world. It leaves little to the imagination concerning the magnitude of the task facing the developing countries.

However superficial some of these basic indicators may be, they do suggest an underlying reality. It is meaningful and revealing that in the World Bank table per capita GNPs span a range from $90 for Laos to $4,910 for Japan (55 times greater). Even larger disparities characterize energy consumption data, which vary from 16 kg of coal equivalent per capita annually for Kampuchea (Cambodia) to 3,622 kg for Japan (226 times greater). To be sure, these are extreme cases. The United Nations uses an average ratio of 12 to 1 between the per capita GNP of the rich, industrialized countries and that of the poor, developing countries. A recent study prepared for the World Bank by Irving Krayis, Alan Heston, and Robert Summers of the University of Pennsylvania's Wharton School concluded that the average ratio is only 7 to 1.[26] Dr. W. Häfele and his associates at the International Institute for Applied Systems Analysis in Laxenburg, Austria, use a factor of 16 as the average ratio between energy consumption per capita in the developed world and that in the developing world.[27]

The gap to be bridged is immense. The amount of resources required to overcome the backwardness of seven-eighths of East and Southeast Asia's population can be illustrated by the following example. Modern industrial societies have sunk a large stock of processed metals and other minerals into their infrastructure. Steel is a particularly valid indicator, being used for a wide variety of purposes in a developed economy, but hardly at all in preindustrial societies. Harrison Brown, of the Resource Systems Institute in Honolulu, has estimated that "we have in use in the United States some 10 metric tons of steel per person. Of this, the greater part exists in the form of heavy structural shapes, reinforcements, pilings, nails, staples, and wire fences. About 8 percent of the steel, or 750 kilograms per person, is in the form of private automobiles, trucks, and buses." Brown also estimated that "for every person in the United States we now have in use about 150 kilograms each of copper and lead, 100 kilograms each of zinc and aluminum, and 20 kilograms of tin."[28]

The processing of metallic ores—which includes reduction to metals, transportation, and manufacturing—requires large amounts of energy. And the total stock of metals and other raw materials imbedded in the American economy continues to grow. Brown estimates that per capita consumption of steel in the United States rose from 140 kg in 1900 to 300 kg in 1910, and is now at about 700 kg annually.

[26] Jay Elliott, "Gap Between Rich, Poor Nations Less Than Believed," *Los Angeles Times*, November 24, 1978.

[27] Lecture at The Rand Corporation, Santa Monica, California, March 30, 1979, summarizing the forthcoming book, *Energy in a Finite World—A Global Systems Analysis.*

[28] Harrison Brown, *The Human Future Revisited*, W. W. Norton & Co., New York, 1978, pp. 53-54. Also, Harrison Brown, James Bonner, and John Weir, *The Next Hundred Years*, The Viking Press, New York, 1957, pp. 17-26.

Table 1

BASIC INDICATORS: EAST AND SOUTHEAST ASIA[a]

	(1)	(2)	(3)	(4)	(5)	(6)	(7)
			GNP Per Capita			Energy	
	Population (millions) Mid-1976	Rate of Population Growth (annual %)	(U.S. dollars) 1976	Average Annual Growth (%) Av. 1960-76	Index of Per Capita Food Production (1965-67 = 100) Av. 1974-75	Average Annual Growth of Production (%) 1960-75	Per Capita Consumption (Kg of coal equivalent) 1975
Low-Income Countries (income per person below $250)							
1. Kampuchea (Cambodia)	8.1	2.8	NA	NA	53	NA	16
2. Laos	3.3	2.4	90	1.8	103	NA	63
3. Burma	30.8	2.4	120	0.7	98	4.5	51
4. Vietnam	47.6	2.2	NA	NA	NA	0.5	NA
5. Indonesia	135.2	2.1	240	3.4	117	8.5	178
Middle-Income Countries (income per person above $250)							
6. Thailand	43.0	2.5	380	4.5	106	17.2	284
7. Philippines	43.3	3.0	410	2.4	108	3.3	326
8. China, People's Republic	835.8	1.7	410	5.2	108	4.6	693
9. Korea, Democratic People's Republic	16.3	2.7	470	3.5	110	9.5	2,808
10. Korea, Republic of	36.0	2.0	670	7.3	104	6.2	1,038
11. Malaysia	12.7	2.9	860	3.9	146	34.6	560
12. Taiwan	16.3	1.9	1,070	6.3	NA	NA	1,427
13. Hong Kong	4.5	2.1	2,110	6.5	84	NA	1,119
14. Singapore	2.3	1.6	2,700	7.5	208	NA	2,151
Industrialized Countries							
15. Japan	112.8	1.2	4,910	7.9	107	-3.9	3,622

[a] Source: The World Bank, *World Development Report, 1978*, Washington, D.C., August, 1978, pp. 76-77; Column (2) is based on the *1976 World Population Data Sheet* of the Population Reference Bureau, Inc.

Much larger amounts of nonmetals such as stone, sand, gravel, and cement are consumed each year. The magnitude of this process is reflected in the fact that in the United States nearly 15,000 ton-km of freight per person are being transported each year.

Assuming that China's population is 1 billion and that—a wild guess—on a per capita basis the present stock of crude steel imbedded in China's economic infrastructure is not more than 10 percent of that in the United States, China would need some 9 billion metric tons of steel to replicate and equal our present economic infrastructure. Whether such an achievement, or even a fraction thereof, is possible is not a question of physical availability of resources in nature. On that issue the National Commission on Supplies and Shortages concluded in December 1976: "We see little reason to fear that the world will run out of natural resources during the quarter century or more that we have defined as the long run."

The Commission, which was chaired by Donald B. Rice, President of The Rand Corporation, based its conclusions on "the large body of evidence that is already available" on long-run supply and demand trends for commodities. Table I of its report shows that in 1970, known reserves of iron ore were 251 billion metric tons.[29]

Even though minerals are physically available in sufficient quantity in the earth's crust to sustain global industrialization at prevailing prices, their availability to a given country depends on where they are located on the political map of the globe, whether a country has the capital resources to mine its iron ore, and what it can offer in exchange for the supplies it needs to import. Another constraint is the rate at which steel manufacturing capacity can be expanded. At a social cost which the present Chinese leadership seems neither willing nor able to incur, the Soviet Union achieved between 1928 and 1937 an annual growth rate of 14.8 percent in the production of ferrous metals, quadrupling its output in ten years.[30]

China is not seeking Stalinist rates of growth in the development of its steel industry. As mentioned earlier, Beijing has recently published—for the first time in about 20 years—exact figures for the year 1978's production of steel. After a period of stagnation in 1976 and 1977 due in part to the Tangshan earthquake, which devastated that nation's principal source of coking coal, steel output increased 33.9 percent, from 23.74 million tons in 1977 to 31.78 million tons in 1978.[31] This spurt was the result of making full use of existing capacity, which had been underutilized. Further expansion will depend on building new steel mills. As mentioned earlier, no expansion is planned for 1979 and the target of the Ten Year Plan may have been reduced to 50 million tons or even less by 1985.

With its present steel-producing capacity of 32 million tons, it would take China some 280 years to produce 9 billion tons. Assuming a level of production of 50 million tons annually by 1985, it would still take China about 180 years to equal the present per capita standing stock of the United States. Furthermore, this crude

[29] National Commission on Supplies and Shortages, Government and the Nation's Resources, Washington, D.C., 1976, pp. 16, 22.

[30] Donald R. Hodgman, Soviet Industrial Production 1928-1951, Harvard University Press, Cambridge, 1954, p. 191. Table 28 shows the revised production index for ferrous metals (1934 = 100) rising from 42.7 in 1928 to 170.2 in 1937. Hodgman noted, "Limitations on available data make the construction of an independent index of Soviet industrial output an especially dubious procedure for the years since 1937. Beginning in 1938, the Soviet government, presumably impelled by considerations of military security, sharply curtailed the publication of annual production statistics for Soviet industry" (p. 81).

[31] State Statistical Bureau of the People's Republic of China, loc. cit., p. 2.

arithmetic does not take into account China's population growth and the need to replenish stock lost through corrosion or by failure to recycle all steel that is no longer in use.

Another figure is relevant in this context: The world's total production of crude steel was 706 million metric tons in 1974.[32] If global production were to be made available exclusively to China, without a nail to spare for anybody else, "catching up" with the United States would take about 12 years.

It may be naive to assume that China will seek to mirror-image the American lifestyle, complete with private automobiles and urban sprawl. But "catching up with Japan" does ultimately imply the adoption of the American lifestyle by successive approximations. Global trends, in countries with free economies and planned economies alike, seem to point in that direction. First the privileged urban elites and gradually the rest of the population seek more comfortable homes, equipped with modern appliances, and private automobiles. Even if China were to shun the extremes of the American way of life and adopt Japanese standards, its future requirements for energy and other natural resources would be staggering. It is hard to visualize the Chinese people being forever content to ride bicycles while satellite TV transmissions from other countries show all people using automobiles, not just the priviliged political elites, as is the case in China today. One can also speculate on the political impact of the tastes that China's young technological elites will acquire while studying abroad.

Furthermore, one cannot ignore the crucial fact that in the coming decade, China will not be the only claimant on natural resources for economic development and modernization. Of the world's population of 4,257 million in mid-1977, the developed countries accounted for 1,154 million. The population of the developing countries totaled 3,103 million, of which China represented 31.6 percent.[33] In any assessment of the magnitude of the global developmental task, it must be assumed that even if one postulates a utopian state of "zero growth" in the developed countries, the developing countries will all try to achieve higher standards of living through industrialization and will therefore claim an increasing share of the world's natural resources.

It would take 43 years, at 1974 global levels of production of crude steel, to create a stock of 10 tons per capita for each person now living in the Third World. The industrialization of the rich countries took longer than that, but available technology and managerial techniques can shorten the time for the currently industrializing countries.

South Korea is an outstanding example. In 1970 it had no steel industry. Today its steel mill at Pohan produces 5.5 million tons and it will produce 8.5 million tons in 1981, while plans for a second steel mill are already under way. All iron ore and coking coal are imported from abroad. Obviously, as more countries try to overcome their backwardness simultaneously and to telescope the stages of economic growth into a short time span, it is likely that competition for natural resources and for other factors of production needed for industrialization, such as capital and skilled foreign manpower, will increase substantially in the 1980s.

By what means will the now developing countries obtain the required re-

[32] Department of the Interior, Bureau of Mines, *Minerals Yearbook 1974, Volume III, Area Reports: International,* Washington, D.C., 1977, p. 25.

[33] Bureau of the Census, op. cit., p. 14.

sources? Can the present international economic system do the job? If not, what alternative methods are likely to be invented? What tensions and conflicts are likely to occur along the way, given the uneven distribution of resources among developing countries? What can be done to channel these processes into constructive and benign channels? Will it be possible for the latecomers to the Industrial Revolution to catch up, or have they missed their chance, at least until the present international economic system undergoes basic structural changes?

It is abundantly clear, after 30 years of experimentation with international economic assistance and governmental economic planning, that sustained growth was difficult to achieve even in the relatively favorable setting of the 1950s and 1960s. In the coming decade, the constraints to be encountered by developing nations are bound to become more stringent. The international economic system seems unable to cope efficiently with the growing cost of energy, capital goods, and technological skills and with restrictions on the flow of goods through the channels of international trade.

In the less crowded and politically less mobilized world of the 1920s and 1930s, the breakdown of the international economic system had a major impact on the security and well-being of mankind. Economic frustrations set the stage for shortsighted and self-serving nationalistic competition. As the global order broke down, isolated instances of military aggression created the state of disarray that engulfed mankind in World War II.

It is certainly in the national interest of the United States to help prevent the breakdown of the present world order, which may be unable to withstand the combined pressures of nationalist, ideological, and economic forces. The impact of American activities on the international economic system is enormous. These activities can amplify or reduce the conflicts inherent in the competition for energy and other economic resources in the Pacific region and elsewhere.

American international economic leverage must be used to maximize the chances for the development and maintenance of a benign global environment. In this respect, the growing interest in the Department of State and in Congressional committees in the concept of a Pacific Economic Community is a salutary symptom, although the implementation of such a concept is not likely to move faster than the creation of the European Economic Community, which reached its present stage through the sustained efforts of a whole generation of leaders.

THE THREAT OF FOOD SHORTAGES

Assuming that the developing countries, including China, fail to become modern industrial societies in the next few decades, can they at least be expected to satisfy the basic human needs of their populations, especially for food? China's emergence as a full member of the international community is sometimes viewed as a threat to other countries' supply of staple foods. The *New York Times* published the following comment at the time of Secretary of Agriculture Bob Bergland's visit to China in November 1978:

> If each of China's 900 million people were to consume just one additional pound of grain a week, it would add 21 million metric tons to the worldwide demand. That tonnage is equal, in terms of wheat, to all the wheat now

grown in Canada each year, or the total annual consumption of wheat in the United States in all forms, from bread to liquor.[34]

The same reporter noted that "today, a Chinese order for 21 million tons of grain would seriously affect the exportable surplus of the United States and create a worldwide shortage." This is surely an exaggeration, in view of the fact that 1978 world grain production was estimated by the U.S. Department of Agriculture at 1,370 million metric tons, in perfect balance with an estimated consumption for the same year of 1,360 million metric tons. According to the same USDA estimate, world grain reserves in 1978 were expected to amount to 190 million metric tons, nearly 60 million more than existed in 1974.[35] Past experience indicates that grain shortages manifest themselves in strong upward price pressures only when world grain reserves drop to a low of about 100 million metric tons, as happened in 1973 and 1974.[36] If the USDA estimates for 1978 were reasonably accurate, additional Chinese grain imports of 21 million metric tons in 1978 would not have created a worldwide shortage. But how long global supply and demand of food grains will remain in balance and whether the countries having a food deficit will be able to pay for the imports they will require is another question. In this respect, the future growth of Chinese agriculture is particularly important to the world as a whole. At present its agriculture is "technologically so backward that it employs 70 percent of the labor force."[37]

Because China is the single largest nation in the world and because it cannot grow all the food it needs, its existence is a particular source of concern to its smaller neighbors. The image that China's "teeming millions" are threatening the welfare of the rest of humanity is just as tenaciously held as the expectation of exporters of manufactured goods that great profits will be made by those who succeed in penetrating the Chinese market. Both anticipations are probably exaggerations, at least in the short run.

During Bergland's visit to China, the press reported that Beijing expected an output of about 285 million metric tons of grain in 1978. This is not a totally reliable figure,[38] but it is good enough for present purposes. With 23 percent of the world's population, China would have produced only 20.8 percent of the world's food grains. U.S. government analysts believe that China has spent more than $1.5 billion on grain imports in the last three years because agricultural expansion has lagged behind population growth.

Robert Michael Field and James A. Kilpatrick, economists at the Central Intelligence Agency, argue that lower population figures than those currently accepted by American demographers would make Chinese grain imports difficult to explain.[39] If China does not succeed in the Malthusian race between population

[34] H. J. Maidenberg, "When China Changes Its Diet, the World Sits Up," New York Times, November 12, 1978, p. F3.

[35] William Robbins, "U.S. Grain Surplus Is Providing New Relief for World and Nation," New York Times, November 11, 1978, p. 28.

[36] Lester R. Brown, In the Human Interest, W. W. Norton & Company, New York, 1974, pp. 53-54.

[37] National Foreign Assessment Center, China: In Pursuit of Economic Modernization—A Research Paper, Washington, D.C., December 1978, p. II.

[38] Fox Butterfield, "China Seen as Bigger Buyer of U.S. Grain," New York Times, November 15, 1978; Jay Mathews, "Poor Grain Harvest Seen Blow to China's Modernization Plans," Washington Post, November 14, 1978.

[39] Robert Michael Field and James A. Kilpatrick, "Chinese Grain Production: An Interpretation of the Data," The China Quarterly, No. 74, June 1978, pp. 379-382. For 1979, China will import 2.5 million

growth and agricultural expansion, this will have a negative impact on China's image among its southern neighbors, where fears about China's future needs for "fertile tropical lands" have deep roots in the past history of Han expansionism.

In the 1950s many political and military leaders in Southeast Asia were very worried that China would be forced by population pressure to conquer their countries in order to gain control of their rice fields. Then, gradually, Mao Zedong's (Mao Tse-tung's) policy of self-reliance and the "green revolution" which seemed to promise all countries agricultural self-sufficiency alleviated Southeast Asia's fears of economically motivated Chinese expansionism. As a French observer of the region remarked recently, "The capitals of the region are more concerned about Moscow than about Beijing, while their peoples fear more, until now, the near-by Chinese than the far-away Russians."[40]

This is partly true, as the governments of Southeast Asia do not seem to fear Chinese hegemony at present, whereas the perceived failure of the United States to arrest the forward movement of the Soviet Union in the Third World does worry them.

At the same time, there is concern about Beijing's commitment to the communist parties of Southeast Asia, which was explicitly reaffirmed by Vice-Premier Deng Xiaoping during his November 1978 visit to Singapore and Malaysia. Furthermore, China's thirty-day military campaign against Vietnam in February 1979 has further eroded Southeast Asia's belief that it is not threatened by its giant neighbor. It is hard to estimate at this time whether the countries of Southeast Asia still derive comfort from the fact that China has been making special efforts to improve its food supply by investing heavily in farm equipment and fertilizer plants bought from the West and is not purchasing military hardware in large quantities. In November 1978 Beijing expressed willingness to exchange agricultural delegations with the United States for the purpose of trading seeds, pest-control methods, and livestock breeding techniques. At about the same time, China was also requesting help from the United Nations Development Program (UNDP) for the modernization of its agriculture and industry.[41]

If China is to escape from its present state of poverty, it will have to overcome major natural and institutional obstacles constraining its agriculture. The target of 400 million tons annual production of food grains set in early 1978 by Premier Hua Guofeng is almost certainly not attainable. It would require an annual growth rate of 4.3 percent in 1978-85, compared with a 3.6 percent average in the eight years before 1976 and 1977, when there was no increase at all. China is not likely to achieve such growth rates with the resources presently available to it.

The recently published Second Asian Agricultural Survey of the Asian Development Bank (ADB), which did not include China as it is not an ADB member, anticipated "low" (realistic) growth rates of agricultural output by 1985 of only 2.3 percent for Bangladesh, 2.8 percent for India, 2.9 percent for Pakistan, 2.4 percent for Sri Lanka, 2.7 percent for Burma, 2.5 percent for Indonesia, 4.0 percent for Western Malaysia, 3.1 percent for the Philippines, 3.4 percent for Thailand, and 2.3 percent for South Korea.

---

tons of wheat worth $285 million from Australia alone, the biggest wheat deal made by Australia with China in 20 years, according to a January 19, 1979 Reuter dispatch from Beijing.

[40] René Vermont, "Déstabilisation de l'Asie du Sud-Est?", *Défense Nationale*, February 1979.

[41] Associated Press, "China Seeks U.N. Assistance in Modernizing Farming and Industry," *Los Angeles Times*, November 16, 1978.

Some of these countries enjoy much more favorable conditions for agricultural expansion than does China. But even under "high" (optimistic) assumptions, only Pakistan, Thailand, and West Malaysia are expected to increase agricultural output by, respectively, 4.3, 4.4, and 5.0 percent per year between now and 1985.[42]

The ADB anticipates that these ten member countries, which collectively had a food grain deficit of less than 8 million tons in 1972, will have a shortfall of 46 million tons in 1985. The ADB survey concluded that the "green revolution" will not be able to raise agricultural output at a faster rate than population growth.[43]

If all of East and Southeast Asia, as well as South Asia, are plagued by growing food deficits in the 1980s, this could have disturbing security implications, although the specific nature of these future crises is hard to visualize. Viewed realistically, countries that cannot feed their own populations are hardly desirable targets for conquest by another country with similar problems.

A look at ADB statistical projections should reassure most East Asian governments that fear conquest by land-hungry neighbors. Only Burma and Thailand are expected to have exportable surpluses of food grains by 1985, and these could cover only 17 percent of the 14-million-ton food-grain shortage Southeast Asia as a whole is expected to have in that year. However enviable their food supplies may be, compared with those of their neighbors, Burma's and Thailand's surpluses would not solve the problems of any of the other countries in the region.

The granaries of the world—Australia, Canada, and the United States—would be the only desirable targets of conquest for countries of East Asia that are unable to pay for their growing food imports. But these three countries are well defended and far away.

Countries lacking the capital and technology required for rapid expansion of agricultural production cannot become military powers capable of conducting transcontinental wars of conquest. Furthermore, it is cheaper to develop scientific agriculture than to become a major military power. Economic rationality precludes military solutions to Asia's future food shortages. The Malthusian race can be won only by determined birth control and vigorous agricultural expansion. China is actively pursuing both goals and is not likely to engage in expansionist adventures.

Unfortunately, the invasion of Vietnamese border areas by Chinese troops on February 17, 1979, and the thirty-day punitive campaign in which they engaged have revived the long-standing apprehensions of the countries of Southeast Asia that Beijing will not hesitate to use military force in pursuit of its national interests.

The Foreign Minister of Singapore, Sinnathamby Rajaratnam, articulated the fears of the smaller countries of Southeast Asia in a recent interview in which he said, "We have moved into an era where Third World imperialism and communist imperialism are the only kinds of imperialism we are likely to encounter, in the coming decades at least . . . . Under the cloak of communism, the practitioners of communism are really xenophobic nationalists fighting like the capitalists of old, for national glory, national aggrandizement, and loot."[44]

It is not inconceivable that Vietnam will use the system of indirect rule it has

---

[42] Asian Development Bank, *Rural Asia, Challenge and Opportunity*, Federal Publications, Singapore, Kuala Lumpur, Hong Kong, 1977, Table II-2.4, pp. 180-181.

[43] Ho Kwon Ping, "Asian Agriculture's Decade in the Wrong Direction," *Far Eastern Economic Review*, September 15, 1978, pp. 47-48.

[44] Quoted in Keyes Beech, "Nationalism Becomes a Plague in Asia's Red Regimes," *Los Angeles Times*, April 1, 1979, Part VIII, p. 1.

established in Laos and Kampuchea for economic gain. The fertile lands irrigated by the Mekong River and its tributaries may be attractive to the economic planners in Hanoi. It is less likely that Beijing will seek territories on the mainland of Southeast Asia for colonial-style cultivation.

A more likely development in case of recurring large-scale food deficits would be the encouragement by Chinese authorities of spontaneous migrations to neighboring countries, on a pattern similar to the influx of Mexicans into the United States, using political influence to prevent efficient border controls by the target countries.

While these are possible developments, they are less probable than expanded concessional exports by the major grain-producing democracies in response to chronic food shortages. Hunger in East Asia will generate strong internal political pressures and great mental anguish in the rich countries, appealing to their humanitarian tradition and their guilt-ridden revulsion against consumerism, and also to the interests of their own farmers.

COMPETITIVE CLAIMS TO SEABEDS AND COASTAL WATERS

Territorial conflicts in East and Southeast Asia are more likely to result from the political ambitions of certain governments and from ethnic antagonisms than from primarily economic causes. A major exception could be competitive claims to oil- and mineral-rich offshore areas, sustained by the worldwide movement for the enclosure of parts of the high seas, which was stimulated by the United Nations Third Conference on the Law of the Sea.

Most countries in East and Southeast Asia have economic and security interests to protect in the framework of the new law-of-the-sea concepts that have been evolving since the end of World War II, when the United States first claimed exclusive rights to the mineral resources of its continental shelf. After the first substantive meeting of the United Nations Third Law of the Sea Conference, held in Caracas, Venezuela, from June to August 1974, the concept "that coastal states should have exclusive economic control over both the living (fish) and non-living (mineral) resources in a 200-mile zone off their coasts" has gained general acceptance among states.[45]

The application of this general principle is complicated by the presence in the waters off the coast of East and Southeast Asia of many islands as well as small exposed rocks and islets, the possession of which by one sovereign state can be used to claim certain areas and to challenge the claim of another sovereign state to a 200-mile exclusive economic zone.

In the Yellow Sea, the East China Sea, and the South China Sea there are various areas where 200-mile exclusive economic zones overlap. Alternative principles of boundary extermination, such as the "median line" criterion favored by Japan or the "natural prolongation of the continental shelf" criterion favored by China, are invoked in support of conflicting national claims.

Some countries, such as Indonesia and its neighbors, have settled most of their

---

[45] U.S. Senate, Committee on Foreign Relations, *The Third U.N. Law of the Sea Conference*, Washington, D.C., February 5, 1975, p. 3. Report to the Senate by Senators Claiborne Pell, Edmund Muskie, Clifford Case, and Ted Stevens, Advisers to the U.S. Delegation, Caracas, June-August 1974.

boundary problems through negotiations. Concerning continental shelf boundaries, Indonesia signed an agreement with Malaysia on October 27, 1969, with Thailand on December 17, 1971, with Australia on May 18, 1971, and with India on August 8, 1974. Concerning territorial waters—an issue complicated by Indonesia's adherence to the "archipelago principle"—agreements were reached with Malaysia on March 17, 1970, with Singapore on May 25, 1973, and with Australia (for Papua-New Guinea) on February 12, 1973.[46]

In the Yellow Sea there are many unresolved claims to offshore areas among China, North Korea, and South Korea; in the East China Sea, among China, South Korea, Japan, and Taiwan; in the South China Sea, among China, Vietnam, Taiwan, the Philippines, Malaysia, and Indonesia; and in the Gulf of Thailand, among Kampuchea, Vietnam, and Thailand. Maps 1, 2, and 3 illustrate the complexity of conflicting claims in the South China Sea and the Gulf of Thailand. As Maps 4 and 5 clearly suggest, the PRC is bound to play a decisive role in the management of conflicts resulting from competitive claims to resources located in offshore areas. Its claims reach deep into the potential 200-nautical-mile exclusive economic zones of its Southeast Asian neighbors. In East Asia, some of the most promising offshore petroleum prospects are north of Taiwan and west of the Okinawa Trough, which China claims on the basis of the "natural prolongation" criterion, taking advantage of the geological characteristics of its very broad continental shelf.

In the Gulf of Thailand and in the South China Sea, some of the conflicting claims exacerbate tensions between countries engaged in armed conflict, such as Vietnam and Kampuchea. Other contests involve countries that distrust and dislike each other, thus reducing the likelihood of compromise or cooperation. China could play an increasingly important role in the resolution of some of these conflicts by creating a doctrine of regional relevance, by setting an example to other claimants, and possibly by mediating between its quarreling neighbors.

Unfortunately, the precedent set by China is not promising. In January 1974, Beijing sought to resolve a long-standing dispute over the Paracel Islands by attacking and capturing the small South Vietnamese garrison stationed on the islands. It then proceeded to install a Revolutionary Committee on the main island in a newly erected four-story building and to claim repeatedly its historic rights over the Paracels and over most other islands in the South China Sea.

The fall of Saigon and the unification of Vietnam under communist rule did not alter China's attitude, although Hanoi continues to assert its rights to the islands, which are included in maps of the territory of the Socialist Republic of Vietnam. Dr. Choon-Ho Park, a leading authority on this topic, concluded on the basis of research into legal and historical arguments that the dispute is "political in nature and susceptible therefore of political resolution only."[47]

The potentially most serious conflicts in the South China Sea and the Gulf of Thailand are between China and Vietnam over areas west of Hainan Island, where oil has been found; between Vietnam and Indonesia over the potentially oil-rich offshore area north of Natuna Island; between Thailand, Vietnam, and Cambodia concerning areas claimed by all three where gas has been found; and between China and the Philippines over Philippine oil explorations in the Reed Bank of the Spratly

---

[46] Information provided by the Centre for Strategic and International Studies, Jakarta, in October 1978.

[47] Choon-Ho Park, "The South China Sea Disputes: Who Owns the Islands and the Natural Resources," *Ocean Development and International Law Journal*, Vol. 5, No. 1, 1978, pp. 30-37.

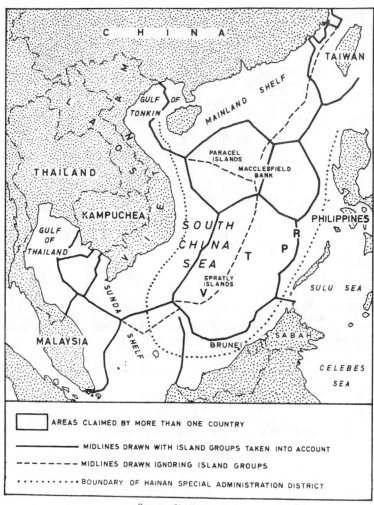

Source: Choon-Ho Park.

P = Thi-tu and 4 other islets held by the Philippines.
R = Reed Bank drilling by a Philippine-Swedish US (Standard Indiana) consortium.
T = Itu-aba and a few other islets held by Taiwan.
V = Spratly Is. and 12 other islets held by Vietnam.

Map 1—Disputed Areas in the South China Sea

Source: Peter Polomka, *Ocean Politics in Southeast Asia*, Institute of Southeast Asian Studies, Singapore, 1978, p. 18. Used with permission.

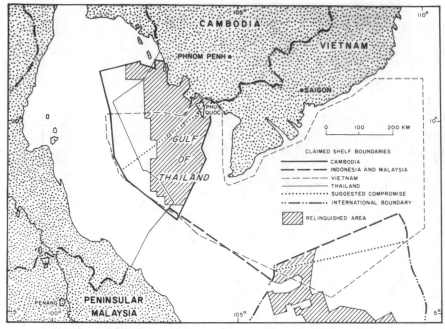

(Modified version of map appearing in *Petroleum News S.E.A.*, February/March
1973. p. 18: used with permission.)

Map 2—Overlapping Shelf Boundary Lines in the Gulf of Thailand
and the South China Sea

SOURCE: Corazón Morales Siddayao, *The Off-Shore Petroleum Resources of South-East Asia*, Oxford University Press, Kuala Lumpur, 1978, p. 78. Used with permission.

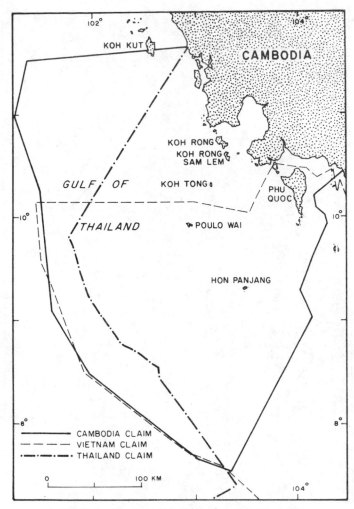

(Modified version of map in *Petroleum News S.E.A.*, June 1973;
used with permission.)

Map 3—Tripartite Gulf of Thailand shelf dispute
SOURCE: Siddayao, op. cit., p. 80. Used with permission.

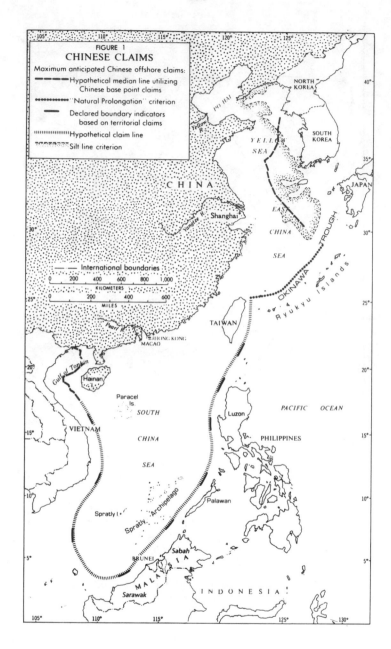

Map 4—Chinese claims

Source: Selig S. Harrison, *China, Oil, and Asia: Conflict Ahead?*, published for The Carnegie Endowment for International Peace, Columbia University Press, New York, 1977. Used with permission.

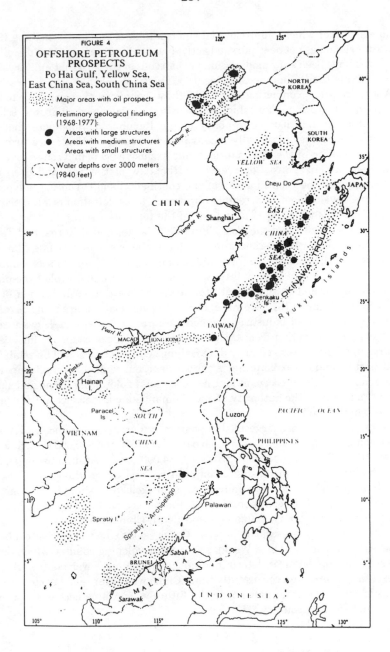

Map 5—Offshore petroleum prospects

SOURCE: Harrison, op. cit.

Archipelago, over which China claimed "indisputable sovereignty" in June 1976.[48] This latter claim has not been pursued actively by Beijing, perhaps because oil finds in the area have been very modest, and perhaps out of concern that military action might activate the Philippine-U.S. Security Treaty of 1951.

Apart from the conflicting claims of those countries that can invoke some principle of international law which happens to suit their particular interests, the special situation and distinctive policy of the Republic of Singapore should be mentioned. As a "geographically disadvantaged country," Singapore firmly opposed the adoption of the "200 nautical mile exclusive economic zone" concept at the United Nations Third Conference on the Law of the Sea, and even more strongly opposed the "continuation of the continental shelf" concept, advocating instead the development of a regional approach to exploitation of all marine resources located outside the 12-mile limit of the territorial sea.[49]

In the Yellow Sea and the East China Sea, Japan, South Korea, and Taiwan had granted—before 1979—concessions to foreign oil companies, while China had "flatly ignored the sustained efforts of Japan and South Korea to seek boundary agreement."[50] In practice, very little was done to explore and exploit the oil and gas resources located in those contested areas before the normalization of U.S. relations with China in 1979. Now that close working relations are being developed between China and all industrial democracies, South Korea and Taiwan can no longer expect cooperation from the oil companies of those countries for offshore ventures in offshore areas contested by Beijing. What patterns will be established for offshore oil and gas exploitation is not yet clear, but conflicts over offshore areas will probably remain quiescent as long as no serious explorations for oil and natural gas take place under the authority of one claimant state in defiance of the counterclaim of another state.

China is also the third largest fishing nation in the world. The Food and Agriculture Organization estimated China's fish catches in 1976 at 6,880,000 tons, following Japan's 10,620,000 tons and the USSR's 10,134,000 tons.[51] As diminishing returns set in, making fishing increasingly competitive, and China's food requirements grow, Beijing might assert maximum claims on exclusive fishing rights, based on the configuration of its continental shelf and on the sovereignty it claims over various islands in the East China Sea and South China Sea.[52]

But this need not necessarily happen. China seems eager to cultivate a benign image, especially in the Third World, as a poor developing country which despite its very large population is determined not to engage in power politics. Beijing's representatives proclaim consistently that "China will never seek hegemony or act like a superpower, neither now nor in the future when China becomes a powerful modernized socialist country."[53]

---

[48] Park, loc. cit., p. 41.

[49] Siddayao, op. cit., pp. 68-69.

[50] Park, loc. cit., p. 53.

[51] The Oriental Economist, *Japan Economic Yearbook 1978/79*, Tokyo, 1978, p. 50.

[52] The State Statistical Bureau in Beijing recorded an output of "aquatic products" of 4.66 million tons in 1978, down 0.9 percent from 1977. Whether this refers to inland ponds or offshore fishing is not clear.

[53] "The International Situation and China's Foreign Policies," speech by Huang Hua, Chinese Foreign Minister and Chairman of the Chinese Delegation to the U.N. General Assembly, *Peking Review*, No. 40, October 6, 1978, p. 5.

But although Beijing has voiced no territorial claims against any of its neighbors, with the exception of the Siberian lands taken by the tsars and retained by the commissars, China will have a hard time convincing smaller and weaker countries in its vicinity that it will never use its superior power against them, especially in view of the takeover of the Paracels by Chinese forces in January 1974 and the thirty-day punitive war against Vietnam in February 1979. Naturally, Asians intently watch the Sino-Vietnamese conflict and developments in Laos and Kampuchea.

As far as offshore territorial claims are concerned, China remained silent on the question of the continental shelf in international law until the early 1970s. It was only in reaction to a proposed joint Taiwan-South Korean-Japan seabed development venture in the vicinity of Taiwan and the Senkaku (Tiaoyu Tai) Islands that the official *People's Daily* raised the issue, on December 4, 1970. In an article entitled "U.S. and Japanese Reactionaries Out to Plunder Chinese and Korean Seabed Resources," it denounced as "aggression" foreign plans to exploit resources on or in "the sea floor of China's vast shallow water areas." The article avoided defining the scope of Beijing's claim to the seabed of the East China Sea and never mentioned the term "continental shelf."[54]

Only after it took over China's seat in the United Nations in late 1971 and joined the U.N. Seabed Committee in March 1972 did Beijing submit its own definition of the continental shelf, as "the natural prolongation of the continental territory." It also linked the extent of its continental shelf with that of the economic zone in which it claimed ownership of all the natural resources, "including living and non-living resources of the whole water column, seabed, and the subsoil."[55]

As Hungdah Chiu has pointed out, unless the delimitation of its exclusive economic zone was based on geological criteria, "China would have to share the continental shelf with Japan or Korea in the Yellow Sea and the East China Sea by the equidistance rule, even though the shelf is the natural prolongation of China's continental territory and not that of Japan or Korea."[56]

Until recently, China seemed determined to assert these maximal claims. After Japan and South Korea signed an agreement on January 30, 1974, concerning the joint development of the continental shelf, the PRC Foreign Ministry issued a statement, on February 4, denouncing the agreement as "an infringement of China's sovereignty" and stating that "according to the principle that the continental shelf is the natural extension of the continent, it stands to reason that the question of how to divide the continental shelf in the East China Sea should be decided by China and the other countries concerned through consultation."

On June 13, 1977, after the Japanese Diet had approved the 1974 agreement with South Korea, the PRC Foreign Ministry issued an even stronger statement, saying, "The East China Sea continental shelf is the natural extension of the Chinese continental territory. The People's Republic of China has inviolable sovereignty over the East China Sea continental shelf .... Without the consent of the Chinese government, no country or private persons may undertake development

[54] Hungdah Chiu, "South China Sea Islands: Implications for Delimiting the Seabed and Future Shipping Routes," *The China Quarterly*, No. 72, December 1977, p. 751.

[55] Chiu, loc. cit., p. 752.

[56] Ibid., p. 753.

activities on the East China Sea continental shelf. Whoever does so must bear full responsibility for all the consequences arising therefrom."[57]

OFFSHORE CLAIMS AND OIL PRODUCTION

China made a major concession to Japan after the conclusion of the Treaty of Peace and Friendship on August 12, 1978. During his October 1978 visit to Japan, Vice-Premier Deng Xiaoping postponed indefinitely the dispute concerning the Senkaku (Tiaoyu Tai) Islands, a promising offshore petroleum zone 215 miles southwest of Okinawa, claimed by Tokyo, Taipei, and Beijing.

Japan had offered several years earlier "to pigeonhole the issue," as a means of advancing the normalization of Sino-Japanese relations, although recognition of Japanese sovereignty over those small uninhabited islands could have considerable legal value in establishing Japan's claim to the resources of part of the continental shelf beneath the East China Sea.[58]

China did not respond. As recently as April 14, 1978, eighteen Chinese fishing boats, some armed with machine guns, anchored in the waters surrounding the Senkakus. Instead of fishing, crewmen displayed signs supporting China's territorial claims to those islands. Following Japanese protests, a spokesman for the PRC Embassy in Tokyo said, "The islands are part of the territory of the People's Republic of China as outlined in a Chinese Foreign Ministry statement of October 31, 1971."[59]

Beijing's action was interpreted by the international press as an additional obstacle to the conclusion of the Sino-Japanese treaty, which had been stalled for years over China's demand for the inclusion of a clause denouncing (Soviet) "hegemony." Then on May 11, 1978, it was announced that Japan's Ambassador to China Shoji Sato and Chinese Vice-Foreign Minister Han Nianlong (Han Nien-lung) had reconfirmed "the attitude of the two countries not to make an issue of these islands,"[60] and the fishing boats departed.

As a final touch, during his press conference in Tokyo, which was televised live throughout Japan on October 25, 1978, Vice-Premier Deng Xiaoping charged that "certain elements" in Japan were attempting to use the dispute over ownership of the Senkaku Islands "to dampen China-Japan relations." He repeated that the two governments had agreed to refrain from discussing the dispute and added that it should be shelved, leaving it for future generations to resolve, because "our generation doesn't have enough wisdom to solve this problem."[61]

It is difficult to forecast whether China will exercise as much forbearance with regard to jurisdictional conflicts over offshore areas in dispute with South Korea and Taiwan in the East China Sea, and with the countries of Southeast Asia—especially Vietnam—in the South China Sea. These conflicts have been described at length by Selig S. Harrison.[62]

[57] Ibid., p. 753, quoting Peking Review, Vol. 20, No. 25, June 17, 1977, p. 17.

[58] Selig S. Harrison, China, Oil, and Asia: Conflict Ahead?, Columbia University Press, New York, 1977, pp. 178-181.

[59] Andrew H. Malcolm, "Japanese-Chinese Dispute on Isles Threatens to Delay Peace Treaty," New York Times, April 15, 1978.

[60] Sam Jameson, "Japan-China End Dispute Over Islands," Los Angeles Times, May 12, 1978.

[61] Sam Jameson, "Teng Sees U.S.-Peking Ties in Due Time," Los Angeles Times, October 26, 1978.

[62] Harrison, op. cit.

According to a detailed survey conducted by the Republic of China's Ministry of Internal Affairs in 1946-47, "the South China Sea has 127 uninhabited islets, shoals, coral reefs, banks, sands, cays and rocks. They are grouped in four mid-ocean coral archipelagos: The Pratas Reef (Tungsha); the Macclesfield Bank (Chungsha); the Paracel Islands (Xisha); and the Spratly Islands (Nansha)."[63] Chinese ownership of the Paracels is contested by Vietnam, and its ownership of the Spratlys is contested by Vietnam, the Philippines, and Taiwan. Hanoi's forces have fortified Pugad Island; Manila flies regular air cover over Parola Island, where it maintains a presence, from its small base at Puerta Princesa on Palawan Island; and Taipei maintains a small garrison on Ligaw Island, whereas Beijing maintains no military presence in the Spratlys.[64]

Seabed resources in the South China Sea are claimed by China, Taiwan, Vietnam, Malaysia, Indonesia, Brunei, and the Philippines. Chiu notes that "China's consistent claim of territorial sovereignty over the mid-ocean Paracel Islands, the Spratly Islands, and the submarine Macclesfield Bank creates a difficult problem regarding the division of the seabed in the area where the islands are situated.[65]

As many of these areas are offshore sedimentary basins with oil prospects, jurisdictional conflicts are not likely to remain quiescent if any of the parties involved engage in prospecting; they may flare up into serious crises if oil is found in commercial quantities. One major recent development is the entry of Vietnam into the market. Petro-Vietnam has granted concessions to Deminex of West Germany, AGIP of Italy, and Bow Valley Ltd. of Canada; and the French company Elf-Aquitaine is also negotiating. Estimates of Vietnam's productive capacity range from 500,000 to 1 million barrels per day.[66]

According to a December 1978 survey of petroleum exploration activities in East Asia, conducted by the President of the Southeast Asia Petroleum Exploration Society (SEAPEX) located in Singapore, Leslie R. Beddoes, Jr., "international offshore boundary disputes are now slowly being resolved, and this assists petroleum exploration by removing the factor of political or sovereignty risk."[67]

Specifically mentioned were maritime boundary disputes that had been resolved between Papua-New Guinea and Australia; between Japan and South Korea (on the southern continental shelf); and between India, Indonesia, and Thailand (offshore of West Thailand). Other boundary disputes were reported to be under negotiation between Indonesia and Vietnam.[68]

The same survey recorded increased exploration activities in the South China Sea in 1978: off the coast of Vietnam, under contracts signed by European and Japanese companies with Petro-Vietnam; off the northwest coast of Palawan Island by American and European companies under contract with the Philippines' Bureau of Energy Development; and by the PRC through its own agencies near Hainan Island, including areas in the Gulf of Tonkin.

The President of SEAPEX concluded that "the geological situation and hydro-

---

[63] Chiu, loc. cit., p. 756.

[64] George McArthur, "Vietnam Fortifies Disputed Island Outpost," Los Angeles Times, June 26, 1977.

[65] Chiu, loc. cit., p. 759.

[66] "Private Firms Slate Tests Off Viet-Nam," The Oil and Gas Journal, January 8, 1979, p. 28.

[67] Leslie R. Beddoes, Jr., "Highlights of Petroleum Exploration Activity in East Asia," paper presented at the Conference on Energy and Southeast Asia, Singapore, December 6, 1978, p. 2.

[68] According to the Oil and Gas Journal, January 8, 1979, "Vietnam and Indonesia reportedly are close to signing a demarcation agreement concerning disputed waters in the South China Sea."

carbon play-types are favorable for large-scale accumulations offshore Vietnam, offshore the People's Republic of China, offshore Malaysia and Brunei, in various parts of Indonesia, and offshore the northwest shelf of Australia."[69]

The Philippines was not rated as a high-potential area, although apparently Cities Services East Asia recently started producing about 40,000 barrels per day from two platforms in the Nido area off Palawan Island. These Philippine oil-related activities in the Spratly Archipelago could create a national security crisis for the United States if Philippine naval ships were attacked by China or Vietnam.

Under the Mutual Defense Treaty of 1951, the United States has a basic commitment to the defense of the Philippines, derived from the following text: "Each party recognizes that an armed attack in the Pacific Area on either of the parties would be dangerous to its own peace and safety and declares that it would act to meet the common danger in accordance with its constitutional processes." An armed attack under the treaty includes "an armed attack on the metropolitan territory of either of the parties, or on the island territories under its jurisdiction in the Pacific or on its armed forces, public vessels or aircraft in the Pacific."[70]

Although the commitment to come to the defense of the Philippines is not automatic, Manila could invoke the 1951 Treaty if Philippine forces defending oil operations in the Spratlys were attacked by Chinese or Vietnamese forces.

At present, although China claims the Spratlys, it has established no military presence in those islands, seven of which are occupied by Philippine troops and three by Vietnamese. Apparently, the two sides did not talk about the Spratlys during Vietnamese Prime Minister Pham Van Dong's visit to Manila in September 1978.[71]

Whereas Beijing has maintained control over the Paracels, after terminating the presence of South Vietnamese forces there in January 1974, no attempt has been made by China to occupy the Spratlys.[72] China did not act even during its punitive military expedition against Vietnam in February 1979, despite the fact that Hanoi has asserted its claim to both the Paracels and the Spratlys.[73] Nevertheless, Hungdah Chiu believes that "while the PRC is willing to make concessions to Third World countries in many international matters, there is so far no indication that it would be willing to give up its claim to the South China Sea Islands."[74]

China's self-restraint with regard to these territorial claims probably reflects Beijing's need to secure foreign capital and advanced technology for the development of its offshore oil resources. It is unlikely that the international oil industry would allocate risk capital for exploration in a contested area against explicit Chinese opposition. If China is cooperative, joint ventures with other regional claimants and foreign oil companies might be feasible. As China is counting on oil

[69] Beddoes, loc. cit., p. 16.

[70] United States Senate, Committee on Foreign Relations, *United States Security Agreements and Commitments Abroad—The Republic of The Philippines*, 91st Cong., 1st Sess., Hearings Before the Subcommittee on United States Security Agreements and Commitments Abroad, Part I, September-October 1969, p. 6.

[71] Rodney Tasker, "A Courteous Rebuff for Dong's Diplomacy," *Far Eastern Economic Review*, September 29, 1978, p. 9.

[72] Harrison, op. cit., p. 191.

[73] Chiu, loc. cit., p. 763.

[74] Ibid., p. 765.

exports to pay for its accelerated program of industrial expansion,[75] its presently dormant claims will have to be activated before too long, and ways will have to be found to resolve pending jurisdictional disputes which create a climate of uncertainty that is detrimental to the investment of risk capital in oil ventures.

Much of the cooperative oil exploration and development that China can undertake offshore will of course be in areas that are not the object of conflicting territorial claims. For instance, the newly created Japan National Oil Corporation (JNOC) reached agreement in principle with Chinese authorities in early August 1978 to undertake joint offshore exploration and development in the Bohai (Pohai) Gulf, northwest of the Yellow Sea,[76] a geological extension of the Daqing (Ta Ch'ing) field, so as to increase oil exports to Japan after 1983.[77] Negotiations on joint exploitation of the oil fields in the Bohai Gulf and at the mouth of the Pearl River started on January 18, 1979, in Tokyo[78] but were suspended when agreement could not be reached on whether the Chinese should pay the Japanese in yen or in dollars.[79]

The quality of Chinese crude oil from the Daqing fields and the adjoining Bohai Gulf creates export problems. It has high specific gravity, is heavy in wax content, and has high concentrations of sulphur and oxides of nitrogen. Senior Japanese power industry executives went on record in October, 1978 opposing increased reliance on Chinese oil,[80] when Toshio Komoto, at that time Japan's Minister of International Trade and Industry, negotiated increased oil imports from China.

Whereas in 1977 Japan had imported 130,000 barrels per day from China,[81] Komoto hoped to increase annual imports from China to 600,000 barrels per day (30 million tons per year) in 1985 and 1 million barrels per day (50 million tons per year) in 1990.

If the oil that can be produced from onshore and uncontested offshore areas in the Yellow Sea and the East China Sea is difficult to export, even to Japanese utilities, which benefit most from the proximity of a source of supply such as the Bohai Gulf, China may be prompted to accelerate exploration and development of higher quality offshore oil deposits in the South China Sea, including areas in the Gulf of Tonkin.

West of Hainan, at least three rigs were operating in very shallow water in November 1978,[82] and light crude has been found there, as well as in the Pearl River delta.[83] Expansion of production west of Hainan may become a major flash point in the ongoing Sino-Vietnamese conflict. The offshore exclusive economic zones of the two countries in that area have not been defined, and given the present

[75] George Lauriat, "Japan's Peace Treaty's Effect on the Oil Industry," *Far Eastern Economic Review*, October 6, 1978, p. 60.

[76] "Miti Hunts the Elusive Gusher," *Economist*, September 2, 1978, p. 90.

[77] Sam Jameson, "Japan Expects Rising but Limited Trade with China," *Los Angeles Times*, September 27, 1978.

[78] "The Exploitation of China's Southern Oilfields," *Wen Wei Po*, Hong Kong, February 3, 1979.

[79] "Doing Business with China," *Oil and Gas Journal*, February 26, 1979.

[80] "Power Industry Refuses to Buy More Oil from China," *Asahi Evening News* (Tokyo), October 3, 1978.

[81] "China Seen Doubling Oil Production," *Oil and Gas Journal*, October 2, 1978, p. 74.

[82] Melinda Liu, "China's Oil Fields," *Far Eastern Economic Review*, November 3, 1978, p. 45; Burt Solomon, "China's Enigma: Can Oil Finance the Future?," *Energy Daily*, November 15, 1978, p. 3.

[83] "The Geologic of China's Oil," *Economist*, March 3, 1979, p. 102.

state of their relations, joint ventures between Beijing and Hanoi with foreign oil companies seem inconceivable.

Until now, China had not initiated explorations in the Gulf of Tonkin in areas that Vietnam could claim under the "median line" principle,[84] despite the fact that in an interview with the managing editor of *Yomiuri Shimbun* on March 4, 1979, Chinese Vice-Premier Li Xiannian had remarked that the Vietnamese "came up with increasingly absurd demands" in the Gulf of Tonkin.

Hanoi apparently had produced a map with its maritime boundary drawn so close to the coast of Hainan Island that the Xisha and Nansha Islands, which "have been Chinese territories throughout history," were shown as part of Vietnam. Li Xiannian remarked that the Vietnamese "are simply conceited" as he explained to the Japanese journalist that in 1956 Vietnamese Premier Pham Van Dong had issued a statement endorsing Premier Zhou Enlai's (Chou En-lai's) proclamation of a 12-mile territorial sea limit "which of course included Nansha and Xisha islands"; but when Li Xiannian asked Pham Van Dong in 1977 on behalf of Premier Hua Guofeng why Vietnam had changed its position, the Vietnamese Premier, "at a loss for words, merely reclined on his sofa and said nothing."

The open hostility between the two communist countries is in striking contrast to Beijing's invitation to U.S. oil firms to participate in the development of China's offshore oil, which a recent CIA study characterized as "the most dramatic policy reversal" in Chinese economic policies since the death of Mao Zedong.[85]

The first American oilman invited to Beijing, J. Hugh Liedtke, Chairman of Pennzoil Co. of Houston, Texas, told the press in August 1978—following a visit to China in June—that Pennzoil would prepare a specific proposal for exploration of a major offshore basin "probably in the South China Sea."[86]

Since then, Exxon, Phillips, Union, Mobil, Amoco, Atlantic Richfield, and others have also been invited to Beijing to discuss possible contracts to develop offshore fields.[87] Western European companies, including Petro-Canada, BNOC, BP, Hispanoil, AGIP, Elf-Aquitaine, and a Norwegian group have also been invited to hold discussions with the Chinese.[88]

By the summer of 1979, no contracts for exploration and development had been signed with foreign oil companies. But a high-level Chinese delegation, headed by Zhang Wenbin (Chang Wen-pin), President of the Chinese Petroleum Corporation, signed a letter of intent in February with British Petroleum to undertake a seismic survey in an area of the Southern Yellow Sea just north of Shanghai.

The same delegation also reached agreement in March with Atlantic Richfield Co. and Santa Fe International for seismic surveys, probably in the South China Sea, although no further details have been disclosed. Pennzoil, the first U.S. oil company to have presented a detailed contract proposal for oil exploration, has not yet been able to conclude an agreement.

On June 3, 1979, Kang Shien (K'ang Hsih-en), a Deputy Prime Minister directing energy and economic planning, stated in Washington that he expected to sign

[84] Statement by Selig S. Harrison at a Pacific Forum Conference on "Political Change and the Economic Future of East Asia," held in Seoul, Korea, on September 8-10, 1979.

[85] National Foreign Assessment Center, op. cit., p. 1.

[86] Hobart Rowen, "China's Oil—Peking Turns to West for Its Technology," *Washington Post,* August 11, 1978.

[87] Burt Solomon, "China Sets Offshore Oil Strategy," *Energy Daily,* March 30, 1979, p. 3.

[88] Beddoes, loc. cit., p. 15.

agreements with American companies "in the coming few days" for geophysical prospecting offshore. Kang Shien had been received by President Carter and had had extended conversations with Secretary of Energy James R. Schlesinger.[89]

Apparently, the Chinese follow a "phase one, phase two" strategy, commissioning geographical surveys before inviting foreign oil companies to offer production arrangements. They use the exclusive proposals they have received to learn as much as possible about the new world of international oil, exploring alternative patterns of foreign participation.[90]

In early August 1979, the Chinese government released for the first time detailed information on the arrangements it has made with foreign oil companies for offshore geophysical surveys. In the Bohai Gulf, Japanese oil companies will conduct the surveys; further south, in the area bordered by South Korea and Japan, French companies will operate; in the East China Sea, opposite Shanghai, British Petroleum will be the leading prospector, together with five other companies; in the area stretching from the southern tip of Taiwan to the coast of Hainan Island and in the Gulf of Tonkin, American companies will be active, with the possible participation of the Italian National Oil Company.

After the seismic data are processed, in mid-1981, China will invite bids for the second stage of exploration and development. The companies that agree to conduct geophysical exploration will do so at their own expense and will receive no guarantees that they will be favored bidders in the subsequent exploitation program. In addition to paying all the costs, foreign oil companies will have to pay 3.5 percent of their total costs as a "service charge" to the China National Oil and Gas Exploration and Development Corporation. They will also have to allow Chinese technicians aboard their survey ships to learn the use of the companies' technology.[91]

China's future role as an exporter of petroleum is difficult to assess accurately, but it can have only a relatively minor impact on global oil supply in the 1980s. After his visit to China in October-November 1978, Secretary Schlesinger told the press in Tokyo that his Department "estimated that China has oil reserves of about 100 billion barrels, some of which has not yet been verified, with about half land-based and half under the sea."[92] This is the highest estimate released until now by the U.S. government.

Schlesinger also said that "China's production of 2 million barrels a day would increase, but whether China would reach its goal of doubling production by 1985 depends upon the 'speed and success of the exploration process.'" He added that "the U.S. government would encourage oil firms to participate in the development of offshore Chinese oil but would not participate directly itself."[93]

The National Council for U.S.-China Trade estimates that the PRC's total oil production was about 102 million metric tons in 1978 (which is indeed 2 million barrels per day) and will increase to between 178 and 232 million metric tons of crude oil (3.5 to 4.6 million barrels per day) in 1985.[94]

[89] Clyde H. Farnsworth, "China Expects Oil-Exploration Pacts," New York Times, June 4, 1979.

[90] Barry Kramer, "U.S. Oil Concerns Step Up Drive to Prod China into Reaching Accords on Drilling," Wall Street Journal, January 25, 1979; "Doing Business with China," Oil and Gas Journal, February 26, 1979; Burt Solomon, op. cit.

[91] Fox Butterfield, "Ten U.S. Companies Join Search for Oil Off China," New York Times, August 6, 1979.

[92] Sam Jameson, "Iran Strife May Force U.S. Oil Curbs," Los Angeles Times, November 8, 1979.

[93] Ibid.

[94] Information obtained by telephone from the National Council for U.S.-China Trade on January 3, 1979.

Vice-Premier Li Xiannian told a group of Japanese businessmen in September 1978 that China's 1978-85 development plan will require investments of about $600 billion,[95] which analysts discount as too high.

According to other estimates, the total cost of the plan amounts to about $350 billion, of which some $40 billion would have to be in foreign exchange, to be used for the importation of Western equipment and technology. Such requirements seem within the capacity of the Chinese economy, although they imply a major effort to increase production and sale of export goods in the next seven years.

The National Council for U.S.-China Trade estimates that China's total exports will increase from $11.2 billion in 1978 to $40.1 billion in 1985. The increase cannot come entirely from the export of crude oil, but as an illustration of the magnitude of the task involved, it may be worth noting that to earn an additional $28.9 billion from oil exports in 1985, China would have to export an average of 3,360,000 barrels per day at a 1979 price of $23.50 per barrel. Japanese oil firms considered $13.20 per barrel excessive in December 1978 when that price was 50 cents higher than good Arabian light crude.[96] China will need increasing amounts of oil for domestic consumption in support of its development program. Exports of 3,360,000 barrels per day in 1985 are probably not a realistic target. And if it seeks to export such quantities of oil, China will not be able to be generous with regard to conflicting claims on offshore oil deposits. To become a major oil exporter, it will need all the resources at its command.

If American oil companies engage in offshore oil production in partnership with the PRC, this may complicate the relations between the United States and other claimants to those offshore oil deposits, unless they become partners in some joint ventures or are compensated in some other form.

The diplomacy of offshore oil claims may have some other facets. Selig Harrison suggested in 1977 that in making its far-reaching boundary claims, "Peking may be actuated not only by specific plans or priorities with respect to oil development as such, but also by a desire to corner oil development rights as a bargaining weapon in dealing with littoral states. If Manila or Kuala Lumpur show a cooperative attitude in matters affecting the Sino-Soviet rivalry, one of the rewards could be corresponding Chinese cooperation with respect to the boundaries of offshore oil concessions or the terms of crude imports."[97]

This was an interesting observation, but I strongly doubt that Beijing will be willing to relinquish claims to substantial offshore oil and gas deposits for some uncertain political gains in its rivalry with the Soviet Union in Southeast Asia. Furthermore, there are no present indications that the ASEAN countries favor the Soviet Union, the patron of Vietnam, in its competition with China, and clear indications to the contrary, such as the unanimous support by ASEAN of Pol Pot's claim to Kampuchea's seat in the General Assembly of the United Nations.[98]

Harrison also stated that "it appears to be only a matter of time before Beijing seeks to dislodge the military garrisons now maintained by Taiwan and the Philippines in the Spratlys, by either political or military pressure or both."[99] The possi-

[95] Takahiro Okada, "China's Eight Year Economic Plan Will Cost 1,000 Billion Yuan, Li Says," *Japan Economic Journal*, September 26, 1978.

[96] Terry A. Anderson, "Japanese Oil Firms Balk at China Deal," *Los Angeles Times*, December 18, 1978.

[97] Harrison, op. cit., p. 195.

[98] Don Shannon, "Pol Pot Retains Cambodia Seat in U.N.," *Los Angeles Times*, September 22, 1979.

[99] Harrison, op. cit., p. 198.

bility certainly exists, but after its attack on Vietnam, China has good reason not to exacerbate the fears of its neighbors. It is more likely that Beijing will tolerate Taipei's troops in the Spratlys until the issue of China's reunification is settled, as it has tolerated the presence of Taipei's forces in Quemoy and Matsu since 1959.

If the oil deposits on which the Philippines have a claim are of marginal importance, it would be rational for Beijing to seek agreements with Manila either for joint ventures or for some equitable boundary settlement, rather than confront the United States with a challenge to its credibility regarding the 1951 Mutual Security Treaty with the Philippines.

Beijing should also want to avoid further accusations of practicing "hegemonism" in the South China Sea. After years of efforts to rally other Asian nations against Soviet hegemonism, this will be a matter of growing urgency as the Soviet Union becomes more deeply entrenched in Vietnam. Chinese diplomacy may even create delicate situations for the United States if the present conflict between China and Vietnam continues and, as geologists seem to expect, rich offshore oil deposits are found in the Gulf of Tonkin and adjoining areas of the South China Sea which China would be reluctant to yield to Vietnam.

But China may decide to be more conciliatory toward other claimants, including even Vietnam, in order to secure the cooperation of foreign oil companies in its offshore oil ventures. Multinationals—whose capital and technology will be required, especially for operations in deep waters—will not invest in offshore ventures prior to the resolution of conflicting claims. It seems unlikely that expensive drilling rigs and production platforms will be set up by experienced operators in locations to which the host government does not have unchallenged title. Even preliminary geological surveys are conducted with much more circumspection today than they were a few years ago when the United States, as the dominant power in the Western Pacific, was expected to protect the operations of American companies against hostile interference.

Political risk is a very important consideration in the making of investment decisions in the international oil industry. Until hydrocarbon deposits become much scarcer than they are today, risk capital will not flow to contested areas, even if they seem geologically promising. Oil companies are, of course, interested in all geological prospects, but exploration and development decisions are made carefully, weighing the comparative advantages of the many basins that have not yet been exploited. Risk capital is scarce relative to the number of available options. Oil production off the coast of China will reach significant proportions only in areas viewed as secure zones by potential foreign investors. The conciliatory statements made by Deng Xiaoping in October 1978 in Tokyo suggest that this is understood in Beijing.

"CATCHING UP WITH JAPAN"

While the United States is the ultimate model of modernity for most Asian countries, Japan is the living reminder that their aspirations are neither utopian nor unadaptable to Asian circumstances. A century ago, Japan was a backward feudal society and its potential for modernization was not viewed as particularly promising. Now, as other Asians witness the increasing Westernization of Japan, that success story sets and legitimizes for them the standards of modern life in an industrial society. Poor countries are neither troubled by Western pangs of conscience over "consumerism" nor impressed by what they see as hypocritical sermonizing about the beauties of "smallness." They all want to be affluent and powerful.

The changes in lifestyle currently taking place in Japan are valid indicators of what the rest of East and Southeast Asia will strive for in coming decades. A recent household survey conducted by the Japanese Prime Minister's office revealed that annual purchases of meat have been sharply increasing in recent years, while those of fresh fish are declining—a trend with obvious implications for future requirements for food grain and meat imports.

Another survey, conducted in February 1977 by Japan's Economic Planning Agency, established that almost all Japanese households possess color TV sets, refrigerators, and washing machines. One out of two Japanese households owns a passenger car. In turn, the Japan Power Survey Committee estimated that electric power consumption in 1977 amounted to 480 billion kilowatt-hours (KWh), or a per capita average consumption of 4,210 KWh.[100] Comparative data on electricity consumption graphically depict the immensity of the resource mobilization and management problems that economic modernization will create in East and Southeast Asia. In the industrialized countries, much electricity is used wastefully, for example, for space and water heating, for cooking, and for industrial processes requiring low heat. But modern life requires electric lights, telephones, radio, TV, small motors, and many electronic processes for which electricity is indispensable.

Average consumption figures for electricity in East and Southeast Asia are misleading, because the populations of that region do not enjoy a homogeneous lifestyle. A small minority live in the Age of Electricity. The vast majority live in a world that has not changed much in the millenia since agriculture was invented. In 1974, when the average per capita consumption of electricity in Japan was 4,137.4 KWh, data collected by the United Nations Economic and Social Commission for Asia and the Pacific indicated that the average per capita consumption of electricity in Indonesia was 25.1 KWh.[101] The figure conceals a fundamental cleavage between two lifestyles: The vast majority of Indonesians do not use 164.8 times less electricity than the average Japanese; they use no electricity at all. There is no electricity in Indonesian villages. According to one recent report, even in the capital city of Jakarta, only one out of 44 persons uses electricity.[102]

If the Indonesians living in the modern sector approximate not Japanese but only Singaporean levels of electricity consumption, which in 1974 reached 1,742.3 KWh per capita (about 40 percent of the Japanese per capita consumption), then the 3,266 million KWh generated in Indonesia in that year would have given a modern lifestyle to only 1.44 percent of the country's total population, which seems plausible on an impressionistic basis.

But even those whose only experience with electricity involves the ubiquitous transistor radio are no longer fully outside the national and global community. They gradually are becoming aware that their material life can be made easier by the products of science and technology. Although processes of cultural change seem

---

[100] The Oriental Economist, *Japan Economic Yearbook 1978/79*, Tokyo, 1978, p. 71.

[101] Work sheets of the Economic and Social Commission for Asia and the Pacific, obtained in Bangkok in October 1977.

[102] Bill Peterson, "The Cities: A Nightmare—But the Poor Keep Coming," *Washington Post*, May 17, 1978, p. 10.

extremely slow to those who have completed the transition to modernity, they are actually extremely rapid in historical perspective, and it is difficult to believe that the more backward segments of mankind will stagnate forever. During its first two centuries, the Industrial Revolution generated a surprising variety of institutional patterns for the achievement of basically similar structural transformations of traditional agrarian societies. There is no reason to believe that human creativity will fail to discover more patterns of modernization, although the countries that are now embarking on the road of economic development are facing greater obstacles than did their predecessors. They have to cope with greater competition for resources, a less favorable international trade system, more complex managerial problems, and lack of time. The latter is particularly intractable. It reflects an acceleration of the historical process of growing expectations, caused by the impact of mass education and mass communications.

In that setting, "catching up" becomes a task of truly forbidding magnitude. For instance, while Japan's power-generating capacity in 1977 was 108,089 megawatts (MW), Indonesia's generating capacity was about 3,500 MW, half of which was supplied by costly and inefficient privately owned small diesel generators.[103] To equal Japan's present capacity, Indonesia, whose population is 20 percent larger, would have to build 50 modern 2,500-MW powerplants, plus transmission and distribution networks. To complete this gigantic task by the year 2000, five such powerplants would have to come on line every two years, beginning in 1981. At a cost set conservatively at $1,000 per installed KW of generating capacity, and assuming constant costs, an investment of $125 billion would be required for the powerplants alone. Naturally, the total cost of electrification would be considerably higher.

Indonesia's Central Bureau of Statistics estimated the country's gross domestic product (GDP) for 1976 at $37.33 billion. If the Indonesian GDP were to continue to grow as it has in recent years, at 7 percent per year in real terms—and this is an optimistic assumption—its 1980 GDP would be about $49.79 billion, and its 1981 GDP would be $53.27 billion, in constant 1976 dollars. If the first group of five 2,500-MW powerplants were to be financed out of the GDP for 1980 and 1981, $12.5 billion of that amount would have to be devoted exclusively to the construction of powerplants. Indonesia could not mobilize resources of that magnitude with its present institutional structure. And the cost could not be spread over a longer period, as five additional plants would have to come on line every two years to reach the hypothetical target of 125,000 MW installed capacity by the year 2000.

To be sure, although Indonesians often express the hope that their country will eventually be as modern and prosperous as Japan, President Suharto and his economic advisors have not set the year 2000 as a target date. Their expressed hope is to keep Indonesia's GDP growing at an average rate of 6.5 to 7 percent through successive five-year plans, doubling total GDP every ten years and increasing per capita income by about 5 percent annually. The Indonesian leadership is also aware of the rather modest resource endowment of their country relative to its population, which is expected to exceed 150 million at the end of the Third Five-Year Plan, in 1984.

[103] Budi Sudarsono, of the Indonesian National Atomic Energy Agency, statement at a seminar on "The Future of Large-Scale Energy Systems," held at the East-West Center in Honolulu, September 17-21, 1979.

The present Chinese leadership, despite its lucid pragmatism, seems bolder in its aspirations. Invoking the authority of the late Premier Zhou Enlai, the task of "catching up" with Japan by the year 2000 through "the four modernizations" has become China's explicit national goal. Even if this "creative myth" is not taken literally, that task is indeed a mind-boggling undertaking, with far-reaching consequences for the world's resource management in the next two decades.

Again using electricity as an indicator—although it was Lenin, not Mao Zedong, who said some sixty years ago that "Communism = Soviets + Electrification"—let us consider briefly the task Beijing is setting for itself. The total installed generating capacity of the PRC is about 50,000 MW.[104]

With a population of about 114 million and 108,000 MW of installed capacity, Japan has a capacity of 947.36 MW per million inhabitants; in contrast, if China's population is 1 billion and it has 50,000 MW of installed capacity, China has 50 MW per million inhabitants. To match Japan's level of electrification, China should have 950,000 MW of installed capacity, without taking into account either the rate of growth of Japan's power industry or that of China's population until the year 2000.

To equal Japan's present generating capacity on a per capita basis, China would have to expand the capacity of its power industry by more than 19 times. In other words, to be where Japan is today in the year 2000, China would have to add to its electricity-generating capacity each year an amount almost equal to its present total capacity (50,000 MW). Past social experiments do not indicate that China has either the organizational or technological capacity to achieve such feats. U.S. government specialists estimate that China's power-generating capacity will expand at best by 6,000 to 8,000 MW per year through 1985.[105]

It is difficult to imagine how that performance could be improved, yet we should not assume that human creativity cannot develop new social mechanisms for a more efficient mobilization of resources. Past failed social experiments such as the Great Leap Forward or the Cultural Revolution are not necessarily conclusive evidence that other, more successful, ways will not be found.

The implications of China's entry into the international economic sphere for global energy prospects have not been fully ascertained. The Workshop on Alternative Energy Strategies, conducted by Professor Carroll L. Wilson of the Massachusetts Institute of Technology, limited its task to the study of future energy supply and demand in what it called the WOCA (World Outside Communist Areas), thereby excluding China. Nevertheless, it concluded gloomily, "When we look ahead over the remainder of the century, our scenarios paint an increasingly disconcerting picture after 1985."[106] China's accelerated modernization can only paint the picture even darker. If China does indeed have oil reserves of 100 billion barrels, as Secretary Schlesinger stated in Tokyo last November, this is not a large resource base for the modernization of a nation of 1 billion people. It amounts to only about 100 barrels of oil per capita. If China consumed oil at the present per

---

[104] Interview with Tong Dalin, Vice-Minister of State, The State Scientific and Technological Commission of the People's Republic of China, in Beijing, on September 17, 1979. In the absence of official Chinese statistics, the U.N. had estimated China's total generating capacity at 40,000 MW. See United Nations, *World Energy Supplies 1972-1976*, Statistical Papers, Series J, No. 21, New York, 1978, Table 18, p. 173.

[105] National Foreign Assessment Center, op. cit., p. 6.

[106] Carroll L. Wilson, *Energy: Global Prospects 1985-2000. Report of the Workshop on Alternative Energy Strategies*, McGraw-Hill, New York, 1977, p. 8.

capita rate of Japan, its reserves would last less than 6 years.[107] China is not a resource-rich country relative to its population. Its modernization policy will unavoidably put additional pressure on the world's "energy budget." Vice-Minister Tong Daling estimated that China's total energy consumption might increase from 0.7 tons of coal equivalent per capita at present to 3.0 tons of coal equivalent per capita by the year 2000. If China's population would increase by the end of the century to 1.2 billion, Tong Dalin stated, China's energy requirements would amount to 3.6 billion tons of coal equivalent. [108] Beijing's decision to "join the world" is rendering past forecasts of supply and demand of energy and other natural resources obsolete. If Beijing's modernization plans succeed—as they should in order to alleviate the great poverty of almost one-quarter of the world's population—will the demand for food grains, industrial raw materials, and sources of energy produced by the other three-quarters of mankind increase sharply? In turn, will the necessity to import primary products deplete China's foreign exchange reserves and constrain the importation of the capital goods needed for rapid modernization?

In the common interest of mankind—not for the sake of playing a dubious "China card" in the geopolitical competition with the Soviet Union—the industrial democracies should assist China in every possible way to increase its domestic food production, extraction of minerals, and development of energy sources. This view is shared by Mr. Kiichiro Kitaura, Chairman of the Nomura Securities Co. of Japan. After telling a symposium on trade issues held in Washington, D.C., on February 8-9, 1979, that China aims at an annual economic growth rate of 8.4 percent,[109] "which is not easy to achieve," he added:

> There are some concerns, however, that these development projects may put China into payment difficulties and make it insolvent. The key to this problem seems to be in the development of Chinese agriculture and oil, and I think U.S.-Japan cooperation in these two areas is most important.[110]

The agreements reached in Beijing in November 1978 by Secretaries Schlesinger and Bergland serve the national interest of the United States, because if China can feed its population and implement its modernization policy, prospects for stability in the Pacific region will be increased, and tensions will be reduced. But we should not overestimate the contribution that the United States can realistically expect to make to the solution of China's immense economic problems. The most ambitious project discussed during Secretary Schlesinger's visit to China was "possible U.S. participation in constructing an awesome hydroelectric dam planned for the Yangtze Gorge on the upper Yangtze River with an ultimate capacity of 25,000 to 30,000 MW; by comparison, China's entire installed electric capacity is estimated at about 40,000 MW."[111]

[107] In early 1978, Japan consumed oil at an annual rate of 305 million kiloliters (1,916 million barrels), equivalent to an annual per capita consumption of 17.7 barrels.

[108] Interview in Beijing on September 17, 1979.

[109] Vice-Premier Yu Qiuli stated on June 21, 1979, that the growth targets for 1979 were 4 percent in agriculture and 8 percent in industry. Loc. cit., p. 7.

[110] Kiichiro Kitaura, "Toward the Development of New U.S.-Japan Economic Relations," *Wall Street Journal*, March 23, 1979, p. 14.

[111] Burt Solomon, "U.S., China Set Tentative Agenda in Energy—Hydro, Coal, Nuclear Physics Head a Long List," *Energy Daily*, November 7, 1978, p. 1.

A rigorous investigation of 1,598 rivers in 1955 established that China's total water-power resources approximate 540,000 MW, of which some 300,000 MW "are suitable for actual development." But "the thinly populated and lightly industrialized Southwest accounts for 73.3 percent of the total (392 gigawatts), while heavily peopled (having almost one-third of China's population) and industrialized east China has only 2 percent of the total hydro potential."[112]

During the years when China was turning its back on modern technology, leading students of China's energy prospects expressed doubts that a 25,000- to 30,000-MW powerplant could be built in the Yangtze Gorge, forgetting perhaps China's great and ancient tradition of building large-scale water works. The likelihood that the Yangtze Gorge project and other hydroelectric works will materialize has increased considerably with the signature in Beijing on August 28, 1979, by Vice-President Mondale of an agreement permitting the U.S. Army Corps of Engineers, the U.S. Bureau of Reclamation, the Tennessee Valley Authority, and the U.S. Department of Energy to provide technical assistance to China in developing its hydroelectric projects. China will pay for the assistance, but the U.S. government is prepared to grant China up to $2 billion in Export-Import Bank credits over the next five years. To make these arrangements possible, the State Department had to declare China a "friendly nation," a status that only one other communist country, Yugoslavia, has previously been granted.[113]

Helping China to replace "traditional building technologies and massed labor"[114] with modern engineering methods in the development of public works such as hydro-electric dams is an appropriate way for the U.S. government to assist China's modernization. Agricultural extension services are also suitable activities for government-to-government cooperation. By assisting in the development of China's renewable energy resources and food production, the U.S. government would contribute to the future welfare and stability of the Pacific region as a whole. China's enhanced self-reliance could reduce competition with other Asian countries for imports of food and energy in the coming decades, when the pressure of the world's most populous area on the earth's resources will increase dramatically. For instance, the ASEAN region alone might require oil imports of 7 million barrels per day by the year 2000—about 13.7 percent of what optimistic analysts expect annual global supply to be at the end of the century.[115] Like the ASEAN region, China will probably have exhausted its oil and gas reserves by the end of the century, unless future discoveries greatly exceed what can be expected on the basis of probability analysis.[116]

The severity of the "energy crunch" that East Asia will experience in the coming decades will be proportional to the success of each country's modernization efforts. The developing countries in the region will also be increasingly in competition with the new industrial countries (South Korea, Taiwan, Hong Kong, and

[112] Vaclav Smil, *China's Energy Achievements, Problems, Prospects*, Praeger Publishers, New York, 1976, p. 69.

[113] Norman Kempster reporting from Beijing to the *Los Angeles Times*, August 28 and 29, 1979.

[114] Vaclav Smil, "Energy in China: Achievements and Prospects," *The China Quarterly*, March 1976, p. 65.

[115] Guy J. Pauker, "The ASEAN Energy Scene in Global Perspective," *Asian Survey*, June 1979, p. 635.

[116] Richard Nehring, *Giant Oil Fields and World Oil Resources*, The Rand Corporation, R-2284-CIA, June 1978.

Singapore) and also with Japan, all of which will depend on their export earnings for the purchase of food, raw materials, and energy.

Japan's future situation should be of particular concern to all of East Asia. To believe that Japan will accept the loss of its present economic strength and dynamism in response to political pressures or because of institutional constraints within the international economic system strains credulity.

Under extreme pressure, Japan's national energy is bound to burst out of the channels through which it flows at present, within the "rules of the game" set by its OECD allies, and seek new solutions. This may involve anti-Western partnerships with China or the Soviet Union or the Third World, a revival of radical nationalism and reliance on military power, or totally new patterns of behavior. At this time, Japan's growing interest in trade with China and its expressions of concern about the future of the countries of Southeast Asia remain set in the framework of the prevailing world order, and Japan accepts its responsibilities as one of the world's most powerful industrial democracies. But this could change under extreme pressure.

It seems axiomatic that it is strongly in the interest of the United States to work out mutually beneficial ways for Japan to maintain its present place in the global power constellation. While East Asia "catches up with Japan," that industrious and energetic nation has to remain able to hold its own and pay its way.

POLICY IMPLICATIONS FOR THE UNITED STATES

As the people of East and Southeast Asia continue to struggle for a better life, the United States will be confronted with a host of difficult policy decisions affecting both the immediate interests of the American people and the future of the prevailing world order. As a producer of food and capital goods for export, as an importer of energy and other natural resources, as the major source of technological innovation, investment capital, and credits, as a major military and political power, and as a cultural and scientific center, the United States influences the shape of things to come in the Pacific region, both by its acts and by inaction.

What policies should the United States pursue to increase the chances that a constructive and benign international environment will prevail in the Pacific region in the coming decades?

First of all, in the absence of international institutions capable of sustaining and protecting an orderly international system, the United States must help to maintain peace and stability in the Pacific region. And without a credible force posture, the United States cannot expect a respectful hearing when it seeks to dampen international conflicts or to facilitate compromises among nations competing for their share of access to natural resources and for business opportunities.

The invasion and conquest of Kampuchea by Vietnam and the devastation of Vietnamese borderlands by China demonstrated not only the inability of the United Nations to prevent the use of force but also the ineffectiveness of American admonitions unsupported by the threat of American military intervention.

Perhaps the response of the United States to these events would have been less restrained if vital American interests had been affected. But in the light of what has happened in Southeast Asia since the Vietnamese invasion of Kampuchea, it can be argued that American wishes will not prevail in the Western Pacific unless the United States is again viewed as forceful and resolute, willing to use its vast resources for sanctions or rewards.

Mild expressions of American displeasure did not stop either Vietnam or China from the use of force in pursuit of their national goals. Yet the adverse impact of these events on the image of the United States as custodian of the prevailing international order in the Western Pacific did not at the same time enhance the status of the Soviet Union in the region. Moscow's November 1978 treaty with Hanoi—which should have carried more weight than American verbiage—did not restrain Chinese leaders from launching an attack on Vietnam after having given public notice that they intended to "teach the Vietnamese a lesson."

The international mechanisms by which regional stability had been maintained in East Asia are no longer effective. Unless the United States regains a position of major influence in the region, the next decades could become a period of political chaos. This would not be conducive to orderly economic growth and would thus eventually be detrimental to the interests of all concerned. The developing nations of East and Southeast Asia need a stable international environment in which to pursue the process of economic modernization and to overcome the great poverty of their populations. American political and military weakness in East Asia would create a sense of uncertainty, to the detriment of the region.

Second, the United States must find ways to reduce competition for resources and markets among developing countries and between the latter and old or new industrialized countries. It is too early to form opinions on whether the agreement reached in Geneva on March 20, 1979, concerning the establishment of a Common Fund to stabilize commodity prices will have a beneficial impact. At first sight, it appears to be a rather modest achievement after five years of efforts by the developing countries, especially in light of the failure of the month-long UNCTAD V Conference held in Manila in May 1979. The developing countries were unable to obtain assurances from the developed countries that the growing tide of protectionism will be reversed and, fearing their economic progress will suffer in the 1980s, demanded "global consultations" by a high-level intergovernmental group of experts on how to restructure international trade, development, money, and finance, while pledging among themselves to follow a policy of "collective self-reliance." The North-South dialogue, which has produced few concrete results in the last five years, has reached a major impasse. The 119 countries of the "Group of 77" are turning their hopes toward intraregional and interregional trade among developing countries. The emerging "South-South dialogue" has ominous implications for the future of the world economic system.[117]

After arguing that credible American military strength will remain an indispensable factor for the stability of the Pacific region in the foreseeable future, it must also be stressed that power alone is not likely to contain explosive pressures, if the one-third of mankind living in East Asia finds its avenues to peaceful change and development blocked. It thus becomes necessary to find concrete and specific answers to the complex analytic and policy questions involved in distributing American resources in the most practical way between military preparedness and economic policies.

[117] Ho Kwon Ping, "Self-Help Is Better Than No Help," *Far Eastern Economic Review*, June 15, 1979.

Intuitively, it would seem obvious that the United States should take the lead in promoting cooperative policies with regard to exploitation of natural resources and international trade in manufactured goods. Although intrinsically costly, this would be cheaper in the long run than the military operations that would be required for the restoration of a destroyed international order. The willingness of the American people and the Congress to invest several billion dollars in an Egyptian-Israeli settlement in the hope of reducing the likelihood of another war in the Middle East is a valid precedent for such international preventive therapy.

Were chaos to prevail in the Western Pacific in the 1980s as the result of conflicts caused by economic competition between developing and new industrialized countries, it is doubtful that the United States could help restore peace with its resources limited to the presently available two carrier task forces, the air wings currently assigned to the Pacific Theater, and the bases and facilities available in Japan, the Philippines, and South Korea.

A significant expansion of the U.S. force posture in the region would probably cost much more, besides requiring substantial lead time in the aftermath of a major crisis, than a dynamic and imaginative economic policy for the region. The United States and the other OECD countries should help China, the ASEAN countries, and—under suitable circumstances—the countries of Indochina with their development plans; they should also act as catalysts for the resolution of conflicting claims and, hopefully, for the development of cooperative patterns leading eventually to a Pacific Economic Community. Such expectations are not necessarily naive. The Marshall Plan provides historically valid evidence that countries that were bitter enemies can cooperate in response to sufficiently attractive material incentives and to purposeful leadership.

In a protectionist world and in the absence of assistance to countries competing for scarce natural resources, sharp political rivalry and even acts of violence among countries may be hard to avoid, even if the Soviet Union were to abstain from using such conflicts for the furtherance of its geopolitical interests.

It is not inconceivable that China, the new industrialized countries, the ASEAN group, the countries of Indochina, and even the Latin American countries of the Pacific region could agree on cooperative patterns of modernization. Vigorously supported by the industrialized democracies with capital, technology, and managerial skills, they might transcend their fears and hatreds to realize tangibly better chances to cope with their economic problems. The obvious corollary of this argument is that the industrial democracies should not aid and abet current rivalries and conflicts in the Pacific region for short-term national gains that are likely to backfire eventually.

More immediately relevant, it seems particularly important to help China's modernization only within the framework of a comprehensive economic policy for East and Southeast Asia, in order to avoid rendering the other, smaller countries in the region vulnerable to Soviet penetration. The latent fear of China and the Soviet Union in the Western Pacific can have, from a Western viewpoint, undesirable repercussions on the alignment of various countries in the region.

It is not in the interest of the United States to assist China in "encircling" the Soviet Union or vice-versa. This requires not only careful scrutiny of any direct or indirect Western contribution to the military strength of the two communist rivals, but also abstention from supporting an uneven pattern of economic development in East and Southeast Asia. If growth is balanced among neighboring nations, peaceful cooperation is more likely to prevail, and the Soviet Union may find it more difficult to retain or recruit allies from among countries lacking alternative options.

Major new initiatives in the policies of the industrial democracies cannot realistically be expected to materialize instantly. A process of public education, international consultation, and mobilization of political support would have to take its time. What can be done in the meanwhile? As a first, preventive step, the U.S. government and American private interests should continue to avoid taking sides in offshore territorial conflicts in the East China Sea and South China Sea and should seek instead to reconcile meritorious conflicting claims. American technology, management, and capital will continue to be in great demand. This circumstance can and should be used as leverage to facilitate conflict resolution, compromise, and cooperation among contending claimants who may otherwise paralyze each other's endeavors, to everybody's detriment.

Because of their global reach and experience, American multinational corporations could play a particularly useful role in helping the countries of East and Southeast Asia overcome jurisdictional conflicts over natural resources. This would require firmness in not accepting at face value China's jurisdictional claims to disputed maritime territories in the East China Sea and the South China Sea. Although American mediation may not succeed in the short run, in the long run patience may prove useful, not only commercially but also geopolitically. It seems preferable to obtain arrangements acceptable to all interested parties—before oil, gas, or other minerals are being extracted—rather than to side with China merely because it is the strongest contending party, thereby forcing its injured opponents to turn for support to the Soviet Union.

The equity principle should also apply to the flow of American investment capital and of credits on concessional or commercial terms into East and Southeast Asia. Resource transfers follow paths determined partly by commercial interests and partly by political considerations. The U.S. government, in cooperation with private American financial institutions, and increasingly—to the fullest extent possible—in consultation with other OECD countries, should balance the financial needs of all eligible East and Southeast Asian countries, so that the recent surge of interest in China will not work to the detriment of the new industrial countries (South Korea, Taiwan, Singapore, and Hong Kong), the developing countries of the ASEAN group, and the countries of Indochina.

China is not yet a stable and predictable factor in the affairs of East Asia. It is currently reassessing the modernization plans it announced with excessive self-confidence a year ago.[118] In the bilateral talks taking place in Hanoi, China is making demands that may be unacceptable not only to Vietnam but also to its other Southeast Asian neighbors. The eight-point plan presented by Chinese Vice-Foreign Minister Han Nianlong (Han Nien-lung) on April 26, 1979, demanded that Vietnam recognize the Spratly and Paracel Islands in the South China Sea as belonging to China.[119] This directly affects the interests of the Philippines and has implications for Malaysia, Brunei, Indonesia, and others.

Although it is clearly in the interest of the United States and of a stable world order to assist China in overcoming poverty and in becoming part of the world

---

[118] Fox Butterfield, "China Reassessing its Liberalization Drive," *New York Times,* April 23, 1979.
[119] "China Rejects Viet Proposal for a DMZ," *Los Angeles Times,* April 27, 1979.

economic system, a premature commitment to plans lacking firm political support within China itself may further erode the confidence of other Asian nations in American leadership.

Finally, widespread and persistent famine is likely to be the greatest single threat to peace, order, and stability in the Pacific region. In the long run, family planning and increased agricultural productivity are the only remedies to this problem. It will take several decades, even under very favorable circumstances, to stabilize population growth; while success in agricultural modernization remains inextricably linked to progress in industrialization.[120]

In the next couple of decades, the two billion people who will be living in East and Southeast Asia will continue to be dependent—probably to an increasing degree—on food imports from the world's major producers, primarily the United States, Canada, and Australia. The 1974 World Food Conference held in Rome contributed only modestly to the establishment of a new institutional framework for dealing with the global maldistribution of food grains. In future years, the need to finance and transport large quantities of food grains between continents will become greater than ever before, as will the pressure on the food crops of the major producers.

The growing demand for American, Canadian, and Australian food grains will have wide economic, social, and ecologic repercussions in the producing countries. Also, although the argument may be repugnant to Western moral sensibilities, the political leverage of the major grain producers is likely to become greater, in the next decades, than that of the oil-exporting OPEC countries. During the next two decades it will be easier, however costly, for the industrial democracies to develop alternative sources of energy than it will be for developing countries to become self-sufficient in food grains. Unfortunately, this situation does not create a symmetrical bargaining situation. The populous developing countries of East and Southeast Asia will not be in a position to barter energy for food, especially if their modernization plans are successful. They will have to import both these resources, using scarce foreign exchange, which they also need to acquire capital goods.

If the OPEC countries and the industrial democracies could agree on a comprehensive plan of international assistance to countries in East and Southeast Asia that are willing to shelve past conflicts and cooperate in joint developmental efforts, this would constitute a giant step toward peace and stability in the Western Pacific.

---

[120] Professor Donald J. Bogue and Dr. Amy Ong Tsui provide new hope that the world's population problem is manageable by vigorous family planning in their article "Zero World Population Growth?," *The Public Interest*, April 1979. They predict that the world's population will stabilize at about 7.4 billion by the year 2025.

Chapter 12

U.S. DEFENSE POLICY, TECHNOLOGY TRANSFERS, AND ASIAN SECURITY

Leslie H. Gelb[1]

INTRODUCTION

Writing about the relationship between the proliferation of technology and Asian security, one runs a high risk of uncovering problems that do not exist and overdramatizing those that do. The spread of technology—conventional arms transfers and the transfers of nuclear capabilities—is not a driving or central factor in Asian security issues. The transfers being made to the region have been taking place at a pace consistent with the absorptive capacities of the countries. The patterns are not unnatural.

This is not to say, however, that the diffusion of technology in Asia will not cause and exacerbate problems; but these problems will not be peculiar to the region. Competitive nations worry about technological imbalances, just as they are concerned about military imbalances; and they worry about the breakout potential of their neighbors and adversaries, just as they keep a watchful eye on the adversaries' knockout punch. The countries of Asia will have new problems as new weapons and new weapons-related technologies are introduced into the region.

Before examining these issues, a few additional cautionary notes are advisable. First, it is hardly possible to treat this subject as an "Asian" problem. In terms of technological prowess, the region includes states running from the supergiants, like Japan, to those countries barely able to maintain modern technology. Even consideration of subregional groupings of states, such as Southeast Asia, tends to suggest a coherence unwarranted by realities. Second, it is difficult to use the term "technology" in a very systematic way. I will confine myself essentially to defense and defense-related technology. That is, I will by and large ignore the sensitive and sometimes crucial area of dual-use technology, such as computers. Thus, in this paper, Asia is used as a vessel of convenience for talking about policies, and the term "technology" is used simply to mean the transfer of arms, arms-related know-how, and nuclear technologies and know-how.

To accommodate these unshapely partners, the analysis is divided into four parts: First, a description is given of trends and problems in the transfers of conventional arms and technology and matters relating to the potential for nuclear-weapons proliferation. China will be discussed separately. Second, future policy problems for China, Northeast Asia, and Southeast Asia are considered. Third, some remarks about the U.S. security stance are offered. Finally, some thoughts are presented on how technology transfers should relate to our basic strategic objectives in the region.

[1] Leslie H. Gelb at present is a Senior Associate of the Carnegie Endowment for International Peace. From January 1977 until July 1979 he was Director of the Bureau of Politico-Military Affairs, U.S. Department of State. Prior to that time he was a diplomatic correspondent for The *New York Times*.

The author wishes to acknowledge the assistance of David Gompert, Priscilla Clapp, S. William Barnett, and Dunn Scott in the preparation of this analysis.

TRENDS IN TECHNOLOGY TRANSFER

Conventional Weapons Technology

Technology transfer is not a clearly defined concept. In the military area, one can distinguish between two types of technologies: the technology of *use* and the technology of *know-how*. By technology of use, we mean the transfer of military training, hardware, and services to support the hardware. Examples would be an armored capability (tanks, APCs), the capability to carry large bombloads a long distance and drop them on a target, or air-refueling capability. By the transfer of know-how, we mean the transfer of the ability to reproduce items of hardware and to manufacture them in a local facility. The transfer of know-how is an irreversible process; once someone learns how to manufacture a rifle, the knowledge cannot be taken back.

Most of the global activity in arms transfers has been the transfer of *use technology*. Figures published by the Arms Control and Disarmament Agency for the period 1967-76 show that approximately $79.1 billion in military goods were transferred by nine major suppliers to over 135 importing countries. Only one Asian country—the People's Republic of China (PRC)—is counted among the nine major suppliers, providing only 3 percent of the transfers in this ten-year period (see Table 1). As recipients of hardware, the countries of East Asia account for $20.8 billion of the $79.1 billion exported worldwide in 1967-76, or 26.3 percent of the total.

The transfer of *know-how technology* has lagged considerably behind the transfer of use technology, and it is difficult to measure. Taking the more sophisticated end of the spectrum, aircraft manufacture, we find that only seven Asian countries have any capability whatsoever. These are Australia, the PRC, Japan, New Zea-

Table 1

BREAKDOWN OF MAJOR ARMS SUPPLIERS, 1967-76

Supplier	Value (billions of U.S. dollars)	Percent
United States	38.3	48
Soviet Union	22.0	28
France	3.8	5
Britain	2.8	4
People's Republic of China	2.2	3
Federal Republic of Germany	2.0	3
Czechoslovakia	1.4	2
Canada	1.3	2
Poland	1.1	1
Others	4.2	5
Total	79.1	—

Source: *World Military Expenditures and Arms Transfers: 1967-1976*, U.S. Arms Control and Disarmament Agency, Washington, D.C., 1978.

land, Taiwan, Indonesia, and the Philippines. Of the seven, Japan is the most advanced, but virtually all of its production is based on U.S. designs, such as the P-2J patrol aircraft, the T-2 jet trainer, the F-4J fighter, or the newer P-3 patrol aircraft and the F-15 fighter.

There are a number of factors limiting the expansion of military production capabilities which will continue to apply over the next decade. The Stockholm International Peace Research Institute lists as the most important of these factors:

- The shortage of financial resources.
- The absence of appropriate materials.
- The limited production capability of defense-related industries.
- The shortage of skilled manpower.
- The higher cost of local production versus imports.[2]

To these considerations must be added the desire of suppliers to protect their own advanced technologies and the policy restrictions that recipient countries (e.g., Japan) might place on themselves.

The countries of the East Asian region can be divided into three groups in terms of their ability to produce and/or absorb modern weapons. Table 2 summarizes U.S. transfers to these countries.

Group 1: Japan, Australia, and New Zealand. These countries are generally at the level of the advanced NATO countries in using state-of-the-art equipment. Japan has the industrial base to produce or co-produce most modern weapons systems.

It is no secret that Japan could be a larger, more advanced military power, but for various reasons it chooses to constrain the capabilities it acquires. Although we do not expect any major changes in the configuration of Japanese defense forces, we do anticipate major qualitative improvements, with particular emphasis on the technology-intensive areas of air defense and air-submarine warfare. Japan will also continue to gradually improve its defense production base.

The PRC probably falls somewhere between the first and second group.

Group 2: North Korea, South Korea, and Taiwan. Shortfalls in skilled manpower, access to advanced production equipment and related raw materials, logistical infrastructure, and command and communications still inhibit the ability of these countries to use and integrate the most modern weapons systems. However, they can use and maintain individual first-line systems, particularly aircraft and anti-aircraft missiles. They have the industrial base for producing conventional weapons systems such as trucks, communications equipment, and artillery. Production of more sophisticated equipment such as radars, missiles, and aircraft is limited to assembly, with components produced elsewhere.

In the coming years, South Korea will continue to increase its stocks of advanced systems, both through the turnover of ground combat equipment from U.S. forces and through purchase, particularly of advanced aircraft. The South Koreans are also determined to increase their own production capabilities, which generally lag behind those of the North; and the United States can be expected to help somewhat in this endeavor through defense industry cooperation, such as co-production arrangements.

---

[2] The Stockholm International Peace Research Institute, *The Arms Trade with the Third World*, Stockholm, 1971, pp. 61-62.

Table 2

SELECTED U.S. WEAPONS TRANSFERS TO EAST ASIA

Recipient	Weapons Systems		
	Aircraft	Missiles	Armor, Other
Australia	A-4 F-111 P-3	Harpoon Redeye Sidewinder Standard Tartar	—
Taiwan	F-5A/E	Bullpup Chaparral HAWK Nike Sidewinder TOW	Tanks APCs Artillery
Indonesia	F-5E T-33 Helicopters	—	APCs Misc. ships
Japan	P-3 F-15	Harpoon HAWK Nike Sidewinder Sparrow Standard TOW	Artillery Tanks
South Korea	S-2 F-4 F-5 Helicopters	Bullpup Harpoon HAWK Maverick Nike Sidewinder Standard TOW	Tanks APCs Artillery
Malaysia	F-5E	Sidewinder	105mm howitzer
Philippines	F-8H	Sidewinder	APCs 105mm howitzers
Singapore	A-4 F-5E	Sidewinder	—
Thailand	F-5E OV-10	Sidewinder	APCs Tanks Artillery

aDescriptions of these weapons systems will be found in *Jane's All the World's Aircraft* and *Jane's Weapons Systems*.

Taiwan will also continue actively to seek advanced military hardware and production capabilities. What it achieves will be limited most significantly by the willingness of suppliers to deal with the island, rather than by limitations in Taiwan's capabilities and resources. As Secretary of State Vance has explained U.S. policy, "We will continue our previous policy of selling carefully selected defensive weapons to Taiwan."[3] The United States will probably remain the principal supplier of defense weapons for Taiwan. For example, the life of the F-5E/F co-production/co-assembly agreement has been extended by another 48 units, which means that the assembly line will now run until 1983. Other countries will probably not be willing to supply advanced equipment to Taiwan; and the island is not likely to turn abruptly to the Soviet Union for military hardware, for fear of disrupting its vital trade relationship with the United States.[4]

Group 3: The Remaining Countries of Asia (the Philippines, Indonesia, Thailand, Malaysia, Singapore, and Vietnam). These countries are more severely limited in their ability to absorb modern arms and have only limited production capabilities. They are what might be termed the "F-5 countries," the countries more or less capable of absorbing relatively simple, easily maintained first-generation equipment. Their production capacity is generaly limited to small arms and ammunition.

The countries of Southeast Asia are unlikely to increase dramatically their demand for arms or military technology, including their capacity to produce advanced weapons, over the next decade. This does not mean that we should expect a *decrease* in the demand; each country has reasons for improving its capabilities. On the other hand, in a region such as this, where arms levels are relatively low and the pace of acquisitions is relatively slow, a single acquisition of new technology, which may seem insignificant in global terms, can have a major impact on security perceptions in the region.

In Southeast Asia, the acquisition of more and better weapons by one of the ASEAN states could act as an impediment to political cooperation by the Association as a whole. But these countries see themselves as sitting on the edge of the Indochina cauldron; and they will view Vietnam with increasing suspicion if and as it consolidates its influence on the Peninsula. A modest improvement in the capabilities of these countries could enhance their own sense of security without increasing the threat each poses to its neighbors. The key here will be responsible national leadership and mutual trust, to minimize both excessive arms acquisitions and misapprehensions about intentions.

Nuclear Technology

Among the Northeast Asian countries, acquisition of nuclear technology has been significant over the past few years. The PRC, of course, is a nuclear military power; but generally speaking, the diffusion of nuclear capabilities in the region has more to do with the pursuit of energy security than military security. Nonetheless,

[3] See Secretary of State Vance's statement at the Conference with Business and Civic Leaders on China Policy at the State Department on January 15, 1979, *New York Times*, January 16, 1979.

[4] Taiwan's armed forces would soon cease to function without reliable supply of American spare parts. The United States has a $550 million business investment on Taiwan and takes 40 percent of Taiwan's exports.

some developments in this area are clearly relevant to military potential and could ultimately affect regional security and politics.

To illustrate my point and to underscore the complexity of the issues, let me briefly describe the role nuclear energy is playing in East Asian countries. As I do so, I think the implications of the other side of the coin—nuclear proliferation—will speak for themselves.

I shall start with Japan, simply because it is the major nuclear nation in the region—and one of the most important in the world. Japan has something like 17,000 megawatts of installed nuclear generating capacity, second in the world only to the United States. It has more than 20 research or experimental reactors in operation, as well. Japan is a world leader in every major aspect of the nuclear fuel cycle: uranium enrichment technology is under development; a pilot-scale nuclear fuel reprocessing plant is in operation; and Japan can fabricate its own fuel. Japan will never be totally independent of foreign suppliers for its nuclear program, as it lacks uranium resources. But through recycling of spent fuel and development of the fast breeder reactor, it hopes to reduce that dependence as much as possible. Japan is also a supplier of components for nuclear power reactors and potentially could become a major supplier of complete nuclear reactor systems.

Japan's "nuclear neuralgia" need not be elaborated on. The sensitivities in Japan, in fact, complicate the government's task in such areas as developing public acceptance of new nuclear installations. Japan is a party to the Non-Proliferation Treaty, and its forswearing of nuclear weapons has been a cornernstone of every government's policy since World War II. But it is clear that Japan could have "the bomb" at any time, and it is this factor among others to which countries in the region pay close attention when considering their own nuclear options.

Ranking just after Japan, Taiwan is the second largest consumer of nuclear power in the region. In the next decade, fully half of the island's electricity will originate in nuclear power reactors. As with Japan, the skills and techniques for harnessing the atom have been under development in Taiwan for decades, and the island's advanced nuclear capabilities also have the potential for application to non-peaceful purposes. These include reprocessing skills at a research scale of effort which could be turned into operating facilities to extract plutonium. Although our formal governmental relationship with Taiwan has come to an end, the United States remains deeply concerned that the island's security not fall into jeopardy and, in the nuclear context, that its capabilities not be directed to nuclear weapons as the "answer" to its security concerns.

South Korea is another case in which the need for nuclear power and the security imperative could mix dangerously. South Korea, too, will be producing half its electricity through nuclear power in the coming decade. This country also has a reprocessing potential; and Korean nuclear scientists are among the best in the world. We think nuclear energy makes sense in South Korea, and the United States is one of the nation's major suppliers of nuclear reactors and fuel. We do not think, however, that nuclear weapons make sense for South Korea, and South Korea's leaders seem to agree with us.

One country in the region that will become a major nuclear supplier in the 1980s is Australia. The country has uranium reserves, still only partially explored, which are the largest known in the region and may prove to be among the largest in the world. For an energy-starved region—and world—the demand for these reserves will become stronger in years to come. The extent of this new uranium supply may make recourse to advanced reactor types such as the breeder unnecessary for a longer period than was earlier predicted. It may also prove possible for Australia to develop as a major reliable supplier to the other nations of the region. In this connection, we have consulted closely with Australia on our approach to nuclear supply issues—how to reconcile transfers of nuclear materials and technology with the risks of proliferation. We are confident that Australia will be a highly responsible supplier of its valuable resources, and that its entry into the nuclear community will be of benefit to all in the region and the world.

Other countries of the region (such as the Philippines and Indonesia) are only beginning to consider nuclear power production.

The People's Republic of China

For the past two decades the Chinese have not imported significant amounts of military-related equipment and technology. There are several reasons for this: the abiding emphasis on self-reliance in the Chinese national character; the "never-again" attitude engendered by the precipitate withdrawal of Soviet assistance in 1960; the shortage of foreign exchange and the competing claims of the civilian industrial sector, which have left little for military imports; and a lack of willing suppliers. Military imports aside, the Chinese have made some efforts in the past 20 years to improve their technological base more generally, through such imports as heavy transport equipment, computers, specialized steels, and various production technologies and plants. But even in these areas, acquisitions have not been vast enough, good enough, or timely enough to prevent a widening of the technological gap that separates China from the USSR, Japan, and the United States.

This gap is especially noticeable and evidently worrisome to the current Chinese leaders as it affects their military modernization plans. The years of Cultural Revolution turmoil and self-reliance have taken their toll. Given the national security goals the Chinese seem to have set for themselves, their military capabilities are far below their requirements. Whether in ground, air, or naval forces, they are incompletely equipped with old systems largely of obsolete Soviet design, along with some adaptations of their own, which are markedly inferior in maintainability and combat use to the modern forces the Soviets deploy near China.

At present Beijing (Peking) is exploring possibilities for military-related imports—both advanced technologies and weapons systems—from Western Europe. This is part of a wider effort by the Chinese to come out of their shell of "self-reliance" and turn to international markets to begin remedying economic, technological, and military weaknesses. The press has reported, *inter alia*, PRC-British talks regarding the Harrier jet fighter and PRC-French discussions concerning anti-tank missiles and a jet fighter. There have been other deals, with more likely to come, in the area of "dual-use" technology which could contribute to advances in Chinese military capabilities. Chinese attitudes about military imports seem to have changed, and Beijing may find more than one willing supplier in the West.

Of course, some things have not changed. Not all the past constraints on Chinese interest in foreign military technology were rooted in a now-receding ideological purism. The Chinese are, at least for now, no more capable of absorbing massive doses of sophisticated military equipment or technology than they were before their recent shopping (or window-shopping) spree. Their foreign exchange picture has not brightened; in fact, given their new interest in purchasing massive amounts of "civilian" industrial technology, greater demands than ever are being placed on roughly constant resources, leaving relatively little for weapons and weapons-production technology. Moreover, I do not belive that the deep Chinese preference for self-reliance has been, or could have been, completely washed away practically overnight.

My own explanation of Beijing's current import strategy—and I emphasize "my own"—is that their top priority remains the acquisition of *production* technology, both civil and military, in order to bring nearer to reality the elusive goal of national self-reliance. Chinese purchases of actual weapons, I believe, serve several purposes: to help with a near-term, but necessarily limited upgrading of forces on the northern border; to open the door to subsequent acquisitions of production technology through licensing, co-production, and, less directly, increased human exposure to sophisticated systems; and, perhaps most important, to show the Soviets and others (including themselves?) that China and the West can and will do business in the military field.

If this explanation is correct, we may see only a few, symbolic deals (even though they may be significant in size and level of sophistication) involving direct arms purchases in the near term, probably tied to longer-term arrangements for tranferring arms-production technology. In turn, these deals will be in the context of—and possibly linked to—still larger, broader arrangements involving trade, credits, technology transfers, and Western investments in China. There is simply no such thing as a "quick fix" for remedying current Chinese military inadequacies.

Even if arms and arms-production technologies prove to have relatively low priority in China's overall acquisition strategy, there are important "gray areas" of technology transfer, which, although ostensibly for the expansion of civilian industrial capacity, are also essential to military industrial capacity. Examples are steel-making, marine turbine engines, computers, propulsion systems, and communications technologies. The PRC is likely to put a great deal of emphasis on acquiring such dual-use technologies because of the greater overall effect they will have on China's total industrial capacity.

In still other areas, Chinese imports will improve the PRC's industrial-technological base in the broadest sense—which of course affects overall Chinese power. This is especially true in the area of energy. Oil recovery technology can help China produce the oil to pay for other imports. In my view, we will see more Chinese interest in this sort of acquisition—and probably greater Western interest as well, since Soviet objections are less likely to be respected in cases where the Chinese are merely trying to build up their country, rather than their army.

Finally, in the nuclear area, the PRC has, in a sense, entered the nuclear age backwards, as compared to other Asian countries. From its first nuclear weapon test in 1964, the PRC has developed for itself a significant military nuclear capability, including thermonuclear weapons. Only now is the PRC looking to the atom for the purpose of energy production pursued elsewhere in the region.

POLICY PROBLEMS FOR THE FUTURE

China

Secretary of State Vance has explained that the United States will not sell arms to the PRC, but that we cannot decide for others what defensive arms they might sell.[5] Even within this policy framework, the prospect of Western military transfers to China raises some major policy questions for us, and some even tougher choices for those of our allies who are considering sales.

There is a major strategic issue imbedded in the question of arms transfers to the PRC, a question which involves the whole structure of U.S. relations with Moscow and Beijing. Our policy has been and continues to be to treat both countries evenhandedly with regard to technology transfers. The extent to which our European allies sell arms to China, and the degree to which we and our allies continue to approve dual-use technology transfers to the PRC that are not also approved for the Soviet Union, will have major strategic ramifications.

The potential Western sellers may see some strategic value in further complicating Soviet military plans and stretching Soviet capabilities thin by helping the PRC to improve its forces. These governments no doubt also recognize the economic benefits to be had. And yet, they have to be a little unsure about what this flurry of Chinese interest will really amount to in terms of actual contracts—about whether they will experience severe political repercussions in their relations with the Soviets, only to learn that the Chinese, having demonstrated that they *could* buy Western arms, lose much of their apparent current enthusiasm for doing so.

Nor do we know what concrete forms Soviet reactions will assume, what linkages the Soviets might make. Would Moscow direct such reactions mainly against Europe, or would it hold the United States accountable for whatever sales occur, our claims of a "hands-off" policy notwithstanding? It is even possible that behind all the rhetoric, the Soviets in practice will show greater interest in areas of cooperation with the West, in hopes of breaking the feared political encirclement implied by Western military transfers to China.

For the United States, the issue of Taiwan—the security of its people—is also touched by the question of Western arms sales to the PRC. As I said earlier, there is no doubt that the top Chinese military priority is to improve PRC capabilities vis-à-vis the Soviet Union. But the fungibility of military systems means that we must examine the possibilities for deployment against Taiwan of whatever Western sales are under consideration. This, in turn, brings me back to a point made in the previous section: that the transfer of *production* technology rather than the sale of arms may prove to be the focus of Chinese transactions with the West and Japan.

[5] Secretary of State Vance stated U.S. arms sales policy toward China as follows: "It is our strong and unequivocal policy that we do not intend to, nor will we, sell military equipment—weapons—to either the People's Republic of China or to the Soviet Union. Insofar as other nations are concerned, this is a matter which each of them must decide for itself." (Press Conference at the Department of State, November 3, 1978.) In expanding on this, President Carter said, "Our publicly expressed and privately expressed advice to the other nations is that the sale of any weapons should be restricted to defensive weapons, and, of course, President Giscard d'Estaing, Prime Minister Callaghan, Chancellor Schmidt would decide with their advisers on what is or is not a defense weapons sale .... The technologically advanced equipment, computers and so forth, would have to be assessed on the basis of each individual item and whether it could contribute in a substantial way to the enhancement of the military capabilities of both the Soviet Union and China. And in general, we will apply the same restraints on that kind of sale to both countries." (White House Press Conference, January 26, 1979.)

From the viewpoint of Taiwan's future security, the former could be just as troublesome as the latter.

A growth in Chinese military capabilities may have a bearing not only on East-West relations and the security of Taiwan but also on the perceived security of other regional states. Insofar as transfers from the West may contribute to growth, we and our allies face yet another complex set of policy issues. For example, how would improved Chinese military capabilities relate to Korean security? Would Beijing be inclined to supply new weapons systems or production technology to Pyongyang? In Southeast Asia, would Chinese force improvements encourage Beijing to play a more active role as a counterweight to Vietnamese military pressures against anxious neighbors?

With regard to nuclear technology transfers, we cannot turn back the clock on China's nuclear weapons capability. But we hope that China will begin to join with us and other concerned nations in recognizing and solving the conflict between peaceful nuclear uses and harmful nuclear potential. For many years, Peking claimed that the spread of nuclear weapons was inevitable and even desirable. In practice, however, it appears that the PRC has avoided contributing to nuclear proliferation. Nuclear technology and materials were not exported, and Beijing turned down requests for nuclear weapons assistance.

China's security interests would clearly not be served by further proliferation in Asia. It is not that any single new nuclear neighbor would necessarily be a military threat to the PRC, but rather that proliferation in Asia could constitute a chain of events that would leave China virtually surrounded by nuclear states of varying size and stability. Thus the PRC must be concerned about the prospects of a nuclear-armed Pakistan, of India "weaponizing" its explosives capability, of South Korea—or most significantly, Japan—going nuclear, and of Taiwan pursuing the development of nuclear weapons. Lately, Beijing has refrained from publicly favoring proliferation. This may be a sign that China is ready to move one step further and adopt a more constructive non-proliferation stance.

One idea which the United States could eventually explore with the PRC would be for Beijing to issue a statement to the effect that it (1) believes that the spread of independent nuclear weapons would be dangerous and destabilizing and (2) will continue a policy of not contributing to the diffusion of nuclear weapons capabilities, including requiring appropriate controls to prevent any peaceful nuclear exports by China from being diverted to military purposes.

Chinese accession to the Non-Proliferation Treaty is not likely to be in the cards in the coming decade. And the PRC will want to avoid compromising its self-proclaimed role as spokesman for the Third World in arguing against "inequitable" arms-control agreements. Nevertheless, given Beijing's self-interest, its new relationship with the United States, and its international role as a nuclear weapons state which is also a member of the U.N. Security Council, it is possible that China might consider undertaking such a public posture on the non-proliferation issue in the near future.

Although only a year ago the Beijing leadership stated publicly that it would find "intolerable" U.S. arms sales to Taiwan after normalization, in fact the PRC agreed to normalization on precisely this basis.[6] The United States will continue to

---

[6] See Hua Guofeng's (Hua Kuo-feng's) comment on U.S. arms sales to Taiwan after normalization at the press conference of December 6, 1978; translated in *Peking Review*, No. 51, December 22, 1978, pp. 10-11.

consider on a case-by-case basis Taiwan's requests for legitimate defensive weapon-ry.

A war in the Taiwan Strait is the last thing we want to see, and we realize that maintaining a credible deterrent on Taiwan can help ensure that we will never see such a war. But normal and steadily improving relations between the United States and Beijing also will contribute to Taiwan's security—in fact, decisively so. Having at last, after thirty years, achieved a normal diplomatic relationship with the United States, Beijing would probably not hazard it for a military adventure against Taiwan—an adventure which would take at least five years to prepare, would require complete revision of present economic and military priorities, and would at the end of that five-year period still not be assured of success. There also remains, of course, the more than 45 Soviet divisions along China's 4,500-mile northern border. Beijing will want to avoid the sort of tempting military opportu-nity that a conflict over Taiwan would present the Soviets.

This is not to say that the question of Taiwan's security will not continue to pose policy dilemmas for us. Decisions on particular weapons and technology transfers will face the United States with the tough call between trying to bolster Taiwan's security directly via transfers and trying to do so indirectly through continued progress in U.S.-PRC relations. Whatever specific decisions we make, however, Taiwan's security will remain an important issue to the American people and their government.[7]

Northeast Asia

In Northeast Asia, the technology trend with the most significance for Asian security and U.S. policy is the expansion of capabilities for the indigenous produc-tion of advanced technologies. While this will not by any means produce self-sufficiency in military production over the next decade, it could seriously challenge the ability of suppliers to restrict levels of technology in the interests of regional stability, arms control, and international security more generally. Specifically, this trend poses three major questions for U.S. policymakers:

1. *How can we influence the rate of acquisition of nuclear technology to mini-mize the impact of proliferation—or "latent" proliferation—on regional security and stability?*

In addition to the problem of proliferation, there is also the issue of the accumu-lation of nuclear material and technology. This phenomenon, call it "latent prolifer-ation," whereby countries steadily reduce the time, effort, and uncertainties in-volved in producing deliverable nuclear weapons, could come to plague security in Northeast Asia during the 1980s. This may be characterized by a combination of inadequate safeguards and the acquisition of reprocessing capacities and long-range delivery systems—seasoned with occasional chatter about possible interest in nuclear weapons.

Japan, South Korea, and Taiwan—three U.S. allies—all have the technical potential to build nuclear weapons. Thus U.S. actions affecting the security of these states will obviously have a direct and essential bearing on whether any one of

---

[7] In acting on the Administration's Taiwan Relations Act, Congress added language strengthening the U.S. commitment to Taiwan's future security. See David Binder, "Pledge to Taiwan Upsets the Chinese," *New York Times*, March 29, 1979.

them exercises that potential. There are several things the United States can do to minimize incentives to proliferate:

- Ensure an adequate defense for these countries through a combination of U.S. military presence in the region and conventional arms transfers.
- Restrain the transfer of sensitive reprocessing and enrichment technologies to the area, but provide adequate supplies of low-enriched fuel for commercial reactors.
- Develop international mechanisms for storing and perhaps ultimately reprocessing nuclear fuel rods. This might begin, for example, with the establishment of a regional fuel storage center. Also, suppliers might offer opportunities for consumer participation in fuel-cycle services from their own plants.
- Encourage Japan to play more of a leadership role in non-proliferation measures such as slowing down its commitment to breeder reactors and the development of large-scale reprocessing facilities. The pace with which Japan moves toward a large national commercial nuclear power operation will affect our ability to influence Korea and Taiwan.
- With Taiwan, in the post-normalization period, we must find ways to continue supplying low-enriched fuel for their nuclear energy program and to ensure that IAEA safeguards remain effectively applied.

2. *As South Korea expands its own technological capability, how can we minimize the risk that new technologies will cause destabilization of the present military balance on the Korean Peninsula?*

The benefits of improved Korean capabilities for self-defense are clear. The U.S. security commitment to Korea will remain, with the air, ground, and naval power necessary to back it up. But the Koreans themselves, during the 1980s, will assume a greater combat role, requiring major improvements in ground forces, air defense, and close air support. Much of the hardware will come directly from the United States, and we shall be able to gauge its effect on the regional balance.

In some important areas, however, Korea appears determined to develop its own technological options, particularly aircraft and missiles. American restraints on the export of relevant U.S. technology will only serve as a holding action; and if applied too harshly, they could cause Korea to turn elsewhere.

3. *What, if anything, do we do about new Asian arms exporters?*

An offshoot of larger regional production capabilities is the possible entry of new exporters into the international arms market. While technological limitations (except in the case of Japan) will constrain the extent and sophistication of any exports, trade restrictions and economic pressures facing some Asian nations may add to their interest in arms exports. There are plenty of markets for relatively unsophisticated but nonetheless potentially destabilizing arms transfers. If it chose to, Japan could probably compete on a level with the United States in high-technology exports (see Tables 3-A and 3-B).

The United States has substantial policy constraints on its exports of high-technology production facilities. In recent years, these constraints have been considerably tightened. At this point, it appears that any further tightening would do very little to inhibit the development of production capabilities and would serve to exacerbate relations with our allies.

Table 3-A

AIRCRAFT CO-PRODUCED IN EAST ASIAN COUNTRIES

Producer	Aircraft
Australia	Bell 206B-1 Jet Ranger II helicopters (completed 1977)
People's Republic of China	Soviet MiG-19 (designated as the Shenyang F-6). Chinese version of Soviet MiG-21, the Shenyang F-8 Shenyang (Tupelov) TU-16 Shenyang F-9, embodying MiG-19-derived technology
Indonesia	Lipnur LT-200, based on Pazmany (U.S.) PL-2 light aircraft
Japan	Bell helicopters Model 47 (program completed) Lockheed P2V-7 (P-2H) Neptune anti-marine aircraft (program completed) Boeing Vertol 107 Model II helicopter Hughes Model 369 helicopter McDonnel-Douglas F-4 (F-4E/J for Japan) BK-117 light multipurpose helicopter (joint development with MBB of the FRG) North American Aviation F-86F (completed) Lockheed P-3C Orion Lockheed F-104J (completed) McDonnel-Douglas F-15 Sikorsky F-55 helicopter (completed) and S-61 series
Republic or Korea	Hughes 500M-D light helicopters
New Zealand	Sargent-Fletcher (U.S.) FU-24 general-purpose light aircraft Transavia (Australia) Airtruk agricultural aircraft
Philippines	MBB (FRG) BO 105C helicopters Britten-Norman (UK) Islander light utility aircraft XT-001 primary trainer, copy of SIAI-MARCHETTI (Italy) SF260MP American Jet Industries TT-1 Pinto trainer, COIN version
Taiwan	Modified version of Pazmany (U.S.) PL-1 turboprop trainer Bell UH-1H helicopter Northrop F-5E[a]

Source: *Jane's All the World's Aircraft, 1977-78*, London, 1978.

[a]While it would take a major effort for Taiwan to reproduce an aircraft like the F-5E after the present agreement expires, the possibility that Taiwan would opt for the program cannot be discounted completely. This would probably require a large diversion of resources and talent earmarked elsewhere in Taiwan and thus would be very costly. However, the PRC accomplished something similar when it copied the MiG-21 and produced a limited number.

Table 3-B

AIRCRAFT PRODUCED IN EAST ASIAN COUNTRIES

Producer	Aircraft
Australia	Nomad[b] N22B, STOL utility Nomad N24, STOL transport Nomad Mission Master, maritime surveillance Nomad Search Master, coastal surveillance
People's Republic of China	Shenyang F-6 (MiG-19) Shenyang F-8 (MiG-21) Shenyang F-9, updated F-6 Shenyang (Tupelov) TU-16
Indonesia	Lipnur single-engine light aircraft
Japan (illustrative)	Fuji T-3 (KM-2B) single-engine primary trainer P-2J patrol (Lockheed Neptune development) C-1, medium-range military transport Helicopters T-2 jet trainer F-1 close-support fighter US-1 SAR amphibian
New Zealand	Single-engine aircraft
Philippines	PADC Islander single transport PAF X7-001, primary training, single-engine
Taiwan	AIDC T-CH-1, turboprop-powered transport AIDC XC-2, twin-turboprop transport

Source: *Jane's All the World's Aircraft, 1977-78*, London, 1978.
[a]Some small, single-engine, propeller-driven aircraft are not included.
[b]Nomads do not appear to be British derivatives.

The United States has been talking with the Soviet Union over the past year about the possibilities for multilateral restraint in conventional arms transfers (CAT). It is not at all clear how applicable CAT would be to the East Asian region, assuming it was feasible at all. This is something that we will continue to review with the countries in the area.

Southeast Asia

The challenges for U.S. policymaking in Southeast Asia have changed fundamentally over the last decade. We remain concerned about and willing to help preserve the security of our non-communist friends—the ASEAN states of Indonesia, Malaysia, the Philippines, Singapore, and Thailand. But now, conflict and confrontation in the area is between the communist countries, rather than between communist and non-communist states: Vietnam-Cambodia, China-Vietnam, and USSR-China, with Laos in the eye of the hurricane.

The non-communist countries have made important strides in creating a basis for political cooperation among themselves, as evidenced by the growing significance of ASEAN. This development can reduce the incidence of dispute and confrontation between non-communist countries, but it cannot, in the near-term, provide real protection from Vietnam, or from being somehow injured by the struggles among the major communist powers in the region.

Even without these continuing security concerns, the demand for arms among our Southeast Asian friends will not abate. A natural updating of forces by these countries will itself pose policy choices for the United States. In particular, there will be an interest in replacing 1960s-vintage U.S.-built combat aircraft (e.g., the F-5) with new generations (e.g., the F-16). But the F-16 is not just newer than the F-5, it is substantially more potent—in fact, probably more potent than is needed by most countries in Southeast Asia and elsewhere. How the United States satisfies the demand for a new fighter could become a major arms-transfer policy question for the Carter Administration.

THE U.S. SECURITY STANCE

Ultimately, our own security posture in East Asia will be essential to stability in the region and thus relevant to the demand for military technology in the coming decade.

The debate over U.S. forces in Korea has obscured the fact that the United States will have considerable military power in East Asia for the indefinite future. To back up our continuing commitment to Korean security, as well as our commitments to Japan and other Asian allies and friends, we will maintain the following forces in the area: nine squadrons of land-based combat aircraft (three of which will be in Korea, with the remainder in Japan); two brigades of the Third Marine Amphibious Force in Japan (Okinawa); and the 20 to 25 forward-deployed combatants of the Seventh Fleet, including two aircraft carriers. American force levels in the Pacific area are generally stable (Table 4), and when qualitative factors are taken into account, it is obvious that U.S. military capabilities in the region have not decreased. We will also maintain the ability to reintroduce in timely fashion whatever additional forces may be required.

Judgments about the sufficiency of these forces should take into account not only future Soviet deployments but also the fact that the role of the PRC in the region has changed dramatically, as has our perception of that role. This allows us to plan, tailor, and, if necessary, concentrate our forces to meet specific threats. While our military presence is smaller than the forces deployed along the Sino-Soviet border, it is generally deemed to be an adequate counter to the Soviet military assets available for deployment beyond the Chinese theater. In light of the qualitative problems facing the Soviet fleet, the capabilities of our allies, and our own strong forces in the region, I believe the U.S.-Soviet balance in East Asia is favorable to us and that the trends are not adverse to that balance.

For the countries of East Asia, a security relationship with the United States remains very important to regional stability. As long as we maintain a military presence at current levels to support these relationships, it is unlikely that the demand for arms and production capabilities will develop too much momentum. The preference of a number of countries for relying heavily on U.S. security commitments engenders some self-restraint. Since the acquisition of nuclear weapons or excessively threatening conventional capabilities would jeopardize the availability of U.S. support, even those regimes that may be tempted to pursue such ends have a strong incentive for restraint.

Table 4

FORCE TRENDS IN THE PACIFIC, 1973-83[a]

	United States			Soviet Union		
	1973	1978	1983	1973	1978	1983
Airpower						
Bombers[a]	14	14	14	270	270	250-290
Land-based tactical aircraft[b]	180	192	192	0	0	0
Sea-based tactical aircraft	720	540	540	0	0	15-25
Land-based ASW aircraft	108	108	108	56	62	60-75
Naval power						
Carriers	9	6	6	0	0	1
Major surface combatants	81	80	85-95	53	62	56-64
General-purpose submarines	40	35	38-43	86	70	67-73
Amphibious forces						
Major amphibious ships	30	33	30-33	15	18	18-21
Marines/naval infantry	29,000	29,000	29,000	4,000	6,000	6,000-8,000
Attached air support	60	60	60	0	0	0

Source: *Military Balance, 1973-1974*, Institute of International Strategic Studies, London; and State Department staff estimates.

[a]Includes Soviet naval aviation and long-range aviation.
[b]Does not include Soviet tactical aircraft deployed along the PRC border.

The American public recognizes that we have important economic, political, and cultural interests in the region. Consequently, there is durable, bipartisan support in the United States for maintaining a military posture of this scale and improving it qualitatively. There is little or no political pressure for diminishing the U.S. role or presence in Asia; if anything, the pressures go in the other direction, as demonstrated by Congressional and public support for maintaining American ground forces in Korea.[8]

Insofar as growing economic and technical potential might lead Asian countries toward greater militarization, the American defense posture in the area can help attenuate these tendencies. True, we cannot police the Far East; but our presence, and the political influence that surrounds it, can help discourage the misuse of military capabilities. We can also directly influence the development of some countries' military posture and their plans to emphasize legitimate self-defense missions —through joint exercises, coordinated planning, training, military-to-military contacts, and, in some cases, command-and-control relationships.

THE FUTURE SECURITY ENVIRONMENT AND U.S. RESPONSES

Finally, let me address in a broader perspective the question of the transfer of defense technologies to Asia, because our response to this question must depend on our fundamental strategic objectives in the region.

We appear to be entering a period of considerable turbulence—even danger—in U.S.-Soviet relations. The Soviets have developed a substantially greater capability to project military power beyond their borders than was the case a decade ago. This is a fact that will increasingly affect Moscow's diplomacy. At the same time, the Soviets have also suffered a number of setbacks—rather important setbacks—over the last few years. They appear to be developing a kind of strategic claustrophobia, a loser's mentality. They have made large investments in several countries, only to be thrown out abruptly. They will be looking for ways to make up for these losses. This suggests that a time of new boldness in Soviet actions lies ahead, and with it a period of great uneasiness and uncertainty in U.S.-Soviet relations.

The basic judgment underlying this analysis is that relations among the communist countries will be the key source of competition and conflict in Asia in the coming decade. Although future tension between the United States and the Soviet Union should not lead to direct confrontations in Asia, it could affect the way the Soviets react or overreact to China and to its new relationship with the West. It will certainly affect situations in other parts of the world—the Middle East, the Persian Gulf, Africa, and the Indian subcontinent—which will have an increasing impact on Asian security.

What basic strategy will best serve the United States and its allies in Asia? Our security posture in the region—as in Europe—is strong. While U.S. military power may not be directly relevant to the rivalries that develop among the communist states in Asia, a strong U.S. presence will be important for keeping these instabili-

---

[8] Congressional opposition to the Carter Administration's early decision to withdraw all U.S. ground forces from South Korea led to a reversal of the withdrawal policy in the context of a reassessment of the strength of North Korea's armed forces. See the official announcement of the President's decision to suspend the ground force withdrawal program in the *New York Times*, July 21, 1979.

ties from threatening the non-communist Asian states. America's military and political posture in Asia will also be important for the ways in which we meet challenges that come from situations in other parts of the world. In order to manage these situations without straining our own resources or placing unnecessary burdens on our allies, we should concentrate on consolidating and expanding our basic positions of strength in Asia, as well as in Europe. This means building on what we have, while avoiding new initiatives or fundamental changes in our current position.

If consolidating and expanding our positions of strength should be our fundamental objective in Asia, what does this mean for technology transfers? Let me make some general propositions:

First, the United States should be responsive to requests for arms transfers and production know-how, more so than we have been in the past. But we should not delude ourselves by thinking that arms transfers can be a substitute for diplomacy or that they can induce the recipients to set aside domestic difficulties. Arms transfers send a signal of support; they assist our basic security stance; but they don't replace diplomacy, and they don't obviate the need for domestic change.

Second, in Southeast Asia we have friends and allies who will be facing a new phase in arms acquisitions. Some of these countries will be looking beyond their current "F-5" level as a response to concerns about an aggressive Vietnam allied to the Soviet Union. We will want to work with them in meeting their security concerns, but in a way which will ensure that we do not exacerbate tensions among our friends and allies that would undermine their political unity. This will require that they work with each other and communicate with each other on these decisions in ways that they are not doing now.

Third, in Northeast Asia, our relationship with Japan is solid and expanding into new areas of technology transfer. We should develop the same approach in our dealings with South Korea, particularly in seeking new areas for co-production activity. The general thrust of our transfers, both arms and production know-how, should be to promote self-sufficiency—not as a substitute for the U.S. commitment to Korean security, but as a means of reassuring the Koreans that they can trust themselves, as well as us, in their own defense. Korean attitudes today seem to reflect a lack of self-confidence in their ability to defend themselves, which ultimately affects their diplomacy.

Fourth, to put the question of nuclear technology transfer in the context of this basic strategic objective, it seems important that we continue our efforts of the past few years to prevent the proliferation of nuclear weapons. This will require both negative and positive responses. On the negative side, we should continue to be firm with our friends about their intentions to develop nuclear weapons capability. They will expect us to be tough. We should not allow ourselves to be blackmailed into providing certain conventional arms in order to buy a country off the nuclear weapons option. Conventional arms are one thing, the nuclear question is another, and the United States should not let itself be put in the position of having to provide unnecessary or destabilizing conventional weapons in order to deal with a threat to go nuclear. On the positive side, there should be no doubt whatsoever about our reliability as a supplier of nuclear fuel. Countries in Asia are becoming increasingly commited to nuclear energy as a source of power. This concerns their economic security, and it is important that the difficult questions we will face together should not raise any doubts about our reliability in assisting in energy security.

Fifth, when technology transfers are related to our basic strategic objective of consolidating existing positions of strength, the toughest question will be that of the best policy for dealing with the PRC. It will have vital implications for our relations with the Soviet Union, for the balance of power in Asia, and for the reliability of U.S. commitments. The Sino-Soviet military balance is anything but a balance. Chinese forces cannot be compared with Soviet forces. But for some years now we have proclaimed a policy of evenhandedness in making technology transfers to the Soviet Union and China. Any deviations from this policy, which might occur sooner or later (not necessarily in arms technology, however), will have the most difficult repercussions on the Soviets. Furthermore, to the extent that we help or acquiesce in improving the PRC's military capability vis-à-vis the Soviet Union, we will also be improving their capability against Taiwan. We cannot ignore this. How we handle the defense of Taiwan will affect the confidence of our other Asian allies in our security commitments to them.

Finally, and most important, what our Asian friends and allies will feel they need in the way of arms and technology will be determined by their trust in the United States. The most tangible way for us to demonstrate the credibility of our commitment to their security will be to maintain our military presence as it is. As I described earlier, the U.S. force posture in Asia is considerable. It is my personal opinion that it should remain at current levels for the indefinite future, with no further troop reductions.

The U.S. public recognizes that we have important economic, political, and cultural interests in the region. Consequently, there is durable, bipartisan political support in the United States for maintaining a military posture of the present scale and improving it qualitatively. There is little or no political pressure for diminishing the U.S. role or presence in Asia; if anything, the pressures go in the other direction.

We should also be careful that our Asian friends are not misled by those voices in the U.S. political debate that predict doomsday. Looking around the world, even a pessimist would have to find mixed signals—both successes and failures for the Soviet Union and the United States. Our allies would be misled if they were to infer from the doomsday sayers that there is something less than full resolve on the part of the United States to meet its commitments in Asia. I think we can now have considerable confidence that the Carter Administration will meet its security commitments in Asia and elsewhere.

Appendix A

PARTICIPANTS IN THE CONFERENCE ON EAST ASIAN SECURITY IN THE 1980s

Held on January 11-13, 1979
at
The Rand Corporation
Santa Monica, California

Dr. Michael H. Armacost
Deputy Assistant Secretary for East Asian
and Pacific Affairs
Office, Assistant Secretary
(International Security Affairs)
Department of Defense

Brigadier General Richard T. Boverie
Deputy Director for Plans and Policy
Directorate of Plans
Office, DCS/Operations, Plans, and Readiness

Admiral Noel Gayler

The Honorable Leslie H. Gelb
Director
Bureau of Politico-Military Affairs
Department of State

Dr. Goh Keng Swee
Deputy Prime Minister and Minister of Defense
Republic of Singapore

The Honorable Philip C. Habib

Dr. Erland H. Heginbotham
Deputy Assistant Secretary
Bureau of East Asian and Pacific Affairs
Department of State

The Honorable Richard C. Holbrooke
Assistant Secretary for East Asian and
Pacific Affairs
Department of State

Mr. Arnold L. Horelick
Central Intelligence Agency

Mr. William G. Hyland

Mr. Herman Kahn
Director
The Hudson Institute

Dr. Paul H. Kreisberg
Deputy Director
Policy Planning Staff
Department of State

Dr. Takuya Kubo
National Defense Council
Japan

Dr. Kim Kyung-Won
Special Assistant to the President
  for International Affairs
Republic of Korea

Mr. Paul F. Langer
The Rand Corporation

Mr. Norman D. Levin
East Asian Institute
Columbia University

Dr. Lim Bian Kie
Department for Public Affairs
Centre for Strategic and International Studies
Indonesia

Mr. Winston Lord
President
Council on Foreign Relations

Mr. Roderick MacFarquhar, M.P.
House of Commons
United Kingdom

The Honorable David E. McGiffert
Assistant Secretary of Defense
  (International Security Affairs)
Department of Defense

Dr. Harald B. Malmgren
President, Malmgren, Inc.

Dr. Alexandro Melchor, Jr.
Director, The Asian Development Bank

Lieutenant Colonel Charles R. Nelson
Office, Director of Net Assessment
Office, Secretary of Defense
Department of Defense

Dr. Guy J. Pauker
The Rand Corporation

Mr. Nicholas Platt
National Security Council

Dr. Jonathan D. Pollack
The Rand Corporation

Professor Lucian W. Pye
Center for International Studies
Massachusetts Institute of Technology

Lieutenant Colonel Alfred K. Richeson
Office of the Secretary of Defense
    (International Security Affairs)
Department of Defense

Mr. Charles W. Robinson
Chairman
Energy Transition Corporation

Mr. Yukio Sato
Secretary to the Foreign Minister
Ministry of Foreign Affairs
Japan

The Honorable Richard L. Sneider

Dr. Soedjatmoko
Bappenas, National Development Planning Agency
Republic of Indonesia

Dr. Richard H. Solomon
The Rand Corporation

Dr. George K. Tanham
The Rand Corporation

Dr. Jiro Tokuyama
Managing Director
Nomura Research Institute
Japan

Dr. Charles Wolf, Jr.
The Rand Corporation

Mr. Donald S. Zagoria
Hunter College

Appendix B

AGENDA OF THE CONFERENCE ON EAST ASIAN SECURITY IN THE 1980s

Held on January 11-13, 1979
at
The Rand Corporation
Santa Monica, California

Introductory Remarks, Donald B. Rice, President,
The Rand Corporation

SESSION I. TRENDS IN EAST ASIAN SECURITY AND THEIR IMPLICATIONS
FOR REGIONAL FORCE PLANNING

Chairman:

Philip C. Habib, former Under Secretary of State,
Diplomat in Residence, Stanford University

Paper:

"Security in Northeast Asia," Takuya Kubo,
Research Institute for Peace and Security,
former Secretary-General of the National Defense Council, Japan

Discussant:

Winston Lord, President, The Council on Foreign Relations

Paper:

"American Defense Planning and East Asian Security:
Choices for a Time of Transition,"
Richard H. Solomon, The Rand Corporation

Discussant:

Lim Bian Kie, Centre for Strategic and International Studies,
Jakarta

Session II. The Great Powers in Asia: Trends and Implications

Chairman:
Alexandro Melchor, Director, The Asian Development Bank

Paper:
"Changing Japanese Security Perspectives: Issues for the Region and the Great Powers," Paul F. Langer, The Rand Corporation

Discussants:
Yukio Sato, Secretary to the Foreign Minister,
  Ministry of Foreign Affairs, Japan;
Nicholas Platt, National Security Council

Chairman:
General Richard T. Boverie, Deputy Director for Plans and Policy,
  Directorate of Plans, United States Air Force

Paper:
"Security Implications of the Soviet Military Presence in Asia,"
Admiral Noel Gayler

Discussant:
Donald S. Zagoria, Hunter College

Paper:
"The Sino-Soviet Conflict," William G. Hyland, Senior Fellow,
  Georgetown Center for Strategic and International Studies

Discussant:
Roderick MacFarquhar, Member of Parliament, United Kingdom

SESSION III. REGIONAL CONFLICTS AND COOPERATION, AND GREAT POWER RIVALRY

Chairman:
George K. Tanham, The Rand Corporation

Paper:
"Vietnam and Big Power Rivalry," Goh Keng Swee,
Deputy Prime Minister and Minister of Defense,
Republic of Singapore

Discussant:
Michael H. Armacost, Deputy Assistant Secretary for East Asian
and Pacific Affairs, Department of Defense

Paper:
"Prospects for Korean Security," Richard L. Sneider,
former U.S. Ambassador to the Republic of Korea

Discussant:
Kim Kyung-Won, Special Assistant to the President
for International Affairs, The Blue House, Republic of Korea

SESSION IV. ECONOMIC/TECHNOLOGICAL TRENDS AND REGIONAL POLITICAL-MILITARY RELATIONS

Chairman:
Charles W. Robinson, Chairman, Energy Transition Corporation

Paper:
"U.S. Security Policy, Technology Transfers, and Asia,"
Leslie H. Gelb, Director, Bureau of Politico-Military Affairs,
Department of State

Discussant:
Charles Wolf, Jr., The Rand Corporation

Paper:
"An Economic Perspective on the Asia-Pacific Region,"
Harald B. Malmgren, President, Malmgren, Inc., and co-editor of
The World Economy

Discussant:
Jiro Tokuyama, Managing Director, Nomura Research Institute,
Tokyo

Paper:
"Security Implications of Regional Energy
and Natural Resource Exploitation," Guy J. Pauker,
The Rand Corporation

Discussant:
Erland H. Heginbotham, Deputy Assistant Secretary,
Bureau of East Asian and Pacific Affairs, Department of State

SPECIAL EVENING PRESENTATION

Keynote Speaker:
The Honorable Richard C. Holbrooke
Assistant Secretary for East Asian and Pacific Affairs,
Department of State

SESSION V. CONCLUDING DISCUSSION: PERCEPTIONS AND TRENDS
IN REGIONAL SECURITY; POLICY DILEMMAS; CHOICES FOR AMERICA'S
FUTURE INVOLVEMENT IN EAST ASIAN SECURITY AFFAIRS

Chairman:
David E. McGiffert, Assistant Secretary of Defense
(International Security Affairs)

Presentation:
"An Asian Perspective," Dr. Soedjatmoko, National Development
Planning Agency, Republic of Indonesia

Presentation:
"An American Perspective," Herman Kahn, Director,
The Hudson Institute

Appendix C
SUMMARY OF DISCUSSIONS[1]

SESSION I

The first session was ostensibly devoted to a discussion of papers dealing with Japanese and American perspectives and policy choices concerning East Asian security in the 1980s. Although both issues were addressed, attention quickly turned to four overall themes: (1) the nature and extent of the changes currently under way in regional security; (2) the utility of the label of "national security" at a time when traditional categories of analysis seem to be eroding; (3) the identification of broader patterns of historical change (political, economic, social, technological, and cultural), both within Asia and in relation to the industrialized nations of the West; and (4) assessments of the respective roles and consequences of the American and Soviet military presences within East Asia.

Pronounced differences of opinion on the degree of flux in present or prospective security arrangements in the region were evident in the discussions. One approach saw recent developments—in particular, the Sino-American normalization agreement, the signing of a Sino-Japanese Treaty of Peace and Friendship, and the continued strengthening of Soviet power, especially the USSR's de facto military alliance with Vietnam—as portending a major shift in both regional alignments and global security issues. In view of the continued retrenchment of American power in Asia (e.g., the decision to withdraw ground forces from the Republic of Korea (ROK), and the severing of the U.S.-Republic of China Mutual Defense Treaty), the U.S. military presence in the region had to be judged far less credible and predictable than it has been in the past. According to this view, the traditional U.S. emphasis on Europe at the expense of Asia, the absence (except in Korea) of any unambiguous Cold War lines of geographic or ideological cleavage, China's potential emergence as a regional military power, and the increased American reliance on an island defense strategy have all contributed to great uncertainty about the future stability of East Asia. Many states in the region have had to consider far more concretely their defense options in a world of economic and military transition, with the United States being far less dependable as a possible security guarantor.

Not all participants were persuaded by such an assessment, however. Others viewed the recent changes in American policy (especially with respect to the People's Republic of China [PRC] and Taiwan) as the logical culmination of a chain of events set in motion nearly a decade ago. Inasmuch as virtually all the states of the region have already acted to rectify these anomalous circumstances, the only concern has been the length of time it took the United States to act. While the role of American ground forces continues to diminish, both the United States and its Asian allies now seem far more agreed on the nature of the security challenges

[1] This summary of the conference discussions was prepared by Jonathan Pollack of The Rand Corporation and Norman Levin of Columbia University.

285

facing them. Even if recent events suggest fluidity, any uncertainties are bounded by an essential American commitment to the security of the non-communist states of both Southeast and Northeast Asia, with the emergent U.S.-PRC relationship considerably reducing any potential instabilities in the overall diplomatic and security equation. At the same time, China's growing links to the non-communist industrialized world and its commitment to economic and industrial development suggest that its preoccupations for the foreseeable future are likely to be domestic rather than external.

Irrespective of such differences in perspective, several participants openly questioned whether long-prevailing conceptions of security were still adequate or even useful tools of analysis. To focus on military capabilities as the predominant instrument for ensuring national security seems increasingly questionable, given that insecurity is rooted at least as much or more in non-military vulnerabilities, such as economic instability or racial or religious antagonisms within multi-ethnic societies. By this logic, therefore, traditional conceptions of security arrangements (e.g., deployment of military forces, alliances, and the like) may simply be inadequate for dealing with the variety of economic and social changes now under way.

The response to such objections assumed several forms. First, no matter how much discussion surfaced about alternative conceptions of national security, analysis and prescription invariably returned to an emphasis on the military component. The use or threatened use of force by great powers seeking to exploit political, economic, or social instabilities is a perennial issue in international politics; it cannot be wished away simply by arguing that military power is now of lessened relevance. Second, the nature and direction of change occurring at other levels of the East Asian scene is far from clear. Under conditions where historical trends are in flux but no clear or certain directions are discernible, it is rather premature to discard past approaches simply because their degree of correspondence to future problems remains unsettled.

References to qualitative and quantitative changes in regional security produced a lively exchange of views on the nature of present historical transformations, and on whether they contribute to stability or instability. The rise of Sinitic power in relation to the West, the destabilizing characteristics of modernization and colonialism, and the unsettling aspects of demographic change were all suggested as key variables explaining present uncertainties and the historic nature of the transformations they indicate. Although overall sentiment never coalesced around a single theme, there was an inchoate sense that major historical changes are now under way, and that the policies of the states of the region are failing to keep pace with them.

The final key topic of the first session concerned the role of American and Soviet military power in East Asia. There was a widespread sense that the U.S. military presence remained vital. Even small increments of power were judged by some participants to provide a critical measure of security for states in the region and in terms of U.S. global interests. Nevertheless, strong residual doubts about both the credibility and relevance of American power for the specific security needs of regional states remained evident in the discussion.

Arguments about Soviet military power focused on both its military and its political utility (or inutility). The growth of Soviet capabilities in East Asia has become an obvious preoccupation of some (though by no means all) Asian states.

Perceptions of this power can and do vary. Americans tend to see such power in its global context or in comparison to the forces in the European theater, whereas most Asians see Soviet deployments in terms of their more immediate regional implications. No matter how one might qualify the impact of these deployments (e.g., by citing Soviet vulnerabilities in other spheres, or their modest or nonexistent relevance to Soviet political objectives), the Soviet Union has become and will remain an Asian and Pacific power in a way that it simply was not a decade ago. Conceptions about security in East Asia must therefore come to grips with this undeniable fact.

Policy Issues

Many of the policy implications of the discussions followed quite directly from these lines of argument. The sense of change perceived by many of the participants and the degree of that change compared to the past were critical to judgments about whether current circumstances merited optimism or pessimism about the future. To some, the declining American military involvement in East Asia was a source of great concern. To those who agreed on the centrality and criticality of the American presence, the belief that the U.S. role was uncertain or worse was highly disconcerting. Others, however, objected that there was no U.S. "loss of will," or that the Soviet Union now could be unfettered in its exercise of power. Disagreements on these pivotal questions directly affected judgments and attitudes on a broad range of subsidiary questions—e.g., the necessity for further (and even abrupt) change in Japanese attitudes toward defense issues, how far the United States should be prepared to go in developing a security relationship with the PRC, whether ASEAN should develop an explicit security component to its economic and political roles, and the need for South Korea and others to weigh more autonomous options in force planning. Fir 'ly, to the extent that some felt the United States to be incapacitated or immobilized, their judgments about America's responsive capacities to a dynamic political, economic, and security environment were directly affected. These issues and arguments, aired at the outset of the proceedings, remained intermittently visible for the remainder of the conference.

Issues for Further Consideration

Several critical issues require further thought and attention in light of the session's discussions. First, conceptions of security and insecurity require much more considered analysis than they have thus far received (although this runs the obvious risk of degenerating into an overly scholastic exercise). With the declining relevance of military power to national security calculations, an exclusively military conception of either security or insecurity ignores many trends in the region that will shape the future.

Second, the analysis of both American and Soviet military power—with attention to constraints, potentialities, and consequences—needs far more systematic assessment than it has thus far received. For example, does the obvious and inescapable growth of Soviet military power in East Asia necessarily argue for a purely military response? What specific political benefits or liabilities accrue to either state through their force deployments? In operational terms, what kinds of capabilities exist, and for what conceivable military missions?

Third, although this was in many ways the least considered issue, analysis must give heightened attention to the perspectives and circumstances of the regional actors themselves. An undue focus on superpower competition loses sight of the transformations now occurring within East Asia, irrespective of American and/or Soviet involvement. Not only are regional states likely to perceive security issues in different terms, their capacities to respond to various potential threats are growing and are likely to be radically different from those of the external great powers.

SESSION II

Session II concerned great-power interactions in Asia. Three broad issues were addressed: (1) the nature of the recent changes in Japanese perspectives on defense and national security; (2) the security implications of Japanese and American normalization of relations with the PRC; and (3) the prospects for future U.S.-Japanese defense relations. A fourth issue, the nature of the Soviet threat in Asia, was raised and addressed in detail in the subsequent session.

The starting point of the discussion concerned recent changes in Japanese security perspectives. These shifts have been largely a result of other changes in Japan's external environment, particularly the growth of Soviet military power and the USSR's international behavior, signs of retrenchment in U.S. Asian and global security policies, and the resulting trends associated with the changing military balance. As a result, a new perception of national security as a political issue has developed in Japan. It has encompassed a broader acceptance of the Self-Defense Forces as a necessary instrument for security, and a recognition and increased appreciation of the U.S. military connection as an essential element in Japan's defenses. With the caveat that immediate, dramatic departures should not be expected, most participants agreed that there has been a significant loosening of Japan's past political immobility on security issues.

Opinions on the substance of Japan's evolving approach to security, however, were less unanimous. Three broad views were discernible. The first school of thought saw recent changes as evidence of a major shift in Japanese defense attitudes. This shift involved a Japanese desire to strengthen its own independent military capability and move toward broadening its diplomatic relations (an "omnidirectional" policy), while trying to slow down as much as possible the U.S. withdrawal from Asia.

The second view, while acknowledging the elements of genuine change, tended to emphasize the limits of this transformation. Although these new perspectives permit greater Japanese acceptance of the need for "self-defense," they do not suggest either acceptance of the need for projection of power or the development of a fully independent military capability. These changes seek to make the U.S. military commitment more credible, while also striving to create the economic and political conditions necessary for broad regional stability. However, they do not indicate full-scale military rearmament and diplomatic realignment.

The third view downplayed the significance of recent attitudinal changes. Proponents of this view saw continued Japanese "self-restraint" and reliance upon the United States as the basic pillars of Japanese security policy. Recent changes enable this policy to operate more freely—for example, in providing greater support for U.S. base activities in Japan, making more equitable burden-sharing arrangements, and providing more extensive measures for defense cooperation. But the basic governmental orientation remains unchanged. Thus, while Japan may be entering a "new era," according to this view it is not doing anything new.

A similar division regarding the substance of the "new era" was present in discussions of the nature and implications of Japanese and American normalization of relations with the PRC. Two basic views were identifiable on this question: a perception of normalization as a dramatic, historic development which has fundamentally restructured relations in Asia and the world; and a perception of it as a more modest, moderate extrapolation of long-developing trends. Those espousing the first view tended to interpret normalization as Japan and the United States "choosing sides" to align with the Chinese in the Sino-Soviet feud, thus raising the possibility of either a Sino-Japanese alliance as an alternative to Japan's reliance upon the United States or a "united front" composed of Japan, China, and the United States directed against the Soviet Union in Asia. The second view, in contrast, tended to minimize the implications of normalization, stressing either the Japanese denials of any intention to align with the Chinese against the Soviets or the inherent economic, political, and strategic constraints upon any such development. Hence, while the Sino-Japanese peace treaty may have some symbolic significance indicating a Japanese "tilt," perhaps, toward the PRC, it does not, according to this view, presage any millennial change with dramatic security implications.

A third broad question concerned the prospects for future U.S.-Japanese defense relations. In general, there was agreement on the basic "good health" of the present relationship, with increasing financial and military cooperation indicating positive changes over the situation that has existed heretofore. Still, a number of participants pointed to possible problem areas. The most keenly felt was the potential for strains stemming from trade and economic imbalances. Pointing to widespread anti-Japanese sentiment in Europe, to the increasing difficulty of moderating U.S. Congressional pressures, and to the resulting inability to successfully compartmentalize defense and economic concerns, several participants warned of major future problems. Others were less displeased with the Japanese, pointing to the general fulfillment or near fulfillment of Japanese promises, and noted the diminished viability of most of the old slogans used to pressure the Japanese. Both groups, however, were concerned about the potential for serious strains in security arrangements that could result from unresolved economic tensions.

The other major potential problem cited was the existence of sentiment within Japan for development of an independent military capability. While this sentiment is still thought to be slight, there is a chance that it could grow—particularly if it became linked to a larger nationalist reaction to foreign pressure. Some participants felt that this sentiment should be drawn upon to encourage a greater Japanese defense buildup and the assumption of a larger regional security role. Others felt that Japan should be encouraged to take as "free" a ride as it likes, arguing that if Japan did rearm, it would do so in a major way. There seemed broad agreement, however, on the need to maintain U.S. credibility vis-à-vis the Japanese and on the desirability of keeping Japan's defense efforts within the Mutual Security Treaty framework. Some participants felt that present Japanese inclinations represent both what the Japanese have promised and precisely what the United States desires.

The final general issue raised in the second session concerned the Soviet threat in Asia. Although some argued that the Soviet Union was the weakest of the major actors in Asia, others felt that Soviet power is already in the ascendancy, with the possibility of some Asian states being linked to the Soviet bloc. According to the latter school of thought, greater attention should be paid to regional security arrangements (including, perhaps, development of a Japanese Pacific fleet as part of Japan's broader defense responsibilities), and less concern should be displayed over "provoking" the USSR.

The subsequent discussion focused in greater detail on the possible implications of an increasing Soviet military presence in Asia. The first issue considered was the functional capability and political utility of Soviet military forces. Qualitative improvements in the Soviet Far East forces and the expansion of Soviet command, control, and intelligence operations were deemed highly significant. It was argued that the Soviet Union can now place major limitations on the freedom of action of any Asian nation, that it can threaten to coerce any nation dependent on overseas trade or Middle Eastern oil, that it can make an important difference in the outcome of factional strife in Asia, and that it can severely constrain U.S. power and influence beyond Guam. While there are limitations to the political utility of the Soviet forces, the United States must seek to counter these developments and devise ways to maintain control of the sea and air lines of communication. This task, it was further suggested, requires access to bases in the Far East, the denial of similar bases to the Soviet Union, and the development of an adequate allied force to contain Soviet submarine, air, and seagoing forces.

Soviet military strategy was discussed in the context of the USSR's growing military power, and three possible strategies were suggested: war with China; sea war with the United States and its allies; and "proxy" wars through the "friendship treaty" ploy. Historical Soviet caution, the risk of alienation from the world communist movement, and the long-range rather than short-range nature of the China problem were seen by most discussants as limiting the possibilities of the first strategy. Another, less sanguine view, however, held that the Soviet geopolitical position in the world has become very weak despite the increasing Soviet military capability. The options available for dealing with this weakness (e.g., pressuring Japan and/or Western Europe, or confronting the United States) would be counterproductive, hence China would be the safest place for the Soviets to use force if they are going to use it at all. In this sense, the heart of the strategic problem facing the Soviet Union has become China itself. If détente does not lead to severe restraints on aid to China's modernization effort, it was argued, the Soviets might very well perceive the military option as the best.

On the second possibility, sea war with the United States, opinions were generally congruent. Except in the context of a global war, such a sea war was considered extremely unlikely.

The bulk of discussion focused on the third possible strategy, war by "proxy." Most participants agreed that this was the likeliest possibility for the expansion of Soviet influence. While the object of this strategy on the part of the Soviets would be to counter a perceived conspiracy to encircle them (the Japan-China peace treaty, normalization of U.S.-PRC relations, European arms sales to the PRC, etc.), the effect might be to draw together precisely the kind of anti-Soviet groupings that the strategy is designed to counter.

While there was broad agreement on the nature of the Soviet military presence in Asia, there was considerable diversity of opinion on how the United States should respond to the possible use of Soviet power. The discussion focused on two main options. The first was described in terms of "linkage," i.e., devising a coherent policy complete with both "carrots" and "sticks," which would convince Moscow that a détente relationship with the United States is impossible in the absence of Soviet self-restraint. "The more restraint, the more détente" and vice versa were suggested as appropriate rules of thumb. This option was felt inadequate by others, however, who argued the need for an apparatus to deal with such situations "on the ground," that is, through U.S. "proxies," if not through direct U.S. involvement. It was suggested that East Asia is less vulnerable than other parts of the world partly because of the security treaties, military commitments, and U.S. presence in the region. Especially given the difference that even a limited number of soldiers can sometimes make, it is essential to demonstrate willingness to commit either American or allied troops. In the absence of such willingness, the Soviets supposedly reap two rewards: (1) at least a temporary Soviet victory, and (2) an indication that they can get away with such conduct freely.

Running through the debate between proponents of these two main options was a common element: a perception that the major source of instability and interventionist pressure in Asia is the Soviet Union, and that the United States should devise a strategy—either "linkage," a major move toward China, including open arms sales and full economic assistance, or development of U.S. "proxies"—to counter Soviet power. Others felt that Asian instability, while manipulated by the Soviet Union, was primarily a natural result of indigenous social and economic conditions. Proponents of this view saw much of the discussion about proxies and the like as "unbelievable" in the light of America's Vietnam experience and in conflict with current circumstances, where traditional forms of power have lost much of their former efficacy. The greatest mistake, it was argued, would be to attempt to match Soviet intervention through parallel U.S. action. Rather, the United States should understand the very real limits operating today on the exercise of influence by external powers and should therefore deal with the basic underlying causes of social change.

Some participants felt that there is great injustice in taking "natural events" and transforming them into global crises. At the same time, it was argued, the United States does not need such a confrontationist mentality. Asia (excluding Vietnam) is one of the few areas where the United States has had a string of "triumphs," including the economic vibrancy of various friendly Asian states and the opening of China. Instead of worrying over the few Asian failures and reverting to an interventionist posture, it was argued, the United States should concentrate on how its successes can be maintained. While the United States should certainly increase the political "opportunity costs" of intervention by the Soviet Union, U.S. intervention or support for "proxy wars" clearly represents the wrong way to go. Thus, the session ended with a basic division over military vs. non-military definitions of security, with the issue left largely unresolved.

Policy Issues

Four principal policy issues emerged from the discussions. The first concerned possible American responses to recent changes in Japanese security perspectives.

Japanese ambivalence or uncertainty regarding the American security guarantee has been a long-term trend, rather than a reaction to a single event. Thus it was felt that U.S. attitudes would be an important determinant of future actions taken by Tokyo. Considerable political sensitivity will be called for on issues such as burden-sharing in defense and arrangements for assuring the uninterrupted flow of natural resources to Japan.

The second issue concerned the potential security implications of U.S.-PRC normalization. Opinions were divided on whether the United States should be prepared to make a full and unequivocal commitment to strengthening the PRC economically and militarily, thereby doing everything possible to keep it firmly in an anti-Soviet coalition. Some felt that more informal cooperation with the PRC was a wiser, less risky course, and that a more "evenhanded" approach to the two communist powers was likely to be less provocative to the Soviet Union and thereby less destabilizing to global security arrangements.

The third policy issue concerned future prospects for U.S.-Japanese defense relations. Concern was expressed about economic tensions spilling over into the defense area, and about the need to minimize Japanese development of an independent military capability outside the Security Treaty framework. The conviction was also expressed that Japan should make a greater contribution (especially in a budgetary sense) to regional security arrangements, although this view was not shared by all participants.

The final issue concerned the overall question of how best to respond to Soviet military activity in the region. Means for strengthening the U.S. strategic position in Asia and for avoiding any impression of a further decline in U.S. security commitments were both discussed. Several participants expressed the view that encouraging or seeking to incite Sino-Soviet tensions was likely to prove highly counterproductive, even as means were being sought to respond to Soviet "proxy war" or "friendship treaty" strategies.

Issues for Further Consideration

As in the first session, an essential cleavage was apparent between those stressing the continued relevance of military power and those who believe that less weight should be placed on the use of force as an instrument of national policy. For the former group, the growth of Soviet capabilities represents an alarming trend which needs to be countered largely by military means. For the latter group, the enormous disparity between the increasing depth, diversification, and sophistication of Soviet forces and the absence of any meaningful political or economic advantages accruing to Moscow should be evidence enough of the shortsightedness of simple calls for more and better arms.

While such a division of view is almost more theological than political, the fact that perceptions of security in Asia and elsewhere are much affected by the relative distribution of military forces among various contending states bears repeating. Inescapably, elites do tend to pose their security concerns in concrete military terms. Thus, the extent to which security is a function of military or non-military means clearly merits further consideration. The constraints as well as the potentialities of relying on military, political, and economic instruments for enhancing regional and national security deserve careful scrutiny.

SESSION III

Session III was devoted to the issue of regional conflicts and great-power rivalry, beginning with Indochina. The discussion of Southeast Asia focused initially on Sino-Vietnamese tensions and their relationship to Vietnam's recent invasion of Kampuchea (Cambodia). Although views on the origin of the quarrel varied, all participants agreed on the centrality of the Soviet role in encouraging Hanoi's attack on Kampuchea. The extremely rapid approval of Vietnam's application for membership in COMECON and the subsequent signing of the Treaty of Peace and Friendship both indicate Soviet encouragement and support for the Vietnamese. Thus, Hanoi was able to launch its attack with the expectation that the Soviet-Vietnamese alliance would deter China from retaliating against Vietnam.

The consequences of a Vietnamese "victory" were considered substantial. A victory would enhance Vietnam's military reputation while closing a festering sore on its borders, although the possibility of a protracted guerrilla war in Kampuchea could not be ruled out. At the same time, the conflict appears to have eliminated a "buffer" between Thailand and Vietnam, thereby increasing the prospects for conflict and posing the need for some new means to guarantee Thai security. The possibility of Thailand seeking this through accommodation with Vietnam or even by moving closer to the Soviets was suggested by several participants.

Other complications also seemed likely to result from Vietnam's attack on Kampuchea, including further delays in Indochina's economic reconstruction and exacerbation of the refugee problem for other Asian states. The attack has also made regional relationships throughout Southeast Asia more uncertain. Polarization between a Vietnamese-led group and ASEAN was suggested as one possibility, which raised the issue of whether ASEAN should develop a military component to its activities. Others challenged this view as overly pessimistic. The division between communists, it was suggested, is a basic fact of life not only in Southeast but in Northeast Asia as well. Moreover, this division is bound to grow, replacing the former "East-West" conflict with a new "East-East" one. As a result, each of the communist countries is likely to attempt to improve its relations with ASEAN, to the disadvantage of its communist antagonists, thereby putting ASEAN in a very enviable position. This alternate view, then, anticipated a situation which could present a great opportunity for ASEAN and for the West within the next year or so.

Important consequences were also perceived for each of the major powers competing for influence in the region. The Vietnamese action has exposed PRC "impotence" and raised the issue of how the Chinese can increase the costs to Vietnam of any future action. At the same time, it has made Chinese cooperation in places like Korea less likely, as Beijing (Peking) will now feel the need to strengthen its relations with Pyongyang. Not everyone accepted the notion of Chinese "impotence," however, and the possiblity for greater U.S.-PRC cooperation in other places (Vietnam, Thailand, Iran, or Pakistan, for example) was also suggested. Vietnam's apparent success has probably strengthened the Soviet-Vietnamese relationship in the short term, although in ways and to a degree that are as yet unclear. There was general agreement among the participants that the United States does not have a sufficiently great stake in Indochina to warrant direct U.S. action. However, Vietnam's actions have compounded difficulties in the U.S.-

USSR relationship and have thrown into relief the need to devise means for responding to such Soviet activity.

Hanoi's future priorities and foreign policy intentions were also addressed, and two broad schools of thought were evident. Some tended to see Vietnamese pressure on Thailand and the attempt to take over control of the Thai Communist Party as the minimum to be expected of a generally outward-oriented, expansionist Vietnam. Such a posture will require close Soviet-Vietnamese relations, both as a deterrent to Chinese military action and as a source of financial and military support. This would result in a Vietnamese threat to Thailand's security, as well as a new opportunity for penetration of Soviet power and influence throughout Asia (for example, future access to Cam Ranh Bay).

The second school of thought viewed Vietnam to be drawing a distinction between Indochina and the rest of Southeast Asia and differentiated Vietnamese from broader Soviet interests. According to this perspective, Vietnam's unwillingness to tolerate the situation in Kampuchea was only to be expected, but Vietnam has neither the intention nor the opportunity for similar expansionist activity outside of Indochina. At the same time, Vietnam's strong desire to maintain its independence and leadership role in Indochina is not identical with the Soviet Union's interest in expanding its influence and containing China throughout East and Southeast Asia. Moreover, the potential for anti-Vietnamese guerrilla warfare, for conflict with China, and for continued strained relations with the United States and the other developed states of the West seriously impedes Vietnam's plans for economic reconstruction.

In such circumstances, there are substantial incentives for the Vietnamese to try to disengage themselves from Soviet control on the one hand and from Chinese pressure on the other. Since even China expects Soviet influence to end within eight to ten years, as the full effects of these divergent interests and debilitating demands are felt, the durability and effect of the Soviet-Vietnamese alliance were considered questionable.

The fourth issue concerned the refugee problem. With another million refugees expected to materialize within the next few years, this problem could have major destablilizing effects throughout Asia. Some participants expected the future problem in Asia to be as great as the Palestinian problem in the Middle East. Others expressed the view that the flow of refugees might diminish. To varying degrees, however, a sense of concern was shared by all.

Some of the participants saw Vietnam benefiting greatly from the refugee flow, despite its isolation and the unattractive image it created for itself by the expulsion of its ethnic Chinese nationals. This group argued that Vietnam was acquiring considerable gold, eliminating its ethnic tensions, and increasing the pressure on ASEAN and the West. The solution, in this situation, would be to bring sufficient direct pressure upon Hanoi to stop the refugee flow.

Other participants viewed the refugee problem not as a situation organized and managed by the Vietnamese government but as one caused by disenchanted citizens conniving with certain government officials to win their freedom. Proponents of this view argued that, on a variety of grounds, the United States should not be put in a position where it obstructs the emigration of these alienated citizens. Rather, attention should be directed to handling the outflow more fairly and effectively.

The final issue concerned the basic American policy orientation to the region. On this issue, the different perspectives reflected contrasting attitudes regarding the Soviet presence in Asia and paralleled, to some extent, the division evident in Sessions I and II between contending definitions of security. Two broad orientations were identifiable. The first saw developments primarily in terms of a purposeful Soviet global strategy that requires a U.S. response. This view emphasized the need for firm support of Thailand; encouragement of ASEAN, including the possible addition of a military component to ASEAN's activities; support of China in its attempt to pressure Vietnam; and closer U.S.-PRC relations as a counterbalance to increasing Soviet influence in Asia.

The second orientation viewed regional developments more in terms of the internal situations of the various regional states themselves (e.g., the instability in Iran and the lack of legitimacy in Kampuchea). While asserting the "discontinuities" in Soviet policy and the relatively limited gains the Soviet Union has achieved from the local instabilities, proponents of this view emphasized the need for a long-term approach designed to strengthen the societal structures of the countries concerned in order to prevent instability, and for a political-economic approach that interprets developing situations more broadly than in terms of military security alone.

Most of the discussion of Northeast Asia concerned the power balance on the Korean Peninsula. The general issues addressed were the factors sustaining the status quo and the prospective problems that might upset it. A number of factors were felt to contribute to the status quo: an overall balance of power between the North and the South, including political and economic as well as military factors; the critical role of the United States both as peacekeeper and as potential peace-maker; the positive contribution of Japan in providing military bases and economic support to the United States and the ROK, respectively; the restraint exercised by China and the Soviet Union over North Korea; and the utility of the formal U.N. peacekeeping machinery. These elements were seen to form a complex and delicate "equation" which, taken as a whole, deters North Korea, the sole power with clearly revisionist ambitions. The U.S. role was given particular stress, however, with the other elements considered complementary or of subsidiary importance. In view of the defensive capability and orientation of the ROK forces, it was argued, it is the perception of the automaticity of the U.S. military response, and of the extreme damage such reprisal would entail, that effectively deters Pyongyang.

A number of problems were suggested, however, that might upset the status quo. The first and most critical question was that of North Korean perceptions regarding the will and intention of the United States to defend the South. This issue was felt to require constant attention. Such developments as the U.S. decision to withdraw its ground troops from Korea, for example, inevitably affect these percep-tions. In this regard, there was broad agreement regarding the potentially destabil-izing effects of the U.S. withdrawal decision. Although there was some difference of opinion regarding the advisability of calling off the withdrawal altogether, there was general agreement on the need to end the fixed timetable presently in effect and to submit the withdrawal decision itself to later review.

There was a conflict of views, however, on the question of how the South should respond to the planned withdrawal. Some suggested the need for the ROK to begin thinking of taking over the deterrent role itself. As long as the North might believe that it could attack South Korea without suffering major damage, the South must begin to consider acquiring its own strategic retaliatory capability. Other participants argued against moving in this direction. To begin with, they said, the ROK is in a good position to successfully defend itself, having a strong defensive posture with both good tactical air capability and the potential for naval air reinforcement. Moreover, the basic assumption must continue to be that U.S. air power would be involved in any hostilities from the very beginning, regardless of the planned withdrawal of American ground forces. In the absence of a complete U.S. military withdrawal, the question of the ROK developing a deterrent capability should be treated with the greatest of caution.

The second problem cited was the growing military vulnerability of the North and the possibility of a future economic "crossover" between the North and the South. The incredible performance of the ROK economy suggests that the North is falling farther and farther behind, both economically and in terms of military technology. By the early to mid-1980s, the situation is likely to look ominous to the North. As a result, alternatives designed to thwart this development might become increasingly attractive to Pyongyang. One possibility, of course, would be an all-out invasion. Another possibility would be a North Korean attempt to seize Seoul and then quickly retreat, a move that could set the South back at least ten years in its economic development. Such temptations, it was argued, will make the period in which the "crossover" occurs an extremely tense and difficult one. The key question will be how the North reacts.

Linked to the increasing vulnerability of the North were the limited prospects for meaningful negotiations with Pyongyang. These prospects are slim, it was suggested, largely because of the nature of the domestic structure in the North. Since Kim Il-sung's claim to political legitimacy rests on his pledge of reunification, any renunciation of this pledge through negotiations would necessarily negate the basis of legitimacy itself. In this sense, it was argued, hopes for meaningful negotiations hinge upon the question of leadership succession.

The final problem regarding maintenance of the status quo concerned the question of continued Soviet and Chinese restraint upon Pyongyang. This problem has two dimensions: the will to restrain North Korea, and the ability to do so. Until recently, it was felt, both China and the Soviet Union have shared with the United States and Japan the desire to maintain the status quo on the Peninsula and have generally acted to restrain the North Korean regime. The will to continue such efforts, however, has become problematical. Recent developments in Southeast Asia and elsewhere have tended to limit China's willingness to take positions that would antagonize Pyongyang. Concerned about possible consolidation of the Soviet position on its Korean flank and a narrowing of its own room for influence, Beijing has shifted its attention away from the question of Korean unification. The will of Moscow to continue to restrain Pyongyang is similarly problematical. On the one hand, the Soviet Union's desire for détente with the West provides an incentive to continue to restrain the North. On the other hand, its desire to increase its leverage vis-à-vis China through the supply of arms and other aid to the North could lead to the opposite effort. Particularly with the emerging "triple entente" of China, the United States, and Japan, the Soviets could come to perceive some kind of proxy conflict in Korea as being in their interest. In either event, it was suggested, the Chinese and the Soviets—regardless of the question of will—might lack the ability to restrain North Korea. Pyongyang possesses a certain independent capability, it was pointed out, and can, if it chooses, "draw in" its reluctant allies.

Policy Issues

The discussion of policy centered on the American choices for friends and adversaries in Southeast and Northeast Asia. Consideration of Thailand focused on the immediate need to strengthen the Thais militarily (e.g., through arms sales), politically (by demonstrating to the Soviet Union and to Vietnam the costs of heightened pressure against the non-communist states of the region), and economically, in order to bolster governmental confidence and dampen local instabilities.

Arguments about Vietnam's external conduct were divided between coercive and conciliatory strategies. Some participants argued for "squeezing" Vietnam, either directly or by encouraging China to take action against Hanoi, while others suggested ways to encourage Vietnamese moderation, focusing in particular on the country's great need for economic reconstruction. Some participants argued that means of diluting the Soviet-Vietnamese relationship must also be sought. Such means might include efforts to avoid further political polarization in Asia (e.g., not encouraging the development of a military component for ASEAN). No proposals were agreeable to all, with the possible exception of an implicit recognition that the United States clearly stands to benefit by not involving itself directly in conflicts between or among the communist powers.

Opinions on policy options in Northeast Asia revealed more consensus. The overall (though not unanimous) sentiment on the decision to withdraw U.S. ground troops from Korea is that the unconditional nature of the original Carter Administration policy and its explicit timetable should both be rethought. Less agreement was apparent on the specific defense requirements of the ROK at present—e.g., whether direct military sales should be expanded, whether or not more advanced fighter aircraft should be transferred to Seoul, and how much encouragement should be given to the development of an indigenous defense industry. Also unsettled was the issue of negotiating objectives and initiatives vis-à-vis the North.

Issues For Further Consideration

Several issues seemed particularly worthy of further consideration. First, the relationship between regional conflicts and external great-power involvements is obviously highly complex. If, as many are prepared to argue, the Soviet Union is playing a largely inciting role in the conflicts in Indochina, why should Soviet behavior in Korea be seen as generally restraining rather than encouraging Pyongyang? Stated more simply, the specific differences on a region-by-region (or even country-by-country) basis tend to contradict the notion of great-power behavior reflecting some grand strategy. A more concrete sense of how and where the interests and objectives of the major powers vary is needed before more systematic attention can be given to future security arrangements.

A second issue apparent in the discussions but rarely explicitly stated was the problem of "looking back rather than looking ahead." No matter how much lip service is paid to the degree and nature of change in East Asia, discussion was more often couched in terms of past conflicts and strategies than in terms of the need to design new policies that may bear only slight resemblance to those of the past. The refighting of old battles (actually and figuratively) suggests that many participants are not wholly persuaded that changes in the region are indeed that profound, or that those changes afford U.S. policymakers much greater latitude and opportunity than in the past.

SESSION IV

Session IV dealt with a diverse range of issues: (1) the military and political significance of U.S. arms transfers to East Asia; (2) the more specific implications (and potential complications) of weapons sales to China, either by the United States or by Western Europe; (3) economic trends in the Asia-Pacific region, both in relation to global patterns and in their more specific regional implications; (4) China's emergent relationships with the world and regional economies; and (5) the potential scarcity of energy, food, and related resources over the coming two decades.

Discussion of the arms transfer phenomenon dealt with both its short- and long-run purposes and implications. While U.S. arms transfers are clearly intended to serve a number of diverse objectives and interests, several ongoing uncertainties were highlighted. In one sense, arms sales are intended as a substitute for an on-site U.S. military presence. Yet, beyond a certain point, this goal cannot be achieved, since a more credible demonstration of an American commitment will ultimately be expected. At the same time, even as the United States seeks to build up the indigenous defense capacities of various emergent regional powers, an abiding interest remains in restraining the acquisition of sensitive technologies, especially as they pertain to nuclear or "near-nuclear" capabilities. It is often difficult to see how the latter concern can be reconciled with the former. Attention to ceilings on arms sales may not be a very meaningful approach to this dilemma, since it does not deal with critical questions related to qualitative technological change (e.g., dual-use capabilities, the frequently ambiguous offensive-defensive distinction, etc.). Finally, the issue of where arms sales fit within a larger security and diplomatic equation requires careful attention, especially as various states of the region begin to move into a more self-sufficient phase of weapons production.

This last concern provided an effective transition to the discussion of possible arms transfers to China. While some participants tended to downplay the military significance of such sales (at least in the short run), the symbolic importance of arms transfers was clearly considered important. Most participants agreed that the willingness to undertake such sales, while not likely to stimulate the creation of a vast and threatening military machine, was potent testimony to the West's commitment to China's broader modernization process. Others placed greater stress on the possible implications (even in the short run) of such sales for U.S.-Soviet relations. The fact that weapons transfers to China would have only a modest impact on the regional balance of forces was seen as small consolation for Soviet policymakers. Thus, the terms and context of possible weapons sales (either by the United States or by third parties) should be weighed for their possible impact on Soviet thinking. For example, making such sales expressly conditional on the degree to which Moscow does or does not undermine the regional or global security interests of the United States would provide a very meaningful incentive for Soviet restraint. At the same time, the United States can let Chinese leaders know that their access to Western defense technology will be conditioned by PRC policy towards Taiwan. Such strategies are based on the assumption that the United States can develop meaningful leverage by its decisions on technology transfer and arms-sales issues.

Discussion in the remainder of the session shifted almost exclusively to nonmilitary components of regional security, beginning with general economic trends in the Asia-Pacific region. The principal concern among the participants was whether the remarkable economic dynamism and prosperity in the region could be maintained into the coming decade. Several conferees suggested that the vibrancy of a number of East Asian economies—in particular, those of South Korea, Taiwan, Hong Kong, and Singapore, all of which are following the Japanese pattern of aggressive expansion of foreign trade—was simply too great to be sidetracked. For major commercial banks, such economies offer low risk and high profitability; thus it is unlikely that funds for capital investment will be unavailable, especially with the continuing decline in capital spending in the West. This conclusion is even further strengthened by the shift of these economies into heavy industry and out of labor-intensive endeavors (e.g., South Korea's major breakthrough in shipbuilding). If there is any threat at all to the remarkable economic growth of these countries, it will come from the growing protectionist sentiment in the West. Because of East Asia's particular dependence on foreign trade, protectionism represents the most evident danger to these upward trends. And, given the fact that the United States is progressively losing more of the market share in East Asia, such a prospect may grow stronger over time.

Attention then turned to the potential emergence of new economic arrangements in the region that would bring together different groups of states. The PRC's increasing involvement in foreign trade and technology acquisition is considered a principal catalyst for such a development. For example, a consortium might develop among China, Japan, and the United States, with the latter two countries providing large quantities of leased machinery. Proposals for joint oil exploration between China and Western firms could well pose a threat to smaller states in the region that are also seeking to move into offshore oil drilling. Nevertheless, expectations of a sudden vast expansion of the "China market" must be tempered by the limited opportunities that do exist in the near term in the Chinese economy, as well as by the essential need to pay continued heed to the concerns of other Asian states. On balance, however, China's increasing involvement in regional trading patterns was considered a positive factor.

The key issues for the immediate future concern the management of interdependence and coping with structural impediments to change within various domestic economies. Nowhere is this more apparent than in the looming trade problems between the United States and Japan. This issue could well develop into a full-blown crisis, with trade becoming at least as much of an issue for Japan's security as any potential military threat. The fact that policies are often made by individual firms rather than governments only compounds the long-term problems of managing economic patterns.

An even more enduring consideration that is certain to affect all the states of the region is the availability of an adequate supply of energy, food, and critical resources in the coming decades. China's new demands deriving from its modernization efforts could well deny resources to other Asian states or could at least make competition for them vastly more acute. The fact that states such as South Korea and Taiwan have grown prosperous through the aggressive expansion of foreign trade does not assure this prospect for other countries operating under increasing conditions of regional and global resource scarcity. Continued expansion of population in many East Asian states can only mean increased demand for food, industrial raw materials, and energy, all potentially leading to an extremely dangerous and destructive pattern of resource competition. Such trends could also spill over into the military area, as states sensitive to control of seabed resources, for example, may come to feel the need to develop capabilities for defending themselves against encroachment.

Not all participants took such a pessimistic view of these issues, however. Some felt that if states are willing to undertake the necessary investments now rather than later for exploitation and development of natural resources, no severe constraints would develop in the future. Perhaps greater concern ought to be addressed to "economic racism" (e.g., growing anti-Japanese sentiment at a time of increasing trade imbalances), which could lead to extremely destructive economic reprisals during the 1980s. Still, the inherent difficulty of projecting trends to the end of the century underscored the problems of economic and social issues that governments may well be unable to cope with.

Policy Issues

A number of policy issues were raised in this session, and uneasiness and uncertainty regarding present U.S. policy directions were evident among the participants. The first issue concerned the adequacy of a surrogate U.S. security role (through arms transfers), with the Soviet military presence becoming more active and visible. Some participants also doubted whether the intensity and virulence of conflict in the communist world necessarily allowed for a relaxed U.S. view of operational military deployments. The overall question of an appropriate military posture for the United States in East Asia thus remained a paramount issue on the conference agenda.

A second policy consideration concerned the terms, objectives, and consequences of U.S.-PRC normalization. It was clear from the conference discussions that full U.S. diplomatic recognition of the PRC had left unresolved a host of key policy issues. These included arms transfers to China and the degree to which an American commitment to Chinese security and to the PRC's modernization effort ought to supplant (or take precedence over) past U.S. policy commitments to other Asian states. The implications of normalization for future U.S.-Soviet relations were also seen as a vital issue on which present U.S. policy seems divided or confused. There were major doubts among the participants about whether the U.S.-China normalization agreement had yet been matched by a systematic consideration of the Sino-American relationship across a broad spectrum of policy concerns.

A final set of issues concerned the management of economic problems in areas such as trade imbalances and resource exploitation. The inherent difficulty of coordinating governmental policy with the interests of private corporations underscores the need for attention to mechanisms for assuring appropriate integration of policy options. Deep concern was expressed about how an issue such as trade relations can be managed without severely straining the U.S.-Japanese relationship.

Issues For Further Consideration

One question that merits further scrutiny concerns the malleability of military power for progressively smaller and yet more expansive security tasks. The United States is arranging arms sales and technology transfers to encourage the development of indigenous military strength among various states in East Asia. At the same time, the emergence of a Sino-Japanese-American quasi-alliance is contributing enormously to the "globalization" of efforts to counter and contain Soviet military power. In both cases, the degree to which such policy initiatives are in accord with U.S. security interests, both global and regional, remains unsettled.

A second key question is that of the relationship between economic and resource issues and the classic conception of national security policy. The contrast between "old" and "new" approaches to the security issue is nowhere more apparent than in this area. Because economic and social well-being clearly affects the stability of various states, this factor must be weighed in any security equation. Nevertheless, the way in which such diverse perspectives can be integrated into a more coherent, comprehensive approach to the security of nations or regions remains unclear.

EVENING SESSION

The starting point of the evening's discussion was a statement of the belief that, from the perspective of American interests, the situation in Asia today is better than it has been in many years. Factors cited as contributing to this favorable situation included the normalization of relations with the PRC; the conclusion of the base agreement with the Philippines; the ending of a triple crisis with the ROK (regarding "Koreagate," the troop withdrawal program, and human rights); the emergence of ASEAN as an impressive organization (both economically and in terms of regional influence) and a significant improvement in U.S.-ASEAN ties; the rise of Congressional sympathy for a continued U.S. presence in Asia; growing support for the Carter Administration's Asia policy; the signing of the Sino-Japanese peace treaty; the emergence of Japan as an important regional actor; and the growth of internal stability throughout Asia. Areas of difficulty were also acknowledged, such as the problems with Taiwan over U.S.-PRC normalization, the signing of the Soviet-Vietnamese friendship treaty, the fall of Kampuchea, the trade imbalances between the United States and various East Asian countries, and the "time-bomb" quality of the refugee issue. However, it was argued, there is no evidence to indicate that the power of the United States in Asia is on the decline.

The first specific issue raised in the discussion related to recent events in Southeast Asia, particularly the Vietnamese invasion of Kampuchea. These events suggested that Vietnam has abandoned its position of non-alignment in the Sino-Soviet dispute, with the Soviet Union gaining influence but not in a major way. The overthrow of the Pol Pot regime, it was stressed, was not a setback for the United States, since the U.S. had no interest in its continuation. As a result of the overthrow, however, Vietnam will now have to maintain troops in all three countries of Indochina. While ASEAN will face a new and major test as a result of these developments, the United States will be in a position to provide greater support. Moreover, the United States and the PRC will inevitably be drawn closer together, sharing with Japan and the ANZUS alliance the objective of restraining the extension of Soviet power. The United States must make it clear to Moscow that, while it accepts the Soviet Union as a Pacific power, attempts by the Soviets to change local situations to their advantage all over the world will be unacceptable and will generate American responses with friendly and allied countries.

In Southeast Asia, the crucial question now concerns Thailand. If Thailand is threatened, a very difficult situation will be created. Depending on how Thai leaders respond to the threat, the United States might provide a small increase in military credits as a gesture of commitment, while adapting specific tactics to the larger strategy of restraining the Soviet Union.

Recent developments preclude any move to normalize U.S. relations with Hanoi in the near future. Although the Vietnamese recently dropped their demand for economic reparations, it will take some time before the issue of establishing diplomatic relations can be addressed.

The second major issue addressed in the evening session was the recent normalization of relations with the PRC. This development, it was suggested, removed many of the restraints and inhibitions on U.S.-PRC interactions. The dramatic evolution of the relationship in the past month attests to the importance of normalization in this regard. The United States is now hopeful that many new possibilities can be explored and that China can be involved in a greater collaborative effort to help reduce regional tensions, particularly in Korea. The only way this new relationship can work, however, is if normal relations can be maintained with Taiwan. Here the problem is not only the PRC but the obstacles represented by Taiwanese unwillingness to support parts of the legislative package required for relations to be maintained. It was stressed that careful management of this issue must receive the highest priority.

Despite the new possibilities suggested by normalized relations with China, the United States does not want an "imbalance" to develop in the U.S.-USSR-PRC relationship. This is the single most important issue facing the United States today. The United States will neither "tilt" excessively toward Beijing nor make a U.S.-PRC alliance a part of its global policy. An example of this determination is the clear posture on the question of arms sales: While its European allies may sell whatever they like to China, the United States will not sell weapons. Thus, the concern apparent in some parts of the Soviet bureaucracy about an alleged "triple entente" is unjustified. The most important U.S. relationships in Asia are those with Japan, the ROK, ASEAN, and ANZUS. Although much depends upon Soviet behavior and its effects on Congressional and public attitudes, the United States will seek equilibrium in its relations with the Soviet Union, not isolation.

A final issue was the question of Korea. Having weathered a very difficult two years, the prospects for U.S.-Korean relations look very good in the coming year. The major problem, it was suggested, is the significantly increased level of North Korean military strength that recent intelligence estimates have revealed. Whether this increased strength is a recent development or a recent "discovery" is not yet clear, but the implications are serious and must be faced.

Two other areas were touched upon briefly: economic problems with Japan, and the refugee issue. Regarding current U.S. economic problems with Japan, it was stressed that nothing is more critical for U.S. policies in Asia than finding a way to diminish the danger of protectionism. One of the Administration's highest legislative priorities in this regard is to get approval of the Multilateral Trade Negotiations, a task which is expected to be as difficult as obtaining ratification of SALT.

On the refugee issue, although some change in the refugee flow may be expected in the next few months (with some refugees going back to Kampuchea, for example), boat people will continue to leave Vietnam and a low-level exodus from

Laos is expected to persist. This, it was suggested, will continue to be a very critical problem, especially for Malaysia, which is bearing the brunt of the burden.

SESSION V

The original intent of the final conference session was to draw together the previous discussions and address overall trends, policy dilemmas, and choices in East Asian security, especially as they pertain to the future American role in the region. Although intermittent attention was devoted to these issues, the emphasis was on contextual factors, many of them not usually included within the conventional framework of international security. The elaboration of such themes continued the dialectic of optimism and pessimism that had been apparent throughout the proceedings. The dominant focus, however, was on difficulties and constraints, not on opportunities.

There was a pronounced difference in perceptions of the nature of political change in Asia; wide variation was noted in abilities to see beyond present circumstances and deal with emergent political, economic, and demographic trends. These trends, it was argued, will ultimately prove far more decisive for regional security than will force planning and military deployment. (One participant suggested that the inability to perceive these changes and plan beyond the present context was a characteristic American problem.) In particular, it was argued that there are long-term limitations on Soviet power (e.g., unfavorable demographic changes which are increasingly apparent in the Soviet armed forces), many of which are simply beyond the capacity of Soviet leadership to manage or control. Leadership uncertainties in the Soviet Union were also noted. Although some participants argued that such focus underestimated Soviet capacities, most agreed that assessments of Soviet power must encompass more than simple appraisals of Soviet military strength.

A long-term process of political change was also perceived to be under way in Japan, encompassing the erosion of the Liberal Democratic Party's past monopoly on political power, pressures for a more autonomous foreign policy, and a concern that the inability to maintain past levels of economic growth will lead to unspecified but destabilizing political change. The prospects for China's modernization drive were deemed similarly uncertain. There appears to be little recognition within China of how unsettling this process could be or of the threat it will pose to long-entrenched patterns of political and institutional power in the region and in the world. Even if the modernization program meets with early success—and that prospect can also be questioned—its political and social consequences simply cannot be foreseen.

A range of other potential problems was also suggested. The North-South dialogue between Asian societies and the West has been far less vitriolic than similar discussions in other regions, but this degree of civility could change rapidly. Tensions between Asia's emerging industrial powers and its less developed countries could also grow in a dangerous and destabilizing manner. (Recent pressures related to economic opportunities and income disparities were seen as early evidence of this phenomenon.) Thus, social forces and social change are the factors that threaten to swamp political and technological change. Such issues cannot be ameliorated in any significant way by the accretion of military power, yet projections about Asia's political future were almost nonexistent.

At a somewhat different level, the issue of cultural and perceptual differences was also given substantial attention. The need for knowledge, communication, and understanding about Asia by Americans, and about America by Asians, was deemed critical. The Asian understanding of the American political process remains very limited and highly confused. At the same time, American power is not perceived as highly credible, particularly as the United States continues to behave like a patron when the limits of its power will prevent the realization of any grandiose objectives. Also looming in the background is the future relationship between a strong, united, powerful China (assuming the realization of the modernization program) and the West. Western expectations of China, and Chinese expectations of the United States and other non-communist nations, remain disconcertingly obscure and could well prove the source of great political confusion and conflict in the future.

Thus, no matter how optimistic or encouraging certain political trends might appear, an uneasy sense remained among many participants that the pace of political and economic change is rapidly outstripping the capacity of either governments or political thinkers to understand, let alone control. The fractionation of the international communist movement has succeeded in denying to the United States and to the non-communist states of the region a coherent sense of the purposes and potentialities of their mutual association. Doubts about the depth and durability of these political, economic, and security ties were in many ways the defining elements in the concluding deliberations.

Policy Issues

Although the concluding session rarely assumed an explicit policy focus, several undercurrents were apparent. First was the overall issue of a strategy for American defense planning in Asia. Despite the extent to which many participants questioned the continued relevance of military power, others were unequivocal in arguing the importance of a continuing U.S. military presence in the Pacific. Undeniably, the recent growth in Soviet power requires an American response, although the response need not be (and could not be) a wholly military one. The continuing credibility of American capabilities remains vital at a time when the diffusion of power is a growing trend. This concern with U.S. credibility was not discussed solely in terms of stemming Soviet influence. The nuclear option has become increasingly real for a number of Asian states. Should proliferation occur, it would clearly be deleterious to U.S. and regional security interests. The continuing commitment of the United States to peace and stability in the Asia-Pacific region will therefore remain vital to retarding this trend. Thus, although the region is clearly far less susceptible to U.S. influence than it was in the past, an effective U.S. security presence must be assured, now and in the future. Although never the object of extended discussion, the need for a concrete assessment of a plausible and necessary defense role for U.S. forces in the 1980s and beyond was clearly apparent to the conferees.

It was generally agreed that the nature of America's dealings with East Asia needs to be more carefully delineated in terms of U.S. policy objectives. The major changes in the Sino-American relationship are only the most recent embodiment of the necessity to define the terms (and limits) of U.S. dealings with allies and quasi-allies, both old and new. Clearly, there is a "proto-coalition" between various Asian states and the United States on security issues, especially in terms of countering Soviet power. But the potentialities and limits of such an alignment, particularly in areas beyond the military realm (e.g., economics), remain undetermined.

A final policy issue, which was intermittently discussed throughout the conference and raised again in the concluding session, concerned the relationship between the United States and Japan. There is clear evidence of growing friction and unease engendered by the trade imbalance, Japan's limited contribution to regional security arrangements, and other issues. As various participants noted, it cannot be assumed without question that the past framework of U.S.-Japanese relations will persist indefinitely. Whether in terms of concrete military ties, Japan's political and economic role in East Asia, or the overall bilateral U.S.-Japanese relationship, the possibility of drift and deterioration in dealings between Tokyo and Washington was an issue of great concern, and one that urgently requires rectification if the positive trends in the region are to be sustained.

Issues for Further Consideration

No conference succeeds in resolving all issues, or even in adequately discussing all key themes, and these sessions were no exception. Several issues stood out as largely unresolved. The first was the need for an adequate comprehension and stocktaking of the nature of political and economic changes occurring within various Asian societies, and in the region as a whole. Conceptions of both national and regional security have been, and will continue to be, extensively recast throughout the area as a result of these changes, yet much of the argumentation at the conference continued to dwell on the past.

What applies to Asia as a whole also needs to be addressed more specifically in terms of the U.S. political and defense role in the region. The American experience in Vietnam remained an obvious (if sometimes understated) preoccupation for a number of conference participants. While the past cannot be wished away, Asia and America on the verge of the 1980s confront a radically different era in terms of the nature of security issues and the forces propelling interstate and intrasocietal change and conflict. The task for future research will be to describe and assess such change within the context of the still potent issues of military power and security planning. This task has just begun and will clearly become a major intellectual and political concern in the 1980s.

INDEX

ACNs. *See* Advanced capitalist nations
Advanced capitalist nations (ACNs), 191. *See also* Developed countries
  conservatism of, 194
  GDP of, 192
Afghanistan
  and Sino-Soviet conflict, 10
  Soviet intervention in, 62
  Soviet relations with, 2, 9
  Soviet treaty with, 46, 50
Africa, expansion of Soviet influence in, 166
Agricultural production
  in Asia, 229-230
  and food shortages, 227-228
  and "green revolution," 229
  in PRC, 220, 229
Aircraft
  East Asian production of, 270, 271
  MiG-23s, 121
  Soviet attack-fighters, 58
Air defense, for Japan, 102
Air Division, 314th, 129
Air Force, U.S.
  in Korea, 128
  qualitative capabilities of, 58
Air Forces
  ROK, 120
  Soviet, 56
Airlifting capability, in Pacific-Asian-Indian Ocean theater, 66
Air-mobile force, Soviet, 56
Airpower, sea-based vs. tactical, 66-67
Air transport, long-range heavy, 66
Alexandrov, I., 44, 45
Angola, Soviet proxy in, 62
Anti-hegemony strategy, China's, 2, 97, 103
Antitechnology movement, 194
ANZUS countries. *See also* Australia; New Zealand
  Oceanic alliance with, 2
  and regional security, 64
"Arc of Crisis," 49
Armed Forces Committee, Senate, 116
Arms control agreements, 141. *See also* Korean negotiations
Arms Control and Disarmament Agency, 259
Arms race
  in Asia, 16
  on Korean Peninsula, 122
Arms sales, 27
  to PRC, 48
  to ROK, 120, 122

Arms suppliers, major, 259. *See also* Weapons transfers
Arms supply, Korean, 135
Army
  Khmer Rouge, 151, 158
  ROK, 120
  Vietnamese, 150
ASEAN (the Association of Southeast Asian Nations), 6, 164. *See also* Indonesia; Malaysia; Philippines; Singapore; Thailand
  Chinese minority in, 164-165
  economic access to U.S. of, 167
  economic concerns of, 163
  and economic growth, 212
  foreign trade of, 209
  impact of new Indochina conflict on, 162-168
  and market competition, 16
  and national diversity, 95
  and oil exploration, 246
  Overseas Chinese in, 164-165
  and regional security, 175-176
  and Sino-Soviet conflict, 10
  and technology transfer, 271
  and Vietnam-Kampuchea conflict, 30-31, 151
Asia, East
  aircraft co-produced by, 270, 271
  American abandonment of, 100
  democracy in, 94
  demographic estimates for, 216
  diffusion of technology in, 258
  domestic stability in, 95
  energy crunch in, 252
  European influence in, 93
  financial market support for, 210
  food shortage in, 230
  Japanese economic role in, 214
  national diversity in, 95
  in 1950s, 35
  in 1960s, 35
  Soviet influence in, 169-170
  Soviet military presence in, 54-62
  territorial disputes in, 199
  in turbulent global economic environment, 207
  U.S. direct investments in, 24
  U.S. exports to, 22
  U.S. imports from, 23
  U.S. military force structure in, 28-29
  U.S. security posture in, 272

307

ABOUT THE EDITOR

Richard H. Solomon heads the Social Science Department of The Rand Corporation, and is director of Rand's research program on International Security Policy. He received his Ph.D. in 1966 from the Massachusetts Institute of Technology, where he specialized in political science and Chinese politics. From 1971 to 1976, he served as Senior Staff Member for Asian Affairs on the National Security Council, having previously been Professor of Political Science at the University of Michigan. Dr. Solomon is a member of the Joint Committee on Contemporary China of the Social Science Research Council, the Board of Directors of the Graphic Arts Research Foundation, and the board of the Committee on Scholarly Communication with the People's Republic of China. He is the author of *Mao's Revolution and the Chinese Political Culture* (1971) and *A Revolution Is Not a Dinner Party: A Feast of Images of the Maoist Transformation in China* (1976). He has also contributed articles to such professional journals as *Foreign Affairs* and *The China Quarterly*.

SELECTED LIST OF RAND BOOKS

Averch, Harvey A., John E. Koehler, and Frank H. Denton. *The Matrix of Policy in the Philippines*. Princeton, N.J.: Princeton University Press, 1971.

Becker, Abraham S. *Military Expenditure Limitation for Arms Control: Problems and Prospects*. Cambridge, Mass.: Ballinger Publishing Company, 1977.

Becker, Abraham S., Bent Hansen, and Malcolm H. Kerr. *The Economics and Politics of the Middle East*. New York: American Elsevier Publishing Company, Inc., 1975.

Clawson, Marion, Hans H. Landsberg, and Lyle T. Alexander. *The Agricultural Potential of the Middle East*. New York: American Elsevier Publishing Company, Inc., 1971.

Cooper, Charles A., and Sidney S. Alexander (eds.). *Economic Development and Population Growth in the Middle East*. New York: American Elsevier Publishing Company, Inc., 1972.

Einaudi, Luigi R. (ed.). *Beyond Cuba: Latin America Takes Charge of Its Future*. New York: Crane, Russak & Company, Inc., 1974.

Goldhamer, Herbert. *The Foreign Powers in Latin America*. Princeton, N.J.: Princeton University Press, 1972.

Gurtov, Melvin. *Southeast Asia Tomorrow: Problems and Prospects for U.S. Policy*. Baltimore, Md.: The Johns Hopkins Press, 1970.

Halpern, Manfred. *The Politics of Social Change in the Middle East and North Africa*. Princeton, N.J.: Princeton University Press, 1963.

Hammond, Paul Y., and Sidney S. Alexander (eds.). *Political Dynamics in the Middle East*. New York: American Elsevier Publishing Company, Inc., 1972.

Hosmer, Stephen T. *Viet Cong Repression and Its Implications for the Future*. Lexington, Mass.: Lexington Books, D. C. Heath and Company, 1970.

Hosmer, Stephen T., Konrad Kellen, and Brian Jenkins. *The Fall of South Vietnam: Statements by Vietnamese Military and Civilian Leaders*. New York: Crane, Russak & Company, Inc., 1980.

Hsieh, Alice Langley. *Communist China's Strategy in the Nuclear Era*. Westport, Conn.: Greenwood Press, 1976.

Johnson, John J. (ed.). *The Role of the Military in Underdeveloped Countries*. Princeton, N.J.: Princeton University Press, 1962.

Johnstone, William C. *Burma's Foreign Policy: A Study in Neutralism*. Cambridge, Mass.: Harvard University Press, 1963.

Langer, Paul F., and Joseph J. Zasloff. *North Vietnam and the Pathet Lao: Partners in the Struggle for Laos*. Cambridge, Mass.: Harvard University Press, 1970.

Leites, Nathan. *The Operational Code of the Politburo*. Westport, Conn.: Greenwood Press, 1972.

Liu, Ta-Chung, and Kung-Chia Yeh. *The Economy of the Chinese Mainland: National Income and Economic Development, 1933-1959*. Princeton, N.J.: Princeton University Press, 1965.

Lubell, Harold. *Middle East Oil Crises and Western Europe's Energy Supplies*. Baltimore, Md.: The Johns Hopkins Press, 1963.

Moorsteen, Richard, and Morton Abramowitz. *Remaking China Policy: U.S.-China Relations and Governmental Decisionmaking*. Cambridge, Mass.: Harvard University Press, 1971.

Quandt, William B., Fuad Jabber, and Ann Mosely Lesch. *The Politics of Palestinian Nationalism*. Berkeley and Los Angeles: University of California Press, 1973.

Robinson, Thomas W. (ed.). *The Cultural Revolution in China*. Berkeley and Los Angeles: University of California Press, 1971.

Rosen, George E. *Democracy and Economic Change in India*. Berkeley and Los Angeles: University of California Press, 1966.

Scalapino, Robert A. *The Japanese Communist Movement, 1920-1966*. Berkeley and Los Angeles: University of California Press, 1967.

Schurr, Sam H., Paul T. Homan, et al. *Middle Eastern Oil and the Western World: Prospects and Problems*. New York: American Elsevier Publishing Company, Inc., 1971.

Stepan, Alfred C. *The Military in Politics: Changing Patterns in Brazil*. Princeton, N.J.: Princeton University Press, 1971.

Tanham, G. K. *Communist Revolutionary Warfare: The Vietminh in Indochina*. New York: Frederick A. Praeger, Inc., 1961.

Trager, Frank N. (ed.). *Marxism in Southeast Asia: A Study of Four Countries*. Stanford, Calif.: Stanford University Press, 1959.

Whiting, Allen S. *China Crosses the Yalu: The Decision to Enter the Korean War*. Stanford, Calif.: Stanford University Press, 1968.

Wolf, Charles, Jr. *Foreign Aid: Theory and Practice in Southern Asia*. Princeton, N.J.: Princeton University Press, 1960.

Wolfe, Thomas W. *Soviet Power and Europe, 1945-1970*. Baltimore, Md.: The Johns Hopkins Press, 1970.

Zasloff, Joseph J. *The Pathet Lao: Leadership and Organization*. Lexington, Mass.: Lexington Books, D. C. Heath and Company, 1973.